T0134963

Universal, Intuitive, and Permanent Pictograms

EBOOK INSIDE

Die Zugangsinformationen zum eBook Inside finden Sie am Ende des Buchs.

Daniel Bühler

Universal, Intuitive, and Permanent Pictograms

A Human-Centered Design Process
Grounded in Embodied Cognition,
Semiotics, and Visual Perception

 Springer

Daniel Bühler
Berlin, Germany

ISBN 978-3-658-32312-7   ISBN 978-3-658-32310-3   (eBook)
https://doi.org/10.1007/978-3-658-32310-3

Responsible Editor: Petra Steinmüller
This Springer imprint is published by the registered company Springer Fachmedien Wiesbaden GmbH part of Springer Nature.
The registered company address is: Abraham-Lincoln-Str. 46, 65189 Wiesbaden, Germany

Acknowledgments

I am grateful for the funding of the design production process by the German Federal Ministry of Education and Research (BMBF) and the VDI/VDE Innovation + Technology GmbH (VDI/VDE-IT) through the Universal Cognitive User Interface project (grant no. 16SV7305K) and for the partial funding of the evaluation studies by the Research Cluster Cognitive Systems at Brandenburg University of Technology Cottbus—Senftenberg.

I would like to thank Jutta and Walter Bühler, Matthias Dübner, Prof. Dr. rer. nat. Carsten Hartmann, Prof. Dr.-Ing. Fabian Hemmert, Prof. Dr.-Ing. Jörn Hurtienne, PD Dr. phil. Dr. rer. nat. habil. Peter Klimczak, Dr. rer. nat. Robert Lieck, Dr. med. Martha Loose, Maxi Matzanke, Prof. Dr. phil. Christer Petersen, Dr. rer. nat. Kati Nowack, Nils Schekorr, and all study participants for their contribution to the project.

Finally, I would like to thank my brother, Denis Bühler, PhD, who has taught me most of what I should know and even more of what I should not.

Contents

List of Abbreviations, Acronyms, and Symbols

ANOVA	Analysis of variance
BES	Best-evidence synthesis
β	Probability of a Type II error
CMT	Conceptual metaphor theory
χ^2	Chi-squared
d	Cohen's d
df	Degrees of freedom
EC	Embodied cognition
η_p^2	Partial eta-squared
F	F-statistic
GUI	Graphical user interface
HCD	Human-centered design
HCI	Human–computer interaction
HITF	Human Inference Task Force
IQR	Interquartile range
IUUI	Intuitive Use of User Interfaces group
iStep	Intermediate step
M	Mean
Mdn	Median
n	Size of sample
n.t.	Not tested
NPR	Non-photorealistic rendering
p	Probability
PPS	Perceptual symbol systems theory
QUESI	Questionnaire for the subjective consequences of intuitive use
QUT	Queensland University of Technology group
R^2	Coefficient of determination
r	Pearson's r
RTD	Research through design
s	Seconds
SD	Standard deviation
STD	Semantic differential technique

τ	Kendall's τ
U	Mann-Whitney U
UCUI	Universal Cognitive User Interface
UIPP	Universal, intuitive, and permanent pictogram

List of Figures

Step 3: Grounding, Deriving, and Evaluating Pictogram Contents

Step 4: Developing a Design System and Producing the UIP Pictograms

Step 5: Evaluating the UIP Pictograms

List of Tables

Step 1: Introduction, Goals, and Summary of the Process

Abstract

Following ISO 9241:210, the first step of a human-centered design process consists in the close examination of previous research, the identification of suitable theories, methods, and resources, and the planning of the process. All subsequent steps are based on this review. Consequently, this introductory chapter discusses existing theories and research, it describes the structure of the UIPP project, and it explains the project goals.

Let me begin with an example. A few years ago, a large German heating system manufacturer began distributing a newly developed heating system in Muslim countries. One function that could be activated via the system's user interface was economy mode. In this mode, the heating system saved energy, thus, it saved money. Economy mode was very popular in Europe. However, in Muslim countries, it was hardly used at all. The manufacturer discovered that Muslim users did not activate economy mode because the pictogram that needed to be touched in the graphical user interface to activate the mode represented a piggy bank. Users preferred not to touch the pictogram because, in Muslim countries, pigs are sometimes considered unclean. Subsequently, the manufacturer replaced the piggy bank with the visual representation of a leaf (M. Roßmann, personal communication, December 12, 2018, J. Zander, personal communication, March 13, 2019).

I suggest that three points are illustrated by the example. First, in the interaction of humans with computers and with each other via computers, graphical user interfaces (GUI) and visual representations are still ubiquitous. This holds although, in the field of human–computer interaction (HCI), today, GUIs and visual representations are sometimes considered to be outdated because of their long

D. Bühler, *Universal, Intuitive, and Permanent Pictograms*,
https://doi.org/10.1007/978-3-658-32310-3_1

history and their restriction to a single sensory channel (e.g., Hurtienne and Israel 2007, p. 127; Ishii and Ullmer 1997, p. 240). Instead, the number of situations in which we encounter them seems to be still growing. Sometimes, scholars even consider visual representations the most important mode of communication and interaction today (Kress 2010; Marcus 2015, p. 59).

Second, the example shows that, in the course of recent technological developments, markets have become increasingly connected just as people's lives. Consequently, it is no longer sufficient to provide systems of interaction that are suitable for individual cultures, groups, and people. Instead, systems are required that allow for interaction between them, independent of culture, age, and capabilities (Bourges-Waldegg and Scrivener 1998, p. 288; Plocher et al. 2012, p. 162; Röse 2006, p. 253).

Third, pictograms and other visual representations are fast and easily recognized and learned (Nakamura and Zeng-Treitler 2012, pp. 535–536; Yamazaki and Taki 2010, pp. 71–72), they are often assumed to be universally and intuitively comprehensible (Massironi 2009, pp. 260–262; Mertens et al. 2011, p. 80). Sometimes, designers seem to hold on to these assumptions, although evidence has been gathered that suggests otherwise, showing that users interpret pictograms differently (Callahan 2005; Cho et al. 2007; Del Galdo and Nielsen 1996), sometimes in dangerous ways (Wogalter et al. 2006, p. 161).

In summary, I suggest, the example illustrates that visual representations are still relevant today. However, here is a lack of understanding of visual representations, there is a lack of research on universal and intuitive design (Marcus 2007, p. 376), and there is a lack of knowledge about how to apply scientific findings to design (Röse 2006, p. 253). This book tries to contribute to their remedy of all three.

Universal, Intuitive, and Permanent Pictogram Project: Two Main Goals

The project that I describe in this book started with the hypothesis that there is a good reason for the continuous use of pictograms and other visual representations in HCI. The reason is that they have the potential to be universally, intuitively, and permanently comprehensible (see Rogers 1989, p. 106). However, they appear to be sometimes arbitrarily, confusingly, or even wrongly designed, because their design is based on incorrect assumptions. Instead, I propose that they might be universally, intuitively, and permanently comprehensible if their design were grounded in scientific research and in empirical data.

The project was part of the Universal Cognitive User Interface project (UCUI). UCUI was a joint research project by numerous German research departments and companies, for example, Agilion GmbH, Chemnitz, InnoTec21 GmbH, Leipzig, Javox Solutions GmbH, Aachen, and XGraphic Ingenieurgesellschaft mbH, Aachen, led by Fraunhofer IKTS, Dresden, and Brandenburg University of Technology, Cottbus—Senftenberg. UCUI was funded by the German Federal

Ministry of Education and Research (Bundesministerium für Bildung und Forschung). The UCUI project aimed for the development of a user interface prototype that facilitates intuitive interaction of users with technical devices while protecting the user's privacy. The goal was to develop an interface system that adapts to the user, in other words, a user interface that does not require the user to adapt to the system. The project followed a universal approach (see Sect. "Definitions of Universality in HCI"). It aimed at users who are less familiar with technical devices or less able to use them. The prototype consisted of a single interface for a heating system with which the user interacted through speech, gestures, virtual keyboard, and pictograms (see, e.g., Jokisch and Huber 2018; Meyer et al. 2019).

Being a part of the UCUI project, the first goal of the project presented in this book was to design universally and intuitively comprehensible pictograms that might be integrated into the UCUI heating system user interface. In addition, the project aimed for permanently comprehensible pictogram prototypes. Let me explain. Modes of interaction that are learned might become intuitive through repeated use (see Sect. "Definitions of Intuitiveness in HCI"). For example, in general, we use language intuitively because we have learned it very early in childhood and because we use it constantly. Also, modes of interaction might become universal, for example, through globalization and standardization. English, for example, is becoming more and more widespread, and more and more people are learning the English language. However, modes of interaction are subject to change. Users transform modes of interaction according to their needs (Bezemer and Kress 2016; Kress 2003, 2010). For that reason, in the case of language, differences between uses of a language in distinct regions exist as much as between distinct user groups in one region. Also, there are differences in the use of a language between certain points in time. We are usually not able to comprehend our first language, as it was used in the Middle Ages. Consequently, even if a mode of interaction were universal and intuitive because of repeated use and standardization, it would transform over time, and future generations might no longer be able to comprehend the previously universal and intuitive mode. This holds for language, and it holds for visual representations, too (see Sect. "Historical and Contemporary Examples of Visual Representations"). For that reason, the project that I present aimed for interactions that are successful in the future, too. That is, it aimed for the design of pictograms that are permanently comprehensible. Thus, I call it the Universal, Intuitive, and Permanent Pictogram project (UIPP).

To be clear, I assume that neither pictograms nor any mode of interaction will ever be completely universal, intuitive, or permanent. Human beings, their physical and cognitive abilities, their bodies, and their personal and cultural experiences are far too complex, and technology is developing too fast to create a single set of pictograms or a mode of interaction that is suitable to everyone and will be forever (Heimgärtner 2013, pp. 67–68). In reality, designers might need to integrate "partially universal, general solutions and partially unique, local solutions to the design of UIs" (Marcus 2007, p. 356) in order for these to be suitable for specific users or user groups at specific times (Miller and Stanney 1997, p. 130). In addition, because of various limitations, constraints, and lacking resources, I assume, no project will be able to achieve such a high goal. For example, a general focus of universal design is on elderly people and people with disabilities (see Sect. "Definitions of Universality in HCI"). Since aging as well as certain disabilities might come with varying physical and cognitive abilities, research that focuses on elderly people and people with disabilities is extremely important. However, this was not a central focus of the UIPP project. Of course, this is a drawback. Nevertheless, the choice had to be made because of limited resources. I chose to focus on cross-cultural design instead of inclusive design because research on cross-cultural design is scarce, too (Hurtienne 2017, p. 16), and I hoped that focusing on similarities between people might provide a good basis for subsequent research on individual capabilities (Mansoor and Dowse 2004, p. 31). Consequently, the goal of the UIPP project was, to produce pictograms that are as universal, as intuitive, and as permanent as possible—considering the constraints on the project.

Besides designing universal, intuitive, and permanent pictograms, the project had a second main goal. Today, while various methods to evaluate designs exist, only few methods and technical processes for designing HCI can be found (Goonetilleke et al. 2001, p. 758). Instead, "the design outcome is highly dependent on the experience and expertise of the designer" (Löffler et al. 2013, p. 1). This is a challenge for less experienced designers, researchers, as much as businesses because they might lack the resources to access expert knowledge. Consequently, the second goal of the UIPP project was, to develop a technical process for the design of suitable pictograms that can be performed by other designers, researchers, and businesses, thus, enabling you, the readers, to adopt the process in your projects.

To achieve this, UIPP had two additional subgoals. In HCI, it is a desideratum to further strengthen the scientific bases to achieve more technical designs. In addition, it is a desideratum to strengthen the empirical bases to arrive at data-driven designs (Costa et al. 2014; Evers 1998, p. 4; Heimgärtner 2017, p. 192; Tan et al. 2017). For that reason, instead of focusing on artistic or designerly conventions (Cavanagh 2005, p. 301; Hurtienne et al. 2015, p. 236), the project aimed for scientifically underpinned processes and guidelines (Hurtienne et al. 2009, pp. 61–62). Furthermore, it aimed for comprehensive explanations of its empirical methods, its procedures, and their outcomes (Hurtienne 2017, p. 16). Consequently, in this book, I discuss in detail the theory, I ground the process in scientific research, and I present empirical data, that is, semiotics ("Step 2: Understanding Visual Representation(s)"), embodied cognition ("Step 3: Grounding, Deriving, and Evaluating Pictogram Contents"), visual perception and research through design ("Step 4: Developing a Design System and Producing the UIP Pictograms"), and empirical approaches in HCI ("Step 5: Evaluating the UIP Pictograms").

Furthermore, in contrast to many studies in HCI, UIPP includes all steps of the design process. As early as in 1998, Wood pointed out: "[W]hile there are some excellent sources of information on user interface design, none contains specific descriptions of how a designer transforms the information gathered about users and their work into an effective user interface design" (p. 10). The issue still exists. It is called the design gap (see Hurtienne et al. 2015, p. 240). In order to contribute to the closure of the design gap and to enable other designers, researchers, and business to perform the UIPP process, this project includes all steps, from theoretical underpinning, to requirements analysis, to design of prototypes, and to evaluation (see, e.g., Sect. "The Pictogram Design Production Process").

If these goals are achieved, I argue, not only will users profit, because their interaction will be more effective, and they will be able to interact successfully with people from all over the world. Researchers will profit, because the findings in this project will contribute to research on universal and intuitive design in HCI. Finally, businesses will profit, because they will be able to apply the technical process to design innovative products (Heß et al. 2013, p. 17), at low cost, to "achieve greater success and increased profitability through (…) global distribution and increased acceptance" (Marcus 2007, p. 376).

The UIPP Design Process and the Chapters of this Book

Shneiderman et al. (2017, pp. 137–141) described three viable approaches to the design of user interfaces and HCI: *participatory design, agile interaction design,* and *human-centered design.* Participatory design focuses on "the direct involvement of people in the collaborative design of the things and technologies they use. The arguments in favor [of this approach] suggest that more user involvement brings more accurate information" (p. 138). However, since only a limited number of users is involved, single users might have too much influence on the design of products that are developed for the public. Furthermore, direct user involvement comes with higher production times and higher costs. In contrast, the approach of agile interaction design aims at fast, flexible, and adaptive development in order to be able to react to fast-changing markets, technologies, and user preferences. For example, Apple introduces new devices every few months (Apple Inc. 2020). However, these rapid changes in the design of interfaces may lead to unwanted confusion in the users. Finally, the approach of human-centered design (HCD) focuses on the users by involving them during the process and taking their wishes into account. Here, instead of direct involvement, the user information is used to scrutinize the designer's assumptions. According to Shneiderman et al. (2017, p. 137), human-centered design leads to easily developed, maintained, and utilized designs. The process has been used successfully in many studies and projects (e.g., Fetzer et al. 2013; Heimgärtner 2013; Hurtienne et al. 2008, 2015; Salman et al. 2012; see Hartson and Pyla 2012, pp. 47–86; Sharp et al. 2019, pp. 37–67, too). Consequently, the UIPP project was structured as a human-centered design process, too.

The UIPP process was based on the ISO 9241:210 standard (International Organization for Standardization 2010) which is a framework for human-centered design. ISO 9241:210 does not define a specific process but mentions six HCD steps that can be adapted according to the goals and requirements of a specific project (International Organization for Standardization 2010, pp. 5–19) (see Fig. 1).

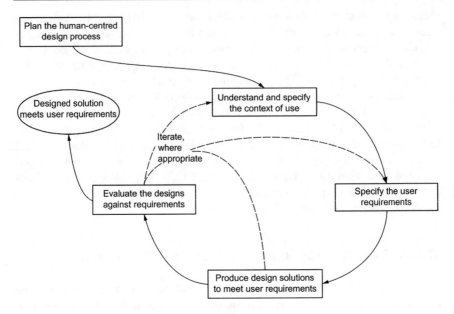

Fig. 1 The six steps in a human-centered design process, according to ISO 9241:210 (International Organization for Standardization 2010, p. 11)

In the following, I describe the HCD steps and I summarize their subsequent application in the UIPP project. The six HCD steps make up the six chapters in this book (see Fig. 2). Although the book presents a complete human-centered

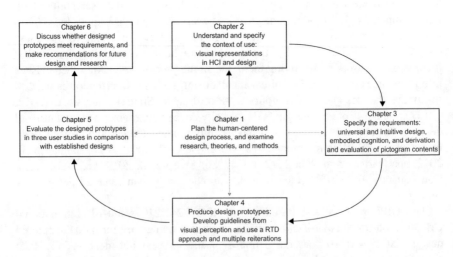

Fig. 2 The UIPP human-centered design process. Each chapter represents one step. Dotted arrows indicate iterations

design process, readers might want to study the chapters separately if they are interested in ideas for specific steps in their design projects:

1. Following ISO 9241:210 (International Organization for Standardization 2010, p. 9), the first step of a human-centered design project consists in the close examination of previous research, the identification of suitable theories, methods, and resources to achieve the goal of the project, and the planning of the project. The subsequent HCD steps are based on the reviews.

   While previous theories and research were examined throughout the UIPP project, in this introductory chapter ("Step 1: Introduction, Goals, and Summary of the Process"), I discuss previous research, and I describe the structure of the project and its goals.

2. In the second HCD step, the context of use, including the users and the user tasks and goals, need to be identified, described, and analyzed.

   Usually, this step consists in a close examination of the real situations in which existing products are used by actual users (e.g., Cooper et al. 2014, pp. 113–117). In UIPP, however, the context of use, the users, and their tasks were specified by the Universal Cognitive User Interface (UCUI) project. That is, the context of use is the universal use of pictograms in HCI, and the pictograms should be comprehensible to all users, independent of culture, age, and capabilities. If this is achieved, the pictograms should be suitable for the UCUI heating system interface, too. For that reason, in UIPP, instead of examining real situations in which users interact with existing pictograms, in Step 2 ("Understanding Visual Representation(s)"), I discuss universal characteristics of visual representations in HCI. That is, I describe in detail the central properties and relations, I discuss existing pictogram systems, and I propose a taxonomy. The goal was to achieve a general understanding of visual representations that might be the basis for the following steps in the process and for other design projects, too. For example, I argue, in order to yield suitable results when designing visual representations, one must always consider two central properties: the design and the reference relation.

3. According to ISO 9241:210, in Step 3 ("Grounding, Deriving, and Evaluating Pictogram Contents"), based on the context of use analysis, requirements for design are specified. Various ways to achieve this exist, for example, through analyses of existing designs, through interviews, and ethnographic observations (Shneiderman et al. 2017, pp. 144–148). Actual users of the designed systems should be involved in the process to provide information, to participate in the design process, and to evaluate the results.

   In UIPP, pictogram contents are considered requirements for pictogram design (as explained in "Step 2: Understanding Visual Representation(s)"). Consequently, following the examples by Hurtienne et al. (2008, p. 242) and Löffler et al. (2013, pp. 5–6), grounding, deriving, and evaluating pictogram contents is considered the HCD analysis of requirements, according to

ISO 9241:210. In Step 3 ("Grounding, Deriving, and Evaluating Pictogram Contents"), first, I present general requirements for universal and intuitive design. Then, I discuss the theory of embodied cognition, and I develop requirements for universal, intuitive, and permanent pictogram contents relying on the theory. Finally, I report two empirical online studies that were conducted to derive and evaluate pictogram contents based on these requirements. Users were involved throughout the UIPP process. In Step 3 ("Grounding, Deriving, and Evaluating Pictogram Contents"), they provided data for the derivation of pictogram content candidates, and they evaluated the candidates.

4. In Step 4 ("Developing a Design System and Producing the UIP Pictograms") of a HCD process, a design team produces prototypes based on previous findings and on existing guidelines. The design team should include people with various disciplinary backgrounds, skilled, for example, in human–computer interaction, user interface design, user research, technical support, and software engineering. According to ISO 9241:210, the designed prototypes should be refined continuously, for example, through iterative evaluations. Reiterations are useful because human–computer interactions are complex, and requirements can hardly be specified in their entirety at the beginning of a design process. Instead, many requirements will emerge only during the process.

In Step 4, I describe the design production process. First, I suggest that the process of visual perception is universal, intuitive, and permanent. Consequently, I derived guidelines for universal, intuitive, and permanent content design from research on visual perception as part of the UIPP project. Then, I report a research through design (RTD) process that was used to produce the pictogram prototypes, following the previously derived guidelines and using the evaluated pictogram contents. All skills mentioned above were found in the UIPP design team, and several iterations were done during the production process.

5. According to ISO 9241:210, in the fifth step, the designed prototypes should be evaluated by real-world users. All requirements should be fulfilled, including requirements that emerge only during evaluation. While evaluations should be part of each HCD step in order to refine continuously the requirements for design, at the end of the project, the designed prototypes should be evaluated thoroughly.

In UIPP, while several evaluation studies were conducted during the entire process, in Step 5 ("Evaluating the UIP Pictograms"), I report four user studies that evaluated in detail the produced UIP Pictograms by comparing them with established manufacturer pictograms. In these studies, three different approaches were used consisting of comprehension tests, direct comparisons, and subjective ratings to determine whether the UIPP prototypes are more suitable than the established pictograms and whether they might be considered universal, intuitive, and permanent. I contend that the evaluation was successful.

6. Finally, ISO 9241:210 suggests that the conformity of the designed prototypes with the requirements should be discussed, and recommendations regarding future designs and processes should be made.

   To that end, in Step 6 ("Conclusion, Implications, and Future Research"), the UIPP design process is summarized, drawbacks are discussed, and recommendations for design and for future studies are made. In conclusion, I propose a technical process for the design of suitable pictograms. See Fig. 2 for the complete UIPP human-centered design process.

Step 2: Understanding Visual Representation(s)

Abstract

In the second HCD step, the context of use, including the users and the user tasks and goals, needs to be identified, described, and analyzed. This step usually consists in a close examination of real situations in which existing products are used by actual users. Since the context of use in the UIPP project was specified by the Universal Cognitive User Interface project, this chapter discusses universal characteristics of visual representations in HCI. That is, it describes in detail central properties and relations, it discusses existing pictogram systems, and it proposes a taxonomy of visual representations. For example, it argues that always two central properties must be considered: the design and the reference relation. The goal of the chapter is to achieve a general understanding of visual representations that might be the basis for the following steps in the process as much as for other design projects.

Various Terms and Definitions

Research on visual representations is vast and variegated. This holds for HCI and for human science and practice in general. As Gittins (1986) said:

> Interest in the use of pictographic symbols is not confined to human-computer interface design. Considerable attention has been focused on iconic communication in human language, cognitive psychology, in signposting for public services, in equipment controls, as well as in graphic arts. (p. 520)

In line with the vast number of studies on visual representations, many, sometimes incoherent definitions and taxonomies exist, and several terms are in use for what I call *pictogram*. I suggest, this variety of definitions and taxonomies indicates a

D. Bühler, *Universal, Intuitive, and Permanent Pictograms*,
https://doi.org/10.1007/978-3-658-32310-3_2

lack of understanding of visual representation in HCI. To illustrate this, I present some definitions in chronological order. Gittins (1986), for example, defined *icons* as "pictographic symbols which are used as part of the dialogue in order to represent processes and data in the computer" (p. 523). Horton (1994) stated that everything on a computer screen "that is not a word label or a window border is an icon" (p. 2). Honeywill (1999) used the terms *icon* and *graphical symbol* interchangeably. Marcus (2003) defined icons as "signs that are self-evident, 'natural,' or 'realistic' for a particular group of interpreters, like a photograph of a person, a 'realistic' painting, or a right-pointing arrow to indicate something should move or is to the right" (p. 38). In addition, he defined *ideograms* as "symbols that stand for ideas or concepts" (p. 38), *phonograms* as representations that refer to a sound, for example, the letter *m*, and *pictograms* as "an icon (or sometimes symbol) [*sic*] that has clear pictorial similarities with some object, like the person or men's room sign" (p. 38). Furthermore, Abdullah and Hübner (2006) defined the concept of pictogram as "an icon sign which represents complex facts, not through words or sounds but through visual carriers of meanings" (p. 11). Wogalter et al. (2006) distinguished *representational symbols*, *abstract symbols*, and *arbitrary symbols*: Representational symbols "refer to the concept fairly directly and generally depict a familiar, easily recognized form" (p. 167). Abstract symbols are similar to the meaning that they represent, however, the relation between representation and meaning is not as direct as in representational symbols. Arbitrary symbols have no "representational relation to the designed concept" (p. 167), and their meaning must be learned by the interpreter. More recently, Massironi (2009) described icons as a category of graphics that is "completely stable and unambiguous, immediately recognizable " (p. 260). Furthermore, he called icons *signals* and counted "ideograms, pictograms, street signals, and other graphic symbols" (p. 260) into this group. Wang et al. (2007) and Nakamura and Zeng-Treitler (2012) provide further reviews.

The amount of distinct taxonomies and definitions for similar or the same concepts suggests that some research in HCI and related fields falls short of an exact understanding of visual representation(s). However, understanding visual representations, their design, perception, and interpretation should be assumed as the basis of subsequent research and design. Moreover, if the process of visual representation is not well understood, I argue, research and design will not yield optimal results. For that reason, in the UIPP project, I analyzed visual representations, I examined existing definitions, and I defined the terms that I use. In this chapter, I present the results. For example, I do not use the term *icon* although it is very common. In general, icons refer to functions in HCI, and they often activate these functions (Gatsou et al. 2012, p. 93; International Organization for Standardization and International Electrotechnical Commission 2010, pp. 1–2; Rau et al. 2013, p. 71). Furthermore, in Ancient Greek, the term icon (i.e., εἰκών, *eikṓn*) refers to an image that is based on similarity. Thus, using the term for visual representations that are based on convention is misleading. Similar holds for the term *graphical symbol*. Symbols are signs that refer to their meaning based on convention, like written language, flags, and so forth (Nöth 1995, pp. 42–45). Consequently, using the term for visual representations that are based on similarity seems inappropriate. Finally, the terms *pictograph* and *pictogram* have the same etymological source: the Ancient Greek verb γράφειν, *gráphein*, which means to write, to draw, or to scratch. While *gráphein* refers to the act of writing, *grámma* refers to the written, drawn, or scratched objects, that is, a picture, written letter, or piece of writing (Elkins 2001, p. 83). As a result, I use the term pictogram because it addresses the designed object. I propose the following definition: Pictograms are single representations that are perceived through the visual sensory channel. They are simple in that their content consists of only few elements. I elaborate on the definition in the following sections.

Defining Basic Concepts: Representation, Similarity, and Sign Relations

Following Giardino and Greenberg (2015), I use the term *representation* to refer to "any event, process, state or object which is a vehicle for content, broadly construed" (p. 2). Consequently, a *visual representation* is an event, process, state, or object that carries meaning and that is perceived through the visual sensory channel. Of course, this is a broad definition. It includes writing, too, because writing is perceived visually and refers to a given meaning. According to Giardino and Greenberg (2015, pp. 1–3), there are two categories of representations that are perceived through the visual sensory channel. The first category is entirely based on convention, for example, written language, signal flags, and Arabic numerals. The second category is based on similarity, like realistic photographs, line drawings, maps, and diagrams. The latter category is the focus of the UIPP project. In the following, for reasons of readability, I use the term visual representation to refer only to the second category.

Of course, the term *similarity* needs further specification. Greenberg (2013) stated: "similarity is defined simply as sharing of properties" (p. 229). On the one hand, according to Lopes (1996, pp. 150–151), similarity or resemblance is representation-dependent. That is, a representation must carry properties that can be interpreted as being shared with an object, creature, or scene that is not the representation. On the other hand, similarity is recognition-dependent. That is, a user must be able to recognize these properties as shared with that object, creature, or scene. This two-fold description indicates that at least two important relations are involved in visual representation: the reference between representation and objects and the interpretation of the representation by a user, based on the design of the representation.

In their discussion of visual representation, Giardino and Greenberg (2015) referred to one approach in particular: Charles Sanders Peirce's theory of semiotics (p. 537). Semiotics is called the "science of signs" (Nöth 1995, p. 3). A *sign* is any phenomenon that is interpreted as conveying or communicating meaning.

Consequently, semiotics addresses representation (Chandler 2018, pp. xvi, 2).[1] Peirce described signs as consisting of three parts. First, an object, idea, or a concept that the sign refers to. He called that part the *referent*. Second, the material part of the representation, that is, the real-world forms and patterns that a human being perceives. He called that the *representamen*. Third, the interpretation that a person makes of the representation. Peirce called this the *interpretant*. Peirce proposed detailed categorizations for the relations between those three parts. Between the referent and the representamen he suggested the notions of *icon*, *index*, or *symbol*; between representamen and interpretant *rheme*, *dicent*, or *delome*; and for the sign and its relations as a whole *qualisign*, *sinsign*, or *legisign* (Nöth 1995, pp. 42–45). While Peirce's categorizations of the relation between representamen and object are comprehensible and widely used especially in studies on visual representation, his other categorizations are difficult to grasp, not directly applicable to visual representation, and subject of discussion among scholars see, e.g., (Chandler 2018, pp. 36–37).

Applying Peirce's Sign Relations to HCI

Barr et al. (2003, pp. 26, 30–31) proposed that Peirce's triadic model can be applied to the design of visual representations in HCI (see Fig. 1).

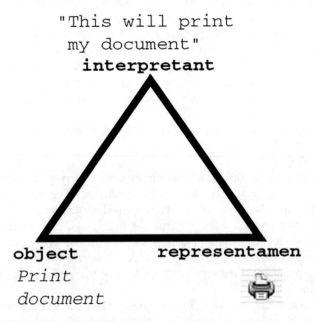

Fig. 1 A diagram of the Peircean triad as applied to a print pictogram (Barr et al. 2003, p. 26)

---

[1]De Souza has argued as early as in 1993 (pp. 771–772) that, in addition to findings in cognitive sciences, semiotics would lead to a better understanding of HCI.

They argued that Peirce's interpretant equals the designer's thoughts and mental representations when designing the visual representation, and it equals the user's individual interpretations when using the visual representation, for example, *This will print my document if I touch it* (on top of the diagram). The representamen equals the graphical user interface and the pictograms, that is, the real-world material representation, its content, and its design, for example, the printer on the bottom right. Finally, the object or referent is the intended meaning that the representation is referring to, for example, the process of printing a file or *print document* (see Fig. 2).

Let me add the following explanation. First, the content of a representation is not the idea, concept, or object that the representation refers to. The content of a visual representation are the patterns, forms, or objects that we recognize or see in the representation. For example, in Fig. 2, in general, we are able to recognize the object *printer*. However, the representation does not refer to the printer as its intended meaning. Instead, it refers to the meaning of printing. Second, I use the term *meaning* differently than it is often used in cognitive sciences or linguistics. In cognitive sciences and linguistics, the term is often used for what I call interpretation. Nevertheless, I use the term for the intended meaning of the representation, that is, the object, idea, or concept that the representation refers to, because this is the lexical definition of the term (The Merriam-Webster.com Dictionary 2019),

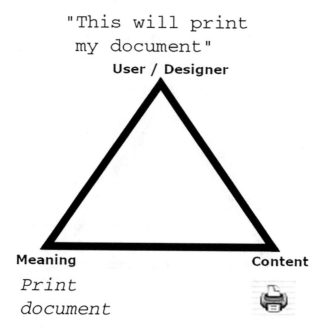

Fig. 2 Adapted diagram of the Peircean triad as applied to a print pictogram adapted from (Barr et al. 2003, p. 26)

it is how the term is commonly used in design, and it corresponds with our everyday usage of the term (see Frege and Textor 2007), too. Third, I use the term meaning not exclusively to refer to propositional meanings, that is, meanings that can be communicated through language, for example, objects, concepts, functions, and so forth. Instead, the term includes emotional states, feelings, and multimodal sensations that might be conveyed through a visual representation, too. As a consequence, following Bourges-Waldegg and Scrivener (1998, p. 299), I argue that meaning is one of the central issues in design and HCI.

In line with Barr et al.'s application of Peirce's triangle, I suggest that three relations are involved in the process of visual representation in HCI that can be described as follows: First, the relation between designer and material representation. The designer starts with some thoughts and ideas that she wants to communicate. In order to communicate these thoughts, she chooses the content of the representation and designs the content in a specific way, that is, the material representation (e.g., the printer in a cartoon style). I call this the *design relation*. Second, the relation between the material representation, that is, its content, and the intended meaning. The representation is referring to the intended meaning in a specific way, for example, in case of the printer through contiguity (see Sect. "Defining Basic Concepts: Representation, Similarity, and Sign Relations"). I call this the *reference relation*. Third, the relation between the intended meaning that the representation is referring to and the user, in other words, the interpretation of the intended meaning by a user, for example, *This will print my document if I touch it.* I call this the *interpretation relation* (see Fig. 3).

Fig. 3 Adapted diagram of the Peircean triad as applied to a print pictogram adapted from (Barr et al. 2003, p. 26)

Fig. 4 Like icon (Cresnar)

The so-called like button may serve as another example (Fig. 4). Here, the abovementioned three relations can be distinguished as follows. The designer designed the content of the pictogram, that is, a clenched hand with a stretched thumb, as a stylized black-and-white line drawing. This is the design relation. The content refers to the pictogram's intended meaning, that is, *to like something*, based on convention—the pictogram's meaning is due to the socially established use of the gesture. This is the reference relation. Finally, the pictogram might be interpreted by a user as referring to the individual liking of a specific content, information, or post on social media. This is the interpretation relation.

I follow Barr et al. in that both the design and the reference relations are crucial for the interpretation relation to be successful. That is, design as much as reference must be realized in suitable ways for the user to be able to comprehend the representation. Only if both the design and the reference relation are suitable, the representation is comprehensible. If only one of the two relations is comprehensible, the pictogram is not. Take, again, Fig. 4. If we are not familiar with the convention of a clenched hand with a stretched thumb meaning *to like something,* the reference relation is incomprehensible to us, and we are not able to interpret the pictogram successfully. If we are not able, for example, to recognize the curved line on top of the hand as a stretched thumb, the design relation is incomprehensible to us, and, again, we are not able to interpret the pictogram successfully. Along those lines, I hypothesize, for a visual representation to be universally, intuitively, and permanently comprehensible, both relations, the design relation and the reference relation, must be universally, intuitively, and permanently comprehensible. If, for example, only one of the two relations is universal, intuitive, and permanent, I argue, the representation is not. For that reason, in the next section, I discuss both relations in more detail.

Conceptualizing the Relations of Design and of Reference

Although there is a large number of designed visual representations and a large number of studies on visual representations, a problem with many approaches is that they do not address the relations of design and of reference separately. They rather conflate them (Nakamura and Zeng-Treitler 2012, pp. 538–540). For example, theoretical scholars often focus on the relation of reference while neglecting the design relation. Designers, in contrast, tend to focus on the design relation while neglecting the other (see, e.g., Isherwood et al.'s (2007) approach). This is a drawback because it renders the approaches less precise. As a consequence (see Sect. "Various Terms and Definitions"), research and design might not yield optimal results. For that reason, in this section, I discuss both relations and their universal, intuitive, and permanent comprehension separately.

Approaching the Reference Relation

In a detailed study, Nakamura and Zeng-Treitler (2012) analyzed 846 health-related pictograms. They argued that it is crucial to understand the relation between the material representation and the meaning of the representation. I called this the reference relation. As described above (see Sect. "Defining Basic Concepts: Representation, Similarity, and Sign Relations"), Peirce distinguished three categories of reference relations: iconic, symbolic, and indexical relations. Iconic relations refer to meanings based on similarity, for example, a depiction of a person. Symbolic relations refer to meanings based on convention, for example, written words and letters. Indexical relations refer to meanings based on cause-and-effect, for example, the smoke of a fire (see, e.g., Nöth 1995, pp. 42–45). In their paper, Nakamura and Zeng-Treitler (2012, pp. 538–540) proposed a taxonomy that they based on Peirce's categorization. However, they suggested an adaptation. While they agreed that one category of reference relations is based on similarity and a second on convention, they argued that the third category of relations is not exclusively based on cause-and-effect. Instead, it contains many more types. They proposed that the third category is based on semantic associations, and they suggested that "prior studies have not yet produced a classification that is granular enough to distinguish among the different types of indirect approaches" (p. 539). For that reason, they provided a detailed description.

In the category of *semantic association,* the reference relation is neither based on similarity nor convention "but mediated as in the case of a picture of a clock used to convey the concept 'time'. Because there are no visual counterparts to the concept 'time', one can create a pictograph not by visual but by semantic proximity. In this case, a device used to measure time, which has an easily identified form, stands for the concept of time itself" (p. 544). The described relation is indirect, or semantic. If the representation were intended to refer to the object of a clock, not to the concept of time, the reference relation would be based on similarity because the content of the representation would be similar to the object clock. Nakamura and Zeng-Treitler described seven types in the category of semantic association. I adapt them slightly:

1. *Comparison or contrast:* A meaning is referred to by using objects as the content of a representation including conventional elements that indicate comparison. For example, arrows might be used to indicate a comparison between two objects.

2. *Exemplification:* Multiple examples of a content are represented to refer to a more general or collective meaning. For example, multiple examples of food are represented to refer to the concept of food.
3. In *physical decomposition,* a part of an object or concept is used to refer to the complete object or concept, for example, a crown that refers to a queen. This type of reference relation is called a synecdoche in language. Nakamura and Zeng-Treitler called it physical decomposition although, for example, a crown is not a physical part of a queen. However, a crown might be considered a part of the concept of a queen.
4. In *semantic narrowing,* the meaning that is referred to cannot be perceived through the visual sensory channel, for example, a smell or the concept of happiness. For that reason, a content is represented that is naturally connected to the meaning but is not an exemplar or a part of the meaning, as in Types 2–3. Take, for example, a smiling face that refers to the meaning of happiness. The face is not happy in itself, but it is naturally connected with people who are happy. A second example is a flower that refers to the concept of smell. Smell cannot be represented through the visual sensory channel. The content of a flower might refer to the concept of smell because, in general, smell is considered naturally connected with flowers. In contrast to Nakamura and Zeng-Treitler (2012, p. 546), I include body language in this type of semantic association because body language is closely connected to the emotion or bodily state that it refers to, for example, facial expressions and body posture. However, gestures like the thumbs-up gesture that Nakamura and Zeng-Treitler mentioned (see Fig. 4) are conventional, thus, part of the second category of reference relations, that is, symbolic relations.
5. *Temporal decomposition* is used to refer to actions or events. In this type, snapshots or excerpts of an action are used as content to refer to the complete action or event as the meaning of the representation.
6. *Metaphor:* Characteristics of one object are mapped onto another. Nakamura and Zeng-Treitler gave the example of a cactus that is drawn over a tongue (see Fig. 10). This visual representation refers to the meaning of *dry mouth.* The cactus refers to the meaning *desert.* The tongue refers to the meaning *mouth.* The desert's characteristic of dryness is mapped onto the tongue's meaning mouth. This type is very common in written and spoken language (see my discussion of conceptual metaphor theory in Sect. "On the Formation of (Abstract) Mental Representations". However, the presented type is a visual metaphor, see, e.g., Forceville 2008, 2009).
7. *Contiguity* is similar to semantic narrowing. However, here, the represented content is not naturally connected to the meaning that the representation refers to. Instead, the content that is used has a human-made connection to the intended meaning. For example, a sphygmomanometer that refers to the concept of blood pressure, or a glass that refers to the meaning of water (Nakamura and Zeng-Treitler 2012, pp. 544–546). According to Nakamura and Zeng-Treitler, contiguity is called metonymy in language. They said, the type can be

distinguished further into the subtypes of physical contiguity, container, source, use, tool, cause or effect, and object.

It is important to note that most visual representations consist of more than one category or type of reference relation. That is, in general, categories and types are combined. I argue that the first category, that is, iconic relations, is a candidate for universal, intuitive, and permanent reference relations because it is based on similarity with real-world objects that everybody might encounter. However, only few meanings can be referred to based on similarity with real-world objects or creatures alone. The second category is based on convention, that is, repeated use or social agreement. On the one hand, by definition, this category of reference relation is culture specific. On the other hand, in order for a user to be able to understand the category, the user requires learning of the convention. For that reason, the second category is not a candidate for universal, intuitive, and permanent reference relations. The third category, that is, semantic association seems the most complex category, as illustrated by the discussion of the various types and subtypes above. At the same time, Nakamura and Zeng-Treitler argued that most meanings are referred to through this category. I propose that some types of this category are candidates for universal, intuitive, and permanent reference relations. For example, it seems likely that most people are familiar with the connection between flowers and smell, as in the type of semantic narrowing. Furthermore, most people might be able to interpret successfully snapshots of certain actions, for example, a snapshot of a running person, as in temporal decomposition. In conclusion, I suggest aiming for categories 1 and 3 in order to achieve universal, intuitive, and permanent reference relations. While Category 1, that is, similarity, seems easy to achieve, designing universal, intuitive, and permanent semantic association might be challenging. Consequently, Step 3 of the UIPP project consists in the development of an approach to the derivation of universal, intuitive, and permanent semantic associations.

Approaching the Design Relation

There are countless ways of designing a visual representation (Greenberg 2013, pp. 238–239, 245, 249). Thus, the question arises, how these design relations can be categorized. Greenberg (2011, pp. 160–163) argued that the designs of representations can be organized along a single axis. This axis has two poles. The first pole consists of visual representations that are designed in a way that makes them appear identical to the objects or scenes that they depict. I call these objects or scenes real-world objects or scenes. Jacob et al. (2007) defined the real world as "the undigital world, including physical, social, and cultural reality outside of any form of computer interaction" (p. 2466). In case of the first pole, the user is not able to distinguish between the three-dimensional real-world objects and their depiction on a two-dimensional surface, for example, in the case of trompe l'oeils and realistic photographs. These representations are often called *concrete* (see, e.g., Curry et al. 1998). In contrast, the second pole consists of visual representations that are designed in a way that makes them appear *abstract*. Here, the design relation is not based on similarity with a real-world object or scene, but it is arbitrary or conventional, for example, in the case of charts, graphs, and Venn diagrams (Giardino and Greenberg 2015, pp. 2–3). I argue that every design relation can be categorized along this axis, although, of course, the axis describes only one property of designs. Nevertheless, this property is central to all designs.

Let me add one aspect. If the design of a representation comes with specific rules and regularities, I call it a *design system*. Take, for example, linear perspective line drawings. Here, two central properties can be distinguished: linear perspective and black (or grey) pencil strokes. Linear perspective is based on optical laws, and it is mathematically defined, that is, it provides precise rules. It is a technique for projecting a real-world scene onto a flat surface (Lopes 1996, p. 129; Willats 2006, p. 1). Consequently, if one uses the technique of linear perspective to represent a scene, the technique determines how the visual representation is designed. Together with black pencil strokes, it contains the central rules of the design system of linear perspective line drawings. Of course, linear perspective is only one of many ways to represent a scene or object on a surface. Other design systems might not include rules of projection that are equally specific or detailed. However, they still come with regularities by which they are characterized, for example, the exaggeration of physical properties in caricatures and the display of various views of an object in a single representation in the case of cubism. These regularities need to be followed if the representation is to be interpreted as belonging to the given design system (Lopes 1996, pp. 129–130). If these rules are not followed, the representation is not. However, designers are free to vary on all other properties. The latter is the reason why every individual design of a representation might be unique.

Design systems do not only contain rules and regularities for the design of visual representations. They also imply rules for interpreting the representations (Giardino and Greenberg 2015, p. 19). This does not require explicit knowledge of the design system and of its rules. Implicit knowledge often is sufficient (see Sect. "Definitions of Intuitiveness in HCI"). That is, often, both designers and users have internalized the properties and rules of a system without necessarily being able to communicate them. It seems evident that many designers are not able to describe the rules that they follow subconsciously when they design. However, they are able to point out when the given rules are violated, which suggested that rules and regularities exist. This is similar to users of GUIs or native speakers of a language who are, often, not able to communicate how a specific GUI works or which grammatical rules they follow when they speak. Speakers and listeners, that is, designers and users, have implicit knowledge of the design systems and, for that reason, are able to use them (Giardino and Greenberg 2015, p. 6).

With regard to the UIPP project, on the one hand, this suggests that pictograms should be designed according to the rules and regularities of a universal, intuitive, and permanent design system. On the other hand, this implies that users need to be familiar with said design system or, as an alternative, be able to derive the rules and regularities of the system intuitively. Since every human being might be familiar with the real world, I suggest, designers should aim for the pole of concreteness in order to achieve universal, intuitive, and permanent designs—in contrast to arbitrary or conventional, that is, abstract designs that require learning. Many studies provide evidence for this suggestion, indicating that pictograms are more comprehensible if they are more concrete, that is, if they are more similar to the real world (Curry et al. 1998; Koutsourelakis and Chorianopoulos 2010; Pappachan and Ziefle 2008, p. 336). However, keep in mind that similarity cannot be easily defined (see Sect. "Defining Basic Concepts: Representation, Similarity, and Sign Relations"). There are no objective criteria in order to achieve similarity. Instead, similarity depends on the design of the representation as much as on the ability of the user to interpret that representation as being similar to a real-world object or scene. That is, it depends on the design system and the user's knowledge of that system. For that reason, Step 4 in the UIPP project consists in the development of an approach to a universal, intuitive, and permanent design system.

Unfortunately, semiotics is not clear about the way the interpretation relation is realized. For example, Peirce stated that interpretation is the outcome or the effect of a sign, creating in the mind of a user an equivalent or more developed sign (Nöth 1995, p. 43). He did not provide a clear account of how this outcome or effect is realized. For that reason, I address interpretation in more detail in the following chapters, in particular from the point of view of cognitive sciences. I take from semiotics that both the design and the reference relations must be suitable for the interpretation relation to be successful. In addition, I hypothesize that for a visual representation to be universally, intuitively, and permanently comprehensible, both the design and the reference relations, must be universally, intuitively, and permanently comprehensible (see Sect. "Applying Peirce's Sign Relations to HCI"). If, for example, only one of the relations is universally, intuitively, and permanently comprehensible, the representation is not. Based on this assumption, I present some historical and contemporary examples of visual representations in the next section, and I examine them in light of my hypothesis. I propose that they are not universal, intuitive, and permanent because they fail to achieve the said in both of the abovementioned relations.

Historical and Contemporary Examples of Visual Representations

Prehistoric cave paintings are considered the first visual representation produced by human beings. Just like pictograms today, they were painted for communication and interaction (Horton 1994, p. 7). Today, although we are still able to recognize the objects that they depict because the paintings are similar to the real-world objects they refer to—this is the design relation—we do not know the exact meaning or purpose of the paintings. The paintings were painted as instructions. Since the conventions on which the paintings were based are lost, the reference relation is unknown to us. As a consequence, the interpretation is not successful, and the paintings are neither universally, nor intuitively, nor permanently comprehensible.

Early *ideographic* scripts were based on pictograms, too. In ideographic writing systems, ideographs represent individual concepts (Bußmann and Trauth 1996,

p. 46; Crystal 2011, p. 235), for example, the cuneiform writing system by the Sumerians. Although originally based on similarity, the design relation of cuneiforms is abstract. Thus, it requires learning for a user to be able to distinguish cuneiforms. In addition, the reference relation between the ideograph and its meaning is conventional. Consequently, the reference relation requires instruction, too. For that reason, I argue, neither of the relations is universally, intuitively, nor permanently comprehensible. Consequently, cuneiforms are not universal, intuitive, or permanent.

Subsequently, ideographic systems were transformed, among others, into Egyptian *hieroglyphs*. Hieroglyphs are a set of approximately 700 visual representations appearing first 3100 BC in the Nile area (Honeywill 1999, p. 16). The design relation of hieroglyphs is based on similarity with real-world objects and creatures. However, the first part of the name of the represented object is a syllable of the word that the hieroglyph is referring to. This is the reference relation. For example, in hieroglyphs, the word *hate* might consist of a representation of a horn and of a tiger. Hieroglyphic writing systems are also called *logographic* (Crystal 2011, p. 289). While the design of a logographic representation might be similar to a real-world object or creature, as it is the case for hieroglyphs, the relation between the representation and the meaning that it refers to is grounded in the culture in which the writing system is used. Accordingly, logographic systems require learning, and they are neither universal, nor intuitive, nor permanent. This is evidenced by the fact that the meanings of hieroglyphs were lost and only deciphered again in the nineteenth century.

In the Renaissance, interest in universal writing systems increased, especially in *pasigraphies*. Parsigraphies are artificial communication systems that strive for universality by using characters that refer to one concept each. An early 19th-century example is Andreas Riem's Synonymicum. Riem suggested assigning to every word in a language a distinct number. The same numbers should be attributed to the same words in different languages. That is, if the number 199 was attributed to the word *house* in English, the word *Haus* in German would have the number 199, just like the word *maison* in French. Combinations of strokes indicated basic grammar. Another example is Anton Schmitt's proposal of a unified alphabet for all peoples in 1866. He suggested introducing the alphabet through visual representations of objects that were pronounced like the letter that the representation was referring to—a suggestion similar to hieroglyphs (Stöppel 2014, p. 25). While potentially being universal because of standardization, both systems were difficult to learn because neither the design nor the reference relations were intuitive. Additionally, the understanding of numbers and the names of objects can hardly be considered permanent.

A more recent example is ISOTYPE (International System Of TYpographic Picture Education) (Neurath and Neurath 1980). ISOTYPE was created by Otto Neurath starting in 1924 with the intention to visualize statistical data in a comprehensive way. In ISOTYPE, basic pictograms can be combined in order to convey more complex information. ISOTYPE is an interesting approach, seems easy to understand, and it is still widely used. Some pictograms are designed similar to their meanings, thus, seem to have the potential to be universally, intuitively, and permanently comprehended. However, other elements referring to more complex and abstract meanings appear to be abstract, and they refer to their meaning based on convention. Consequently, they impede universal, intuitive, and permanent comprehension.

The Human Interference Task Force (HITF) researched visual representations with a different intention. HITF was a group of scientists from distinct disciplines, among others, the psychologist Paul Ekman and the linguist and semiotician Thomas Sebeok. The task force was introduced in the 1980s when it was requested by the U. S. Department of Energy to design a system of warning symbols to warn about radioactive waste sites. Since languages and other communication systems transform over time, the special goal of the group was to create a system that should be capable of conveying the intended meaning after 10,000 years. In the end, the system was considered not successful because it was incomprehensible to users who were not previously instructed. In 2004, the system was revised. Two pictograms of human faces referring to certain emotional states were added to the HITF sign system to increase universal, intuitive, and permanent comprehension. The signs were installed at the Waste Isolation Pilot Plant in New Mexico, USA (see Christian 2017, pp. 125–127, 133, 201, 214).

Although visual representations as elements of GUIs are ubiquitous today and most users take them for granted, they were introduced only in 1981 with the Xerox star (MacKenzie 2013, pp. 11–14, 22). In 1984, the first Apple Macintosh included approximately 250 pictograms. Since then, their number increased substantially. Marcus (2003) wrote:

> 1982 to 1985, when we first started designing icons for computeraided design and manufacturing applications, it was not unusual for companies to brag that they had somewhere between 5,000 and 15,000 signs (they sometimes were not sure of the exact number and had no easy way to find out). (p. 39)

In addition, the pictograms "were poorly designed. To be more specific, they were illegible, unreadable, with poor usability (efficiency, effectiveness, and satisfaction), and poor internal system consistency (visual syntax, semantics, and pragmatics)" (p. 39). For comparison, in Standard Mandarin, a person must be able to use approximately four thousand of the language's logograms in order to be considered literate (Norman 1988, p. 73), and Mandarin characters were developed over hundreds of years.

An early system of visual representations that was used in HCI is Bliss or Semantography (Bliss 1978). Bliss was developed by Charles Bliss since 1942. It is based on linguistics and holds a lexicon of 100 basic symbols which can be combined in order to create new words and sentences. Some of the pictograms are fairly similar to the real-world objects that they refer to, however, other pictograms are conventional and bear almost no resemblance (see Fig. 5). Accordingly, they require learning, and they cannot be considered universal, intuitive, or permanent. Bliss contains pictograms for nouns, and it contains elements of pictograms conveying additional meanings like the plural form and gender. Charles Bliss asked the United Nations to adopt the system, but his request was declined. Today, Bliss

Fig. 5 Bliss symbol *hand*. (Blissymbolics Communication International 2019)

symbols are implemented in computer systems for disabled persons in order to help them communicate (Beardon 1995, pp. 190–191; Horton 1994, pp. 11–13; Marcus 2003, p. 42).

A similar example is LoCoS (Lovers Communication System). LoCoS was designed by Yukio Ota in the 1960s with the intention to improve cross-cultural communication (Ota 1973). LoCoS consists of mostly conventional signs which bear minor similarity with the related concept. More complex meanings and sentences are formed by combination (Ota 2011, pp. 3–4).

Many more recent pictogram systems for HCI follow the same approaches, for example, Minspeak (Baker 1982) and IconText (Beardon 1995). IconText is one of the few that uses animation. A pictogram system by Takasaki and Mori (2007) continuously adds new pictograms if needed (Cho and Ishida 2011, p. 145). Besides being based on convention many of these visual representation systems consist of basic pictograms with a fixed meaning and fixed rules for combining these pictograms in order to convey more complex meanings. Apparently, the creators of the systems assumed that repeated use and standardization would lead to universal and intuitive visual representations. However, this was not the case (see, e.g., Beardon 1995, pp. 190–191). For every system, at least one of the relations of design or reference is not universal, intuitive, or permanent.

Some current examples of pictograms in industry applications are presented in Fig. 6. The contents of these pictograms are recognizable, a *group* or *several people*. However, their designs are rather abstract. Although the design relation is based on the silhouettes and contours of real people, the way of designing the content is stylized and appears to be arbitrary, created by one designer or a small group of designers. While some users might argue that the design appears intuitively comprehensible to them, I counter that this is only the case because these users are familiar with the pictograms. Users that are not familiar with the pictograms, for example, elderly users or users from non-western cultures, might have more difficulties interpreting the

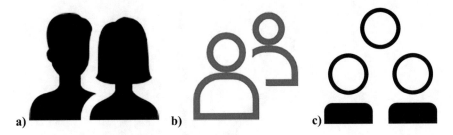

Fig. 6 **a**) Apple TabBar *contacts* (Apple Inc. 2019). **b**) SAP *group* (SAP SE). **c**) IBM *group* (IBM)

pictograms (Mertens et al. 2011). As a consequence, I argue, these pictograms are not universally, intuitively, and permanently comprehensible.

Finally, the International Organization for Standardization (ISO), the International Electrotechnical Commission (IEC), and the Unicode Consortium intend to produce visual representations comprehensible through universal standardization (see, e.g., International Organization for Standardization 2011, International Organization for Standardization 2014, International Organization for Standardization and International Electrotechnical Commission 2011, International Organization for Standardization and International Electrotechnical Commission 2017, which are in development since the 1960s) (see Fig. 7).

The Unicode standard is especially interesting because it is an encoding system that claims to consist of visual representations of

> all the characters for all the writing systems of the world, modern and ancient. It also includes technical symbols, punctuations, and many other characters used in writing text. The Unicode Standard is intended to support the needs of all types of users, whether in business or academia, using mainstream or minority scripts. (Unicode Consortium 2019, para. 2)

However, the standards are created by small groups of internationally renowned experts almost exclusively from western cultures. Consequently, they are culture

Fig. 7 **a**) Unicode *thumbs up* (Microsoft Windows 10 OS version) (Unicode Consortium 2019). **b**) ISO *manual control activation*. (Deutsches Institut für Normung and International Organization for Standardization 2008, p. 113)

specific, and they require learning from users who are not familiar with the conventions of the corresponding cultures (see also Beardon 1995, p. 191). That is, the standards are neither intuitive nor permanent. I discuss standardization in more detail in Sect. "One Design for All" (Sect. "Definitions of Universality in HCI").

Categories of Visual Representations

The discussion in the previous section indicates that producing universal, intuitive, and permanent visual representations is not an easy task. With the intention to better understand visual representations, in this chapter, so far, I have discussed the concept of representation, both the design and the reference relation, and important characteristics of these relations. In conclusion, I propose a taxonomy of visual representations that I use subsequently in the UIPP design process.

The starting points for a taxonomy of visual representations are markings on a surface. Ittelson (1996, pp. 171–172) defined markings as patterns on real-world objects that have no reference relation with said objects. Markings do not appear naturally. They are produced or caused by human beings. They are perceived as two-dimensional while objects are three-dimensional. While ordinary perception is exploratory and strives to make sense of the real world, the perception of markings—although closely related to ordinary visual perception (see Sect. "Visual Perception and Perception of Visual Representations")—strives to make sense of the meaning of the markings. In other words, it tries to interpret the information that the producer of those markings intended to convey. As a result, if markings can and are interpreted as referring to a meaning independent of the real-world material representation, they are visual representations of said meaning.

Following Giardino and Greenberg (2015), I defined visual representation as an event, process, state, or object that carries meaning and is perceived through the visual sensory channel—or, more precisely, is interpreted as carrying meaning. I pointed out that there are two categories of visual representations. The first category is based on convention, the second is based on similarity. I said, in this book, I address the second category as visual representations because it is the focus of the UIPP project (see Sect. "Defining Basic Concepts: Representation, Similarity, and Sign Relations"). Now, I am able to adapt the definition of the first category as follows: Both the design relation and the reference relation are either based on abstraction or on convention. For example, the design of letters or written words is abstract. In addition, their relation to the meaning that they refer to is conventional. In contrast, in the second category, at least one of the two relations is based on similarity (see Table 1).

Using the distinctions that I made in the previous sections regarding the reference and the design relation, I propose the taxonomy in Tab. 1. I argued that it is possible to distinguish three categories of reference relation. The categories are based on similarity, convention, or semantic association. For the design relation, two poles can be identified: concreteness and abstraction. I suggest that visual representations can be categorized using these distinctions. However, keep in mind

Table 1 Poles and categories of design and reference relations, including examples of corresponding visual representations

Reference / Design	Similarity	Convention	Semantic association[4]
Concreteness	Trompe-l'œil[2]	Like button[2]	Print icon[2]
Abstraction	Diagram[2]	Written word, heart icon[1]	Data visualization[3]

Notes: [1]First category of visual representations. [2]Second category of visual representations. [3]Data visualizations are not discussed in this book. However, they are an important topic in HCI and other scientific fields (e.g., Hansen and Johnson 2011; Kosslyn 2006; Munzner 2015; Sedig and Parsons 2013; Spence 2014; Tversky 2011; Ware 2013). I propose that they might be a third category of visual representations. [4]Seven types: comparison or contrast, exemplification, physical decomposition, semantic narrowing, temporal decomposition, metaphor, contiguity

that representations might include multiple categories at once. For example, in the case of trompe-l'œils, both relations are based on similarity. Realistic photographs, too, are based on similarity but not exclusively because their reference relation is also based on semantic association through cause and effect. The design relation of maps and architectural drawings is based on similarity, too—although humans might not be able to perceive the similarity (Tversky et al. 2002, p. 248). In their case, the projection of the represented landscape or building is more abstract than, for example, a photograph of the same landscape or of the building. However, it is still similar to the real-world object or scene. Consequently, I argue that the design system of maps should be situated closer to the pole of abstraction on the axis of the design relation, and photographs and line drawings should be situated closer to the pole of concreteness. Let me analyze some pictograms that are used in HCI.

Take again the like button (Fig. 4). The pictogram is frequently used in social media. It depicts a clenched hand with a stretched thumb as its content. The design relation is based on similarity, but it includes abstraction, too. On the one hand, the content of the pictogram is similar to a real-world object. On the other hand, only the contours of the hand are depicted by a thick black line. The reference relation, however, is not based on similarity. The meaning of this pictogram is not *clenched hand with stretched finger*. Instead, the meaning is approximately *to like something*. I argue, for the like button, the reference relation is based on convention because users understand the meaning due to socially established use of the gesture and due to repeated use of the pictogram.

The reference relation of the pictogram in Fig. 8 is identical to the reference relation of the like button in Fig. 4. The meaning of the pictogram is approximately *love*. The representation refers to the meaning based on convention. The design relation, however, is slightly different. While the pictogram content might have initially been derived from a real human heart, I argue that nowadays the content is not designed with the intention for it to be similar to a real-world heart. Instead, the pictogram content is an abstract shape. Consequently, I argue that the pictogram in Fig. 8 should be categorized into the first of the two categories of visual representations along with written language, signal flags, and numerals, because it is based on convention and abstraction.

Fig. 8 Heart icon (Cresnar)

Fig. 9 Detail of "A diagram of the Peircean triad as applied to a Print icon" (Barr et al. 2003, p. 30)

The pictogram in Fig. 9 was introduced in Sect. "Applying Peirce's Sign Relations to HCI". Similar to the like button, the design relation is based on similarity. The reference relation, however, is not based on convention unlike in the case of the like button. According to Barr et al. (2003, p. 26), the meaning of the pictogram is *print document*. Since most users know that printers print documents, that is, that printers are the source or the cause of printing, the representation refers to its meaning based on semantic association, to be precise, based on contiguity.

Fig. 10 is a more complex example by Nakamura and Zeng-Treitler (2012) that was already discussed in Sect. "Approaching the reference relation". Nakamura and Zeng-Treitler argued that this is an example of the semantic association type metaphor. This holds for the reference relation between the pictogram contents mouth and cactus and the intended meaning of *dry mouth*. However, in case the elements that point towards the tongue represent flashes and that they are supposed to mean *something is hurting*, I argue, the reference relation is based on the semantic association type semantic narrowing because *hurt* is an integral part of the impact of flashes on a human being. In addition, of course, the words *dry mouth* written on the bottom of the pictogram are based on convention. The pictogram illustrates that various categories and types of relations can be combined in a single visual representation.

Fig. 10 Pictogram with the meaning *dry mouth*. Detail of "Examples of representation through semantic association: Metaphor" (Nakamura and Zeng-Treitler 2012, p. 546)

Finally, I argue that diagrams, graphs, and organization charts belong to the second category of visual representations, that is, representations that are based, at least partially, on similarity. Their design relation, of course, is abstract. Diagrams are not designed in a way that they resemble visually a real-world object or scenes. However, their reference relation is based on similarity. That is, they refer to a scene, information, or meaning based on similarity with the scene's, information's, or meaning's inherent or internal structure (see also Giardino and Greenberg 2015, p. 4), that is, through structural similarity. As a result, they belong to the second category of visual representations because they are perceived through the visual sensory channel and at least one of the design or the reference relation is based on similarity.

Summary and Conclusion of the Chapter

According to ISO 9241:2010, the second step of a human-centered design process consist in the description and analysis of the context of use by examining real situations in which existing products are used by actual users. To achieve this, various approaches exist, for example, contextual inquiry, creative methods, expert evaluation, focus groups, interviews, observation, questionnaires, and think-aloud protocols (Böhm and Wolff 2013; Holtzblatt and Beyer 2015; International Organization for Standardization 2002; Kompetenzzentrum Usability Mittelstand 2019). Analyzing the context of use is important and foundational. In UIPP, the context of use was specified as the universal use of pictograms in HCI. That is, the pictograms should be comprehensible to all users, in all contexts, independent of culture, age, and capabilities. By producing such pictograms, I propose, the pictograms should be suitable for the UCUI heating system interface, too. Consequently, instead of examining real situations in which users interact with existing pictograms, I discussed universal characteristics of visual representations in HCI. That is, I described the process of visual representation, the relations involved, I discussed existing pictogram systems, and I proposed a taxonomy. The

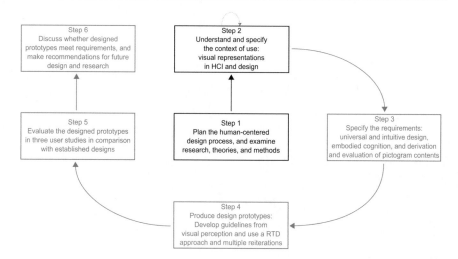

Fig. 11 The UIPP human-centered design process. Step 2 is completed. Dotted arrows indicate iterations

goal was to achieve a general understanding of visual representations that might serve as a basis for the next steps in the process and for other design projects, too. Nevertheless, keep in mind that more specific projects, that is, projects that address more narrow contexts of use than the UIPP project require a thorough analysis of the contexts, by using the methods mentioned above. Then, the analysis of that context of use is part of the UIPP process (see Sect. "Conclusion and the UIPP Technical Process").

This chapter constitutes the second step in the UIPP design process (see Fig. 11). I argued that both the reference and the design relations must be universal, intuitive, and permanent for a pictogram to be universally, intuitively, and permanently comprehensible. Consequently, Step 3 and 4 in the UIPP process consist in the derivation of such reference and design relations. I present the steps in the following two chapters.

Step 3: Grounding, Deriving, and Evaluating Pictogram Contents

Abstract

According to ISO 9241:210, in Step 3, requirements for design are specified, based on the context of use analysis. Various ways to achieve this exist, for example, through analyses of existing designs, through interviews, and through ethnographic observations. In UIPP, grounding, deriving, and evaluating pictogram contents is considered the HCD requirements analysis. Consequently, this chapter, first, presents general requirements for universal and intuitive design. Then, it discusses the theory of embodied cognition, and it develops requirements for universal, intuitive, and permanent pictogram contents relying on the theory. Finally, this chapter reports two empirical online studies that were conducted with 1,967 participants on four continents to derive and evaluate pictogram contents, based on the requirements.

In this chapter, I describe Step 3 in the UIPP process. The third step consists in the UIPP approach to the reference relation and the subsequent derivation of contents candidates for universal, intuitive, and permanent pictograms. The step is composed of three parts. In the first part, I discuss approaches to universality and intuitiveness in HCI, and I present approaches that are suitable. These approaches are grounded in the theory of embodied cognition. As consequence, in the second part, I present the theory of embodied cognition, and I develop requirements for the UIP Pictogram contents from the theory. In the third part, I report two empirical online studies that were conducted to derive and evaluate universal, intuitive, and permanent pictogram content candidates.

D. Bühler, *Universal, Intuitive, and Permanent Pictograms*,
https://doi.org/10.1007/978-3-658-32310-3_3

Approaches to Universality and Intuitiveness

Definitions of Universality in HCI

According to The Merriam-Webster.com Dictionary (2019), the term *universality* addresses "all or a whole collectively or distributively without limit or exception (…) present or occurring everywhere" (para. 1). In general, in HCI, when the term is used, all users across the world are addressed: "Universal design addresses potentially all users and usage-contexts—anyone, anyplace, anytime. Its main objective is to ensure that each end-user is given the most appropriate interactive experience, supporting accessible and high-quality interaction" (Savidis and Stephanidis 2004, p. 244). Two foci can be distinguished: on the one hand, universality with regard to all ages and all physical and cognitive abilities, on the other hand, universality with regard to all cultures. In this book, I call the first focus *inclusive design* and the second focus *cross-cultural design*.

Approaches to Inclusive Design

In line with the abovementioned definition of universality, inclusive design aims at designs that are "usable by the widest range of users, regardless of their personal background, knowledge or abilities" (Hurtienne et al. 2015, p. 236). Consequently, inclusive design focuses on elderly people and on people with physical, mental, cognitive, or sensory disabilities (Marcus 2015, p. 48). Several similar terms are in use for this besides inclusive design, for example, *design for all* and *universal design*. These terms are often used interchangeably and sometimes defined just with slight differences, according to the context in which they are used. For example, the term inclusive design is mostly used in the United Kingdom, and it includes the concept of reasonableness, that is, it considers "that the inclusion of people with disabilities can be disregarded if considered too difficult to achieve or too costly" (Persson et al. 2015, p. 509). The term design for all is used primarily in the EU. In contrast, universal design is used primarily in the United States, and it was defined in relation to architecture to address barrier-free and accessible design. In this book, I use the term inclusive design for a general focus on elderly people and people with disabilities, and I use the term universal design as an umbrella term for both foci on cross-cultural and on inclusive design.

Although inclusive design has been researched since the 1950s, it became a central topic in HCI only in the 2000s (Ostroff 2011). On the one hand, this is because of the ongoing demographic transformation and an increasingly aged population (Czaja et al. 2019, pp. 5–6). On the other hand, this is due to the increasing consideration of people with disabilities worldwide. The latter was expressed, for example, through the ratification of the Convention on the Rights of Persons with Disabilities (CORD) by the United Nations in 2007. Inclusive design addresses that older users as much as users with disabilities have difficulties when interacting with contemporary technology. Their interaction is slower, and they commit more errors than younger users and users without disabilities (Czaja et al.

2019, pp. 15–31; Hurtienne et al. 2010, p. 476). Blackler et al. (2012, p. 575) argued that this is for two reasons. First, elderly users and users with disabilities might be less familiar with contemporary interfaces. Second, often, they have less physical and cognitive ability to interact with these interfaces. Although it is agreed that inclusive HCI is important, there is still a lack of research on inclusive design (this holds for inclusive pictogram design, too, see Schröder and Ziefle 2008, p. 91). Unfortunately, the studies in UIPP were not designed to explicitly address elderly users and users with disabilities. On the one hand, I hoped that a focus on similarities between people might provide a good basis for subsequent research on their individual capabilities (i.e., on inclusive design). On the other hand, an explicit focus on inclusive design would have exceeded the scope and resources of the project. Consequently, the UIPP project focuses on cross-cultural design. Nevertheless, I suggest, the evaluation studies in Step 5 confirm the slower and less accurate comprehension of interface pictograms by older users (see Sect. "General Discussion and Conclusion"). Furthermore, they suggest that the UIPP process might be suitable for inclusive design (see Chap. "Step 6: Conclusion, Implications, and Future Research"). However, this needs further investigation.

Approaches to Cross-cultural Design

Cross-cultural HCI focuses on designs that suit multiple cultures at once or integrates solutions for multiple cultures in one design. There are various and sometimes contradicting definitions of the concept of *culture* (Callahan 2005, pp. 258–263; Heimgärtner 2014, p. 1). I use a general definition, that is, a definition that includes objective as well as subjective characteristics: Objective characteristics are "the institutions and artifacts of a culture, such as its political structures, economic system, social customs, arts, crafts, and literary works. Subjective culture encompasses the psychological features of the culture, values, assumptions, and patterns of thinking." (Callahan 2005, pp. 259–260; cf. Kövecses 2005, p. 1). Cultures are often related to countries or languages. However, they are not determined by them, and borders of cultures, in general, are fuzzy and fluid. In HCI, cross-cultural design became an important topic in the 1990s (Evers 1998, pp. 4–5; Heimgärtner 2013, pp. 62–63). In that context, two categories of research can be distinguished: studies that focus on the analysis of cultural differences and studies that address the production of cross-cultural designs. I present some examples in the following.

Research on Cultural Differences

In HCI, various kinds of differences between cultures have been researched (see, e.g., Callahan (2005); Del Galdo and Nielsen (1996); Plocher et al. (2012) for reviews). In this section, I only discuss findings that focus on GUIs and visual and pictogram design in order to illustrate the challenges for the UIPP project. For example, differences between cultures exist in the presentation of amounts, time, and dates. In Europe, decimals are signaled using a comma while units of thousand are separated with a point. In the United States, decimals a signaled with a point, and thousands are separated with a comma. In Europe, time is presented in a 24 h format. In the United States, time is presented in a 12 h format using a.m. and p.m. as indicators of morning and afternoon. In Europe, dates are presented in the format day, month, year, in the United States as month, day, year. Languages, of course, are distinct. As a consequence, differences in reading direction exist, for example, left to right in Romance languages, right to left in Arabic, and top to bottom in traditional Chinese. These differences strongly influence the user inter-action and the layout of websites (Callahan 2005, pp. 286–287; Marcus 2007, p. 358). For example, Schmid-Isler (2000, p. 4) showed that Chinese homepages are often separated into independent blocks. She argued that this recalls Chinese painting and Art. In contrast, U.S. websites are laid out orthogonally focusing on a central image that is supposed to attract attention. Schmid-Isler argued that this "recalls the western quest for the true perspective, be it in painting, be it in the layout of printed matter or, of course, of webdesign" (p. 4). Walton et al. (2002) showed that hierarchical tree diagrams which are common in western cultures are not readily understood by South African students because of their "exclusion from the hegemonic cultural conventions which govern the organisation of specific domains" (p. 531). Visual representations are interpreted differently in distinct cultures, too. For example, Lee et al. (2014) showed that significant differences in medical pictogram interpretation between U.S., South Korean, and Turkish par-ticipants exist. Brugger (1990, p. 87) showed that Japanese did not comprehend correctly the letter i as indicating information nor the Red Cross as indicating first-aid. Instead, pictograms that are supposed to be international are often adapted in order to suit the specific culture's needs. For example, Sukaviriya and Moran (1990) argued that the trash can pictogram that is used internationally is not suit-able for use in Thailand because, according to them, flies hover over Thai trash cans. For that reason, they proposed an adaption of the pictogram that included flies. Colors are used and interpreted differently, too. Colors that are sacred in the western Christian cultures, for example, blue, red, white, and gold, are not sacred, for example, in Buddhist or Islamic cultures. In Buddhism, the color yellow is sacred, in Islam the color green (Marcus and Gould 2000, p. 34). Callahan (2005) presented another example: "In North America a blue ribbon signifies the best or first in a given class and a red ribbon signifies second; in the U.K. it is the oppo-site" (p. 285). Finally, Duncker et al. (2000, p. 22) conducted a study in which international students could choose among different colors to create a website. English students chose pastel colors with gray and low contrast. Scandinavians used dark colors with low contrasts. Jamaican students used bright colors with high contrasts, and African students chose black as the background color and added brighter colors.

The abovementioned studies focused on specific characteristics of HCI. In con-trast, Geert Hofstede (1997, 2001) developed an approach that enables to analyze complete products by using abstract cultural dimensions that underly the design of these products. Hofstede was an anthropologist who worked with IBM in the 1970s and 80s. Through interviews with large numbers of IBM employees world-wide and subsequent analyses of the gathered data, he was able to distinguish patterns of thinking, feeling, and interacting that were either similar or different across cultures. He argued that cultures vary according to six dimensions: power distance, uncertainty avoidance, collectivism vs. individualism, femininity vs. masculinity, long- vs. short-term orientation, and indulgence vs. restraint. Hofstede defined power distance as the various approaches to human inequality in a culture. He understood uncertainty avoidance as the ways in which a culture approaches the unknown future. Collectivism vs. individualism describes how individuals are integrated into groups. Femininity vs. masculinity addresses the distinct roles that are attributed to women and men. Long-term vs. short-term orientation indicates whether people focus on the present or on the future in a culture. Finally, indulgence vs. restraint is related to the gratification or control of human desires in a culture (Hofstede 2011, pp. 8–16). The dimensions are not considered distinct, and they might overlap. Hofstede suggested rating cultures on indices ranging from 0 to 100, with regard to these dimensions. Hofstede's approach has been used widely in HCI (Callahan 2005, p. 289). For example, Marcus and Gould (2000, p. 35) investigated how the dimensions are reflected in websites in multiple cultures (see Robbins and Stylianou 2002, too). Marcus (2015) showed differences between Western and Chinese websites and Lachner et al. (2018) between German and Vietnamese. Knight et al. (2009, 27, 33) conducted a study revealing that distinct interpretations of visual representations can be analyzed according to Hofstede's dimensions. The proceedings of the International Conference on Cross-Cultural Design provide many further examples (see, e.g., Rau 2013, pp. 367–484; 2018, pp. 285–384).

Approaches to Cross-cultural Design

Similar to inclusive design, for cross-cultural design, there are several terms in use with similar definitions. In addition, distinct design methods might use similar terms, or similar methods might use distinct terms (Heimgärtner 2013, 63–64, 68). Through a cursory literature review, I distinguished four models of cross-cultural design that I describe in the following. I present methods that follow these models, and I explain the terms that are used.

Different Designs for Different Cultures

Several methods exist that follow the *different design for different cultures* model. For example, Jagne et al. (2006, pp. 302–304) proposed a four steps method that aims at cross-cultural design by creating individual designs for individual cultures. They called their method a *cross-cultural design strategy*. They proposed to first investigate the users in the targeted cultures in order to determine cultural characteristics. Second, models of the targeted cultures should be created based on the findings in the first step, and similarities and differences between the targeted cultures should be distinguished. Third, the culture models should be used to produce local design products. In the fourth step, the prototypes are evaluated. A similar method was proposed by de Souza (2005). She called it *semiotic engineering*. Using this method, design products are considered metacommunication artifacts: "They are one-shot messages from designers to users about the range of messages users can exchange with systems in order to achieve certain effects" (de Souza et al. 2001, p. 55). Semiotic engineering distinguishes two parts in an HCI process that must be investigated in order to achieve successful interaction: the designer-to-user communication and the user-system interaction. This holds for every designer and every user, thus, for every culture that a design product is produced for. The goal of the method is to promote culture-sensitivity and cultural diversity (de Castro Salgado, Luciana Cardoso et al. 2013, p. 37). A third method is *intercultural HCI* (Heimgärtner 2013, p. 64). This method emphasizes culture-specific design that is based on the analysis and comparison of multiple cultures to create suitable designs for each culture. Finally, terms that are commonly used in the context of the different designs for different cultures model are *localization* and *internationalization*. Localization is the adaption of products to specific local needs and markets, for example, through language translation. Marcus (2007) said, localization takes place "usually at a scale smaller than countries, or significant cross-national ethnic 'regions'" (p. 357). Internationalization is the adaptation of code, data, and other technical variables of a design product to standards and formats of other regions, countries, and cultures cf. (Callahan 2005, p. 266).

Multi-Layer Design

In 2002, Shneiderman promoted a multi-layer design method that provided different layers for users with different skills and needs. A similar method was proposed by Savidis and Stephanidis (2004). They called it the *unified design method*. They said that designing universal interfaces "implies making alternative design decisions, at various levels of the interaction design, inherently leading to diversity in the final design outcomes. (…) [A] design method leading to the construction of a single interface design instance is inappropriate" (p. 243). According to Savidis and Stephanidis (2004), a systematic approach is needed that integrates alternative designs for different needs "even for the same specific design context (such as a particular sub-task)" (p. 244). Consequently, the unified design method focuses on polymorphic designs to provide various, optional ways of interacting.

One Design for All

The *one design for all* model is the most frequent. A term that is commonly used in this model is *globalization*. Globalization "refers to the entire process of preparing products or services for worldwide production and consumption and includes issues at international, intercultural, and local scales" (Marcus 2007, p. 357). That is, it emphasizes the standardization of already designed products for worldwide distribution (see my discussion of standardized visual representations in Sect. "Historical and Contemporary Examples of Visual Representations"). Standardization has two major advantages. First, it is efficient because a design product does not need to be adapted to various cultures or markets. Second, it is easier for users to use the product if they are familiar with the standard, and users in distinct regions are able to communicate and collaborate if they use the same standards. However, standardization comes with drawbacks, too. For example, if a standard is developed in one country or culture, it might not coincide with the standards and regularities in other countries or cultures. Hsieh et al. (2009) stated that "[t]he majority of current web-based applications assume a one-size-fits-all model (North American model), whereas people from different cultures interact and communicate according to their [the U.S.] cultural context" (p. 712). It can be assumed that this is mostly because of the technology market leadership by U.S. companies. However, U.S. designs are not necessarily suitable for other cultures. Consequently, the habits of one culture (the U.S. culture) are imposed on another and the potentials in the second culture are ignored and not taken advantage of. As an example, users are often excluded if they do not speak English. In addition, standards are often very basic in order for everybody to understand them, and they must be adapted subsequently to each culture in order to be useful. Finally, they are often not very appealing (Callahan 2005, 264, 267).

Universal Model

Instead of transferring one design from one culture to all cultures or integrating various, distinct designs for distinct cultures, the *universal model* aims at a single design that suits all cultures. This is the model followed by the UIPP project. Developing a design according to the universal model seems beneficial at least because of two reasons. First, producing one design that is universal instead of various designs for each user, user group, or culture is much faster and less costly. Second, in an increasingly globalized world with increasing fast and direct interaction between cultures, it seems no longer sufficient to design products that are suitable to each individual group or culture. Instead, designs are needed that allow for interaction and communication between groups and cultures. This seems more likely to be achieved if users share the same design, instead of everyone using distinct designs (Bourges-Waldegg and Scrivener 1998, p. 288).

In the 1970s, single design GUIs, window, icon, menu, pointer (WIMP) interfaces, and the desktop metaphor, that is, an interface that represents a real-world desktop and corresponding functions (Blackwell 2006), were introduced. Many designers and researchers thought them to be natural and universal (e.g., Lodding 1983, pp. 19–20), according to the universal model. However, in the 1990s, through extensive research (as described in Sect. "Research on Cultural Differences"), realization grew that, instead, comprehension of and interaction with these interfaces are influenced by culture. Researchers realized that these interfaces were, in fact, one design for all model designs, instead of universal model designs (Evers 1998, p. 5; Evers et al. 1999, p. 1). Maybe for that reason, recent approaches are much more cautious with regard to claims to universality (see my own discussion in Sect. "Universal, Intuitive, and Permanent Pictogram Project: Two Main Goals"). However, I submit, the intention is still discernable when Kaushik and Jain (2014) said that there is "a broad range of gestures that are almost universal" (p. 143) and Jacob et al. (2008) argued that "these themes apply to most people and most cultures, [although] they may not be entirely universal" (p. 2). Examples of these approaches can be found under the headlines of *natural user interface, tangible computing, embodied interaction,* and so forth. I suggest, in general, the approaches have two central foci: on the everyday and on sensorimotor experiences (Jacob et al. 2007). That is, they "take advantage of users' well-entrenched skills and expectations about the real world", and they "draw strength by building on users' pre-existing knowledge of the everyday" (Jacob et al. 2007, p. 2466). Mostly, the approaches are based on findings in embodied cognition. They yield good results, and they are increasingly important (Dourish 2001; Ishii and Ullmer 1997). Nevertheless, universal design remains a difficult task. On the one hand, the abovementioned approaches might not be able to address all aspects of HCI because experiences had in the context of HCI might lack an equivalent in the everyday real world (Hurtienne et al. 2015, pp. 236–237). On the other hand, it seems difficult to develop a design that suits every user worldwide and those users' individual needs (Hsieh et al. 2009, p. 713)—while, at the same time, preventing cultural confusion (de Souza et al. 2001, p. 12). In Sect. "Embodied Cognition: The UIPP Approach to Suitable Pictogram Contents", I discuss the UIPP project's approach to universal design in more detail.

Definitions of Intuitiveness in HCI

Intuitive is defined by The Merriam-Webster.com Dictionary (2019) as "directly apprehended (…) readily learned or understood" (para. 1). In 1994, Raskin complained that intuitive was a buzzword that was used in marketing but rarely in research in HCI. Regarding interfaces, the term suggests "that normal human 'intuition' suffices to use it, that neither training nor rational thought is necessary, and that it will be 'natural'" (Raskin 1994, p. 17). However, on closer examination, these claims are not fulfilled. Instead, a designed product appears to be intuitive if it is similar to a product that a user has already interacted with. For that reason, we should "replace the word 'intuitive' with the word 'familiar'" (Raskin 1994, p. 18). Today, intuitive is still considered a buzzword (Blackler and Popovic 2015, p. 203). Hurtienne (2011, pp. 15–16) argued that this is the case because of at least four trends: First, products have increasingly more functions, and these functions become more complex. Second, machines turn into software. That is, interaction with controls, buttons, levers, and so forth, turns into interaction with user interfaces. Third, new fields of application come with the necessity to manage abstract and virtual data while the interfaces remain concrete and spatial. Finally, in an increasingly global market, everybody should be able to use interfaces correctly and with little effort, regardless of their culture, age, or ability. The buzzword intuitiveness addresses all four trends by suggesting that less training, thus, time, motivation, and ability are needed to interact successfully with a product that is designed for intuitive use. Consequently, intuitiveness is especially useful "when learning to use new technology, when technology is used only sporadically, and when errors incur high costs (e.g. in safety–critical systems)" (Hurtienne 2017, p. 3). In contrast, it is less important when a lot of time for practicing is available and conscious reasoning is the goal.

Defining Intuitive Use: Prior Knowledge and Automatic Processing

In HCI, research on intuitive use has developed since the year 2000 (Blackler and Popovic 2015, p. 203). Here, intuitive use is commonly defined as the "unconscious use of prior knowledge" (Blackler and Hurtienne 2007, 49). *Unconscious, non-conscious*, or *subconscious use* refers to the automatic or partially automatic cognitive processing of knowledge (Hurtienne 2011, p. 33). *Automatic* means that people are not aware of the process (Blackler et al. 2010, pp. 73–74). Either an automatic process exists since birth, for example, in the case of reflexes, or it has become subconscious through repetition, for example, in the case of knowledge that has been encoded and retrieved many times. Take our use of language. Language is a conventional system of communication, but we are able to use it automatically. This is the case because we have encoded and retrieved our knowledge about language many times. Automatic processing results in lesser cognitive work, and it becomes faster and more probable if the process has been conducted many times (e.g., Blackler and Hurtienne 2007, p. 45, Still and Still 2019, pp. 46–47). *Prior* or *past knowledge*, and so forth, are considered the mental representations of previous experiences that are stored in long-term memory. The process of storing these experiences is called learning. In general, there are two ways of learning: *explicit* and *implicit*. Direct instruction, for example, by a teacher, and the conscious effort of a person are called explicit learning. Their result is explicit knowledge, which is accessible to conscious reasoning. Implicit, tacit, or experiential learning is the incidental and indirect exposure to patterns and regularities that are internalized subsequently and stored in memory by a person. In general, the person is unaware of that process. Implicit learning results in implicit knowledge, which is stored in long-term memory, too, but not accessible to conscious scrutiny or communication. Implicit knowledge can only be recalled in action. One example is our learning of language during childhood. We internalize the regularities of language as children mostly through indirect exposure. At the same time, in general, we are not capable to communicate the rules of language that we have internalized previously. Later, in school, we learn explicitly the grammar of language in order to improve further our use of language (see, e.g., Anderson 2014, 137–141, 144–145, 175–179).

I follow Löffler et al. (2013, p. 1) in their suggestion that intuitive use does not imply that no practice at all is needed. Instead, a short period of training is acceptable if it leads subsequently to more efficient interaction. However, I add, this training should not involve direct instruction. The users should be able to comprehend the interaction or representation exclusively through the application of prior knowledge. In cognitive sciences, sometimes, only the automatic application of implicit knowledge is called intuition, not the application of explicit knowledge (Still and Still 2019, p. 43). I do not make this distinction. Instead of addressing the way of learning the knowledge (i.e., explicit versus implicit learning), I focus on the source of the knowledge, for example, sensorimotor experiences, cultural experiences, and so forth (see Sect. "The Intuitive Use of User Interfaces Group" and "Reality-Based Interaction"). In research on intuitive use, at least two strands can be distinguished: subjective and objective measures (Blackler et al. 2019, pp. 70–76). I describe these in the following.

Subjective Measures of Intuitive Use

Subjective measures approaches aim to assess the subjective experience of users when interacting with a given product. One example is the holistic and phenomenological approach by Diefenbach and Ullrich (2015, p. 229). The authors consider intuitive use a subjective and experiential phenomenon "in between thinking and feeling, which may consist of completely unconscious knowledge transfer but also memorable and verbalizable interaction steps" (p. 229). They distinguish four aspects of intuitive use that they call gut feeling, verbalizability, effortlessness, and magical experience. They have developed an questionnaire to assess these subjective measures (Ullrich and Diefenbach 2010), using the semantic differential technique (SDT) (Osgood et al. 1957; Stoutenborough 2008). The questionnaire consists of 16 questions. For example, participants rate on 7-point Likert-type scales statements like "Using the product... ...was nothing special./...was a magical experience" (Ullrich and Diefenbach 2010, p. 254) (see Study 3.3, p. 304, for my use of the SDT). Another example is the questionnaire for the subjective consequences of intuitive use (QUESI) by Naumann and Hurtienne (2010). Naumann and Hurtienne suggested assessing subjective mental workload, perceived achievement of goals, perceived effort of learning, familiarity, and perceived error rate. QUESI consists of 14 questions designed as bipolar 5-point Likert scales ranging from *fully disagree* to *fully agree* (see my adaptation of one questionnaire item in Sect. "Study 3.3: Subjective Ratings", too). A third example is the approach by Antle et al. (2009, p. 71). The authors used individual, subjective statements on ease of learning, on intuitiveness of learning, and on the amount of concentration required to learn that the participants gave in a post-session questionnaire. In addition, they used the intrinsic motivation inventory (IMI) subscales for enjoyment, interest, and perceived competence (Ryan 1982). These subscales were developed to assess the subjective experience of participants in laboratory studies. In HCI, researchers are increasingly suspicious of subjective measures because several studies have shown that subjective measures are often not reliable (Still and Still 2019, pp. 56–58). They are more positive, culture-specific, and sometimes even suggest the opposite of what is actually used or indicated by behavior (see my discussion in Sect. "General Discussion and Conclusion"). For that reason, in general, objective measures are recommended (Blackler et al. 2019, pp. 75–76).

Objective Measures of Intuitive Use

Objective measures approaches aim to collect objective data on intuitive use, for example, completion time, accuracy and error ratings, latency, or coded videos of participants, in order to assess the intuitiveness of a given product. Two research groups have most influenced the focus on objective measures: the Queensland University of Technology group (QUT) in Australia, that is, Alethea L. Blacker and colleagues, and the German Intuitive Use of User Interfaces group (IUUI), in particular Jörn Hurtienne and colleagues.ss

The Queensland University of Technology Group

The QUT conducted a literature review on intuition in design, cognitive psychology, and HCI in order to arrive at the following definition: "Intuitive use of products involves utilizing knowledge gained through other experience(s). Therefore, products that people use intuitively are those with features they have encountered before" (Blackler and Popovic 2015, p. 203). Following this definition, the QUT focuses on characteristics of products. For example, they conducted studies showing increased accuracy and speed if a user completes a task with a product that shares characteristics with familiar products (Blackler et al. 2010). In line with these findings, the QUT defined a variable that they called *technology familiarity* (TF). *Familiarity* is a sensation that a user has if she encounters a new situation that is similar to her mentally stored knowledge. This sensation increases with repeated exposure to that situation (Gatsou et al. 2012, p. 98; Still and Still 2019, p. 44). Technology familiarity represents how frequently a user uses a given product and how many of the product's functions she uses. The variable is assessed using a questionnaire with items ranging from *never* to *every day* and from *all of them* to *none* respectively (Blackler et al. 2010, 76–77, 86–90). In addition, if a given age group is familiar with a technology because that technology was popular during the formative years of the group, the QUT calls the age group a *technology generation* (Docampo Rama 2001, pp. 4–5).

Based on their findings, the QUT proposed three basic guidelines for the design of intuitive products. First, symbols, functions, and locations should be used that are familiar to a user. Second, if new characteristics are introduced, they should be explained by using familiar characteristics. Third, the same characteristics should be used repeatedly throughout an entire product (Blackler 2008, pp. 217–219). To that end, they developed a tool for the design of intuitive products (see Fig. 1):

According to the tool, in the beginning, the group of users must be analyzed, and the technologies, products, symbols, and functions with which the group is familiar must be determined. Subsequently, the tool proposes an axis of characteristics of products that can be designed to achieve intuitive use. The most basic characteristic of a product are *body reflectors*. Body reflectors are "products or parts that resemble or mirror the body because they come into close contact with it" (Blackler 2008, p. 221). In general, users are familiar with theses bodily aspects since very early in their life. For that reason, body reflectors appear to be self-evident, and every human being might be familiar with them. The next level of characteristics are *population stereotypes*. Population stereotypes are common ways of interacting in a specific culture. They are internalized by human beings very early in life, too, but later than bodily aspects, and they are often cultural conventions, "[f]or example, clockwise movement for progression or increase, and colour codes such as red for stop and green for go" (Blackler et al. 2014, p. 8). However, in other research strands, the term *population stereotype* might refer to ways of interacting in general, and they might be based on innate or sensorimotor

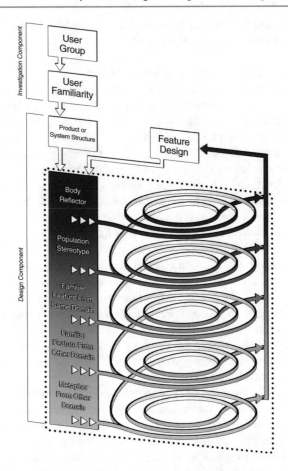

Fig. 1 "Conceptual tool for applying intuitive interaction during the design process" (Blackler et al. 2014, p. 9). The spirals that are part of the tool represent iterations in the design process

knowledge, too (e.g., Hurtienne 2017). At the next two levels, similar features from the same product domain or from a different product domain should be designed in order to allow for intuitive interaction with the designed product. Finally, on the highest level, Blackler (2008) argued that *metaphors* should be used for completely new products and designs. That is, the "retrieval of useful analogies from memory and mapping of the elements of a known situation, the source, and a new situation, the target" (p. 222). I discuss the concept of metaphor in more detail in Sect. "Conceptual Metaphor Theory".

The tool suggests that technology familiarity is the central aspect in the QUT approach. New products should be designed in ways that render them familiar to users. Since only the most basic and established products can be used based on bodily reflectors and population stereotypes, new products need to integrate features of established products. As a consequence, new products should be designed similar to established products in order to be intuitively usable. I suggest, this is a drawback because products will always be designed for a specific group of users with a certain technology familiarity. If users have a high TF regarding the product, they will be able to use the product intuitively. Then, the approach yields good results (Blackler et al. 2012; Blackler et al. 2014). However, if a user group is familiar with a different kind of technology and the group's TF is low, the group will not be able to use the product intuitively. In response, Blackler (2008) argued that "if the design is done well, and if tools and principles suggested here are used, it should be possible to design an interface at any of these levels which people with differing levels of technology familiarity could use intuitively" (p. 224). However, subsequent studies show that this is extremely difficult. In particular, elderly people that are familiar with older technologies are not able to use new designs intuitively in contrast to younger people. This is so because the former are less familiar with new technologies than the latter (Blackler et al. 2012, p. 575, O'Brien et al. 2012). It appears, this might be at least partially related to TF (Blackler et al. 2014, p. 24). In addition, producing designs according to established knowledge of specific user groups goes against all the trends that I mentioned at the beginning of this section. That is, it impedes the development of new technologies, of new interfaces, of new ways of interaction, and, most of all, of designs for all ages, abilities, and cultures, which is the goal of the UIPP project. For example, it does not address differences of TF with regard to cultures that do not (yet) have certain technologies or that use the technologies differently. Consequently, it excludes these cultures. The way to approach this might be to design individual products for each technology generation, following the different designs for different cultures or the multi-layer design model (see Sect. "Approaches to Cross-Cultural Design"). However, as argued above, these are not suitable models for UIPP. Consequently, I do not consider the QUT approach appropriate for the UIPP project.

The Intuitive Use of User Interfaces Group

The IUUI also conducted a literature review. In addition, they conducted interviews and workshops with designers, researchers, and users of HCI. They defined that a system is intuitively usable if the system facilitates effective interaction through the subconscious application of knowledge by the user (Mohs et al. 2006, p. 130) [309]. Later, Hurtienne (2011) described intuitive use as "the extent to which a product can be used by subconsciously applying prior knowledge, resulting in an effective and satisfying interaction using a minimum of cognitive resources" (p. 29). Hurtienne et al. (2015) argued that in principle there are two ways to achieve the subconscious application of knowledge, either through extensive training or "by drawing on knowledge from elsewhere that has been implicitly learned and repeatedly used" (p. 236). The first principle is based on familiarity. It was critiqued by Raskin and improved by the QUT. However, as argued above, that approach comes with an important drawback. That is, products will always be designed for a specific user group with a certain technology familiarity. Consequently, Hurtienne (2017) suggested following the second principle, that is, to use "basic knowledge structures derived from everyday experiences shared by many users" (p. 13). I describe this approach next.

Similar to the QUT, Hurtienne and the IUUI categorized prior knowledge that can be applied in HCI along a continuous axis. However, in contrast to the QUT categorization, the IUUI axis does not focus on the design product but on the domain that is the source of the knowledge (see Fig. 2).

The IUUI categorized prior knowledge from innate, to sensorimotor, to cultural, to expert. *Innate knowledge* is considered to be "'acquired' through the activation of genes or during the prenatal stage of development" (Hurtienne 2011, p. 34), for example, reflexes and instincts. *Sensorimotor knowledge* is acquired very early in life through interaction with the real world, for example, concepts of motion, speed, gravitation, human faces, and so forth. *Cultural knowledge*is learned by interacting with members of a specific culture. Since cultures vary, cultural knowledge can vary, too, for example, concerning values, ways of communicating, and ways of behaving. Finally, *expertise* is considered specialized knowledge, which is developed later in life, for example, in academia, professions, or hobbies. Examples of expertise are knowledge of research methods, medical treatments, and building of complex models. Hurtienne (2011, pp. 34–35) added that the use of tools is distinct because tools might be based on all the upper categories of source domains of knowledge. For example, sensorimotor tools are very simple, like sticks that are used to poke or hit. Tools on the cultural level are more complex, for example, pens that are used to communicate in writing. Expert tools are the most complex, for example, statistical software or robotic surgical systems.

As described above, the earlier knowledge is acquired and the more frequently it is used, the higher is the probability that it will be used automatically, that is, intuitively. Since lower knowledge categories are innate or learned very early, and,

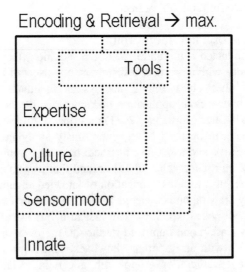

Fig. 2 "Continuum of knowledge in intuitive interaction" (Hurtienne and Blessing 2007, p. 2)

thus, are used very frequently, they are more likely to be applied automatically. The higher the level, the lower the probability is. In addition, for lower categories, it can be assumed that more people have acquired the same knowledge. For example, almost everyone will comprehend the concepts of weight and temperature, in contrast to concepts like multivariate analysis of variance or the pancreaticoduodenectomy which are only known to experts. Consequently, Hurtienne and Blessing (2007, p. 3) argued that focusing on the lower categories of knowledge when designing HCI is advantageous: "Instead of being required to analyse the prior knowledge of the specific target user group, designers might simply refer to rules generated from findings about the general structure of human knowledge (i.e. general human knowledge on the sensorimotor level)" (p. 3). Both Blackler and Hurtienne (2007), that is, the QUT and the IUUI, agreed "that the simpler levels on both continua will apply to more people and applying them where possible rather than the familiar features or expertise levels will make an interface more universally usable" (p. 50).

The IUUI approach has been successfully applied to HCI design in several studies (Hurtienne and Meschke 2016; Hurtienne et al. 2008; Hurtienne et al. 2015; Löffler et al. 2013). In addition, studies suggested that the approach is suitable for the design for all cultures, all ages, and all abilities (Hurtienne et al. 2010, pp. 482–483)—although, of course, further research is needed (Hurtienne 2017, p. 9). With regard to the abovementioned trends in HCI, I propose that the approach addresses all of them. It does neither impede the development of new technologies, nor of new ways of interaction, nor of designs for all ages, abilities, and cultures. Instead, it challenges established HCI and improves it. Consequently, I consider the approach suitable for the UIPP project.

Hurtienne's and colleagues' approach is based on findings in embodied cognition, especially on conceptual metaphor theory (CMT). This is the same basis that suitable approaches to universal designs use, as discussed in Section *Universal model* (Sect. "Definitions of Universality in HCI"). Since suitable approaches both to universal and to intuitive design are grounded in embodied cognition, the theory seems suitable for UIPP, too. For that reason, in the next section, I discuss the theory of embodied cognition in more detail.

Embodied Cognition: The UIPP Approach to Suitable Pictogram Contents

Suitable approaches to universal design and to intuitive design are grounded in embodied cognition (EC). In this section, I discuss the theory of embodied cognition, and I explain why I use it as the theoretical framework for the UIPP approach to the reference relation. Finally, I develop requirements for pictogram contents from the theory. These requirements are used subsequently in the derivation of universal, intuitive, and permanent content candidates.

Basic Claims by Embodied Cognition

Embodied cognition is a theory that has been developed in contrast to the traditional theory of human cognition. The traditional theory, also called *standard*, *Cartesian*, or *cognitivist theory*, holds that cognition happens exclusively in the mind of a person, separate and independent from the body. This view has also been called the philosophical position of *dualism* (Marshall and Hornecker 2013, p. 145). In traditional theory, cognitive processes and mental representations are considered to be amodal and abstract, developed without relation to the sensorimotor experience of a person (Barsalou 2008, p. 618; Gibbs 2005, pp. 80–86). Consequently, these processes and representations are said to be only arbitrarily and statically connected to the objects, concepts, and so forth that they refer to (Wilson and Foglia 2017, para. 4). For that reason, from the traditional point of view, a common way of describing the mind and the brain is that of a processor of symbols, similar to the software and hardware of computers (Antle et al. 2009, p. 66; Shapiro, 2019, p. 47).

In contrast, from the point of view of embodied cognition, it was argued that cognitive processes are grounded in sensorimotor experience. Subsequently, four basic claims were derived from this basic argument:

1. The body of a person, its constitution, motion, and perception, influence and shape the cognition of a person (Wilson and Foglia 2017, introduction, para. 3).
2. Since motion and perception always happen in certain contexts and environments, cognitive processes, in general, are shaped by the physical and social environment (Antle et al. 2009, p. 66; Hurtienne 2017, p. 1).
3. Since cognition in general is shaped by the environment, individual cognitive processes are also influenced and shaped by the specific situation in which they are conducted (Wilson 2002, p. 626).
4. Since the body of a person influences and shapes that person's cognition, the body also constraints cognition. That is, some processes will be easier to conduct, and other processes will be more difficult or even impossible because the body of that person lacks the necessary features or capabilities. For that reason, differences in bodies might explain variation in cognition (Shapiro 2019, pp. 119–120).

Based on these claims, scholars in embodied cognition argued that mental representations in human beings are not amodal or static, as in the traditional view on cognition, but they are grounded in action and perception, thus, they are multimodal and dynamic. EC claims that this holds not only for mental representations of real-world objects but for mental representations of abstract concepts, too (Gibbs 2005, p. 11).[1] On the one hand, it is argued that completely abstract mental representations are rare because even mental representations of abstract concepts

---

[1]This had been previously coined the symbol grounding problem (Harnad 1990).

"are distributed over modality specific domains and involve reactivation of states in sensorimotor systems" (Wilson and Foglia 2017, para. 5). On the other hand, it is emphasized that even completely abstract mental representations are based on sensorimotor experience. I present two theories of EC that explain the formation of these abstract mental representations in the next section. I do so to lay out the theoretical framework for the UIPP approach to the reference relation and for the subsequent derivation of pictogram contents in Studies 1 and 2. Although these EC theories describe the process of formation differently, both share the underlying claim that people's abstract conceptualization of the real world is grounded in basic sensorimotor experiences. Shapiro (2019) called this "the 'trickle up' from basic concepts, through familiar concepts, and onward to more abstract concepts" (p. 120).

Before I present the theories, let me add one aspect. Some scholars, for example, Wilson and Golonka (2013) argued that it is not correct to use the term *embodied cognition* for the claims that I presented above. From their point of view, embodied cognition goes further and implies that "the brain is not the sole cognitive resource we have available to us to solve problems. Our bodies and their perceptually guided motions through the world do much of the work required to achieve our goals" (p. 1). That is, the authors claimed that the body replaces entirely complex internal mental representations, which is also called the *replacement hypothesis* or *radical embodiment* (Lyre 2013). For that reason, the above-described approaches should be called *grounded cognition* (Barsalou 2008, p. 619; Borghi and Caruana 2015, p. 421). A third view on embodied cognition is called *extended cognition* or the *constitution hypothesis*. This view holds that the environment does not only shape cognition but is an integral part of a person's cognitive system: "[C]ognitive systems themselves extend beyond the boundary of the individual organism [and] (…) features of an agent's physical, social, and cultural environment can do more than distribute cognitive processing: they may well partially constitute that agent's cognitive system" (Wilson and Foglia 2017, para. 1). Finally, Wilson (2002) subdivided EC even further into six approaches. In this book, however, I use the term *embodied cognition* for the basic claims presented above. That is, I use it as an umbrella term that "refers to a diverse group of theories and approaches that challenge different aspects of the Cartesian view of cognition" (Marshall and Hornecker 2013, p. 149). Furthermore, in Sect. "Embodied Cognition and HCI", I address some approaches that are established in HCI (again, see Marshall and Hornecker 2013).

On the Formation of (Abstract) Mental Representations

Conceptual Metaphor Theory

The first theory explaining the formation of abstract mental representations is conceptual metaphor theory (CMT). CMT was initiated by George Lakoff and Mark Johnson with their seminal book *Metaphors We Live By* (2003), which is often considered the first major publication in the field of embodied cognition (Barsalou

2008, p. 621; Wilson and Foglia 2017, para. 2). CMT was developed in contrast to traditional metaphor theory. Traditional metaphor theory assumes that metaphors are linguistic phenomena. Thus, metaphors are said to only occur in language, they are considered to be always newly produced, and, therefore, a special case of poetry that does not occur in everyday language. In contrast, CMT assumes that metaphors are a mode of thought and not a mode of language. Metaphors are cognitive processes in which structures and features of one cognitive, that is, mentally represented domain—the source domain—are mapped onto or transferred to another domain, the target domain. This process is indicated by an increasing number of empirical evidence (Barsalou 2008, p. 621). Subsequently, the cognitive mappings can be communicated through language or other modes of communication and interaction. CMT assumes that people understand and conceptualize their environment in general in metaphorical ways. For example, common concepts such as time and love are understood by means of metaphors, that is, by means of cognitive feature mapping. Time is understood spatially, that is, features from the domain of space are mapped onto the domain of time. Time can be in front of us or behind us. Love is understood as a possibly arduous journey that people can take together, and people can part ways again when love ends, that is, features from the domain of journeys are mapped onto the domain of love (Wilson and Foglia 2017, para. 2).

In this context, CMT distinguishes at least four different categories of metaphors. The first category contains *conventional metaphors*. Conventional metaphors are cognitive metaphors that have been established historically in a given culture and subsequently fixed. People learn and internalize them in the course of their lives as members of that culture. Conventional metaphors are used mostly unconsciously and automatically. For that reason, they structure how people think and act in that culture. Take, for example, the previously mentioned metaphor *love is a journey*. In western cultures, this metaphor structures strongly how we think of love and how we act in relationships. Sometimes, conventional metaphors are called *dead metaphors*. However, Lakoff and Johnson (1999) argued that conventional metaphors are still cognitively alive. In contrast, dead metaphors are "linguistic expression[s] that came into the language long ago as a product of a live conceptual metaphor. The conceptual mapping has long since ceased to exist" (p. 117). They give the example of the English word *pedigree*. The word *pedigree* stems from the French *pied de gris*, foot of a grouse. It was based on the cognitive mapping of the shape of a grouse's foot onto a family tree diagram. Thus, family tree diagrams were designed like the feet of grouses, and they were called *pied de gris*. Over time, the word was transformed into the English word *pedigree*. Today, the cognitive mapping of the shape is no longer a part of our cognitive system, and English speakers are not aware of the word's origin. Consequently, the metaphor can be called dead.

In contrast to conventional metaphors, *novel metaphors* are cognitive metaphors that are newly produced by a person. Thus, the cognitive mappings are new, and they have not (yet) been established in a culture. The definition of new metaphor is close to the traditional view on metaphors. New metaphors are considered to be poetic, and they do not occur in everyday language. One example is the metaphor *love is a collaborative work of art*. The metaphor is not established, however, it is a cognitive mapping of features that shapes our concept of love in a certain way (Lakoff and Johnson 2003, pp. 139–146).

The metaphors that we use most often are *complex* or *compound metaphors*. Complex metaphors are made up of other, simpler metaphors. That is, they are combinations of multiple, more basic cognitive mappings (Grady 1997, pp. 37–74; Lakoff and Johnson 1999, pp. 63–74). Gibbs (2005, pp. 78–79) gave the following example: The complex metaphor *theories are buildings* is made up of at least three more basic metaphors, *persisting is remaining erect, structure is physical structure*, and *interrelated is interwoven*. The combination of all three basic metaphors.

> nicely motivates the metaphorical inferences that theories need support and can collapse (...). In a similar way, the combination of STRUCTURE IS PHYSICAL STRUCTURE AND INTERRELATED IS INTERWOVEN gives rise to a different metaphorical compound for theories, namely, THEORIES ARE FABRICS. (Gibbs 2005, p. 79)

Although complex metaphors are either novel or conventional metaphors, that is, they are either individual or culture specific (Evers et al. 1999, 1, 4), there is evidence that complex metaphors are often similar across cultures (Kövecses 2005). CMT holds that this is the case because complex metaphors are grounded in primary metaphors.

Primary metaphors are considered the most basic metaphors (Grady 1997). They are learned through repeated experience of co-occurrences in the world. That is, they are motivated by a sensorimotor experience by a person that comes together repeatedly with a subjective and abstract interpretation by the same person (Hurtienne 2017, p. 2). Through repeated co-occurrences of experience and interpretation in different contexts, the co-occurrences become generalized and lead to automatic cognitive mappings (Hurtienne et al. 2010, p. 477). MacKenzie (2013, pp. 86–88) called these *natural relationships*, in contrast to *learned*, that is, *conventional relationships*. Take, for example, the primary metaphors *more is up* or *affection is warmth*. It is a frequently occurring experience that a material expands vertically with quantity, for example, the level of water in a glass or a pile of sand. Here, the source domain of the metaphor is our sensorimotor experience. That is, we have the described experience because we perceive increasing levels of materials in the real world (Wilson and Foglia 2017, para. 2). The target domain is our subjective interpretation of increasing quantities. Consequently, we map features and characteristics from the source domain of increasing levels onto the target domain of increasing quantities. In the metaphor *affection is warmth*, the source domain is our experience of body warmth. We frequently have the experience that people who are emotionally close to us are physically close, too, for example, our parents who carry us when we are children. Thus, we feel their body warmth. As a consequence, we map the sensorimotor experience of warmth onto the abstract concept of affection, which is the metaphor's target domain (Lakoff and Johnson 1999). Primary metaphors are considered to be atomic. That is, unlike complex metaphors, they cannot be divided into simpler metaphors. They are learned by us automatically during childhood, and they structure subsequently our cognitive system (Hurtienne et al. 2010, p. 477).

Following CMT, in the formation of abstract mental representations three consecutive steps can be distinguished. First, basic concepts are formed through mappings of sensorimotor experiences of co-occurrences in the real world, that is, through primary metaphors. Then, mappings of these basic concepts are combined in order to form more complex and compound metaphors, that is, more complex and abstract concepts. Finally, these complex metaphors are combined again to form the most abstract concepts (Lakoff and Johnson 1999, pp. 63–74; Zwaan and Madden 2005, p. 240). As a consequence, CMT argues that even the most abstract mental representations are based on sensorimotor experience: They represent concepts that are formed through the combination of complex metaphors which are themselves combinations of primary metaphors, and primary metaphors are mappings of sensorimotor experiences in the real world (Lakoff 2012, pp. 776–777). For that reason, abstract concepts such as time and love are understood by means of sensorimotor experience.

Perceptual Symbol Systems

The second theory explaining the formation of abstract mental representations based on sensorimotor experiences that I present the theory to lay out the theoretical framework of the UIPP project is perceptual symbol systems theory (PSS) by Lawrence Barsalou (1999, 2003). Similar to CMT, Barsalou argued that abstract concepts are formed from basic mental representations of sensorimotor experience. However, according to Barsalou (2008, p. 622), instead of being the result of rather straightforward cognitive mappings, abstract concepts are the results of complex simulations in the cognitive system.

PSS holds that the most basic mental representations are formed from perceptual input. That is, stimuli are perceived by us and represented in our brains. Subsequently, we store these *perceptual representations* in memory, and we use them in cognitive processes. Many findings suggest that perceptual representations exist. For example, when a person uses a mental representation of an object in absence of the real-world object, the same areas in the brain are activated as when the real-world object is perceived by that person. That is, stored mental representations and perceptual processes (re-)activate the same sensorimotor areas in the brain (Wilson and Foglia 2017, para. 4). As a consequence, PPS argues that mental representations are not amodal, and their relationship with their referents in the real world is not arbitrary, as argued by the traditional view on cognition. Instead, they are grounded in sensorimotor experience.

Perceptual representations are not restricted to inputs from one sensory channel. Instead, they integrate inputs from various senses, for example, from vision, hearing, touch, and proprioception (i.e., representations of a person's own bodily (re-)action and movement). Consequently, perceptual representations are multimodal. However, they do not necessarily represent the complete initial perceptual input. Instead, they might focus on certain parts, thus, storing in memory only certain characteristics of a stimulus. For example, "selective attention might focus on the form of an object, storing only its shape in memory, and not its color, texture, position, size, and so forth" (Gibbs 2005, p. 86). Subsequently, the cognitive system performs certain operations with and on these perceptual representations. These processes are called *perceptual simulations*. In these processes, perceptual input is re-enacted, and certain characteristics might be selected, extracted, and combined for further processing. These simulations are often complex and, at the same time, partial compared to the initial perceptual inputs—in contrast to cognitive metaphors that tend to be straightforward and complete.

Through these operations and simulations, more abstract mental representations are formed. These abstract representations are called *perceptual symbols*. Perceptual symbols are often unconscious. For example, when people are asked to categorize an object, they do not imagine the abstract category including abstract representations of its characteristics, that is, perceptual symbols. Instead, they imagine a real-world object of that category (Ross et al. 1990). Nevertheless, perceptual symbols are represented in the perceptual cognitive system (Barsalou 2003). For example, the concept of *chair* might not be available to conscious thinking as an abstract mental image of a typical representative of that category. However, it might be represented as a combination of neural activity in the perceptual system in the brain. Thus, while being an abstract representation, it preserves the perceptual characteristics of chairs, thus, our multimodal sensorimotor experience with chairs. As a consequence, more abstract mental representations still share certain characteristics with the perceptual representations on which they are based. That is, they are not arbitrary or amodal. Instead, they are similar to the multimodal perceptual input of real-world objects and scenes.

According to PSS, even the most abstract mental representations are not amodal. They rather include multiple representations of perceptual inputs. This has been suggested by various studies. For example, visual perceptual areas in the brain are active when accessing abstract, conceptual knowledge (Kan et al. 2003). In addition, proprioceptive perception is included in abstract emotional concepts (Wilson 2002, p. 634). For example, the concept of beauty involves our visual perception of instances of beauty, along with internal, bodily states that we feel produced during these instances. Consequently, PSS claims that even the most abstract concepts are based on sensorimotor experience. They are formed through the manipulation of perceptual representations and perceptual symbols in cognitive processes and simulations (Gibbs 2005, p. 90).

The Interpretation of Visual Representations is Based on Sensorimotor Experience

In general, in embodied cognition, it is assumed that there is a close connection between recurring sensorimotor experience, abstract concepts, and the ways these concepts are represented in the real world, for example, through language (Gibbs 2005, pp. 79–80). As I mentioned earlier, cognitive metaphors constitute a mode of thought, but they might be represented through language and other modes of communication and interaction, for example, through visual representations (Forceville 2008, 2009). At the same time, not only the representations of cognitive metaphors are grounded in sensorimotor experiences, but also the interpretations of these representations are. That is, embodied cognition claims that users automatically activate sensorimotor experiences and the mental representation that are based on the latter to interpret modes of communication and interaction (Borghi and Caruana 2015, p. 420; Harnad 1990, 340, 345). I contend that this holds for pictograms, too. Evidence for this has been gathered by various studies (Gibbs 2011, pp. 541–542). For example, Giessner and Schubert (2007) conducted a study in which participants interpreted a visual representation of a manager and her employees. The study participants interpreted the manager as more powerful when the manager was placed vertically higher in the representation, in greater distance to the employees. This is in accordance with the cognitive metaphor *good/more is up*. Casasanto (2009, p. 140) showed that spatial proximity influences participants when judging visual stimuli regarding their functional similarity, that is, with regard to conceptual similarity. Furthermore, in line with CMT, research on visual metaphor is quickly growing in many scientific disciplines, (e.g., Fahlenbrach 2016; Forceville and Urios-Aparisi 2009; Greifenstein et al. 2018; Ortiz 2011).

Of course, neither the use nor the analysis of metaphors in visual representations (e.g., in GUIs) is a novel approach. In fact, visual metaphors have been designed and analyzed for many decades, and they still are in use today (Kennedy 1982; Marcus 2015; Sharp et al. 2019, pp. 78–80). The most prominent example might be the desktop or office metaphor in computers (Gittins 1986, p. 531). However, these approaches come with several drawbacks (see Neale and Carroll 1997 for the most comprehensive study on visual metaphors in HCI; see Blackwell 2006; Carroll et al. 1988, too). In general, in HCI, two categories of approaches to visual metaphors exist. First, approaches that focus on the design of metaphors. I suggest that these approaches are often not based on empirical research, and they do not consider the cognitive and semiotic implications of visual metaphors. Take for example Madsen (1994) who said that only "little research on systematic use of metaphor in this area exists" (p. 57). In addition, Hiniker et al. stated as recently as in 2017 that "the characteristics that make a visual metaphor effective are not well understood" (p. 1). Instead, these approaches often just assume that metaphors are effective (e.g., Marcus 1998, pp. 48–49), considering them to "enable people readily to understand the underlying conceptual model and know what to do at the interface" (Sharp et al. 2019, p. 78). Although some empirical approaches address the design of metaphor, they come with problems, too. For example, they focus exclusively on complex visual metaphors (e.g., Gatsou et al. 2011), that is, metaphors that take cultural experiences as their source domain— not basic sensorimotor experiences as it seems suitable for universal design (Alty et al. 2000; Miller and Stanney 1997; Wang and Huang 2000). Furthermore, these approaches build on existing metaphors that are already established in HCI, that is, conventional metaphors (e.g., Madsen 1994). As Hurtienne et al. (2015) noted:

The theory is often used as a justification for why user-interface metaphors should be intuitive to use, but it is mostly applied to complex compound metaphors (...). Relying too much on complex real-world metaphors, however, can get designers stuck with unwanted constraints the metaphor introduces. (p. 239)

The second category of approaches to visual metaphors focuses on the analysis and the classification of the metaphors. Consequently, the approaches do not address metaphor design. Mostly, these approaches consist either in complex categorizations that are drawn from the literature (Barr et al. 2002; Marcus 1998, pp. 44–45), or they propose abstract frameworks for metaphor analysis (Averbukh et al. 2007; Barr et al. 2004). It appears, a central drawback of these approaches is that they focus exclusively on existing, complex and conventional metaphors—not universal metaphors that are based on sensorimotor experiences. Also, the frameworks seem difficult to apply in metaphor design. I discuss some of the approaches to visual design in more detail in Sect. "Review of Existing Guidelines for Pictogram Design").

So far, I have introduced EC as the theoretical framework for the UIPP approach to the reference relation and for the subsequent derivation of pictogram contents. Although, of course, contrary views exist, for example, the traditional view on cognition, I take two claims from this discussion. First, the most basic claim is that cognitive processes are grounded in sensorimotor experience (see Sect. "Basic Claims by Embodied Cognition"). To support this, I have presented two theories (CMT and PPS) that explain how even completely abstract concepts are formed from sensorimotor experience. Consequently, the first claim that I take from this discussion is that abstract concepts are grounded in sensorimotor experience. In this section, I have explained EC's view on visual representations, and I have discussed other research on visual representations. Although, again, contrary views exist, I take the following second claim from this discussion: EC is a valid approach to visual representations, and the design and interpretation of visual representations are grounded in sensorimotor experiences, too.

Embodied Cognitive Processes Might be Universal, Intuitive, and Permanent

Following my discussion, the question remains, whether embodied cognitive processes might be considered universal, intuitive, and permanent. In PSS, unfortunately, research does not address universality or intuitiveness of embodied mental representations and processes. Following Landau et al. (2010), this might be because PSS focuses on intraconceptual processes, that is, on the question, which sensorimotor experiences are involved in abstract concepts and their mental representations. For that reason, it is used in social psychology, among others (Niedenthal et al. 2005, p. 206). However, PSS does not predict how or in which way these perceptual inputs are used to form mental representations. Consequently, it does not address whether the process of formation might be universal, intuitive, or permanent. In contrast, Landau et al. (2010, p. 1054) argued that CMT is an interconceptual theory. CMT explains how abstract mental representations are formed by mapping more basic concepts onto more abstract concepts. Consequently, CMT is able to predict the formation of abstract mental representations to a certain degree—by analyzing the basic experiences and representations from which these more abstract concepts and representations are formed. In addition, it is able to address whether this process might be universal, intuitive, or permanent. I discuss whether embodied cognitive processes might be considered universal, intuitive, and permanent in line with CMT in this section.

Let me address the question of universality first. While many researchers hold that higher cognitive processes are influenced by culture, it is, in general, agreed that basic processes are universal (e.g., Mansoor and Dowse 2004, p. 31). Take the example of Nisbett et al. (2001). They found that

> [n]aive theories of mechanics and physics (...), naive theories of biology (...) and naive theory of mind (...) appear so early and are apparently so widespread that it seems quite likely that at least some aspects of them are largely innate and resistant to social modification. [Furthermore, t]heories of causality—both highly general ones (...) as well as highly specific ones (...)—are clearly a part of the organism's biologically given cognitive equipment. (p. 305)

Along those lines, CMT claims that primary metaphors are universal because they are based on universal co-occurrences in the real world (Hurtienne et al. 2015, p. 239; Lakoff and Johnson 1999, p. 59). As Kövecses (2005) said:

> Probably no one would be surprised to hear that affection is universally conceptualized as warmth, rather than coldness. To learn such 'primary' metaphors is not a choice for us: It happens unconsciously and automatically. Because this is a universal bodily experience, the metaphor corresponding to it may well be universal. In other words, universal primary experiences produce universal primary metaphors. (p. 3)

This holds for people of distinct ages because younger people have the same basic sensorimotor experiences during childhood that elderly people had previously (Hurtienne et al. 2010, p. 477). Furthermore, it might hold for people with distinct capabilities, as long as they have the same basic experiences—however, see EC's claim about the body as a cognitive constraint in Sect. "Basic Claims by Embodied Cognition". At the same time, CMT suggests that basic, universal sensorimotor experiences do not necessarily lead to more complex mental representations and cognitive processes that are universal, too. Variations and differences between cultures as much as differences between individuals exist (Kövecses 2005, pp. 3–4). For that, CMT gives two main reasons. First, sensorimotor experiences might be used only partially and selectively to form more complex mental representations, depending on individual or cultural preference (Hurtienne 2011, pp. 60–61). Second, basic sensorimotor experiences might be overruled by specific environmental, cultural, or situational contexts. Take to following examples: Barsalou (1993) showed that in the definition of the categories *bird* and *chair* only

44% of the characteristics were similar across study participants. Furthermore, the definitions by each participant varied when being asked two weeks later. Consequently, the participant's mental representations varied due to different individual contexts and preferences (see Wilson and Foglia 2017, para. 4–5, in addition to my discussion of basic-level categories in Sect. "How to Choose Which Exemplar of a Pictogram Content to Represent (G34)"). Kövecses (2005, pp. 39–43) explained that the metaphor *angry person is a pressurized container* is similar across languages. Most likely, this is so because it is closely based on the sensorimotor experience of increasing skin temperature and pulse rate, which is believed to be a universal physiological process of humans in anger. However, in Chinese, the metaphor does not involve hot fluid or gas, and, in Japanese, the container of the pressure is the belly, in Zulu the heart, and the whole body in English. It might be assumed that this is due to different environments and cultural preferences (see Plocher et al. 2012, pp. 165–166, for further examples). In addition, differences in metaphors increase if differences in bodies exist, for example, between right-handers and left-handers (Casasanto 2011; Casasanto and Chrysikou 2011) (again, see the fourth claim of EC in Sect. "Basic Claims by Embodied Cognition"). Nevertheless, much research on "metaphorical expressions across different languages supports the claim that many conceptual metaphors are largely universal, particularly in cases where the metaphors are based on recurring bodily experiences" (Gibbs 2011, p. 540). For example, Cienki (1998) showed that the sensorimotor experience of straightness is used in various languages, for example, American English, Russian, Hungarian, and Japanese, to form very similar metaphors, like *unaltered is straight, an uninterrupted sequence is straight*, and *control is straight*. Neumann (2001) showed that 106 analogous metaphors exist in German and Japanese. More recent research regarding metaphors in HCI confirms these results (e.g., by Hurtienne et al. 2010; Hurtienne 2011; Löffler 2017). Kövecses (2005) reviewed a large number of studies and concluded that metaphors "are potentially universal or can be near-universal. In particular, these metaphors [that] are 'simple' or 'primary' metaphors and/or complex metaphors that are based on universal human experiences" (p. 64). I draw the following conclusion from this for the UIPP project: Since embodied cognitive processes appear to be universal if they involve basic sensorimotor experiences, the UIPP process should aim for these basic sensorimotor experiences in order to be able to achieve universally comprehensible pictogram contents.

Second, regarding the question of whether embodied cognitive processes might be considered intuitive, I have described earlier that intuitive use is commonly defined as the "unconscious use of prior knowledge" (Blackler and Hurtienne 2007, 49). Either intuitive use is innate or repeated activation might lead to automatic processing (see Sect. "Defining Intuitive Use: Prior Knowledge and Automatic Processing"). In general, the literature agrees that embodied cognitive processes are automatic and unconscious (Gibbs 2011, p. 542; Lakoff 2009, p. 13). Since intuitive processing becomes faster and more robust with increasing repetition (e.g., Blackler and Hurtienne 2007, p. 45; Still and Still 2019, pp. 46–47), it seems more likely to achieve intuitive cognitive processing with mental representations and processes that are learned by people very early in life (Hurtienne et al. 2010, p. 477). Since basic sensorimotor experiences are had very early in life, and they are repeatedly activated due to constant co-occurrence in the real world, again, I conclude that the UIPP project should aim for the most basic sensorimotor experiences because they might lead to intuitively comprehensible pictogram contents, too. This is in line with the IUUI approach (Sect. "Definitions of Intuitiveness in HCI").

Third, I contend that it is appropriate to aim for the most basic sensorimotor experiences to achieve permanently comprehensible pictogram contents. This is so because it can be assumed that the most basic sensorimotor experiences, like the co-occurrence of height and quantity and the co-occurrence of warmth and intimacy, are permanent in human history—given the assumption that basic physics in the world and basic properties of human bodies do not change significantly. If these basic sensorimotor experiences do not change, it seems plausible that humans will use the same sensorimotor experience throughout history in order to interpret and conceptualize the world.

In summary, I derive the following requirements for pictogram contents from this discussion: First, the UIPP project should focus on sensorimotor experiences that we have in the real world. Second, it should focus on sensorimotor experiences that we have very early in childhood. I hold that these experiences might be the bases of universal, intuitive, and permanent cognitive processes. As such, they might be candidates for universally, intuitively, and permanently comprehensible pictogram contents. In the next section, I present three HCI approaches that further specify these most basic sensorimotor experiences.

Embodied Cognition and HCI

In HCI, since Paul Dourish's book *Where the action is* (2001), embodied cognition and research on physical interaction with computers has become increasingly important (Marshall and Hornecker 2013, p. 148; Rogers 2012, p. 76). Dourish emphasized the understanding and integration of our interaction with the physical and social environment into the design of user interfaces and interactive systems. He said, "[w]e cannot escape the world of physical objects that we lift, sit on, and push around, nor the consequences of physical phenomena such as gravity, inertia, mass, and friction" (2001, p. 99). For that reason, HCI should draw "on the way the everyday world works or, perhaps more accurately, the ways we experience the everyday world" (p. 17). Dourish called his approach *embodied interaction*. In this section, I discuss three approaches that have been established in the field of HCI since Dourish's book. I do so to specify further the sensorimotor experiences that might be content candidates for universal, intuitive, and permanent pictograms (see Marshall and Hornecker 2013, pp. 151–154, for additional approaches to embodied interaction).

Image-Schematic Design

In Sect. "The Intuitive Use of User Interfaces Group", I have already described a suitable HCI approach: the IUUI approach by Jörn Hurtienne and colleagues. The IUUI categorized prior knowledge from innate to expert knowledge and argued that innate and sensorimotor knowledge should be focused on in order to achieve intuitive design. The approach is based on conceptual metaphor theory. More precisely, it is based on the CMT assumptions concerning *image schemata* (Rogers 2012, p. 78). Image schemata were described first by Mark Johnson in his book *The Body in the Mind* (1987). According to Johnson, an image schema is a "recurring, dynamic pattern of our perceptual interactions and motor programs that gives coherence and structure to our experience" (1987, p. xiv). Take, for example, the image schema *balance*. Balance and imbalance, that is, the even or uneven distribution of weight, are central properties of the world. Based on repeated sensorimotor experiences, humans learn very early in childhood what even or uneven distributions of weight are. Thus, they learn implicitly the abstract schema of *balance*. Subsequently, humans use this image schema to structure their experiences and to conceptualize the world:

> Our experience of bodily balance and the perception of balance is connected to our under-standing of balanced personalities, balanced views, balanced systems, balanced equilibrium, the balance of power, the balance of justice, and so on. In each of these examples, the mental or the abstract concept of balance is understood and experienced in terms of our physical understanding of balance. (Gibbs 2005, p. 70)

Since image schemata are based on a person's sensorimotor experience with the real world, image schemata tend to be universal. Since they are subconscious, they are considered to be intuitive. Other examples of image schemata are *center–periphery*, *container*, *counterforce*, *near–far*, *path*, and *up–down* (Grady 1997, p. 180).

Image schemata are closely related to primary metaphors. Since primary metaphors are mappings of basic sensorimotor experiences to more abstract domains, some scholars argue that primary metaphors are image-schematic metaphors (Hurtienne et al. 2015, p. 238) or that image-schematic metaphors are a subclass of primary metaphors (Hurtienne 2017, 1, 3). Grady (1997, pp. 179–189) drew the following distinction. Image schemata are considered large and abstract structures. For example, the image schema of balance includes all instances and experiences of balance, but it is considered independent from these single instances. Subsequently, image-schematic metaphors draw on these larger structures as source domains to map them onto other domains. In contrast, primary metaphors are based on specific, more concrete *primary scenes*. That is, local structures that might be motivated by distinguishable situations in our life and that include details of these situations (Grady 1999, pp. 84–85). Subsequently, these more local structures are the source domain for metaphorical mappings. Take an example by Lima (2006). The abstract image schema of *container* might include all instances of containers. For that reason, it includes primary scenes that involve containers, too, for example, *going into a room* and *taking something out of a box*. However, only these distinct primary scenes can lead to distinct primary metaphors (Lima 2006, p. 115). For example, the scene *going into a room* involves the sensorimotor experience of going into a container-like space. The scene *taking something out of a box* involves the interaction with a container-like object. Although primary scenes might be schematic to some extent, they are not abstract. Instead, they are mental representations of concrete re-occurring experiences.

Hurtienne and colleagues have used extensively image schemata in their studies. For example, the *up–down* image schema, based on the experience of verticality, was used by Hurtienne (2011, pp. 91–120) to evaluate the application of image-schematic metaphors to user interface design. In the IBIS project (Löffler et al. 2013), Hurtienne and colleagues redesigned the graphical user interfaces of software based on image-schemata in a human-centered design process. The redesigned interfaces were rated higher and more intuitive than the existing interface. As a result of their research, Hurtienne and colleagues were able to show that the application of image schemata to HCI leads to more efficient and more intuitive use (Blackler 2019, p. 5).

From this discussion, I take the following additional requirement for sensorimotor experiences that the UIPP project should aim for in its derivation of pictogram contents: The UIPP project should focus on image schemata, that is, schematic mental representations of re-occurring experiences in the real world. These schematic representations have been be used to successfully design HCI. In addition, since image schemata are abstract representations of larger structures, primary scenes might be suitable for UIPP, too. This is so because primary scenes include more concrete situations in the real world, and concrete situations might be easier to represent visually than abstract schemata (see Hurtienne 2011, pp. 87–88, for a critique of image schemata regarding these aspects). I further discuss this requirement in the derivation and evaluation studies in the next section (see Study 1, Sect. "Results", and "Discussion, Limitations, and Future Research").

Reality-Based Interaction
A second suitable approach that I have already addressed is reality-based interaction (RBI). In 2007, Jacob et al. argued that current approaches to HCI might seem disparate, but "they share salient and important commonalities, which can help us understand, connect, and analyze them" (p. 2466). These commonalities are the focus on the everyday and the focus on sensorimotor experiences. The first focus addresses that designs "draw strength by building on users' pre-existing knowledge of the everyday, non-digital world to a much greater extent than before" (Jacob et al. 2008, p. 1). The second focus addresses that designs draw on the skills and the ways of interacting with the world that people have internalized (Jacob et al. 2007, p. 2466). Approaches do so with the intention to reduce the necessary cognitive effort by a user when interacting with a system and to reduce the time necessary to learn how to interact (Jacob et al. 2008, 4). Based on a review of current literature and on interviews with researchers, Jacob et al. proposed a categorization of emerging approaches in HCI. They distinguished four

| Naïve Physics | Body Awareness & Skills | Environment Awareness & Skills | Social Awareness & Skills |

Fig. 3 The four basic kinds of sensorimotor knowledge according to RBI (Jacob et al. 2008, p. 3)

categories of everyday sensorimotor experience that they considered to be potentially universal (Jacob et al. 2008, p. 2) (see Fig. 3):

- *Naïve physics* refer to a person's general knowledge about the physical world which is based on their everyday experiences with the world, "in other words, common sense knowledge about the physical world. This includes concepts like gravity, friction, velocity, the persistence of objects, and relative scale" (Jacob et al. 2008, p. 3).
- *Body awareness and skills* address people's knowledge about their own body, the functioning of their body, and how to control their body. "For example, a person is aware of the relative position of his or her limbs (proprioception), his or her range of motion, and the senses involved in perceiving certain phenomena" (Jacob et al. 2008, p. 3). In addition, people learn very early in life how to coordinate their movements, that is, how to move their limbs, head, and so forth in order to perform a specific action.
- *Environment awareness and skills* address that people are aware of "their surroundings and possess skills for negotiating, manipulating, and navigating within their environment" (Jacob et al. 2008, p. 3). Since the world is shaped in a certain way and is populated with objects and other people who are physical, too, people have to learn very early in life how to perceive, interpret, and react to their environment. For example, they learn that the sun and moon may give them clues on direction and time and that the size of objects and the color of the air may give them information concerning distances and sizes.
- *Social awareness and skills* refer to people's ability to apprehend and interact with other people, for example, to communicate with them, to collaborate, to trade, and so forth (cf. the term *social signifier* by Norman 2008, pp. 18–19).

I propose that RBI is in line with my discussion of EC, CMT, and Hurtienne's image-schematic approach. It integrates the necessary prerequisites for universal and for intuitive use (Jacob et al. 2008, p. 2). At the same time, RBI offers more detailed categories for sensorimotor experiences. Thus, it is useful in the identification of knowledge about the world that is learned very early in life and that is shared by everybody (Hurtienne et al. 2015, pp. 236–237). Consequently, as a

requirement, I suggest that the four categories should be applied in UIPP's derivation of pictogram contents.

Hierarchical Mental Metaphors Theory

The third approach that I present is the hierarchical mental metaphor theory
(HMMT) by Daniel Casasanto (2013, 2014, 2017). In addition to CMT, Casasanto
distinguished two categories of metaphors, *analogical* and *correlational metaphors*. Analogical metaphors are cognitive mappings that are based on a creative
act by a person. That is, the source domain and the target domain do not co-occur
in the real world. Take for example the metaphor of *loan shark*. In the real world,
creditors and sharks may not be experienced together. For that reason, the cognitive mapping from shark to creditor is a creative act by a person. Subsequently,
analogical metaphors can be communicated and conventionalized in a culture.
Since other people can learn the metaphor only through communication, communication is crucial with analogical metaphors (Casasanto 2013, pp. 8–10).
Correlational metaphors are based on co-occurrences that can be experienced in
the real world. These metaphors do not need to be communicated. According to
Casasanto, examples of correlational metaphors are primary and image-schematic
metaphors.

Casasanto (2013, pp. 4–5) argued that correlational metaphors have three
stages: the stage of innate cognitive mappings, mappings that are based on co-
occurrences in the real world, and the subsequent shaping of these metaphors
through cultural experience. According to Casasanto, there is no evidence that
innate cognitive mappings exist. Studies showing cognitive mappings in infants
are not able to provide evidence that these mappings are not learned, for example, through pre-linguistic experiences with co-occurrences in the real world.
Nevertheless, it seems plausible that innate mappings exist because some cognitive mappings are important for survival (e.g., *important is big*). Regarding the
second stage, Casasanto agreed with the underlying assumption of CMT that the
most basic cognitive metaphors are based on experiences of co-occurrence that are
learned universally and very early in life. However, he specified, these basic mappings of sensorimotor experiences are in fact sets of multiple mappings. That is,
basic metaphors, like *more time is more distance*, integrate multiple mappings, for
example, *time is front or back*, *time is left or right*, and *time is volume*. Casasanto
said, all basic metaphors are sets of cognitive mappings. The third stage of metaphors begins when people are exposed to cultural regularities and conventions. Due
to experiences in a culture, basic sensorimotor mappings are modified. That is, a
specific part of the set of basic mappings developed in the second stage becomes
emphasized and strengthened. This happens because a person repeatedly activates
that specific subordinate mapping due to exposure to cultural regularities and conventions. At the same time, other parts of the superordinate set of basic mappings
are weakened because they are not activated (Casasanto 2014, p. 265; Casasanto
2017, p. 49). Because of this process, Casasanto argued, metaphors are constructed
hierarchically. The result of the process is the variation that we can find in more
complex metaphors—although these metaphors are based on similar universal

sensorimotor experiences: "Even if superordinate families are universal, the specific [subordinate] mappings that get used most frequently or automatically can vary across individuals and groups" (Casasanto 2017, p. 49).

Based on this description, HMMT is able to explain why cognitive mappings might change rapidly if people are primed accordingly. This might happen because weaker, subordinate mappings are reactivated instead of being newly created. In contrast, mappings that do not yet exist will be more difficult to achieve because they are not part of an early-established superordinate set of mappings (Casasanto 2013, pp. 10–15; Casasanto 2017, pp. 49–50).

I draw three conclusions from HMMT. First, in the derivation of pictogram contents it is important to focus on experiences that can be had in the real world, as in the case of correlational metaphors. Analogical metaphors that a based on creative acts and communication should be avoided. This is in line with the requirements that I already formulated. Second, it is important to derive superordinate sets of experiences and distinguish them from subordinate experiences because the latter have been emphasized by culture. Third, in general, it can be assumed that complete sets of superordinate mappings are available in individuals as much as in cultures. Even if individuals and cultures have strengthened certain cognitive mappings in contrast to other mappings, these other, weaker mappings might be reactivated. I take the following requirement from these conclusions: The UIPP project should focus on superordinate sets of sensorimotor experiences that can be had in the real world.

Summary: Requirements for the Derivation of Pictogram Contents

In the first part of this chapter, I have described suitable approaches both to universal and to intuitive design, and I have argued that they are based on embodied cognition. In the second part of this chapter, I have described the theory of embodied cognition, I have explained its basic claims, and I have discussed how abstract concepts are formed according to embodied cognition. EC holds that cognitive processes and mental representations are grounded in basic sensorimotor experiences had in the real world. As a consequence, mental representations and cognitive processes are not amodal but multimodal, and the design and the interpretation of visual representations and other modes of communication and interaction are based on sensorimotor experience, too. From this discussion, I derive five requirements for the subsequent derivation of candidates for universal, intuitive, and permanent pictogram contents. First, the UIPP project should aim for the most basic sensorimotor experiences had in the real world. Second, it should aim for sensorimotor experiences had very early in childhood. Third, following my discussion of approaches in HCI, the UIPP project should focus on schematic mental representations of sensorimotor experiences, that is, image schemata or primary scenes. Fourth, these schematic mental representations should represent naïve physical, bodily, environmental, or social experiences. Fifth, they should consist of superordinate sets of sensorimotor experiences that can be had in the real world. In the remainder of this chapter, I add a sixth requirement, and I report two studies in which these requirements were used to derive and evaluate content candidates for universally, intuitively, and permanently comprehensible pictograms.

Deriving UIP Pictogram Meanings

In order to be able to derive pictogram contents, intended meanings for the pictograms are required. As described, UIPP was a subproject of the joint research project UCUI (see Sect. "Universal, Intuitive, and Permanent Pictogram Project: Two Main Goals"). UCUI's goal was to develop a user interface that allowed for intuitive interaction of users with technical devices. As a case study, UCUI developed a single user interface prototype for a heating system with which the user interacted via speech, gestures, virtual keyboard, and pictograms. Since the UIP Pictograms should be part of the interface prototype, UCUI prescribed the meanings for the UIP Pictograms. However, instead of specifying exact meanings, UCUI provided scenarios. Scenarios are narrative descriptions of situations in which "a user engages the interactive system to solve a particular task" (Shneiderman et al. 2017, p. 147). Scenarios describe the actions by the user and the user goals in order to allow for subsequent identification of and reflection on the system requirements (Sharp et al. 2019, p. 408). Consequently, a process was performed to derive UIP Pictogram meanings from the UCUI scenarios. I describe the process in the following (see Sect. "Appendix A" for the full list of the UCUI scenarios, the actual states, target states, and derived meanings).

To my knowledge, at the time, no procedure to derive pictogram meanings from scenarios existed. Consequently, I developed a three-step process to derive the UIPP meanings. The process was carried out by two researchers, a cognitive psychologist working in HCI and a design researcher working in HCI with experience in cognitive sciences. First, with the intention to derive the most suitable meanings for the UIPP project, the researchers agreed on four requirements for the meanings:

1. The meanings should be simple.
2. The meanings should be modular.
3. The meanings should be specific enough to be suitable for the UCUI prototype and, at the same time, general enough to be suitable for universal use.
4. The meanings should be similar to meanings of established manufacturer pictograms in order to be able to compare subsequently the UIP Pictograms with established pictograms (see "Step 5: Evaluating the UIP Pictograms").

In the second step, based on the requirements, the researchers derived independently from each other meanings that suited the UCUI scenarios. Since UIPP's discussion of the reference relation is closely based on Nakamura and Zeng-Treitler (2012) (see Sect. "Conceptualizing the Relations of Design and of

Reference"), the researchers used Nakamura and Zeng-Treitler's taxonomy of pictogram meanings in their derivation process. In the taxonomy, Nakamura and Zeng-Treitler (2012, pp. 541–542) distinguished four basic categories of words that can be used to refer to pictogram meanings: Standalone lexical words which they separated into (a) nouns and (b) verbs; (c) modifiers, such as adjectives and adverbs; and (d) grammatical function words, for example, conjunctions and prepositions. They argued that grammatical functions words should be excluded from pictogram meanings because these words only exist in verbal communication. Consequently, following Nakamura and Zeng-Treitler, the two researchers derived meanings that consisted of one of the abovementioned three basic categories: nouns, verbs, or adjectives/adverbs. Finally, in the third step, the researchers compared their independently derived meanings, discussed conflicts, and agreed on the most suitable meanings for the UIPP project.

Let me give an example. One scenario that was specified by UCUI was *I am cold!*. For this scenario, UCUI prescribed two system states. The so-called actual system state was *current room temperature in the entire house is perceived as too low*. The target state was *system informs users about current room temperature*. The meanings that were derived for this scenario were: *coldness, everywhere*, that is, the meaning *coldness* which is a noun, and the meaning *everywhere* which is an adjective or adverb. The meanings were derived in German and translated subsequently to English. Translations were done by the same two researchers in a similar process. That is, they translated independently and discussed conflicts subsequently in order to arrive at an agreement. In addition, in the translation process, other researchers with English as a first language were consulted and dictionaries and translation software were used (DeepL GmbH, Messinger and Fellermayer 2007; PONS GmbH, The Merriam-Webster.com Dictionary). In the following, the derived meanings (20) are presented in alphabetical order of first major words.[2] Brackets indicate that a meaning requires additional specification (see Sect. "Appendix B" for meanings in German):

- [Something or someone] is absent, not here
- [Something] is bad, negative
- [Something] begins
- [Something or someone] is busy
- Coldness
- [Something] is dangerous
- Day
- [Something] is decreasing
- [Something] ends
- [Something] is everywhere
- [Something] is good, positive

---

[2]According to the American Psychological Association (2013, pp. 101–102), major words are verbs, nouns, adjectives, adverbs, and pronouns.

- [Something or someone] is here, on-site
- [Something] is important
- [Something] is increasing
- Night
- Power
- Several, a group of [some things or some people]
- [Something or someone] is single, solitary
- Warmth
- [Something] goes wrong, is wrong

Study 1: Deriving Pictogram Content Candidates

Based on the requirements developed in the previous parts of this chapter, two empirical studies were conducted to derive and evaluate candidates for universal, intuitive, and permanent pictogram contents. In this section, first, I report the study that was conducted to derive the content candidates. Then, in the next section, I report the study that was conducted to evaluate the candidates. In Section *Approaching the Reference Relation* (Sect. "Conceptualizing the Relations of Design and of Reference"), I have argued that two categories of reference relations are suitable for universally, intuitively, and permanently comprehensible pictograms, iconic relations and semantic associations. The first category is based on similarity. Through this category, only few meanings can be referred to, for example, concrete real-world objects, actions, and creatures. In order to refer to more abstract meanings, the second category is required, that is, semantic association. In that category, reference relations are indirect or mediated. The category of semantic association is central because most meanings are abstract meanings, according to Nakamura and Zeng-Treitler (2012, p. 536). Consequently, the research question of the first study was the following: Which content candidates can be derived from cross-culturally and intuitively provided participant data, fulfilling the previously described requirements, that might allow for universal, intuitive, and permanent semantic association.

Let me elaborate. In the previous parts of this chapter, I suggested that people universally and intuitively interpret and conceptualize the real world based on sensorimotor experiences. Even the most abstract concepts are based on these experiences. However, universal sensorimotor experiences do not necessarily lead to universal concepts. Variations and differences between cultures as much as between individuals exist (see Sect. "Embodied Cognitive Processes Might be Universal, Intuitive, and Permanent"). From the discussion, I take four assumptions for the following studies. First, if certain sensorimotor experiences have been used to form a given concept or meaning, then, users should associate these sensorimotor experiences with the concept or meaning. Second, if users associate certain sensorimotor experiences with a given concept or meaning, then, pictogram contents using these sensorimotor experiences might be interpreted as referring to that concept or meaning. Third, if users associate sensorimotor experiences with a given meaning universally and intuitively, then, pictograms that have these sensorimotor experiences as content might be interpreted universally and intuitively as referring to that meaning. Finally, if the following studies are able to identify a single sensorimotor experience as being associated the strongest—universally and intuitively—with a given meaning, then, this experience might be most suited as content for a universal and intuitive pictogram for that meaning. In short, if a sensorimotor experience is universally and intuitively associated by users with a meaning, and this experience is used as the content of a pictogram for that meaning, then, users might be universally and intuitively able to comprehend the pictogram as referring to that meaning. This should hold despite variations and differences between cultures and individuals, and it should hold permanently because the physical world and the sensorimotor experiences on which the associations are based are permanent, too. In that case, I argue, the reference relation is based on universal, intuitive, and permanent semantic association.

The following studies were conducted with an additional goal. The second goal was to develop a technical process for the derivation and evaluation of suitable contents that might be used in other projects. To that end, first, I explain UIPP's experimental approach in detail, then, I report the derivation study. Let me begin with UIPP's experimental approach to universal pictogram contents.

Crowdsourcing Cross-Cultural Studies for Universal Associations

To derive pictogram contents that might be universally comprehensible, I argue, sensorimotor experiences that participants associate cross-culturally with given meanings must be collected (see Sect. "Approaches to Cross-Cultural Design"). While many researchers recruit participants in person and on-site (e.g., Choong and Salvendy 1998; Evers 2002; Löffler et al. 2014), online testing has become a viable option at least since the end of the 1990s. However, in online testing, too, recruiting participants might be a problem if researchers are not present (Rau et al. 2011, p. 692). To solve this problem, in UIPP, I used a crowdsourcing approach. In the following, I explain crowdsourcing, and I describe the process that was performed in the UIPP project.

While studies on pictogram design that use crowdsourcing are still rare (see Laursen et al. 2016, p. 2), crowdsourced online testing has become increasingly important in cognitive sciences (Stewart et al. 2017, p. 736). Brabham (2013) defined crowdsourcing as "an online, distributed problem-solving and production model that leverages the collective intelligence of online communities to serve specific organizational goals" (p. xix). To participate in a crowdsourcing process, users register on an online crowdsourcing platform, for example, Amazon's Mechanical Turk (Amazon 2018) or microWorkers (Weblabcenter, Inc. 2020). Either registered users are employers and create tasks through the crowdsourcing platform, or they are workers and complete tasks (Hirth et al. 2011). In contrast to traditional outsourcing processes, in the crowdsourcing model, employers cannot choose which crowd worker will complete the task. However, the employer might be able to specify worker characteristics (e.g., regarding age, gender, first language, place of residence, and so forth). Instead, workers choose among many tasks by various employers which task they would like to complete. After successful completion, the workers are paid an amount previously specified by the employer through the platform. The platform charges a service fee. Usually, many thousand workers a registered with crowdsourcing platforms. For example, Amazon's Mechanical Turk claims to have more than 500,000 registered workers (although the actual number might be lower, see Difallah et al. 2018 and Stewart et al. 2017, p. 743). In addition, these workers are situated in various countries and regions of the world. Again, Amazon allows registrations from people in 59 verified countries. Because of these large numbers, crowdsourcing comes with several advantages for empirical studies: First, crowdsourced studies can draw from a far more diverse population than the traditional on-campus experiments. Second, samples can be larger because payments of workers are much cheaper than in traditional approaches. Third, studies can be conducted much faster because workers are constantly available, and they complete the tasks simultaneously.

Several criticisms of crowdsourced online testing were raised, too, as well as recommendations were made in response to those criticisms. The most important criticism might be that crowdsourced online studies do not provide enough control over participant groups and participant behavior. For example, Clemmensen et al. (2007) argued that hidden user groups might be a problem, that is, groups of people with distinct characteristics in a sample. As an example, participants recruited through a crowdsourcing process are expected to have lower educational levels than the average population (Rau et al. 2011, p. 692). To avoid hidden user groups and misleading results, it is recommended that demographics should be controlled, and known user groups should be outbalanced when designing the study (see Study 3 in this project, Sect. "Participants"). Furthermore, non-laboratory settings of online studies raised criticism because they prevent control by experimenters over the participant's behavior during the experiment. For example, there is almost no possibility for the participants to interact with the researchers. Thus, in order to enable successful completion of the task and, consequently, high-quality data, it is necessary to provide participants with exact and unambiguous instructions. Finally, in a study by Chandler et al. (2014, p. 117), 27% of participants reported not to be alone, and 18% reported watching television. For that reason, researchers recommend including attention checks, that is, distinct tasks or questions that are explicitly verifiable. Only if these tasks or questions are completed correctly, the participant should be included in the study (Laursen et al. 2016, p. 3; Kittur et al. 2008, pp. 455–456). Nevertheless, regarding the lack of control over participants, on the one hand, many researchers argued that they never have control over participants' doing or thinking during a study, even in laboratory settings (Rubinstein 2013, p. 541). On the other hand, several empirical studies showed that "results derived from convenience samples like Amazon's Mechanical Turk are similar to those obtained from national samples" (Coppock 2018, abstract, cf. Levay et al. 2016, 1, 11). For example, Rubinstein (2013) argued that results obtained through online testing are "not qualitatively different from those obtained by more conventional methods" (p. 541). Behrend et al. (2011) even concluded that "the reliability of the data from the crowdsourcing sample was as good as or better than the corresponding university sample" (p. 800), and Heer and Bostock (2010, pp. 211–212) said that crowdsourcing is a viable approach to researching visual perception and visual design. Consequently, in UIPP, a crowdsourcing process was used, and recommendations were followed. That is, instructions were optimized, participants were asked to refrain from distracting behavior during the trials, and attention checks were included.

At least three further criticisms exist regarding crowdsourced online surveys. First, crowdsourcing processes often lack ethical pay rates. In general, the remuneration of crowd workers is low. At first, this might seem an advantage because studies with large samples remain cheap for the employer, that is, the researcher or business. However, it might involve taking advantage of disadvantaged people. In addition, with low pay rates, workers might strive to complete the tasks faster, thus, produce low-quality data. However, at the same time, Stewart et al. (2017) argued that "higher pay rates (…) may also attract the most keen and active participants, crowding out less-experienced workers (…) and shrinking the population being sampled" (p. 713; see Göritz 2014, too). Consequently, in the UIPP studies, crowd workers were remunerated according to the German legal minimum wage which was between €8.50 and €9.19 per hour at the time. German minimum wage seemed appropriate as an ethical payment that allowed high-quality studies at a reasonable price. Second, another problem with online tests is attrition, that is, high drop-out rates by participants. To reduce attrition, Zhou and Fishbach (2016, 9, 11) recommended increasing payment. However, Göritz (2014) showed higher remuneration did not increase completion rate. For that reason, as mentioned above, in UIPP German minimum wage was paid. Reips (2000) proposed three further strategies to reduce attrition: prewarning participants, that is, informing them about the study and their task; personalizing the study, that is, asking for personal information while, at the same time, protecting the participants' privacy; and appealing to the participant's conscience, that is, telling them that it affects badly the outcome of the study if they drop out. All recommendations were followed in the UIPP studies. Finally, Reips (2000) suggested avoiding multiple submissions by individual workers, although multiple submissions are rare. In UIPP, this was prevented through a mechanism on the crowdsourcing platform and by collecting the participants' personal information.

In order to collect cross-cultural data, in UIPP, participants were recruited through a crowdsourcing process. The UIPP project was based in Germany. The crowdsourcing platform that was used is based in Germany, too. It is called Clickworker (clickworker GmbH). U.S. crowdsourcing platforms were not an option because they required U.S. credit cards. Furthermore, a German crowdsourcing platform seemed advisable in the case that questions or necessary adaptations arise during the recruiting process. Since Clickworker provided only limited options for tailoring surveys, it was used exclusively for the recruitment of participants. The survey and materials were hosted on a different webspace.

According to Clickworker, at the time of the studies, the platform's crowd consisted of more than 800,000 workers all over the world. Workers in the following countries were active: Argentina, Australia, Austria, Belgium, Brazil, Canada, Chile, Colombia, Costa Rica, Czech Republic, Denmark, Egypt, Finland, France, Germany, Greece, Hungary, India, Indonesia, Italy, Ireland, Israel, Kenya, Malaysia, Mexico, Netherlands, New Zealand, Nigeria, Norway, Pakistan, Peru, Philippines, Poland, Portugal, Romania, Russia, Saudi Arabia, Serbia, Singapore, South Africa, South Korea, Spain, Sweden, Switzerland, Thailand, Turkey, United Arab Emirates, United Kingdom, United States, Vietnam. For the selection of countries in which participants should be recruited, I defined five criteria: First, in order to be able to collect cross-cultural data, the selection should include as many countries as possible. Second, in order to collect data worldwide, the selection should include countries on as many continents as possible. Third, at the same time, it should include countries with as few first languages spoken as possible in order to reduce required resources for the studies. Fourth, the selected countries should represent a large population of active workers to increase study validity. Fifth, the selected countries should represent a wide range of cultural dimension values, according to Hofstede (1997, 2011) (see Sect. "Definitions of Universality in HCI"), to ensure cultural diversity. Finally, I included seven countries in the recruitment process: Australia, Austria, Canada, Germany, South Africa, Switzerland, and the United States. Consequently, four continents were included (Africa, Australia, Europe, and North America), with two distinct first languages spoken: English and German. In these countries, at least 96,800 workers were active, that is, 21,050 in Austria, Germany, and Switzerland, 70,950 in Canada and the United States, 3,200 in South Africa, and 1,600 in Australia (L. Protze, personal communication, October 19, 2018). In addition, these countries represent a wide range of cultural dimension values (between 62 and 27 in range), according to Hofstede et al. (2010) (see Table 1). Although, of course, these countries do not represent all cultures worldwide, I propose that they provide a suitable basis for the collection of cross-cultural data.

User Utterances and Word Associations Tests for Intuitive Associations

To collect the sensorimotor experiences that people intuitively associate with meanings, I argue, the mental representations of sensorimotor experiences should be collected that participants automatically activate when presented with these meanings. Hurtienne (2017, pp. 30–32) suggested that the most common approach to achieving this is extracting mental representations from user utterances. To that end, user interviews are conducted and recorded. Then, the interviews are transcribed and analyzed subsequently by researchers in order to extract the underlying mental representations. A variation of the approach consists in think-aloud protocols. In think-aloud protocols, utterances of users are not necessarily recorded during an interview but during the users' use of a system. Then, protocols

Table 1 Hofstede's cultural dimension values per country and per dimension (1–100)

Dimension / Country	PDI	UAI	IDV	MAS	LTO	IRI
Australia	39	51	90	61	21	71
Austria	11	70	55	79	60	63
Canada	39	48	80	52	36	68
Germany	35	65	67	66	83	40
South Africa	49	49	65	63	34	63
Switzerland	34	58	68	70	74	66
United States	40	46	91	62	26	68
Highest value	49	70	91	79	83	71
Lowest value	11	48	55	52	21	40

Notes: PDI = power distance, UAI = uncertainty avoidance, IDV = collectivism vs. individualism, MAS = femininity vs. masculinity, LTO = long- vs. short-term orientation, and IRI = indulgence vs. restraint. Values and abbreviations are taken from Hofstede et al. (2010)

are transcribed and analyzed (Blackler et al. 2019, pp. 76–78; Clemmensen et al. 2009, 214–218). Hurtienne et al. (2015, p. 239) used the approach to conduct contextual interviews and code them subsequently into categories of image schemata. The IBIS project, too, used contextual interviews with engineers and end-users and analyzed the transcribed interviews (Löffler et al. 2013, 28–29, 47–53). Maglio and Matlock (1999) conducted interviews with users after they navigated the website *Yahoo!*.

Since experimenters could not be present during the trials in the UIPP studies, because the studies were conducted using a crowdsourcing process, utterances needed to be self-recorded by participants. To achieve this, a refined word association test was used. In a word association test, experimenters assess which concepts or scenes participants have linked internally to a presented word. They do so by asking the participants to write sentences that describe the mental association that they have when being presented with the said word (Gunstone 1980, pp. 47–48). In the UIPP studies, participants were presented with the meanings derived from UCUI. Usually, in word association tests, participants have about one minute for each response. In UIPP, participants were asked to describe what first came to their minds because it was assumed that the mental representations that are the fastest, thus, the easiest accessible have the highest associative strength (Fazio et al. 2000; Wood and Grafman 2003), and meanings with the highest associative strength are the most intuitive. Gatsou et al. (2011, p. 277) also argued that those should be used subsequently for visual design.

Let me add one aspect. In Section *Approaching the Design Relation* (Sect. "Conceptualizing the Relations of Design and of Reference"), I have argued that only pictogram contents are suitable for UIPP that might be designed based on similarity because only those are candidates for universal, intuitive, and permanent comprehension. Consequently, in the UIPP studies, sensorimotor experiences were targeted that might be perceived through the visual sensory channel. Let me give three examples. First, people might associate a flame with warmth because flames usually co-occur with warmth in the real world. When the experience is had, the flame is perceptible through the visual sensory channel. For that reason, the flame can be used as the content of a visual representation that refers to the meaning of warmth. Second, the proximity to loved people might be associated with warmth because the experience of proximity to people often co-occurs with warmth in the real world. Since only people's bodies can be perceived through the visual sensory channel—not the feeling of love—only bodies can be represented as the content of a visual representation. Third, in a hypothetical example, if microwaves were associated with warmth because of the frequent use of microwave ovens, the ovens could be used as the content of a pictogram, not the microwaves, because microwaves cannot be perceived visually. Consequently, in the word association tests, participants were asked for mental associations that can be perceived through the visual sensory channel. I add this as the sixth requirement for the derivation of pictogram contents: Contents should be perceptible through the visual sensory channel.

Experimental Materials and Data: Linguistic, Not Visual

Since the UIPP studies aimed for the design of visual representations and asked for mental associations that can be perceived visually, the question arises, whether it is suitable to present participants with linguistic stimuli and to ask for linguistic responses. A different approach might be asking participants to create visual representations of their associations or of the meanings with which they were presented. As Löffler (2017) pointed out: "[T]he design of the experimental materials greatly affects the results" (p. 190). In addition, in cross-cultural studies, language is a central issue. Although the definition of culture is complex (see Sect. "Approaches to Cross-Cultural Design"), language is a central part of culture. At the same time, languages do not necessarily correspond with individual cultures (Plocher et al. 2012, pp. 170–173). In the UIPP, people with two distinct first languages were recruited, German and English. Consequently, meanings as much as instructions and tasks needed to be translated (Plocher et al. 2012, pp. 173–174). This is a drawback because translated words might refer to several other meanings at the same time, thus, they might lead to deviations in subsequent results. In order to address the question, whether it is suitable to present linguistic stimuli and collect linguistic data, in the following, first, I argue why it appears not to be a disadvantage to present linguistic stimuli. Second, I discuss why it seems an advantage to ask for linguistic responses, instead of visual representations.

Let me explain my first argument. In Sect. "Basic Claims by Embodied Cognition", I have described that mental representations are multimodal, according to the theory of embodied cognition. When experiences are had, inputs from all sensory channels are integrated and stored in memory (Lalanne and Lorenceau

2004; Löffler 2017, pp. 58–61). Later, when these memories are activated, multimodal representations are activated, that is, not a single, sensory-channel-specific characteristic of these representations. Barsalou (2008) gave the example of a chair. When a person has the experience of sitting in a chair, the person integrates input from all sensory channels to memorize the experience

> (e.g., how a chair looks and feels, the action of sitting, introspections of comfort and relaxation). Later, when knowledge is needed to represent a category (e.g., chair), multimodal representations captured during experiences with its instances are reactivated to simulate how the brain represented perception, action, and introspection associated with it. (Barsalou 2008, pp. 618–819)

In other words, when a person is presented with the visual representation of a chair, the person activates the previously had multimodal experiences with chairs, not exclusively the visual experiences with chairs (McDougall et al. 2009, pp. 66–67). The same holds for presentations with linguistic representations of chairs, that is, with presentations of the word *chair*. The word *chair* activates multimodal mental representations of sensorimotor experience with chairs not solely experiences with linguistic representations of chairs. Consequently, I argue, it is not a disadvantage to present participants with linguistic representation because they activate multimodal mental representations—as do visual representations. In addition, studies showed that language and visual mental representations are closely related (Borghi and Caruana 2015, p. 422; Barsalou 2008, p. 628). Nowack (2018) stated, "[r]egardless of whether an event is physically reexperienced or simply recalled in verbal interaction (i.e., talking about feeling low), concrete-abstract associations are retrieved automatically and fast from semantic memory without the need of more controlled and strategic cognitive processes" (p. 6). Even when participants are presented with linguistic stimuli and asked not to use visual mental simulations, they perform spontaneously mental imagery (Gibbs 2005, p. 88). For example, Zwaan and Madden (2005) showed that sentences read by participants significantly influenced the visual mental representations that they activated subsequently. They argued that this is due to co-occurrence in the real world, as in the case of cognitive metaphors. As sensorimotor experiences co-occur, linguistic utterances often co-occur with them (Zwaan and Madden 2005, pp. 227–229). For that reason, "[w]ords and grammar are viewed as a set of cues that activate and combine experiential traces in the mental simulation of the described events" (p. 224). As a consequence, I argue that it is not a disadvantage to present participants with linguistic stimuli because they activate multimodal mental representations of sensorimotor experience. In addition, they are especially suited to activate representations of visual experiences.

Second, let me explain why it seems an advantage to ask for linguistic responses instead of visual representations. Multimodal mental representations are complex because they integrate inputs from various senses. For that reason, I suggest, skill and experience are necessary to communicate them comprehensibly to other people. In general, people are very experienced with language. As

I have discussed earlier (see Sect. "Defining Intuitive Use: Prior Knowledge and Automatic Processing"), people internalize their first language very early in childhood. Over the years, they gather experience to a degree that they are able to use that language skillfully and intuitively although they might not be able to explain explicitly the rules and regularities. Nevertheless, studies have shown that the information integrated by multimodal representations often is too complex to verbalize (e.g., Solomon and Barsalou 2001). That is, although people are very skilled in using language, their skill is not sufficient to communicate their multimodal mental representations. In contrast, only few people are experienced in creating visual representations. Very few are formally trained—apart from the most basic drawing exercises in kindergarten or school—and only experienced designers and artists might have developed expertise. For that reason, I argue that asking participants to draw their multimodal mental representations would yield worse results than asking them to communicate them through language. This is so because, in general, participants do not have the skill to create these visual representations (Barsalou 2008, p. 627). Take, for example, a study by Rogers and Oborne (1987). The authors asked participants to draw certain verbs in order to conduct subsequently research for pictogram design. Rogers and Oborne emphasized that it was difficult for the participants to create drawings for abstract meanings, thus, suggesting that participants were not able to visually represent complex mental representations. In addition, even drawings for simpler, more concrete meanings were extremely basic, and I question their suitability for subsequent pictogram design, especially in contrast to rich linguistic data (Rogers and Oborne 1987, p. 105). Another example is a study by Schröder and Ziefle (2008, pp. 138–140). In the study, participants exclusively reproduced conventional pictograms instead of the personal experience that they might have associated with a linguistic term. In a similar study, Jung and Myung (2006, pp. 178–179) collected exclusively complex culture-specific experiences, not basic sensorimotor experiences. In addition to insufficient skill and experience, switching from one mode of communication to another comes with certain disadvantages. First, switching modes of communication comes with cognitive costs for study participants "analogous to the cost of switching attention from one modality to another in perception" (Barsalou 2008, p. 627). Since study stimuli and instructions can only be presented in written language because of study design, asking participants to switch modes of communication could lower response quality—irrespective of the participants' personal skills in creating visual representations. Second, asking participants to create visual representations would require a second switch of modes of communication either in the analysis of the data because established approaches to coding and quantifying visual data do not exist (Hurtienne 2011, p. 212) or in the subsequent evaluation of the contents (in Study 2). Consequently, in order to be able to use established approaches of analysis and to evaluate without multiplying errors in the results, I hold, the presentation and collection of linguistic data was the most appropriate approach for the UIPP project. I report the studies in the next sections.

Study 1.1: German-Speaking Participant Group

As described above, to be able to collect mental associations of sensorimotor experiences that are as universal and intuitive as possible, and to subsequently derive content candidates from these associations, a computer-assisted multi-stage process was performed including a crowdsourced survey with open-ended questions and quantitative and qualitative analyses of the obtained data (see Hurtienne et al. 2008, p. 242, for a similar approach). In this section, I report the first study that was conducted with German-speaking participants.

Method

Participants
Three hundred and thirty-seven participants were included in Study 1.1 ($n = 337$), ranging in age from 18 to 67 years ($M = 35.69$, $SD = 11.51$). Participants were 49.6% female, 50.4% male, none stated *diverse* as gender. Participants were recruited and remunerated through a crowdsourcing process as described in Sect. "Crowdsourcing Cross-Cultural Studies for Universal Associations". Participants were not remunerated if their answers were erroneous. Since online screen testing was used, only participants with normal or corrected-to-normal vision were allowed to participate. In addition, only participants who were registered on the crowdsourcing website as living in Austria, Germany, or Switzerland and with German as a first language were included.

Materials
Materials were presented in German. In the following, they are translated into English where appropriate.

Stimuli
Stimuli consisted of 20 UIPP meanings (see Sect. "Deriving UIP Pictogram Meanings") that were presented separately including a free-form text entry field for open-ended responses by participants (see Fig. 4). Stimuli were clearly legible and not distorted. This was clarified through pretesting. Presentation of the stimuli was randomized. All stimuli were presented to every, individual participant. In order to prevent erroneous answers due to hastiness, participants could only proceed to the next meanings after 10 s (Kittur et al. 2008, p. 456). However, they could proceed without responding. In addition, two attention check questions were included after 33% and after 66% of the survey in which participants were asked to write an exact phrase. If a participant did not respond correctly to the questions, the survey was aborted and the participant was not remunerated (Meade and Craig 2012; Oppenheimer et al. 2009).

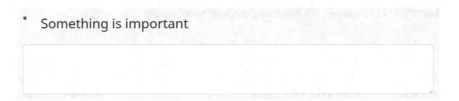

Fig. 4 Presentation of the meaning *[something] is important*. This is the English version of the presentation (see Study 1.2). In Study 1.1, the German translation was presented

Instructional Page

On the instructional page, participants were neither informed about the UIPP project nor about the purpose of the study. They were asked to read the meanings and close their eyes immediately after. It was assumed that this would improve their ability to answer questions by allowing them to disengage from their environment and redirect cognitive resources to knowledge retrieval (Glenberg et al. 1998, p. 657). In addition, they were asked not to listen to music, watch TV, or similar that could distract them (see Sect. "Crowdsourcing Cross-Cultural Studies for Universal Associations"). Participants were instructed to describe extensively the images that came to their minds within the first 15 s after reading each meaning, without evaluating their mental images nor checking them for potential criticism. Participants were instructed not to name abstract concepts, emotions, couple terms, analogies, opposites, or such, in order to be able to collect the basic sensorimotor experiences that people associate with UIPP meanings (see Sect. "User Utterances and Word Associations Tests for Intuitive Associations"). It was recommended to start the response with the clause *I see…*. Furthermore, participants were instructed to proceed to the next page when they could not think of anything more. Finally, participants were told that their response was not to be judged in any way. However, only serious and careful answers were to be remunerated.

Demographic Questionnaire

The study included a demographic questionnaire with three items: gender (*female*, *male*, or *diverse*), German as a first language (*yes* or *no*), and normal or corrected-to-normal vision (*yes* or *no*).

Apparatus

LimeSurvey Version 2.72.4+1171110 open-source online survey software was used for the creation and design of the study materials (LimeSurvey GmbH 2017).

Since a crowdsourcing process was used in the study, participants used their own personal computers in locations of their choice. The survey was designed to support all common computer systems and internet browsers (Andrews et al. 2003, p. 3).

Pretests

Following the guidelines for pilot studies by Andrews et al. (2003, pp. 15–16), 39 consecutive pretests were conducted with individual participants in order to optimize the procedure regarding introduction, instructions, stimuli design, questionnaires, and phrasing of the word association test. After each pretest, the participant was interviewed and the material was adapted (Stahl-Timmins 2017, pp. 458–459).

Design

Open-ended participant responses were collected as free-form text data.

Procedure

Participants were informed about the study on the Clickworker website through an introductory text (see Sect. "Crowdsourcing Cross-Cultural Studies for Universal Associations"). If the participants chose to participate in the study, they were provided with a link to the online survey that was hosted on a different webspace. On the survey website, participants were presented with the instructional page and with the demographic questionnaire. Then, participants were presented successively with the stimuli in randomized order. Participants gave their responses in the free-form text entry fields. After one third and two-thirds of the survey, participants were presented with attention check questions. In the survey, open-ended responses were collected. The test was self-paced. The complete survey took about 29 min. After the session, participants were presented with a thank-you message and a code. They were forwarded to the Clickworker website where they could use the code to receive their payment through the platform.

Data Selection and Cleaning

Erroneous and incoherent responses were deleted. That is, if participants responded random letters or if they gave the same, unrelated answer for multiple questions, their responses were not included. As a consequence, 1.78% of participants' responses were excluded.

Results

Data analyses and coding were conducted using the software TreeTagger 3.2.1 (Schmid 2017), AntConc 3.5.8 (Anthony 2019), and Microsoft Excel 365 Version 1906 (Microsoft Corporation 2019).

In total, 64,529 words were collected as open-ended response data. Raw response data consisted of a vast mixture of descriptions of abstract concepts and of concrete scenes (see Table 2 for word counts and Sect. "Appendix D" for an example of the collected open-ended responses).

In the analysis of the responses, an approach by Maglio and Matlock (1999) was followed. Consequently, the analysis involved two steps: first, a quantitative analysis, then, a qualitative analysis. In the quantitative analysis, raw data for every meaning was lemmatized using the software TreeTagger and the German parameter file that is part of the software (Schmid 1995, 2017). The result was a

Table 2 Count of words collected as open-end responses per meaning in Austrian, German, and Swiss participant group

Meaning	Words
[Something or someone] is absent, not here	3,245
[Something] is bad, negative	3,140
[Something] begins	3,411
[Something or someone] is busy	3,845
Coldness	3,013
[Something] is dangerous	4,415
Day	3,014
[Something] is decreasing	2,989
[Something] ends	3,185
[Something] is everywhere	2,798
[Something] is good, positive	3,302
[Something or someone] is here, on-site	3,175
[Something] is important	3,046
[Something] is increasing	2,924
Night	2,972
Power	2,770
Several, a group of [some things or some people]	3,600
[Something or someone] is single, solitary	3,160
Warmth	2,859
[Something] goes wrong, is wrong	3,665
Total	64,529

Notes: Meanings and responses were presented and collected in German

nominal data set. Then, the software AntConc (Anthony 2019) was used to count lemmatized words and *n*-grams as much as to generate word and *n*-gram frequency lists (see Table 3 for an excerpt).

In the qualitative analysis, raw data and the frequency lists were analyzed in order to identify response patterns. These patterns were coded subsequently into categories (see Maglio and Matlock 1999, pp. 161–163). According to Popping (2015), categories "should fit to the question, should have relevance and semantic validity (they must represent what respondents had in mind saying)" (p. 128). Furthermore, they should be formulated "in a neutral way, in common language, must be specific and concrete and the formulation is as short as possible. The categories should be mutually exclusive, the whole set should be collectively

Table 3 Ranks and frequencies of lemmata and n-grams in the response data for the meaning *[something] is important* in German (Total word count: 3,046)

Rank	Frequency	Lemma	Frequency	N-Gram
1	200	eine	29	ich sehen
2	198	die	25	in die
3	111	ich	24	auf die
4	97	und	16	mit eine
5	96	sein	13	sehen eine
6	66	mein	13	sein wichtig
7	57	in	12	ich sehen eine
8	56	mit	11	an die
9	46	auf	11	auf eine
10	43	wichtig	11	eine rot
11	41	zu	11	ich sehen mein
12	39	an	11	mein familie
13	37	sehen	11	rot ausrufezeichen
14	35	rot	11	sehen mein
15	32	ausrufezeichen	10	in eine
16	32	familie	9	es sein
17	31	haben	9	sein die
18	25	es	9	sein eine
19	25	nicht	8	die hand
20	21	werden	8	nicht vergessen
21	20	termin	8	und die
22	18	für	7	an eine
23	17	schwarz	7	eine rot ausrufezeichen
24	17	sie	7	eine termin
25	16	vor	7	mein freund
26	15	hand	7	sein ich
27	14	freund	7	vor ich
28	14	kind	6	eine wichtig
29	14	stehen	6	mein kind
30	13	dass	6	und eine
31	13	etwas	6	und mein
32	13	geld		
33	13	liegen		
34	12	er		

(continued)

Table 3 (continued)

Rank	Frequency	Lemma	Frequency	N-Gram
35	12	weiß		
36	11	müssen		
37	11	sich		
38	11	vergessen		
39	10	alle		
40	10	gesundheit		
41	10	können		

Notes: Only lemmata with ten and above and *n*-grams with six and above mentions are listed

exhaustive and contain a logical ordering" (p. 128). See Table 4 for the complete list of categories that were coded for the meaning *[something] is important* (including categories that were subsequently excluded because they do not fulfill the requirements).

Table 4 Response categories including details coded for the meaning [something] is important

#	Category
1	Red (35), however, almost exclusively in connection with marks (11, 2-g) and markings
2	Family (32), as an important concept; friends (14), and children (14), life (7)
3	Exclamation marks (35), as a conventional symbol of importance
4	Appointments, deadlines (20), calendars (17), work (8), as important events
5	Black (17), in connection with writing, white (12), in connection with pages, grey (5)
6	Money (13)
7	Big (8), thick (2), in relation to objects
8	Color (7), no specific relations
9	Yellow (7), exclusively in relation with cultural objects, like postal service
10	High (7), exclusively in relation with abstract concepts, like priority and attention
11	On top [German: oben] (6)
12	Small (6), however, no distinct connection with a specific object, concept, or such
13	Middle and in the middle (6)
14	A circle (3), encircling (2)
15	Blinking (3), however, in relation with technologies
16	Shining (2), bright (3)

Notes: Responses were given in German (see Table 3). Coded categories are translated to English. Word frequency is indicated in parentheses

Subsequently, pictogram content candidates were derived from the categories, based on the requirements developed in the previous parts of this chapter (Woike 2010). I repeat the requirements as follows:

1. The content should be a basic sensorimotor experience had in the real world.
2. The content should be a sensorimotor experience had very early in childhood.
3. The content should be a schematic representation of an experience, that is, an image schema or a primary scene.
4. The content should represent a naïve physical, bodily, environmental, or social experience.
5. The content should represent a superordinate set of experiences (see Sect. "Summary: Requirements for the Derivation of Pictogram Contents").
6. The content should be perceptible through the visual sensory channel (see Sect. "User Utterances and Word Associations Tests for Intuitive Associations").

In addition, I adapted the word taxonomy described in Sect. "Deriving UIP Pictogram Meanings" to further specify the contents. Let me explain. In their taxonomy, Nakamura and Zeng-Treitler (2012, pp. 541–542) distinguished between standalone lexical words, that is, nouns and verbs, and modifiers, for example, adjectives and adverbs, that might refer to pictogram meanings. In my adaption, I used four categories for pictogram contents: (a) actions instead of verbs, (b) characteristics instead of modifiers, and objects or creatures instead of nouns which I separated further into (c) countable objects and creatures, that is, objects that have distinct borders, for example, animals, plants, and buildings (i.e., one cat, two firs, and three airports), and (d) uncountable objects "which are without such boundaries and to which the indefinite article or a number cannot be applied in linguistic descriptions" (Thompson et al. 2011, p. 595), for example, materials, liquids, and gases (i.e., wood, water, and air). I made these distinctions because characteristics and actions cannot be represented visually without an additional object or creature. That is, they must be represented by the means of representing an object or creature that has the characteristic or that performs the action:

> For example, the concept 'thin' can only be graphically represented by also representing the modified entity. That is, it is possible to draw a thin person or a thin object but it is virtually impossible to graphically convey the concept 'thin' in isolation in a manner that would be easily comprehended. The same applies for the transitive sense of a verb. For example, a snapshot-like picture of a person in a running posture could represent the intransitive verb 'run'. (Nakamura and Zeng-Treitler 2012, pp. 541–542; see Yamazaki and Taki 2010, pp. 71–72, too)

In addition, I hold that uncountable objects must be represented by means of another object, too, for example, water must be represented in a vessel, wood as a trunk, and so forth. This needs to be considered in the subsequent pictogram design production process (see Sect. "Design Answers: Report of the UIPP Design Production Process").

Furthermore, the contents were separated into image schemata and primary scenes. As described in Sect. "Image-Schematic Design", primary scenes are more local and concrete, however, still schematic situations. They can be considered parts of image schemata. Image schemata are larger, more abstract schemata. I argue that most characteristics that were collected, for example, the concept of thin, which was discussed by Nakamura and Zeng-Treitler, correspond to image schemata (the concept thin to the image schema *big–small*, see Hurtienne 2017). However, as much as the concept of thin—and its antonym thick—the image schema *big–small* requires an instantiation in order to be visually representable. In contrast, primary scenes are often described through actions or combinations of actions, objects, creatures, and characteristics (e.g., as *n*-grams), thus, they are already visually representable—as in the categories *birth, baby, newborn* and *sun rising, new day, sunrise* for the *meaning [something] beings*. Along those lines, in the above-given example, Category 7 can be interpreted as being included in the more abstract image schemata of *big–small*, 10−11 as included in *up–down*, 13 in *center–periphery*, and 14 in *container* (Hurtienne 2017). The Categories 15−16 can be interpreted as being included in the image schema *bright–dark* or as a description of a primary scene.

Based on the derived requirements and the adapted taxonomy, the previously coded categories were analyzed, and suitable pictogram contents were derived. For example, in the case of the already discussed meaning *[something] is important*, Categories 3, 4, and 6 (exclamation marks, appointments, and money) were excluded because they were considered not to fulfill the requirements of being basic sensorimotor experiences had in the real world and very early in childhood (Requirements 1 and 2). Category 2 (family) was considered a description of abstract emotional relations that is not visually perceptible (Requirement 6). The colors in Categories 5 and 8 (black and varied) are only contingently connected to objects, thus, not specifically connected to the presented meaning. Consequently, they are neither considered naïve physical, bodily, environmental, nor social experiences (Requirement 4). Finally, Categories 13 and 14 (middle and circle) were assumed to address the same superordinate set of experiences of something in the middle that is necessarily encircled by something different (Requirement 5). Consequently, they were conflated. In conclusion, the following candidates for the content of a visual representation of the meaning *[something] is important* were derived:

- [Something] is big (German: [etwas] ist groß)
- [Something] is bright, shining (German: [etwas] leuchtet, ist hell)
- [Something] is flashing, blinks (German: [etwas] blinkt)
- [Something] is in the middle (German: [etwas] ist in der Mitte, mittig)
- [Something] is on top (German: [etwas] ist ganz oben)
- [Something] is red (German: [etwas] ist rot)

See Table 5 for the full list of meanings, abbreviated categories that meet the requirements, and subsequently derived content candidates. For each meaning,

Table 5 Meanings, abbreviated categories, and content candidates (80) for German-speaking participant group

Meaning	
Categories (Frequency)	Content candidates
[Something or someone] is absent, not here	
Empty (50) To sit (31), seat (23) To stand (19) Woman (17), man (8) Away (15, far away 7) Alone (9) Long (6)	An empty seat A person is standing alone and far away
[Something] is bad, negative	
Face (19) Black (23), dark (20) Man (11) Downwards (11) in connection with mouth, thumb, arrow Sad (7), to cry (3) Child (6) Overcast, cloudy sky (4), rain (8) Rotten (6), bad (food) (5) Pale, furious, angry (3)	An angry face [Something] is dark / black An overcast, rainy sky A sad face Spoiled food
[Something] begins	
Sun rising (8), new day (12), sunrise (8) Birth (10), baby (6), newborn (2) Lights go off and on (8), something becomes brighter (2) Yellow (4) Bright (8), shining (2)	A baby being born [Something] becomes bright, brighter The rising sun
[Something or someone] is busy	
Hand (14) Many [viele] (29), [mehrere] (5) Again and again (2) Hectic (4), fast (2) At the same time [während] (8), [gleichzeitig] (3)	An action is repeated over and over again Hands performing an action Many [people or things] perform many actions, all at the same time
Coldness	
Snow (67), ice (59), winter (49), snowflake (9) White (34), blue (34) Wind (23) Polar bear (15) (Snowy) landscape (21), winter landscape (8) Tree (11, bare, snowy) Sky (10) To fall (10) Iceberg (9), ice cube (8) Water (9, blue, cold) Mountain (9) Blue background (3) Everywhere (3)	Blue background Snow, ice Snowflake A snowy landscape with mountains [Something] is white, blue

(continued)

Table 5 (continued)

Meaning	
Categories (Frequency)	Content candidates
[Something] is dangerous	
Tiger (35), lion (16), snake (12), shark (10), animal (23) Big (27) Black (25), red (24) Teeth (21), jaws (10), open (5) Fire (19) Dark (19), night, by night (17) Deep (15), abyss [Klippe] (14), [Abgrund] (14) To approach (7) Running (7)	An animal that could kill a human being [Something] is big [Something] is dark, black Fire Doing something by night A deep abyss [Something] is red [Something or someone] is running fast and approaching Teeth and jaws
Day	
Sun (129), sunshine (19) Sunrise (9) Bright, brightness (80), light (15) Sky (blue) (52) Shining (sun) (51) Blue (39, sky) Cloud (21) Meadow (14), flower (5) Green (11), yellow (9)	The blue sky Brightness and light A meadow with flowers The shining sun
[Something] is decreasing	
Glass (37), related to drinking, water (32) Becoming less and less (31), becoming empty (15) Sand (21), related to hourglass Big, large (12), in connection with becoming smaller Taking a piece away (9) To sink (6), down (6) To melt (8)	Something big is getting smaller and smaller Bit by bit [something] is taken away A full container is emptied continuously
[Something] ends	
Black (19), dark (10) A path, track, or road that ends (19) The last of a quantity (12) Slowly doing something (9, light being turned off or on (5)) Tear(s) (7) Humans leaving (6)	[Something] gets slowly darker until it turns black The last of a row or a set A path or a road ends People leave a place Tears
[Something] is everywhere	
Air (63), wind (15), oxygen (5) Dust (6), pollen (7) Ants (4), fly, flies, mosquitos, wasps (4) Sky (20), blue (12), clouds (14)	Air Particles suspended in the air The blue sky

(continued)

Table 5 (continued)

Meaning	
Categories (Frequency)	Content candidates
[Something] is good, positive	
Sun (35), shining (18) Somebody is pleased, glad (20), smiling face (17) Smiling [lachen] (24), [lächeln] (27) Light and colorful colors (10) Green (18) Meadow (9) Child (16), girl (4), daughter (4), young (6) Woman (8), mother (4)	The face of a laughing / smiling girl A green meadow Light and bright colors The shining sun A smiling face
[Something or someone] is here, on-site	
Something or someone is standing someplace (53) To sit (25) To arrive at or come in (10), enter (3) Somebody is waiting someplace (8) Something is standing in front (5) or beside (3) oneself	[Someone or something] is arriving, entering [Someone] is sitting someplace [Someone or something] is standing in front or next to oneself [Something or someone] is standing someplace
[Something] is important	
Red (35) Big (8), thick (2) High (7) On top (6) Middle, in the middle (6) A circle (3), encircling (2) Blinking (3) Shining (2), bright (3)	[Something] is big [Something] is bright, shining [Something] is flashing, blinks [Something] is in the middle [Something] is on top [Something] is red
[Something] is increasing	
Getting bigger (29), higher (6) Water (26, glass (18)), pile (13), dough (10), sand (8) To rise (9) Growing family (16)	[Something] is getting denser [Something] is growing upwards Pregnancy, birth
Night	
Star (87), starry sky (35), night sky (8) Shooting star (5) Dark (99), black (35), dark blue (10) Moon (68), full moon (16) Shining (24), light (22), bright (19, moon, stars) Sleeping (29)	[Something] is dark, black, blue Many stars shining bright The moon shining bright

(continued)

Table 5 (continued)

Meaning	
Categories (Frequency)	Content candidates
Power	
Muscle (45), muscular (18), biceps (12) Arm (11) Man (50) Tense (14) Schwarz, dunkel (11) Tree (6), oak (3), redwood (1) Elephant (5)	A dark tree A male arm with tensed biceps muscle A tree
Several, a group of [some things or some people]	
Human (59), person (20) Group (56), crowd of people (11), gathering (7) Standing (55) Many (38), together (22), with each other (8) Friend (26) Square (10) All (23, doing the same or look the same), team (10) A circle (16, of people) Colorful (13, crowd)	[Some people or some things] standing together, all doing the same thing [Some people or some things] standing together, all looking the same [Some people or some things] standing together in a circle [Some people or some things] standing together, each in a different color [Some people or some things] standing together randomly in a square
[Something or someone] is single, solitary	
To stand (64) Alone [alleine] (39), [einsam] (30), [allein] (28), single (63) Person (38), human (27)	A person standing alone
Warmth	
Sun (84), shining (29), summer (22) Fire (30), campfire (9), fireplace (24) Orange, yellow (15), red (23) Blue (12), in connection with sky White (16), in connection with man-made objects Bright (11) Sweat (8)	Fire A red fire Sun A sweating person
[Something] goes wrong, is wrong	
Something falls down, crashes, collapses (38) Red (14) Hand (8) To fall down from something (11)	[Something] collapses [Something] falls and breaks, shatters Hands dropping [something] that breaks, shatters [Something] is red

Notes: Word frequency is indicated in parentheses. *N*-Grams frequency is omitted. In categories, brackets indicated ambiguous translations. Meanings and responses were presented, collected, and coded in German. Categories are ordered according to frequency. Contents are in alphabetical order of first major words

collected data and coded categories were analyzed, and suitable candidates were derived as described. The results are discussed in Sect. "Discussion, Limitations, and Future Research", together with the results of Study 1.2.

Study 1.2: English-Speaking Participant Group

Method

Participants
The English-speaking participant group consisted of three subgroups: a North-American subgroup, a South African subgroup, and an Australian subgroup. Three hundred and ten participants were included in the North American (Canada and United States) subgroup ($n = 310$), ranging in age from 18 to 73 years ($M = 31.1$, $SD = 11.23$). North American participants were 44.2% female, 55.8% male, none stated *diverse* as gender. Two hundred fifty-one participants were included in the South African subgroup ($n = 251$), ranging in age from 18 to 70 years ($M = 30.63$, $SD = 10.24$). South African participants were 45.8% female, 54.2% male, none stated *diverse* as gender. One hundred and seventeen participants were included in the Australian subgroup ($n = 117$), ranging in age from 18 to 64 years ($M = 35.69$, $SD = 9.61$). Australian participants were 48.7% female, 51.3% male, none stated *diverse* as gender. Participants were recruited and remunerated as described in Study 1.1. Only participants who were registered on the crowdsourcing website as living in the respective countries and with English as a first language were included.

Materials
Stimuli, instructional page, demographic questionnaire, and apparatus were identical to the material in Study 1.1, except they were presented in English. The same translation process was applied as described in Sect. "Deriving UIP Pictogram Meanings".

Design
Study design was identical to Study 1.1.

Procedure
The procedure was identical to the procedure in Study 1.1. However, in Study 1.2, the complete survey took about 25 min, and 2.21% of participants' responses were excluded. Each subgroup completed the survey individually.

Results
The data was analyzed, coded, and interpreted as described in Study 1.1. In total, 78,923 words were collected as open-ended response data (see Table 6 for word counts per group and meaning).

Table 6 Count of words collected as open-end responses per meaning in North American (NA), South African (SA), and Australian (A) participants subgroups (Total: 78,923)

Meaning	NA	SA	A
[Something or someone] is absent, not here	1,579	1,880	813
[Something] is bad, negative	1,475	1,558	702
[Something] begins	1,505	1,910	781
[Something or someone] is busy	1,740	1,879	831
Coldness	1,646	1,617	697
[Something] is dangerous	1,546	1,513	616
Day	1,444	1,516	744
[Something] is decreasing	1,435	1,623	681
[Something] ends	1,700	1,775	663
[Something] is everywhere	1,511	1,453	595
[Something] is good, positive	1,527	1,503	594
[Something or someone] is here, on-site	1,647	1,932	653
[Something] is important	1,434	1,759	674
[Something] is increasing	1,608	1,535	598
Night	1,483	1,568	774
Power	1,462	1,595	599
Several, a group of [some things or some people]	1,621	1,732	633
[Something or someone] is single, solitary	1,785	1,702	798
Warmth	1,581	1,805	689
[Something] goes wrong, is wrong	1,571	1,967	666
Total	31,300	33,822	13,801

Notes: Meanings and responses were presented and collected in English

Quantitative and qualitative analyses were conducted as described in Study 1.1. Data of North American, South African, and Australian participant subgroups were analyzed and coded individually, however, categories and content candidates are presented conflated in Table 7. This is so because the derived pictogram content candidates were almost identical, and they were presented subsequently as a complete set to all three English-speaking subgroups for evaluation in Study 2. Frequency in individual subgroups is indicated in parentheses.

Table 7 Meanings, conflated and abbreviated categories, and content candidates (104) for English-speaking participant group

Meaning	
Categories (Frequency NA/SA/A)	Content candidates
[Something or someone] is absent, not here	
Class, student (17/16/12) Room, space [empty] (15/9/3) White (8/11/5) Sit [people] (5/13/4) Chair, seat [empty] (11/5/5) Yellow, blue, brown (3/9/6) Black (7/6/2) Wooden (5/4/2) In the middle (3/4/1) Hole (2/5/0) Row (2/0/2)	[Something] is black A hole in the middle An empty seat in an empty room An empty seat in the middle of sitting people An empty space in the middle [Something] is white
[Something] is bad, negative	
Black, dark, darkness (25/26/22) Face [frowning, sad, angry, disgusted], cry, tear (16/18/7) Red (19/12/5) [Prohibition] sign (4/9/3) Fight [people], yell [people, at each other] (7/2/3) Food [bad, spoiled] (5/3/0) Cloud [dark] (4/3/1) Dirty (4/2/2) Big [black, red] (2/4/1) Room [dark] (6/0/1) Night (3/0/2)	An angry, frowning face [Something] is black Dark clouds People fighting and yelling at each other [Something] is red A sad, crying face Spoiled food
[Something] begins	
Baby, birth, life [new], to bear (36/22/14) [Starting] line, gun [race] (11/19/11) Morning, day [new], sunrise (17/8/3) Movie [beginning] (5/1/10) Book [being opened] (10/4/1) Grow [plant], little [plant], flower [bloom] (8/5/2) Blank (6/1/0) Light [beginning to shine] (4/4/1) Egg [hatch] (3/0/2) Smile (3/1/0) Spring (0/4/1)	A baby being born A hatching egg The rising sun A sprouting plant

(continued)

Table 7 (continued)

Meaning	
Categories (Frequency NA/SA/A)	Content candidates
[Something or someone] is busy	
Work, office (39/42/10) Telephone (19/17/13) Look [someone at something], stare at (13/10/5) Run around [someone or something], run, walk (6/12/6) Around (6/17/1) Black [business dress] (4/11/5) Talk [people] (5/6/7) Rush, fast, quick (8/4/6) Mother [working] (9/7/0) Sit at [something] (8/4/1) Bee (0/8/1) Pile (2/3/3) Constantly [doing the same thing] (1/2/2) Back [and forth] (2/2/0) Queue (1/2/1)	Bees are flying around [Someone or something] is doing the same over and over again Hands performing an action [Someone or something] is moving around fast [Someone or something] is moving back and forth [Some people or some things] perform actions all at the same time [Some people or some things] are standing in a queue
Coldness	
Ice, snow, glacier, snowflake (106/68/27) White, [light] blue (33/31/16) Water, air [cold] (15/12/6) Mountain, landscape [snow covered] (10/15/1) Ice cube, icicle (14/5/5) Dark, darkness, black (8/9/4) Frost, frozen (8/4/1) Ocean [cold] (1/5/4) Breath (5/0/1)	Breath freezing [Something] is dark, black Ice and snow Icicle Glacier A snow-covered mountain Snowflake [Something] is white, blue
[Something] is dangerous	
Bear, snake, animal, dog, tiger, shark, lion (36/33/14) Gun, knife (16/18/5) Black, dark (22/6/7) [Warning] sign (12/15/5) Fire (13/15/3) Red (12/12/8) Car, road (11/10/2) Run [people], [moving] towards [something] (7/4/4) Tooth (7/6/0) Cliff (3/6/2) Sharp [tooth and other] (5/3/0) Skull (3/2/2) Face [angry, panicked] (3/2/2)	An animal that could kill a human being [Someone or something] is approaching very fast [Something] is black A cliff Fire Knife [Something] is red Sharp teeth and jaws

(continued)

Table 7 (continued)

Meaning	
Categories (Frequency NA/SA/A)	Content candidates
Day	
Sun [yellow, white], shine, sunny, sunlight (123/92/41) Sky, [white] cloud (68/36/23) Bright, light (44/39/14) Blue (32/21/12) Tree [green], grass, flower, field, meadow (29/23/11) Sunrise, the sun rises (10/12/4) Bird (6/12/5) Window (8/2/3) Beach (3/1/2) Clock (1/1/5) Ocean, [sun over the] ocean (3/2/0) Coffee (1/3/1)	The blue sky Light shining bright through an opening in the wall A meadow with flowers and trees The shining sun
[Something] is decreasing	
Down, downward, go down (36/21/15) Graph, line, chart (29/16/14) Water (14/26/9) Money, bank, stock (23/16/3) Get less, get small, shrink (11/10/4) Small (9/9/5) Slowly, slow (11/9/3) Arrow (6/7/4) Emptying [something] (2/3/5) Time (3/5/2) Level [go down], [level] drop, low (1/9/0) Away [farther], distance (2/7/1) Sand [hourglass] (4/2/3) Run out (0/4/3) Size [decreasing] (2/4/1) Air [balloon lets out], balloon (1/0/5) Sun [set] (5/1/0) Ocean [water flowing back to the] (3/1/0)	[Something or someone] is going farther away The level of [something] is sinking Piece by piece [something] is taken away The size of [something] is shrinking A vessel is emptying
[Something] ends	
Black, dark, white (21/12/8) Movie [ending], credits (16/19/5) Road [end] (11/16/6) Rope [end of], [end of] string, cut [rope, string] (9/13/2) [Stop] sign (8/7/4) Away [someone walk], [someone] leave (8/9/1) Come to a [stop, end, movement] (8/6/1) [Finish] line (7/4/2) Funeral, coffin (4/13/4) Death (5/5/0) [Into the] ground (4/1/2) Stand [someone] (3/2/0)	[Something] becomes continuously darker until it is black The end of a rope or string The last of a row or a quantity The linear movement of [someone or something] comes to a stop A road ends [Someone] walks away

(continued)

Table 7   (continued)

Meaning	
Categories (Frequency NA/SA/A)	Content candidates
[Something] is everywhere	
Tree, grass [green], field, flower (27/14/10) Sky [blue], cloud (21/17/5) Air (13/16/8) Light [shine] (14/6/5) Spread [all over a surface], floor (11/8/6) White (13/8/3) Water (11/7/3) Room [that is full] (4/9/4) Ocean, sea (3/8/2) World, planet earth [from outer space] (6/1/5) Fly [around] (5/1/4) Dust, particle [in air, light] (6/2/1) Sand, beach (0/7/2) Bright (3/1/1) Ant (3/1/0)	Air Ants The blue sky Light shining bright Ocean Particles in the air or light [Something] is spread all over a surface
[Something] is good, positive	
Food, meal, [ice] cream, chocolate, cake, apple (41/28/12) Smile, [smiling] face, laugh (23/24/12) Brown, yellow, blue, pink, gold (17/19/5) Green (6/11/3) Sit [people, to eat] (10/4/5) White (9/3/4) Child (3/7/4) Flower, field (3/5/2) Sun (3/4/2) Bright (3/2/2) Hug (3/2/0) Together (2/2/1)	A flower Tasty food [Something] is green People sitting together eating A smiling, laughing face The shining sun [Something] is white
[Something or someone] is here, on-site	
Construction, worker (24/26/24) [Hard] hat (6/5/5) Arrive [someone] (2/5/1) Shadow (3/2/1) Behind [something or someone] (2/5/1) In front of (5/3/1)	[Someone or something is arriving [Someone or something] is standing behind someone or something else [Someone or something] is standing in front of oneself
[Something] is important	
Paper, document (17/14/7) Red (10/14/6) Family (9/16/7) Exclamation mark (8/9/2) Big, large (7/9/2) Black (4/10/2) Money (5/7/3) Office (4/5/2) Light, flash (4/0/0) Gold (3/3/0) Bold [letters] (3/1/1)	[Something] is big [Something] is black [Something] is bright [Something] is flashing [Something] is red

(continued)

Table 7 (continued)

Meaning	
Categories (Frequency NA/SA/A)	Content candidates
[Something] is increasing	
Up, [get] high, rise (31/32/13) Large, [grow] size, [get] big (18/25/3) Water (10/20/7) Arrow, graph (12/14/6) Grow (13/10/3) Money, stock (12/13/9) Level [rise], fill (10/10/4) Number (4/10/3) Temperature, thermometer (6/5/4) Rapidly, [increasing] speed (8/1/1) Pile [something falling onto] (4/2/2) Rain [increasing] (5/3/0) Mountain (6/0/1) Balloon [expand] (4/1/2) Upwards [arrow, graph] (1/6/3) Flood (2/1/2)	[Something] is falling onto a pile while the pile is getting bigger [Something] is growing upward The level of [something] is rising
Night	
Star, sky, million [stars], starry (131/87/55) Dark, black, darkness, dark blue (79/62/31) Moon, full [moon] (59/46/22) Streetlight, lamp, headlights (7/4/9) White [moon, stars], yellow (13/10/4) Shine [moon or stars], [star] twinkle (11/6/2) Tree [hardly seen, blocking view] (7/7/3) Bed (4/7/4) Cloud [none] (4/6/2) Sleep (1/6/2) Silver (1/3/0) Owl (4/1/4)	Bright moon and stars Clouds in the dark sky [Something] is dark, black, blue An owl
Power	
Electricity, electrical (25/18/12) President, government, king (16/12/4) Light (19/16/9) Strong man, tall, large (4/13/0) Lightning, thunder (6/7/1) Black [various] (5/4/4) Muscle, biceps, muscular arm, flex (2/10/0) Suit (5/4/2) Fire, smoke (2/8/0) Power plant (4/0/6) Sky (6/3/0) God (6/3/0) Money (5/3/0) Fist (6/0/1) Spark (3/4/0)	A big, muscular man A fist A male arm flexing biceps Lightning bolt

(continued)

Table 7 (continued)

Meaning	
Categories (Frequency NA/SA/A)	Content candidates
Several, a group of [some things or some people]	
Crowd, flock, team (19/19/8) Together (9/19/5) Stand (9/17/5) Around [something] (8/9/5) Walk [a group] (7/9/6) Sit (6/9/3) Laugh [several people] (5/7/4) Circle (8/4/3) School (8/2/5) All [doing the same] (2/6/3) Play (3/4/2) Large [group] (5/2/1) In front [of, stand] (4/3/0) All [look the same] (3/0/2) Row (3/2/0)	[Some people or some things] jointly moving around [Some people or some things] standing together in a circle [Some people or some things] standing together jointly doing the same [Some people or some things] standing together looking the same
[Something or someone] is single, solitary	
Alone, single, solitary, lonely (74/60/21) Man, person, woman, someone (60/54/19) Sit (32/17/6) Stand, standing (21/16/5) Black, white [various] (14/13/5) Bed, bench, table (12/14/6) Room (10/6/6) Empty (7/3/4)	A person standing or sitting alone
Warmth	
Fire, fireplace, campfire (59/32/36) Yellow, orange, red (31/48/19) Sun, shine (44/39/10) Blanket, curl up, bed (38/24/13) Bright, light (13/12/4) Hot drink, chocolate, coffee, mug, marshmallow (9/20/7) Beach, sand (11/13/2) Glow (8/9/3) Mother [her child], family (7/7/3) Embrace, hug (9/3/2)	Fire Beach Blanket A drinking vessel with a hot drink [Something] is red The shining sun [Something] is yellow

(continued)

Table 7 (continued)

Meaning	
Categories (Frequency NA/SA/A)	Content candidates
[Something] goes wrong, is wrong	
Car, road, bus (27/58/14) Break [something, collapse], [car] crash (13/12/10) Red (11/9/9) Burn [something], smoke, fire (9/8/4) Light [go on, flash] (8/5/5) Black [various] (7/8/2) Face [sad, angry, panicked] (7/5/2) Fire (5/2/4) Over [spill, drop, ground, floor] (6/1/2) Cry [person, baby], tear (5/3/0)	[Something] collapses [Something] falls and breaks Fire [Something] is flashing brightly [Something] is red [Something] spills over onto the ground A sad, crying face

Notes: Word frequency is indicated in parentheses: (NA = North America/SA = South Africa/A = Australia). *N*-Grams frequency is omitted. Brackets indicate additional descriptions. Categories are ordered according to word frequency sum. Contents are in alphabetical order of first major words

Discussion, Limitations, and Future Research

In Study 1, multiple surveys were conducted in a computer-assisted multi-step process to derive suitable pictogram content candidates. In the first step, mental associations that participants had with presented meanings were collected. The study aimed for the collection of mental associations that were activated universally and intuitively by asking for open-ended responses on four different continents, in seven different countries, and in two languages. In the first survey, 337 German-speaking participants living in Austria, Germany, or Switzerland were included, and 64,529 words were collected as open-ended responses. In the second to fourth survey, 948 English-speaking people living in Australia, Canada, South Africa, and the United States participated, and 78,923 words were collected. Raw response data consisted of a vast mixture of descriptions of abstract concepts and of concrete scenes. In the second step, the data were analyzed and coded using software for tagging and annotating linguistic data. In the third step, based on the coded categories, the previously developed requirements, and an adapted content taxonomy, 80 suitable pictogram content candidates for the German-speaking group and 104 contents for the English-speaking group were derived for the 20 UIPP meanings. I consider these candidates the answers to my research question: Which content candidates can be derived from cross-culturally and intuitively provided participant data, fulfilling the previously described requirements, that might allow for universal, intuitive, and permanent semantic association.

While conventional and abstract concepts and scenes were excluded because they did not fulfill the requirements, the analysis revealed many categories and subsequent content candidates that appear to be similar to image schemata and primary scenes. In addition, response data indicate that people activated multimodal representations of sensorimotor experiences when they were presented with the meanings. This is in line with the argument by embodied cognition that people imagine concrete scenes or situations when asked for categories of objects or concepts (Gibbs 2005, pp. 88–89; Vallée-Tourangeau et al. 1998; see Yee et al. 2012, pp. 836–837, too). The coded categories and the derived contents from the English-speaking group are very similar to those of the German-speaking group. Sixty-one of the content candidates derived in the German-speaking group were derived identically in the English-speaking group, that is, 76.3% (see Tables 5 and 7). The high degree of agreement between the groups was a surprise considering that the four participant subgroups are located on four different continents: Africa, Australia, Europe, and North America, and in seven countries, Australia, Austria, Canada, Germany, South Africa, Switzerland, and the United States. However, this was predicted by embodied cognition. EC claims that basic sensorimotor experiences are universal and that they are used subsequently to conceptualize and interpret the world. For that reason, I consider the claims to be validated, and I maintain that the derived contents are suitable candidates for universally, intuitively, and permanently comprehensible pictograms. In Study 2, these content candidates were evaluated.

I propose that the presented process might be used, in principle, for any required meaning. That is, the study design seems appropriate for the use with other meanings that require to be represented visually in a human–computer interaction system. At the same time, the process might also be used for localization, for example, if only contents were derived from the responses of a specific, local population, for a specific context of use (see, e.g., Hsieh et al. 2009, pp. 712–713; Averbukh 2001, p. 232). In addition, the process might be adaptable to other representations, for example, to contents of auditory representations. As Stevens et al. (2009, p. 84) suggested, natural indicators, that is, so-called caricatures of everyday sounds or auditory icons, can be used to design auditory warning signals because they are faster and more correctly interpreted. It seems plausible that the process that was described in Study 1 can be adapted to contents of auditory representations by asking participants to describe the sounds that they associate with a given meaning or to describe the situations or scenes that they imagine in which they hear the sounds. Then, the auditory mental associations of sensorimotor experience that people have would be collected and analyzed following the process that was described. Furthermore, the process and the obtained rich data might be usable as a resource for researching image schemata, primary metaphors, and populations stereotypes (Hurtienne et al. 2009) because the results indicate that image schemata and primary metaphors that were previously confirmed in the literature can be found in the data, and further analysis might reveal metaphors that have not yet been described.

Although the studies have yielded good results, there are some important drawbacks to consider. While I argue that the process can be adapted to other meanings, in this study, only contents for simple meanings were derived. It remains to be evaluated whether the process is suitable for more complex meanings in HCI that might have no equivalent in the real world. As Hornecker (2012) insisted:

"Digital systems are *not* the real world; it is their very strength to offer functionality unavailable in the real world" (p. 178).

Another important drawback of the studies is that only one person coded and analyzed the data. Interpretation of linguistic data is complex. Although a quantitative analysis was conducted and results were verified in Study 2, the qualitative analysis and interpretation formed a decisive part, and a lack of linguistic proficiency might have led to errors (Hurtienne and Meschke 2016, pp. 330–331), in particular with English–German translations. In order to detect and avoid errors, in future studies, at least two researchers should interpret the data—as is it was done for the derivation of the UCUI meanings—and intercoder reliability should be calculated (Hurtienne 2017, p. 13).

Furthermore, the survey might have been too lengthy (Baatard 2012, p. 104). Some erroneous responses suggest that fatigue with some participants was high. Although possible lower quality of responses for meanings presented at the end of trials was outbalanced by randomizing the presentation, future studies should split surveys into several parts, as it was done in Study 2.

Finally, disabilities of participants were not assessed. Participants with vision not normal or not corrected-to-normal were not included, and it can be assumed that people with other physical or cognitive disabilities did not participate in the study either. Consequently, their mental associations were not collected, and they are not represented in the data. This is an important drawback, especially with regard to inclusive design. However, in UIPP, the choice was made to focus on cross-cultural design because of limited resources. Nevertheless, in order to consider people with disabilities, appropriate additional studies should be designed in the future.

Study 2: Evaluating the Content Candidates

In Study 2, the previously derived content candidates for universal, intuitive, and permanent pictograms were evaluated. Consequently, the research question of Study 2 was the following: Which content candidates are evaluated the closest connected to their meanings by cross-cultural study participants that might allow for universally, intuitively, and permanently comprehensible pictograms?

To assess the most intuitive contents, the study evaluated the association strength of the previously derived pictograms contents with their associated meanings. The associative strength was evaluated by asking study participants to rate how closely they consider the content and the meaning to be connected. Along those lines, I considered the contents with the highest ratings to have the highest associative strength, thus, to be the most intuitive candidates. To assess the most universal pictogram contents, again, I conducted surveys with participant groups form four different continents, in seven countries, and with two first languages. I assumed that the contents that were rated highest in most groups were universal candidates. In addition, I assumed that these candidates should be the most permanently comprehensible, too, because the physical world and the sensorimotor experiences on which they are based are considered not to change. In conclusion, I created a ranking of the contents based on the ratings in all groups. The ranking was used in the subsequent design production process of the pictogram prototypes in Step 4 of the UIPP project.

Study 2.1: Austrian, German, and Swiss Participant Group

Method

Participants
Austrian, German, and Swiss participants were divided into four subgroups to reduce fatigue effects. In Subgroup E.1 (Europe 1), two hundred forty-seven participants were included ($n = 247$), ranging in age from 18 to 81 years ($M = 36.34$, $SD = 12.34$). Participants in Subgroup E.1 were 54.3% female, 45.7% male, none stated *diverse* as gender. In Subgroup E.2, two hundred and three participants were included ($n = 203$), ranging in age from 18 to 67 years ($M = 35.22$, $SD = 10.97$). Participants in Subgroup E.2 were 49.8% female, 50.2% male, none stated *diverse* as gender. In Subgroup E.3, Two hundred and four participants were included ($n = 204$), ranging in age from 18 to 67 years ($M = 35.68$, $SD = 11.56$). Participants in Subgroup E.3 were 49.0% female, 51.0% male, none stated *diverse* as gender. In Subgroup E.4, two hundred participants were included ($n = 200$), ranging in age from 18 to 68 years ($M = 35.02$, $SD = 11.98$). Participants in Subgroup E.4 were 5.0% female, 50.0% male, none stated *diverse* as gender. Since online screen testing was used, only participants with normal or corrected-to-normal vision were included. Following Study 1, only participants who were registered on the crowdsourcing website in Austria, Germany, or Switzerland, and with German as a first language, were included.

Materials
Materials were presented in German. In the following, they are translated into English where appropriate.

Stimuli
Stimuli consisted of 79 content candidates (see Sect. "Study 1.1: German-speaking Participant Group") that were presented individually including the associated meaning, the task, and a Liker-type scale. The task was to rate how closely connected content and meanings are. While the original Likert scale is a symmetrical 7-point scale from *strongly disagree* to *strongly agree* (Joshi et al. 2015, p. 397), for this test, a bipolar, asymmetrical 7-point Likert-type scale that ranged from *not at all* to *immediately, i.e. extremely closely* was used. While the literature is inconclusive whether 7-point Likert-type scales should be used over 5-point Likert-type scales (Joshi et al. 2015, pp. 398–399), 7-point scales were used because they allow more fine-grained divisions. If the connection was rated

*Please, picture the following term/scenario before your 'inner eye' first, then rate:
How is the first term/scenario connected with the second term/scenario?

a sad, crying face

something is bad, negative

not at all ○ ○ ○ ○ ○ ○ ○ ○ immediately, i.e. extremely closely

Fig. 5 Presentation of the stimulus for the meaning *[something] is bad, negative* and the content *a sad, crying face*. This is the English version of the presentation in Studies 2.2. to 2.4. In Study 2.1, the German translation was presented

as close, Likert-type score was high. Ratings of less close connections resulted in lower scores. To reduce test time and minimize fatigue, the content for the meaning *[something or someone] is single, solitary*, was not evaluated because only a single content was derived for this meaning. Stimuli were presented as shown in Fig. 5. Stimuli were clearly legible and not distorted. This was clarified through pretesting. Presentation of the stimuli was randomized. All stimuli were presented to each participant. To prevent erroneous answers due to hastiness, participants could only proceed to the next meanings after at least 10 s (Kittur et al. 2008, p. 456). Furthermore, they could not proceed without responding. Two attention check questions were included after 33% and after 66% of the survey in which the participant was asked to write an exact phrase. If the participant did not respond correctly to the questions, the survey was aborted and the participant was not remunerated (Meade and Craig 2012; Oppenheimer et al. 2009).

Instructional Page
On the instructional page, participants were neither informed about the UIPP project nor the purpose of the study. They were asked to read the meanings and visualize the contents and meanings mentally, then, to rate on a Likert-type scale the connection between content and meaning. In addition, participants were asked not to listen to music, watch TV, or similar that could distract them. Finally, participants were told that their response was not to be judged in any way. However, only serious and careful answers were to be remunerated (see Sect. "Appendix E").

Demographic Questionnaire
The study included a demographic questionnaire with three items: gender (*female*, *male*, or *diverse*), German as a first language (*yes* or *no*), and normal or corrected-to-normal vision (*yes* or *no*).

Apparatus

LimeSurvey Version 2.72.4 + 171110 open-source online survey software was used for the creation and the design of the study materials (LimeSurvey GmbH 2017).

Since a crowdsourcing process was used in this study, participants used their own personal computers in locations of their choice. The survey was designed to support all common computer systems and internet browsers (Andrews et al. 2003, p. 3).

Pretests

Following the guidelines for pilot studies by Andrews et al. (2003, pp. 15–16), 11 consecutive pretests were conducted with 62 participants in order to optimize the procedure regarding introduction, instructions, and stimuli design. Participants were interviewed, the data was analyzed, and the material was adapted accordingly (Stahl-Timmins 2017, pp. 458–459).

Design

One dependent variable was collected, Likert-type scale rating with *not at all* = 1, increasing in one-unit steps up to *immediately, i.e. extremely closely* = 7. All effects were reported as significant at $p < 0.05$.

Procedure

Introductory procedure was the same as in Study 1. On the survey website, participants were presented with the task, that is, to rate the connection between the presented contents and meanings, and with stimuli in randomized order. To reduce fatigue, each subgroup was present with a specific set of stimuli, as indicated in Table 8. Sets were randomized. After one third and two thirds of the survey, participants were presented with attention checks. In the survey, Likert-type scale ratings by participants were collected. The test was self-paced. However, participants could only proceed after 10 s. For each subgroup, the complete survey took about 7:30 min. The concluding procedure was the same as in Study 1.

Data Selection and Cleaning

There were no missing data because only complete tests were included in the analysis. Consequently, no data were imputed. However, incoherent responses were deleted, that is, responses by participants who rated all connections identically or who used recognizable rating patterns. Consequently, 1.05% of participants' responses were excluded.

Reliability

A reliability test was performed with North American participants in Study 2.2 (see Sect. "Study 2.2: Canadian and U.S. Participant Group").

Results

Data analysis was conducted using JASP Version 0.10.2 (JASP Team 2019) and Microsoft Excel 365 Version 1906 (Microsoft Corporation 2019).

See Sect. "Appendix F" for median ratings per content candidate including *IQRs*. Non-parametric Friedman tests of differences among content ratings and Conover's post-hoc comparison tests were conducted. Results for Friedman tests are reported per meaning in Table 8. In addition, Wilcoxon matched pairs signed-ranks tests were conducted for all contents per meaning. For each content pair, Hodges–Lehmann estimate of median difference was calculated. Based on the results, rankings of content candidates for each meaning were created according to five rules that I developed during the analysis. I present the rules in the following:

1. The highest-rated content is ranked first.
2. If there is a significant difference between the ratings of the highest-ranked content and the ratings of the second highest ranked content, the second highest rated content is placed on the second rank.
3. If there is no significant difference between the ratings of the highest-rated and the second highest rated contents, the second highest rated contents is placed below the highest-rated content but on the same rank, that is, also on the first rank. In that case, Hodges-Lehman estimate of location is used to determine rating tendency (Green and Salkind 2014, p. 340).
4. If there is a significant difference between the third highest rated content and the second highest rated content, Rule 2 applies accordingly. That is, the third highest rated content is placed on the third rank. As such, Rule 2 applies to all consecutive contents.
5. If there is no significant difference between the ratings of the first content and the second content, and there is no significant difference between the ratings of the second and the third content, but there is a significant difference between the ratings of the first and the third content, then the third content is placed on a lower rank, that is, in this example, the second rank. This applies to all consecutive contents, too.

The rules were applied to all contents and rankings. Let me give an example. For the meaning *[something] is bad, negative* the content *spoiled food* was rated highest. Thus, it was placed on Rank 1. There is no significant difference between the ratings for the content *spoiled food* and the ratings for the content *a sad face*, however, matched-pairs Wilcoxon signed-ranks test and Hodges–Lehmann estimate of median difference indicate that ratings for *spoiled food* are higher. Thus, the content *spoiled food* is placed above *a sad face* but on the same rank. Furthermore, there is no significant difference between the ratings for the content *a sad face* and the content *an angry face*. However, there is a significant difference between the ratings for *spoiled food* and *an angry face*. Thus, an *angry face* was placed on a lower rank, here, Rank 2. In Table 8, the results of Wilcoxon matched pairs signed-ranks test including Hodges–Lehmann estimate of the content in the same line and the content in the line below are reported.

Table 8 Friedman tests and Matched-pairs Wilcoxon signed-ranks tests for content candidates and meanings in Austrian, German, and Swiss participant group

Meaning (Subgroup)		χ^2		p
Rank	Contents	W	p	Hodges-Lehmann Estimate
[Something or someone] is absent, not here (E.4)		39.03		< .001
1	An empty seat	8632	< .001	1.5
2	A person is standing alone and far away			
[Something] is bad, negative (E.4)		366.8		< .001
1	Spoiled food	3470	.096	0.0
	A sad face	3067	.454	0.0
2	An angry face	13,937	< .001	2.0
3	An overcast, rainy sky	4946	.630	0.0
	[Something] is dark, black			
[Something] begins (E.1)		278.4		< .001
1	A baby being born	10,804	< .001	1.0
2	The rising sun	16,162	< .001	2.0
3	[Something] becomes bright, brighter			
[Something or someone] is busy (E.3)		70.71		< .001
1	Hands performing an action	7839	< .001	1.5
2	An action is repeated over and over again	4965	.401	0.0
	Many [people or things] perform many actions, all at the same time			
Coldness (E.3)		504.3		< .001
1	Snow, ice	3485	< .001	1.0
2	A snowy landscape with mountains	2818	.503	0.0
	Snowflake	14,346	< .001	2.5
3	[Something] is white, blue	7990	< .001	1.0
4	Blue background			
[Something] is dangerous (E.2)		815.6		< .001
1	An animal that could kill a human being	5382	< .001	1.0
2	A deep abyss	5410	< .001	1.0
3	Fire	7481	< .001	1.5
4	Teeth and jaws	6294	.066	0.5
	[Something or someone] is running fast and approaching	6726	< .001	0.5
5	[Something] is red	5522	.003	0.5
6	Doing something by night	5014	.046	0.0
7	[Something] is big	4543	.039	0.5
8	[Something] is dark, black			
Day (E.3)		302.5		< .001
1	The shining sun	2530	.001	1.0
2	The blue sky	3646	.066	0.0
	Brightness and light	14,110	.001	2.5
3	A meadow with flowers			

(continued)

Table 8 (continued)

Meaning (Subgroup)		χ^2		p
Rank	Contents	W	p	Hodges-Lehmann Estimate
[Something] is decreasing (E.4)		80.38		< .001
1	A full container is emptied continuously	1156	.567	0.0
	Bit by bit [something] is taken away	4867	< .001	1.5
2	Something big is getting smaller and smaller			
[Something] ends (E.4)		250.4		< .001
1	A path or a road ends	4557	< .001	1.0
2	The last of a row or a set	6898	< .001	1.0
3	People leave a place	6032	.001	0.5
4	[Something] gets slowly darker until it turns black	7583		1.0
5	Tears		< .001	
[Something] is everywhere (E.1)		187.4		< .001
1	Air	10,564	< .001	1.0
2	Particles suspended in the air	14,743	< .001	1.5
3	The blue sky			
[Something] is good, positive (E.4)		249.6		< .001
1	A smiling face	1846	.060	0.0
	The face of a laughing, smiling girl	5914	< .001	1.0
2	The shining sun	4849	< .001	1.0
3	Light and bright colors	4584	.045	0.5
4	A green meadow			
[Something or someone] is here, on-site (E.3)		260.4		< .001
1	[Someone or something] is standing in front or next to oneself	8141	< .001	1.5
2	[Someone or something] is arriving, entering	12,306	< .001	2.0
3	[Someone] is sitting someplace	3099	.624	0.0
	[Something or someone] is standing someplace			
[Something] is important (E.2)		185.3		< .001
1	[Something] is flashing, blinks	7201	< .001	0.5
2	[Something] is on top	4499	.800	0.0
	[Something] is red	5386	.001	0.5
3	[Something] is bright, shining	6668	.024	0.5
4	[Something] is big	6620	< .001	1.0
5	[Something] is in the middle			
[Something] is increasing (E.1)		16.88		< .001
1	[Something] is growing upwards	9993	< .001	1.0
2	Pregnancy, birth	10,275	.429	0.0
	[Something] is getting denser			

(continued)

Table 8 (continued)

Meaning (Subgroup)		χ^2			p
Rank	Contents	W		p	*Hodges-Lehmann Estimate*
Night (E.3)		124.9			< .001
1	The moon shining bright	1732		.439	0.0
	Many stars shining bright	8027		< .001	1.5
2	[Something] is dark, black, blue				
Power (E.1)		325.8			< .001
1	A male arm with tensed biceps muscle	20,563		< .001	2.5
2	A tree	10,130		< .001	1.5
3	A dark tree				
Several, a group of [some things or some people] (E.2)		122.8			< .001
1	[Some people or some things] standing together, all doing the same thing	2523		.262	0.0
				.449	0.0
	[Some people or some things] standing together in a circle	2847		< .001	1.0
	[Some people or some things] standing together, all looking the same	6030		< .001	1.5
2	[Some people or some things] standing together, each in a different color	7486			
3	[Some people or some things] standing together randomly in a square				
[Something or someone] is single, solitary					
	A person standing or sitting alone			n.t.	
Warmth (E.1)		207.8			< .001
1	Sun	1563		.215	0.0
	Fire	5016		< .001	1.0
2	A red fire	10,672		.001	1.0
3	A sweating person				
[Something] goes wrong, is wrong (E.3)		283.8			< .001
1	Hands dropping [something] that breaks, shatters	2473		.462	0.0
	[Something] falls and breaks, shatters				
2	[Something] collapses	5020		.018	0.5
3	[Something] is red	15,544		< .011	3.0

Notes: n.t. = not tested

Study 2.2: Canadian and U.S. Participant Group

Method

Participants
The Canadian and U.S. participant group was divided into four subgroups to reduce fatigue effects. In Subgroup NA.1 (North America 1), fifty-nine participants were included ($n=59$), ranging in age from 18 to 68 years ($M=38.39$, $SD=12.60$). Participants in Subgroup NA.1 were 50.8% female, 49.2% male, none stated *diverse* as gender. In Subgroup NA.2, fifty-nine participants were included ($n=59$), ranging in age from 18 to 68 years ($M=37.25$, $SD=11.89$). Participants in Subgroup NA.2 were 50.8% female, 49.2% male, none stated *diverse* as gender. In Subgroup NA.3, fifty-three participants were included ($n=60$), ranging in age from 21 to 67 years ($M=37.40$, $SD=12.04$). Participants in Subgroup NA.3 were 50.0% female, 50.0% male, none stated *diverse* as gender. In Subgroup NA.4, sixty participants were included ($n=61$), ranging in age from 18 to 69 years ($M=37.01$, $SD=11.3$). Participants in Subgroup NA.4 were 50.8% female, 49.2% male, none stated *diverse* as gender. Following Study 2.1, only participants who were registered on the crowdsourcing website in Canada or the United States and with English as a first language were included.

Materials
Stimuli consisted of 103 contents (see Sect. "Study 1.2: English-speaking Participant Group"). The presentation of the stimuli, the instructional page, the demographic questionnaire, and the apparatus were identical to Study 2.1, except they were presented in English. The same translation process was applied as described in Sect. "Deriving UIP Pictogram Meanings") (Plocher et al. 2012, pp. 173–174).

Design
Study design was identical to Study 2.1.

Procedure
The procedure was identical to the procedure in Study 2.1. However, in Study 2.2, the complete survey took each subgroup about 8:30 min, and 1.67% of participants' responses were excluded.

Reliability
A nine-week test–retest reliability test was performed with time as the only known source of variance ($n=12$) (Salkind 2010, pp. 1237–1242). Because of the interval between two tests, I assumed that participants would not remember the ratings of the connections from the first test. The test had a significant test–retest reliability, Kendall's $\tau=0.62$, $p<0.001$ (Pearson's $r=0.73$, $p<0.001$). The reliability is considered *strong* (Akoglu 2018, p. 92; Dancey and Reidy 2017, pp. 181–189).

Results

Data analysis was conducted as described in Study 2.1. See Sect. "Appendix G" for median ratings per content candidate including *IQRs*. See Table 9 for results and rankings.

Table 9 Friedman tests and Matched-pairs Wilcoxon signed-ranks tests for content candidates and meanings in Canadian and U.S. participant group

Meaning (Group)		χ^2		p
Rank	Contents	W	p	Hodges-Lehmann Estimate
[Something or someone] is absent, not here (NA.4)		86.38		< .001
1	An empty seat in the middle of sitting people	245.5	.793	0.0
		308.0	.863	0.0
	An empty space in the middle	455.0	.054	1.0
	An empty seat in an empty room	808.5	< .001	2.5
2	A hole in the middle	427.5	.134	1.0
3	[Something] is black			
4	[Something] is white			
[Something] is bad, negative (NA.4)		127.9		< .001
1	People fighting and yelling at each other	245.5	.793	0.0
	An angry, frowning face	176.5	.704	0.0
	A sad, crying face	248.0	.512	0.5
	Spoiled food	666.0	.002	1.5
2	Dark clouds	706.0	< .001	1.5
3	[Something] is red	455.5	.965	0.0
	[Something] is black			
[Something] begins (NA.2)		10.71		.013
1	A baby being born	298.5	.074	1.0
	A sprouting plant	195.5	.869	0.0
	A hatching egg	300.5	.296	0.5
2	The rising sun			
[Something or someone] is busy (NA.3)		38.90		< .001
1	[Someone or something] is moving around fast	590.0	.014	1.0
		471.5	.592	0.0
2	Hands performing an action	445.5	.632	0.0
	[Some people or some things] perform actions all at the same time	377.0	.701	0.0
		431.0	.380	0.5
	Bees are flying around	624.0	.065	1.0
	[Someone or something] is moving back and forth			
3	[Someone or something] is doing the same over and over again			
	[Some people or some things] are standing in a queue			

(continued)

Table 9 (continued)

Meaning (Group)		χ^2		p
Rank	Contents	W	p	Hodges-Lehmann Estimate
Coldness (NA.2)		223.8		< .001
1	Ice and snow	139.0	.063	1.0
	Glacier	148.0	.252	0.5
2	Icicle	96.0	.649	0.0
	Snowflake	161.5	.095	0.5
	Breath freezing	211.5	.851	0.0
	A snow-covered mountain	1106.0	< .001	3.0
3	[Something] is white, blue	367.6	.113	1.0
	[Something] is dark, black			
[Something] is dangerous (NA.2)		170.5		< .001
1	An animal that could kill a human being	290.5	.224	0.5
	Sharp teeth and jaws	494.0	.141	0.5
2	Fire	341.0	.278	0.5
	Knife	300.5	.492	0.0
	A cliff	670.5	.006	1.5
3	[Someone or something] is approaching	940.0	< .001	1.0
	very fast	627.5	.010	1.0
4	[Something] is red			
5	[Something] is black			
Day (NA.2)		71.89		< .001
1	The shining sun	282.5	.005	1.0
2	The blue sky	719.0	< .001	1.0
3	Light shining bright through an opening	1019.5	< .001	1.5
4	in the wall			
	A meadow with flowers and trees			
[Something] is decreasing (NA.3)		62.56		< .001
1	The size of [something] is shrinking	256.0	.037	1.0
2	Piece by piece [something] is taken	335.0	.169	0.5
	away	365.0	.409	0.5
3	The level of [something] is sinking	915.0	< .001	2.0
	A vessel is emptying			
4	[Something or someone] is going farther			
	away			
[Something] ends (NA.4)		44.08		< .001
1	A road ends	397.0	.087	1.0
	The end of a rope or string	332.0	.354	0.5
2	The linear movement of [someone or	373.5	.524	0.0
	something] comes to a stop	591.5	.076	1.0
	The last of a row or a quantity	557.5	.098	1.0
	[Someone] walks away			
3	[Something] becomes continuously			
	darker until it is black			

(continued)

Table 9 (continued)

Meaning (Group)		χ^2		p
Rank	Contents	W	p	Hodges-Lehmann Estimate
[Something] is everywhere (NA.1)		95.98		< .001
1	Air	376.5	.083	1.0
	[Something] is spread all over a surface	670.5	.002	1.0
2	Particles in the air or light	450.0	.249	0.5
	The blue sky	419.5	.903	0.0
	Ocean	349.0	.079	0.5
	Light shining bright	614.0	.041	1.0
3	Ants			
[Something] is good, positive (NA.4)		106.7		< .001
1	A smiling, laughing face	351.5	.003	1.0
2	Tasty food	399.5	.076	0.5
	The shining sun	427.0	.604	0.0
3	People sitting together eating	461.5	.476	0.0
	A flower	679.5	.012	1.0
4	[Something] is green	568.0	.031	1.0
5	[Something] is white			
[Something or someone] is here, on-site (NA.3)		9.08		.011
1	[Someone or something is arriving	631.5	.009	1.5
2	[Someone or something] is standing in front of oneself	357.0	.709	0.0
	[Someone or something] is standing behind someone or something else			
[Something] is important (NA.1)		76.79		< .001
1	[Something] is flashing	638.5	.002	1.5
2	[Something] is big	547.0	.063	1.0
	[Something] is bright	495.0	.790	0.0
	[Something] is red	931.5	< .001	1.5
3	[Something] is black			
[Something] is increasing (NA.2)		15.04		< .001
1	The level of [something] is rising	352.5	.003	1.0
2	[Something] is growing upward	456.0	.529	0.0
	[Something] is falling onto a pile while the pile is getting bigger			
Night (NA.1)		32.09		< .001
1	Bright moon and stars	264.5	< .001	1.5
2	An owl	586.5	.041	1.0
3	Clouds in the dark sky	466.0	.643	0.0
	[Something] is dark, black, blue			

(continued)

Table 9 (continued)

Meaning (Group)		χ^2		p
Rank	Contents	W	p	*Hodges-Lehmann Estimate*
Power (NA.2)		16.04		.001
1	A big, muscular man	367.0	.389	0.5
2	Lightning bolt	375.0	.722	0.0
3	A male arm flexing biceps	516.5	.010	1.0
	A fist			
Several, a group of [some things or some people] (NA.3)		22.13		< .001
1	[Some people or some things] standing together in a circle	219.0	.266	1.0
		296.5	.339	0.5
2	[Some people or some things] standing together jointly doing the same	533.0	.016	1.0
3	[Some people or some things] standing together looking the same			
	[Some people or some things] jointly moving around			
[Something or someone] is single, solitary				
	A person standing or sitting alone		n.t.	
Warmth (NA.1)		137.9		< .001
1	Blanket	154.0	.176	0.5
	Fire	235.0	.703	0.0
	A drinking vessel with a hot drink	293.5	.354	0.0
2	The shining sun	575.0	.002	1.0
3	Beach	873.0	< .001	2.0
4	[Something] is yellow	472.0	.026	0.5
5	[Something] is red			
[Something] goes wrong, is wrong (NA.1)		120.3		< .001
1	[Something] collapses	309.0	.845	0.0
	[Something] falls and breaks	345.5	.845	0.0
	A sad, crying face	808.0	.003	1.0
2	[Something] spills over onto the ground	703.0	.032	1.0
3	Fire	600.5	.214	0.5
	[Something] is flashing brightly	771.5	.001	1.2
4	[Something] is red			

Notes: n.t. = not tested

Study 2.3: South African Participant Group

Method

Participants
The South African participant group was divided into four subgroups to reduce
fatigue effects. In Subgroup SA.1 (South Africa 1), fifty-nine participants were
included ($n=58$), ranging in age from 18 to 48 years ($M=29.43$, $SD=7.96$).
Participants in Subgroup SA.1 were 51.7% female, 48.3% male, none stated
diverse as gender. In Subgroup SA.2, fifty-nine participants were included
($n=59$), ranging in age from 18 to 60 years ($M=29.85$, $SD=8.86$). Participants
in Subgroup SA.2 were 52.5% female, 47.5% male, none stated *diverse* as gender. In Subgroup SA.3, fifty-three participants were included ($n=58$), ranging in
age from 18 to 60 years ($M=29.14$, $SD=7.98$). Participants in Subgroup SA.3
were 51.7% female, 48.3% male, none stated *diverse* as gender. In Subgroup
SA.4, sixty participants were included ($n=60$), ranging in age from 18 to 69 years
($M=30.50$, $SD=9.21$). Participants in Subgroup SA.4 were 50% female, 50%
male, none stated *diverse* as gender. Following Study 1, only participants who
were registered on the crowdsourcing website in South Africa and with English as
a first language were included.

Materials
Stimuli, instructional page, and apparatus were identical to the material in Study
2.2.

Design
Study design was identical to Study 2.2.

Procedure
Procedure was identical to the procedure in Study 2.2. In Study 2.3, 1.28% of participants' responses were excluded.

Results
Data analysis was conducted as described in Study 2.1. See Sect. "Appendix H"
for median ratings per content candidate including *IQRs*. See Table 10 for results
and rankings.

Table 10 Friedman tests and Matched-pairs Wilcoxon signed-ranks tests for content candidates and meanings in South African participant group

Meaning (Group)		χ^2		p	
Rank	Contents	W	p	Hodges-Lehmann Estimate	
[Something or someone] is absent, not here (SA.4)		155.1		< .001	
1	An empty seat in the middle of sitting people	344.0	.021	1.0	
2	An empty seat in an empty room	364.5	.416	0.5	
	An empty space in the middle	603.0	< .001	1.5	
3	A hole in the middle	823.0	< .001	2.5	
4	[Something] is black	312.5	.001	2.0	
5	[Something] is white				
[Something] is bad, negative (SA.4)		94.24		< .001	
1	A sad, crying face	271.5	.892	0.0	
	People fighting and yelling at each other	231.5	.292	0.5	
	An angry, frowning face	445.5	.146	0.5	
2	Spoiled food	676.5	.033	1.0	
3	Dark clouds	560.0	.006	1.5	
4	[Something] is black	476.5	.757	0.0	
	[Something] is red				
[Something] begins (SA.2)		4.57		.206	
1	A baby being born	159.0	.271	0.0	
	A sprouting plant	131.5	0.880	0.0	
	A hatching egg	239.0	.214	0.5	
	The rising sun				
[Something or someone] is busy (SA.3)		34.69		< .001	
1	Hands performing an action	318.0	.967	0.0	
	[Someone or something] is moving around fast	371.0	.357	0.5	
	[Some people or some things] perform actions all at the same time	390.0	.368	0.5	
	[Someone or something] is moving back and forth	429.0	.586	0.0	
2	[Someone or something] is doing the same over and over again	494.5	.799	0.0	
	Bees are flying around	619.0	.014	1.5	
3	[Some people or some things] are standing in a queue				
Coldness (SA.2)		221.3		< .001	
1	Ice and snow	156.0	.152	0.5	
	Breath freezing	216.0	.771	0.0	
2	Icicle	228.5	.331	0.0	
	A snow-covered mountain	100.0	.863	0.0	
	Snowflake	217.0	.286	0.5	
3	Glacier	1149.5	< .001	2.5	
4	[Something] is white, blue	865.5	.001	1.5	
5	[Something] is dark, black				

(continued)

Table 10　(continued)

Meaning (Group)		χ^2		p
Rank	Contents	W	p	Hodges-Lehmann Estimate
[Something] is dangerous (SA.2)		154.0		< .001
1	An animal that could kill a human being	342.0	.022	1.0
2	Sharp teeth and jaws	357.0	.167	0.5
	Knife	263.5	.765	0.0
3	Fire	402.0	.151	0.5
	A cliff	490.0	.279	0.5
4	[Something] is red	527.5	.111	0.5
	[Someone or something] is approaching very fast	845.0	< .001	2.0
5	[Something] is black			
Day (SA.2)		81.60		< .001
1	The shining sun	290.5	.013	1.0
2	The blue sky	864.5	< .001	1.5
3	Light shining bright through an opening in the wall	711.0	.004	1.5
4	A meadow with flowers and trees			
[Something] is decreasing (SA.3)		79.15		< .001
1	The size of [something] is shrinking	144.0	.304	0.0
	Piece by piece [something] is taken away	498.5	.007	1.0
2	The level of [something] is sinking	394.0	.003	1.0
	A vessel is emptying	761.0	< .001	2.0
3	[Something or someone] is going farther away			
[Something] ends (SA.4)		36.10		< .001
1	A road ends	244.5	.175	0.5
	The end of a rope or string	624.0	.121	0.5
2	The last of a row or a quantity	393.0	.339	0.5
	The linear movement of [someone or something] comes to a stop	689.0	.297	0.5
	[Something] becomes continuously darker until it is black	650.0	.130	0.5
3	[Someone] walks away			
[Something] is everywhere (SA.1)		87.81		< .001
1	Air	280.5	.524	0.0
	[Something] is spread all over a surface	694.0	.007	1.5
2	Ocean	528.0	.909	0.0
	Particles in the air or light	437.5	.714	0.0
	The blue sky	786.0	.007	1.5
3	Light shining bright	536.0	.838	0.0
	Ants			

(continued)

Table 10 (continued)

Meaning (Group)		χ^2		p
Rank	Contents	W	p	Hodges-Lehmann Estimate
[Something] is good, positive (SA.4)		73.81		< .001
1	A smiling, laughing face	447.5	< .001	2.0
2	Tasty food	278.0	.797	0.0
	The shining sun	613.5	.087	0.5
	People sitting together eating	328.5	.385	0.0
	[Something] is green	424.5	.630	0.0
	A flower	605.0	.002	1.0
3	[Something] is white			
[Something or someone] is here, on-site (SA.3)		20.20		< .001
1	[Someone or something is arriving	462.5	.041	1.0
2	[Someone or something] is standing in front of oneself	516.0	.004	1.5
3	[Someone or something] is standing behind someone or something else			
[Something] is important (SA.1)		91.33		< .001
1	[Something] is flashing	605.0	.002	1.0
2	[Something] is red	572.0	.028	1.0
3	[Something] is big	332.0	.784	0.0
	[Something] is bright	932.0	< .001	2.0
4	[Something] is black			
[Something] is increasing (SA.2)		9.78		0.008
1	The level of [something] is rising	206.5	.036	1.0
2	[Something] is falling onto a pile while the pile is getting bigger	210.0	.881	0.0
	[Something] is growing upward			
Night (SA.1)		48.34		< .001
1	Bright moon and stars	478.0	< .001	1.5
2	An owl	447.0	.146	1.0
	[Something] is dark, black, blue	567.0	.569	0.0
	Clouds in the dark sky			
Power (SA.2)		36.30		< .001
1	A big, muscular man	247.0	.058	1.0
2	A male arm flexing biceps	685.5	< .001	1.0
3	A fist	588.0	.161	0.5
	Lightning bolt			
Several, a group of [some things or some people] (SA.3)		14.83		.002
1	[Some people or some things] standing together in a circle	154.0	.918	0.0
	[Some people or some things] standing together looking the same	196.0	.356	0.0

(continued)

Table 10 (continued)

Meaning (Group)		χ^2		p
Rank	Contents	W	p	Hodges-Lehmann Estimate
	[Some people or some things] standing together jointly doing the same	292.5	.011	1.0
2	[Some people or some things] jointly moving around			
[Something or someone] is single, solitary				
	A person standing or sitting alone		n.t.	
Warmth (SA.1)		182.0		< .001
1	Fire	74.0	.771	0.0
	Blanket	94.0	.983	0.0
	The shining sun	354.5	.002	1.0
2	A drinking vessel with a hot drink	670.0	< .001	2.0
3	Beach	679.0	.004	1.0
4	[Something] is red	489.0	.847	0.0
	[Something] is yellow			
[Something] goes wrong, is wrong (SA.1)		108.3		< .001
1	A sad, crying face	229.5	.067	1.0
	[Something] collapses	333.5	.035	1.0
2	[Something] falls and breaks	623.0	< .001	1.5
3	[Something] spills over onto the ground	613.5	.087	0.5
	[Something] is flashing brightly	424.0	.635	0.0
4	Fire	265.5	.736	0.0
	[Something] is red			

Notes: n.t. = not tested

Study 2.4: Australian Participant Group

Method

Participants
The Australian participant group consisted of four subgroups to reduce fatigue effects. In Subgroup A.1 (Australia 1), fifty-nine participants were included ($n = 59$), ranging in age from 18 to 58 years ($M = 33.72$, $SD = 11.57$). Participants in Subgroup A.1 were 49.2% female, 50.8% male, none stated *diverse* as gender. In Subgroup A.2, fifty-nine participants were included ($n = 59$), ranging in age from 18 to 60 years ($M = 34.57$, $SD = 11.13$). Participants in Subgroup A.2 were 49.2% female, 50.8% male, none stated *diverse* as gender. In Subgroup A.3, fifty-three participants were included ($n = 53$), ranging in age from 18 to 59 years ($M = 34.15$, $SD = 11.24$). Participants in Subgroup A.3 were 54.7% female, 45.3% male, none stated *diverse* as gender. In Subgroup A.4, sixty participants were included ($n = 60$), ranging in age from 18 to 62 years ($M = 33.68$, $SD = 11.3$).

Participants in Subgroup A.4 were 50% female, 50% male, none stated *diverse* as gender. Following Study 1, only participants who were registered on the crowd-sourcing website in Australia and with English as a first language were included.

Materials
Stimuli, instructional page, and apparatus were identical to the material in Study 2.2.

Design
Study design was identical to Study 2.2.

Procedure
The procedure was identical to the procedure in Study 2.2. In Study 2.4, 0.43% of participants' responses were excluded.

Results
Data analysis was conducted as described in Study 2.1. See Sect. "Appendix I" for median ratings per content candidate, including *IQRs*. See Table 11 for results and rankings.

Table 11 Friedman tests and Matched-pairs Wilcoxon signed-ranks tests for content candidates and meanings in Australian participant group

Meaning (Group)	χ^2		p
Rank Contents	W	p	Hodges-Lehmann Estimate
[Something or someone] is absent, not here (A.4)	114.3		< .001
1 An empty seat in the middle of sitting people	475.0	.024	1.0
2 An empty seat in an empty room	513.5	.037	1.0
3 An empty space in the middle	553.5	.107	1.0
A hole in the middle	88.0	< .001	2.5
4 [Something] is black	674.5	.001	1.5
5 [Something] is white			
[Something] is bad, negative (A.4)	173.4		< .001
1 People fighting and yelling at each other	268.5	.042	1.0
2 An angry, frowning face	245.5	.160	0.5
A sad, crying face	609.5	.042	1.0
3 Spoiled food	586.5	.041	1.0
4 Dark clouds	721.0	< .001	1.0
5 [Something] is black	617.5	.036	1.0
6 [Something] is red			

(continued)

Table 11 (continued)

Meaning (Group)		χ^2		p
Rank	Contents	W	p	Hodges-Lehmann Estimate
[Something] begins (A.2)		7.37		.061
1	A hatching egg	282.0	.985	0.0
	A sprouting plant	209.5	.889	0.0
	A baby being born	445.0	.074	1.0
	The rising sun			
[Something or someone] is busy (A.3)		37.90		< .001
1	[Someone or something] is moving around fast	563.5	.001	1.5
2	Bees are flying around	430.5	.570	0.0
	Hands performing an action	404.0	.424	0.0
	[Some people or some things] perform actions all at the same time	268.0	.946	0.0
	[Someone or something] is doing the same over and over again	405.5	.247	0.5
3	[Someone or something] is moving back and forth	624.5	.357	0.5
	[Some people or some things] are standing in a queue			
Coldness (A.2)		238.2		< .001
1	Ice and snow	131.0	.038	1.0
2	Glacier	126.5	1.000	0.0
	Icicle	204.0	.714	0.0
	Breath freezing	323.0	.428	0.0
	Snowflake	271.5	.410	0.0
3	A snow-covered mountain	1175.0	< .001	2.0
4	[Something] is white, blue	880.5	< .001	2.0
5	[Something] is dark, black			
[Something] is dangerous (A.2)		189.7		< .001
1	An animal that could kill a human being	329.0	.213	1.0
	Sharp teeth and jaws	669.5	< .001	0.0
2	Knife	524.5	.527	1.0
	Fire	603.0	.483	0.5
	A cliff	593.5	.032	0.0
3	[Someone or something] is approaching very fast	658.0	.197	0.0
	[Something] is red	906.0	< .001	2.0
4	[Something] is black			
Day (A.2)		108.1		< .001
1	The shining sun	281.5	< .001	1.5
2	The blue sky	76.0	< .001	1.5
3	Light shining bright through an opening in the wall	856.0	< .001	1.5
4	A meadow with flowers and trees			

(continued)

Table 11 (continued)

Meaning (Group)	χ^2		p
Rank Contents	W	p	Hodges-Lehmann Estimate
[Something] is decreasing (A.3)	68.65		< .001
1 The size of [something] is shrinking	193.0	.401	0.0
Piece by piece [something] is taken away	498.5	.007	1.0
2 The level of [something] is sinking	317.5	.973	0.0
A vessel is emptying	923.5	< .001	2.0
3 [Something or someone] is going farther away			
[Something] ends (A.4)	26.42		< .001
1 A road ends	514.0	.081	1.0
[Something] becomes continuously darker until it is black	372.0	.988	0.0
2 The linear movement of [someone or something] comes to a stop	42.0	.896	0.0
The last of a row or a quantity	381.5	.877	0.0
The end of a rope or string	65.0	.130	0.5
[Someone] walks away			
[Something] is everywhere (A.1)	90.99		< .001
1 Air	504.0	.007	1.0
2 [Something] is spread all over a surface	426.0	.412	0.0
Particles in the air or light	776.0	.009	1.0
3 Ocean	56.0	.172	0.5
The blue sky	567.5	.573	0.0
Ants	630.5	.860	0.0
4 Light shining bright			
[Something] is good, positive (A.4)	141.9		< .001
1 A smiling, laughing face	518.0	< .001	1.5
2 The shining sun	571.5	.025	0.5
3 Tasty food	442.0	.080	0.5
A flower	292.5	.832	0.0
People sitting together eating	741.0	.112	0.5
4 [Something] is green	658.0	.024	1.0
5 [Something] is white			
[Something or someone] is here, on-site (A.3)	10.84		.004
1 [Someone or something is arriving	681.5	.028	1.0
2 [Someone or something] is standing in front of oneself	345.0	.116	0.5
[Someone or something] is standing behind someone or something else			

(continued)

Table 11 (continued)

Meaning (Group)	χ^2		p
Rank Contents	W	p	Hodges-Lehmann Estimate
[Something] is important (A.1)	88.36		< .001
1 [Something] is flashing	1005.0	< .001	1.5
2 [Something] is big	659.5	0.310	0.5
[Something] is red	640.5	0.591	0.0
[Something] is bright	1152.0	< .001	1.5
3 [Something] is black			
[Something] is increasing (A.2)	8.85		.012
1 The level of [something] is rising	335.0	.172	0.5
[Something] is falling onto a pile while the pile is getting bigger	371.0	.098	1.0
2 [Something] is growing upward			
Night (A.1)	80.98		< .001
1 Bright moon and stars	693.0	< .001	1.0
2 An owl	746.0	< .001	1.5
3 [Something] is dark, black, blue Clouds in the dark sky	694.5	.164	0.5
Power (A.2)	35.96		< .001
1 A big, muscular man	496.5	.008	1.0
A male arm flexing biceps	54.0	.077	1.0
2 Lightning bolt A fist	366.0	.602	0.0
Several, a group of [some things or some people] (A.3)	13.86		.003
1 [Some people or some things] standing together in a circle	294.5	.345	0.0
[Some people or some things] standing together looking the same	243.5	.560	0.0
[Some people or some things] standing together jointly doing the same	227.5	.071	1.0
2 [Some people or some things] jointly moving around			
[Something or someone] is single, solitary			
A person standing or sitting alone		n.t.	
Warmth (A.1)	164.0		< .001
1 Fire	187.5	.746	0.0
The shining sun	358.0	.148	0.5
Blanket	247.5	.058	1.0
2 A drinking vessel with a hot drink	736.5	< .001	1.5
3 Beach	586.0	.017	1.0
4 [Something] is red [Something] is yellow	537.5	.160	0.5

(continued)

Table 11 (continued)

Meaning (Group)		χ^2		p
Rank	Contents	W	p	Hodges-Lehmann Estimate
[Something] goes wrong, is wrong (A.1)		113.5		< .001
1	A sad, crying face	364.0	.852	0.0
	[Something] collapses	354.0	.513	0.0
	[Something] falls and breaks	767.0	.004	1.0
2	[Something] spills over onto the ground	692.0	.008	1.0
3	[Something] is flashing brightly	551.5	.340	0.5
	Fire	506.5	.686	0.0
	[Something] is red			

Notes: n.t. = not tested

Discussion, Limitations, and Future Research

In Study 2, 952 people on four continents rated 182 content candidates. Based on the individual rankings in each study, I created a comprehensive ranking of the highest-rated contents for all participant groups, including their ranks in each group (see Table 12). I consider this ranking the answer to my research question: Which content candidates are evaluated the closest connected to their meanings by cross-cultural study participants that might allow for universally, intuitively, and permanently comprehensible pictograms?

Instead of a list of the single highest-rated contents, for the subsequent design production process, a comprehensive ranking of contents seemed advisable. This is so because the research through design (RTD) approach that was used in the production process might require to use contents that are ranked lower, for example, if the lower-ranked contents are more suitable for design. For example, a baby being born as the content of a visual representation of the meaning [something] beings might be difficult to design in relation with another object or creature that specifies the meaning, like [warmth] begins. A pictogram representing [warmth] being born like a baby might not be interpreted as intended. Furthermore, higher-rated contents might create confusion with other contents and meanings if they are mentioned multiple times, for example, sun and faces. Finally, sometimes, slight variations of rankings between the groups exist. This means that the ranking is not definite.

However, as much as in the derivation of contents in Study 1, the comparison of rankings in each group revealed many similarities. In fact, the differences between rankings are marginal. Across all groups, that is, across all continents, countries, and languages, rankings had the same tendencies. This was predicted by EC. For that reason, I suggest that the highest-ranked contents might be candidates for universally comprehensible pictograms. Furthermore, all contents that were ranked high were rated as having a close connection with the meanings, that is, a median

Table 12 Comprehensive ranking of the highest-rated contents for all participant groups

Meaning Rank	Contents	A/G/S	C/US	SA	A
[Something or someone] is absent, not here					
1	An empty seat (in the middle of sitting people)	1	(1)	(1)	(1)
2	An empty seat (in an empty room)	1	(1)	(2)	(2)
3	An empty space in the middle		1	2	3
[Something] is bad, negative					
1	A sad, crying face	1	1	1	2
	People fighting and yelling at each other		1	1	1
2	An angry, frowning face	2	1	1	2
	Spoiled food	1	1	2	3
[Something] begins					
1	A baby being born	1	1	1	1
	A sprouting plant		1	1	1
	A hatching egg		1	1	1
2	The rising sun	2	2	1	1
[Something or someone] is busy					
1	[Someone or something] is moving around fast		1	1	1
2	Hands performing an action	1 ,	2	1	2
3	(Many) [people or things] perform actions, all at the same time	(2)	2	1	2
4	An action is performed over and over again (by someone or something)	2	(3)	(2)	2
Coldness					
1	Ice and snow	1	1	1	1
2	Breath freezing		2	1	2
	Snowflake	2	2	2	2
	Icicle		2	2	2
3	Glacier		2	3	2
[Something] is dangerous					
1	An animal that could kill a human being	1	1	1	1
2	(Sharp) teeth and jaws	4	(1)	(2)	1
	Knife		2	2	2
	A cliff (or abyss)	(2)	2	2	2
3	Fire	3	2	3	2
4	[Someone or something] is approaching very fast	4	3	4	3

(continued)

Table 12 (continued)

Meaning Rank	Contents	A/G/S	C/US	SA	A
Day					
1	The shining sun	1	1	1	1
2	The blue sky	2	2	2	2
3	Light shining bright (through an opening in the wall)	2	(3)	(3)	(3)
4	A meadow with flowers and trees	3	4	4	4
[Something] is decreasing					
1	Piece by piece [something] is taken away	1	2	1	1
	The size of [something] is shrinking	(2)	1	1	1
2	The level of [something] (in a vessel) is sinking	(1)	2	1	2
[Something] ends					
1	A road ends	1	1	1	1
2	The end of a rope or a string		1	1	2
	The last of a row or a quantity	2	2	2	2
	The linear movement of [someone or something] comes to a stop		2	2	2
3	[Something] becomes continuously darker until it is black	4	3	2	1
[Something] is everywhere					
1	Air	1	1	1	1
2	[Something] is spread all over a surface		1	1	2
3	Particles in the air or light	2	2	2	2
[Something] is good, positive					
1	A smiling, laughing face	1	1	1	1
2	The shining sun	2	2	2	2
	The face of a laughing, smiling girl	1			
3	Tasty food		2	2	3
[Something or someone] is here, on-site					
1	[Someone or something] is arriving	2	1	1	1
2	[Someone or something] is standing in front of oneself	1	2	2	2
3	[Someone or something] is standing behind someone or something else		2	3	2
[Something] is important					
1	[Something] is flashing	1	1	1	1
2	[Something] is red	2	2	2	2
3	[Something] is bright	3	2	3	2

(continued)

Table 12 (continued)

Meaning Rank	Contents	A/G/S	C/US	SA	A
4	[Something] is big	4	2	3	2
[Something] is increasing					
1	The level of [something] is rising		1	1	1
2	[Something] is growing upward	1	2	2	2
	[Something] is falling onto a pile while the pile is getting bigger		2	2	1
3	Pregnancy, birth	2			
Night					
1	Bright moon and stars	1/2	1	1	1
2	An owl		2	2	2
	[Something] is dark, black, blue	2	2	2	3
Power					
1	A big, muscular man		1	1	1
2	A male arm with flexing biceps	1	2	2	1
	Lightning bolt		1	3	2
3	A tree	2			
Several, a group of [some things or some people]					
1	[Some people or some things] standing together in a circle	1	1	1	1
	[Some people or some things] standing together, jointly doing the same	1	1	1	1
2	[Some people or some things] standing together, all looking the same	1	2	1	1
[Something or someone] is single, solitary					
1	A person standing or sitting alone	n.t	n.t	n.t	n.t
Warmth					
1	Fire	1	1	1	1
2	Blanket		1	1	1
	(The shining) sun	1	(2)	(1)	(1)
[Something] goes wrong, is wrong					
1	[Something] falls and breaks	1	1	2	1
	[Something] collapses	2	1	1	1
	A sad, crying face		1	1	1
2	Hands dropping [something] that breaks, shatters	1			

Notes: Parentheses in contents indicate that a different, but very similar, wording was used in some groups. The groups in which the different wording was used are indicated with parentheses in group rankings. A/G/S = Austria, Germany, and Switzerland. C/US = Canada and United States. SA = South Africa. A = Australia. n.t = not tested

rating of 6 or higher (see Sect. "Appendices F–G"). This is in line with the predictions by EC, too. For that reason, I suggest that these contents might be considered candidates for intuitively comprehensible pictograms. Finally, since the sensorimotor experience on which the contents are based are considered not to change, I suggest that the candidates might be permanently comprehensible, too. In conclusion, I contend that the comprehensive ranking in Table 12 represents suitable content candidates for universal, intuitive, and permanent pictograms.

There were several drawbacks to the study. For example, in general, characteristics, like colors, were rated lower than the average, and contents that describe more concrete scenes and situations were rated higher or even highest. We can assume that the scenes that were rated higher include the characteristics that were rated lower. I argue that this is in line with the argument by embodied cognition that people imagine concrete scenes or situations when asked for categories of objects or concepts (Gibbs 2005, pp. 88–89; Vallée-Tourangeau et al. 1998; see Yee et al. 2012, pp. 836–837, too). Since people imagine scenes, it might have been difficult for the study participants to visualize colors without being presented with a scene or situation at the same time. This is a drawback because it might have affected the results. Future studies should create study designs that assess the perceived connection between characteristics and meanings and scenes and meanings alike. A further drawback was that not all contents were rated in all groups. That is, although they are very similar, there were differences between the contents that were rated in the German-speaking group and the contents that were rated in the English-speaking groups. This is so because distinct contents were derived in Study 1. Creating a comprehensive ranking of contents for all groups would have been even more straightforward if all contents had been rated in all groups. In Table 12, some doubts remain because some contents were rated high in the German-speaking group but were not rated at all in the English-speaking groups because they were not derived in the latter groups and vice versa. In future studies, I suggest, all contents should be rated in all groups even if the contents were not derived previously. Finally, rankings in English-speaking groups are less distinct than rankings in the German-speaking group supposedly because of smaller samples. Future studies should use larger samples.

Summary and Conclusion of the Chapter

Hurtienne (2011) suggested that three approaches to design, using EC and CMT, exist. In the first approach, researchers "take informed decisions based on theoretical considerations. If a good line of argumentation can be created for the grounding of specific metaphors in basic experience and many people share these basic experiences across cultures, then universality may be assumed" (p. 75). Subsequently, in that approach, the theoretically derived assumptions are evaluated in cross-cultural studies. In the second approach, researchers examine users in order to assess "their tasks and mental models, to discern what conceptual metaphors they use in their language and thought and to determine what image

schemas are underlying these metaphors" (p. 75–76). Third, researchers "empirically test hypothetical metaphors across cultures" (p. 75), that is, they present previously derived metaphor candidates to various cultures in order to assess whether
the candidates are suitable for design. I suggest that all three approaches were used
in this chapter. I derived basic requirements for universal, intuitive, and permanent
pictogram candidates from the theory of embodied cognition, in line with the first
approach. Following the second approach, I collected users' mental associations
with the given meanings in Study 1. 143,446 words were given as responses by
1,015 participants in seven countries on four continents, and content candidates
were derived subsequently based on the previously developed requirements. Third
and finally, in Study 2, I evaluated empirically the derived content candidates in
a cross-cultural study to assess whether they are suitable. Nine hundred fifty-two
participants on four continents rated 182 content candidates. The high degree of
similarities between the groups was remarkable. In conclusion, I created a comprehensive ranking of contents for subsequent pictogram design. I contend that the
highest-ranked contents are candidates for universally, intuitively, and permanently
comprehensible pictograms, based on semantic association.

In the beginning of Study 1 (Sect. "Study 1: Deriving Pictogram Content
Candidates"), I described that the presented studies had an additional goal, besides
the ranking of content candidates. The second goal was to develop a process for
the derivation and evaluation of suitable contents that might be used in other projects. This seemed advisable because most research on design that uses embodied
cognition rather "deconstructs existing systems than (…) generates guidelines for
informing the design of such systems" (Antle et al. 2009, p. 66). Instead, according to Antle et al. (2009), research should address "the question: How does an
embodied view of cognition (and interaction) inform the way we design interaction for hybrid physical and digital environments?" (p. 66). I propose that I have
addressed this question by explaining UIPP's experimental approach and by
reporting the studies in detail. Thus, I described a process that can be performed
and adopted by other designers, researchers, and businesses in their projects. First,
I hold that the presented process might be used, in principle, for any required
meaning. That is, study design can be adapted to meanings that other designers,
researchers, and businesses might want to represent in a human–computer interaction system, for example, if stimuli are adapted accordingly (see, e.g., Sect. "Study
1.1: German-speaking Participant Group"). Second, the process might be used for
localization, too. To do so, data should be collected from a more specific, that is,
a more local population than in UIPP (see Sect. "Crowdsourcing Cross-Cultural
Studies for Universal Associations"). Third, the process can be adapted to a
more specific context of use—in contrast to the UIPP approach—if study participants are instructed accordingly (see, again, Sect. "Study 1.1: German-speaking
Participant Group"). Finally, the process might even be adapted to other categories
of representations, for example, to contents of auditory representations. To achieve
this, participants should be asked to describe the sounds that they associate with a
given meaning, rather than the visual experience, or to describe the situations or
scenes that they imagine in which they might hear that sounds. Then, the auditory

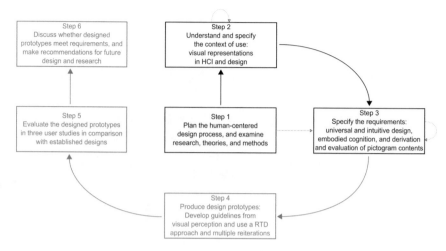

Fig. 6 The UIPP human-centered design process. Step 3 is completed. Dotted arrows indicate iterations

mental associations of sensorimotor experience that people have might be collected, analyzed, and evaluated following the process that was described.

This chapter constitutes the third step in the UIPP process, that is, the approach to the reference relation. According to ISO 9241:210 (International Organization for Standardization 2010), in the third human-centered design step, the requirements for subsequent design are specified (see Sect. "The UIPP Design Process and the Chapters of this Book"). I consider this achieved in this chapter. I propose that the step is completed (see Fig. 6). In the next chapter, I describe the approach to the design relation and the design production process of the UIPP prototypes. This is Step 4 in the UIPP process.

Step 4: Developing a Design System and Producing the UIP Pictograms

Abstract

In Step 4 of a HCD process, a design team produces prototypes based on previous findings and on existing guidelines. As a consequence, this chapter describes the design production process. First, it suggests that the process of visual perception is universal, intuitive, and permanent. Second, it derives guidelines for universal, intuitive, and permanent pictogram content design from research on visual perception. Third, it reports a research through design process that was conducted to produce the pictogram prototypes, applying the previously derived guidelines and using the evaluated pictogram contents. Finally, the chapter presents the produced prototypes and the developed UIPP design system.

In the previous chapter, I have described the UIPP approach to the reference relation, and I have derived content candidates for universal, intuitive, and permanent semantic association. This is Step 3 in the UIPP process. However, as explained in Sect. "Applying Peirce's Sign Relations to HCI", both the reference and the design relation must be universally, intuitively, and permanently comprehensible for a pictogram to be universally, intuitively, and permanently comprehensible. Consequently, once the content candidates are derived, the question remains, how to design the contents in order to achieve universal, intuitive, and permanent design relations (Hurtienne 2017, p. 15). This question is not easily answered. Hornecker (2012) pointed out that mapping sensorimotor experience that we have in the real world onto user interfaces does not suffice. Instead "designers have to design a grammar of interaction" (p. 178), that is, a suitable system to design the contents. In Sect. "Approaching the design relation", I explained that a design system contains rules and regularities for the design and interpretation of representations. Design systems do not require explicit knowledge. Implicit knowledge of the relevant rules and regularities often is sufficient. Designers as much as users often have internalized the rules of the system without necessarily being able to

D. Bühler, *Universal, Intuitive, and Permanent Pictograms*,
https://doi.org/10.1007/978-3-658-32310-3_4

communicate them. For the UIPP project, on the one hand, this suggests that the pictogram contents should be designed according to the rules and regularities of a universal, intuitive, and permanent design system. On the other hand, this implies that users require to be familiar with said design system or, as an alternative, be able to derive intuitively the rules and regularities of the system.

This chapter constitutes the fourth step in the UIPP process. First, I review existing design guidelines for pictogram design. Second, I explain the UIPP approach to a universal, intuitive, and permanent design relation, which is grounded in visual perception. Third, I propose guidelines for a design system derived from research on visual perception. Fourth, I describe the design production process of the UIP Pictogram prototypes that followed a research through design (RTD) approach. Finally, I present the design system developed during the production process, and I present the produced prototypes. This is in line with the fourth step in a human-centered design process, as described by ISO 9241:210 (International Organization for Standardization 2010) (see Sect. "The UIPP Design Process and the Chapters of this Book").[1]

Review of Existing Guidelines for Pictogram Design

There is a vast amount of literature on pictogram design in particular and on visual design in general. Consequently, I conducted a cursory review of several handbooks, books, and papers to arrive at a consensus of basic design guidelines (Caplin and Alastair 2001, Cooper et al. 2014, pp. 411–432, Gittins 1986, pp. 539–540, Honeywill 1999, International Organization for Standardization and International Electrotechnical Commission 2010, Rau et al. 2013, pp. 71–95). In my review, I did not take into account guidelines that address technical constraints, for example, pixel resolution, color depth, or software (e.g., Caplin and Alastair 2001, pp. 132–149. I summarize the guidelines as follows:

1. Research the users of the design and understand their knowledge and needs.
2. Represent familiar objects and utilize well-known pictograms.
3. Use mostly realistic representations and rarely abstract ones.
4. Design coherent entities and closed forms.
5. Create simple, clear, and efficient designs that are recognizable.
6. Use designs that draw attention to the relevant elements.
7. Be consistent, for example, with regard to function and location.
8. Use structure, balance, and flow.
9. Use color scarcely and with purpose.

---

[1]Parts of this chapter have been previously published as Bühler et al. (2020). For this book, they have been revised and adapted.

The respective authors of guidelines might distinguish subcategories of guidelines by describing specific applications or by providing distinct names, for example, Marcus (1995, pp. 426–427) who considered consistency, screen layout, relationships, and navigability subcategories of Guideline 8. However, all authors seem to share the same, abovementioned guidelines as their basis.

Problems with Existing Guidelines

While many designers produce suitable pictograms based on their tacit knowledge (Agrawala et al. 2011, p. 62), my review of the literature on visual design in general and on pictogram design in particular revealed several problems with existing guidelines . First, the guidelines are sometimes vague (see, e.g., Watzman 2003, p. 283). As Agrawala et al. (2011) pointed out: "Design principles are usually not strict rules, but rules of thumb that might even oppose and contradict one another. (...) Designers usually do not directly apply an explicitly defined set of design principles" (p. 62). Consequently, readers of existing guidelines might remain uncertain about when to apply the guidelines and how to apply them. For example, Mullet and Sano (1995, pp. 19–28) indicated that visual design should result in a coherent whole, focus on essential aspects, and be appropriate for the task, without explaining what this means and how this can be achieved. McKay (2013, pp. 170–171) stated that the recognition of pictograms should be efficient—without defining the concept of efficiency nor explaining how efficiency can be accomplished. Marcus (1995) said: "[D]esign all components so that their meaning is not ambiguous" (p. 428) without defining the concept of ambiguousness. Even more recent guidelines by leading multinational technology companies are not more specific. Apple Inc. (2019), for example, stated that a designer should "[c]reate simple, recognizable designs. Too many details can make an icon appear sloppy or unreadable. Strive for a design most people will interpret correctly and won't find offensive" (para. 2), without providing further specification.

Second, often, the guidelines are not based on empirical evidence, and they do not provide scientific reference (see, e.g., McKay 2013, pp. 169–180, and Watzman 2003). The literature is often written by designers for designers (Horton 1994, p. iii), drawing on guidelines by other designers or basing the guidelines on personal experience: "The principles are a form of tacit knowledge that designers learn by creating and studying examples" (Agrawala et al. 2011, p. 62). On the one hand, sometimes, this results in practical recommendations that might appear strange to other designers and, in particular, to scientists. Take the following example: "Close one eye and squint at the screen with the other eye to see which elements pop out, which are fuzzy, and which seem to be grouped. Changing your perspective can often uncover previously undetected issues in layout and composition" (Cooper et al. 2014, p. 414). On the other hand, this might result in inefficient designs, especially considering the increasingly close connection between cultures today. As Röse (2006) pointed out: "It is now unrealistic for [designers] to rely only on their intuition and personal experience" (p. 253). Cultures and people are just far too complex for one designer or a group of designers to have knowledge and understanding of them all.

Third, as a consequence, the guidelines are often culture specific—just like the resulting designs. Since personal experience is always had in a specific culture, guidelines that are based on personal experience can only be culturally specific. In addition, guidelines exist that even discourage derivation from convention (Watzman 2003, p. 283). For example, Maassen (2015), an SAP designer, stated:

> Use familiar icons that have become an industry standard. We all know that a little floppy disc icon is 'save'; you can't make that any easier or clearer. (…) Even if it's hard, we should accept if there's a cultural agreement on what an icon means (para. 1–2).

Along those lines, Marcus (1995) recommended: "[D]eviate from existing conventions only when doing so provides a clear benefit to the user. In other words, have a good reason for being inconsistent!" (p. 427).

In conclusion, I contend that the existing guidelines are not suitable for UIPP. They are sometimes vague, not based on scientific evidence, and, consequently, may not be considered universal.

Guidelines for Universal Visual and Pictogram Design

In Sect. "Definitions of Universality in HCI", I have described general approaches to universal design. However, to date, explicit guidelines on universal visual and pictogram design are still rare. In 2007 (p. 376), Marcus stated that cross-cultural theory was still not an accepted element in visual design. In 2019, IBM simply stated that "[a]ll pictograms should be understandable by a global audience of users, regardless of nationality or language" (para. 2), without providing any further guidance on how universality might be achieved. Nevertheless, there are three exceptions among existing guidelines that are in use in UIPP, too. I present them in the following.

The first exception are Gestalt laws (see, e.g., Chang and Nesbitt 2006, pp. 4–9, Graham 2008, Ware 2013, pp. 181–198, Yee et al. 2012, p. 837). Gestalt laws were discovered through empirical research on visual perception and adapted subsequently to visual design through collaborations of both fields (Drucker 2014, pp. 39–42). Gestalt laws are, in fact, not laws but heuristics (Goldstein 2010, p. 109). That is, they do not consist in strict rules, but they propose certain procedures. They describe how humans perceive and interpret certain visual patterns, based on prior experience (Gómez Reynoso and Olfman 2012, p. 3). Gestalt laws are considered universal and appear to be intuitive (Hurtienne and Blessing 2007, p. 4). They are proven to be useful (Gómez Reynoso and Olfman 2012, p. 8), and they have become extremely influential, for example, through Rudolf Arnheim's work (e.g., Arnheim 1974). Gestalt laws are still in use today, for example, in interface design and in the design of instructional manuals (Graham 2008, Hurtienne 2011, pp. 207–208, Moore and Fitz 1993). They are also part of the guidelines presented in Sect. "Guidelines for Designing Universal, Intuitive, and Permanent Pictogram Contents".

The second exception are guidelines for universal design that are obtained through deductive reasoning. These guidelines focus on cultural and gender neutrality (see, e.g., Horton 1994, pp. 241–268). For example, they suggest that a designer should avoid cultural stereotypes, gender roles, distinct female or male bodies, and skin color in order to be able to design universally comprehensible visual representation. Language and text should be avoided as much as representing an event in a certain reading direction because distinct cultures as well as illiterate people might use distinct directions. Furthermore, gestures should be avoided because they are culture specific, too. Along those lines, Horton (1993, pp. 683–689) recommended not representing hands if they are not manipulating anything because they might have a culture-specific meaning, for example, "[i]n some Arabic cultures the left hand is for unclean tasks" (p. 689). In general, these guidelines recommend that people should be represented as generic as possible, unnecessary details should be avoided, and objects should be generalized.

The third exception is a publication by Lidwell et al. (2010). In the publication, the authors present 125 design principles that they claim to be universal. For each principle, they provide a short description, an application, and—in many cases— reference to scientific research on which the guideline is based. Unfortunately, only few of the guidelines apply to pictogram design. Nevertheless, I use these guidelines, and I follow their example in my presentation of design guidelines in Sect. "Guidelines for Designing Universal, Intuitive, and Permanent Pictogram Contents".

Grounding Visual Design in Visual Perception

Based on the previous discussion, I hold that precise and scientific guidelines for universal, intuitive, and permanent pictogram design do not yet exist. Consequently, the goal of the following section is to develop an approach that might lead to such guidelines, and, subsequently, to a universally, intuitively, and permanently comprehensible design relation. The approach is grounded in visual perception. The process of visual perception is the reception, interpretation, and experience of visual stimuli in the environment. Visual perception seems an appropriate basis for universal, intuitive, and permanent visual design because, in general, the process of visual perception is assumed to be universal, intuitive, and permanent. This is so because most human beings are equipped with the same optical system, and they share similar processing of visual information in the brain (Goldstein 2010, p. 5). In the following section, I describe the process of visual perception first. Then, I show that perception, recognition, and interpretation of visual representation is based on visual perception. Finally, I argue that a universal, intuitive, and permanent design system should be grounded in the process of visual perception.

In visual perception, two systems can be distinguished: *measurement* and *inference*. The systems are closely interrelated, and they interact (Cavanagh 2011, p. 1539). The measurement system receives and transduces visual stimuli, that is, light that is emitted or reflected by objects in the environment. Light is received by the receptors in the eyes. The patterns of the received light are transformed by the receptors into electric signals, a process that is called transduction. Subsequently, the electrical signals are transmitted to the brain. During the transmission, the signals are processed by specialized neurons. Some characteristics that are measured by this system are the intensity of the light that is received in the eye (i.e., brightness), patterns of intensity (i.e., contours), and wavelengths (which lead to the experience of color). These measurement processes are also called bottom-up processes.

The system of inference takes the measurements and interprets them. Based on the processed signals, objects and scenes are identified as much as their characteristics. These processes are also called top-down processes or knowledge-based processes because the identification and classification of objects are based on knowledge, that is, prior experiences and mental representations. Subsequently, the processes of inference lead to our experience of the environment (Goldstein 2010, pp. 5–11).

The process of inference is neither a mathematical procedure nor a wild guess. Instead, "[i]t is a rule-based extension from partial data to the most appropriate solution" (Cavanagh 2011, p. 1539). Since measured visual stimuli are ambiguous, the objects and events inferred are those "that [are] most likely to have caused the pattern of stimuli we have received" (Goldstein 2010, pp. 118–119). In some cases, inference can lead to wrong conclusions, for example, in the case of optical illusions. However, in most cases, the process of inferences yields correct results (Palmer 1999, pp. 23–24). The rule-based extensions are considered heuristics. They are derived from our experiences of similar situations, and they are unconscious. The development of perceptual heuristics is similar to the acquisition of language. As children, based on innate capacities, we learn how to speak through the experience of other people speaking to us or with each other. We identify patterns in language, and we internalize these patterns subsequently. Later, as adults, we are able to formulate complex sentences without knowing the exact syntactical rules. Instead, we reproduce the regularities in language that we have experience beforehand (see Sect. "Definitions of Intuitiveness in HCI"). In visual perception, too, we use unconsciously our experience with regularities in the real world. However, we use these experiences to infer a three-dimensional visual experience from ambiguous two-dimensional visual stimuli received in our eyes. According to Barsalou (2008, pp. 624–625), these processes of inference are embodied cognitive processes (see Sect. "Embodied Cognition: The UIPP Approach to Suitable Pictogram Contents").

Regularities in the Real World and Cultural Influences on Perception

In general, two kinds of regularities in the real world can be distinguished: *physical regularities* and *semantic regularities*. Physical regularities are physical characteristics of the environment that appear frequently:

> For example, there are more vertical and horizontal orientations in the environment than oblique (angled) orientations. This occurs in human-made environment (for example, buildings contain lots of horizontals and verticals) and also in natural environments (trees and plants are more likely to be vertical or horizontal than slanted) (…). It is, therefore, no coincidence that people can perceive horizontals and verticals more easily than other orientations. (Goldstein 2010, p. 115)

As a result of the repeated experience of vertical and horizontal orientations, more neurons are developed that respond to horizontal and vertical orientations. Another example is partial occlusion: If an object partially covers a second object, we perceive the second object as continuing behind the first object although we do not receive any visual stimulus from the covered part of the second object. However, we infer that the second object continues behind the first object because we have previously had the experience of objects not ceasing to exist behind other objects.

Semantic regularities are regular occurrences in scenes and events. People encounter them when repeatedly performing the same actions in the same environment, for example, in the bathroom after waking up, in the office while working, and in the kitchen when cooking. Goldstein (2010) stated: "[o]ne way to demonstrate that people are aware of semantic regularities is simply to ask them to imagine a particular type of scene or object" (p. 117). People easily visualize familiar situations, and they can visualize them in detail. They have knowledge of the objects and events that usually occur in these scenes. Subsequently, humans use this knowledge to predict other events and objects in other scenes and to recognize and remember them (Hollingworth 2005). That is, they derive perceptual heuristics from semantic regularities.

While visual perception is based on the human optical system and on certain processes in the brain, both physical and semantic regularities influence the visual perception of human beings through perceptual heuristics that are based on these regularities. In other words, perception is influenced by experience . As a consequence, since experience is always had by a person in a specific culture, that specific culture influences the visual perception of that person (Miyamoto et al. 2006, p. 116). This holds not only for obvious cases, for example, visualizing work environments, but for perceptual inference processes like visual attention and the perception of depth and color, too (Masuda 2010, Miyamoto et al. 2006). Culture influences even the most basic bottom-up processes (Palmer 1999, pp. 611–613), and it can lead to measurable changes in physiological responding and neural responses (Goldstein 2010, p. 12, Kourtzi and DiCarlo 2006), without the awareness of the perceiver (Pappachan and Ziefle 2008, pp. 331–332). Take the camouflage of an insect as an example. If the camouflage imitates the pattern of a plant that the insect is sitting on, a laywoman might not be able to recognize the insect because she might not be able to identify the insect's contours. The laywoman will only recognize the plant. In contrast, based on her experience, an expert in biology might have developed previously more neurons that are able to process the different patterns of light reflected by the insect and by the plant. As a consequence, she might be able to identify correctly the insect.

Visual Perception and Perception of Visual Representations

There is considerable debate about whether, on the one hand, human beings must learn how to perceive visual representations or, on the other hand, the perception of visual representations is an innate capacity. Gibson (1978), for example, proposed that learning is not needed because the perception of visual representations is grounded in the general process of visual perception. In contrast, Goodman (1976) argued that visual representations are conventional, thus, they must be learned, for example, through experience. I follow DeLoache et al. (1998) and DeLoache et al. (2003) in their claim that both positions are correct:

> [L]earning is not necessary for the perception of simple pictures: Infants automatically perceive pictures, seeing through them to the objects depicted. However, Goodman and his supporters were also right that infants must learn about pictures; although they can see a picture's surface (its two-dimensionality), they have to learn what that surface signifies. (p. 210)

Let me elaborate. Empirical studies have shown that humans are able to recognize the content of visual representations from an early age on (Bovet and Vauclair 2000, 143, 147–148). Yonas et al. (1978), for example, showed that children as young as 22 to 26 weeks develop the capability of seeing depth in a visual representation (see also Arterberry 2008, Yonas et al. 1986), a capacity that seems to be shared by all cultures and even other species. Although cross-cultural studies on the perception of visual representations are inconclusive and difficult to conduct, in general, they report that adults who have not been previously presented with visual representations are at least able to comprehend the representation successively when given cues (Bovet and Vauclair 2000, pp. 144–151; see also my definition of intuitive use, Sect. "Defining Intuitive Use: Prior Knowledge and Automatic Processing", indicating that the perception of visual representations "cannot result from learning a convention of representation" (Cavanagh 2005, p. 304). Instead, it appears to be grounded in the general process of visual perception.

In fact, in the perception of visual representations, the same heuristics seem to be applied as in visual perception in general. For example, the capacity of young children to detect similarities between a real-world object and its photographic representation "is most likely based on detection of similarities in the visual information projected to the eyes by objects and photographs of the same objects"

(Yonas et al. 2005, p. 165). That is, the heuristics that are used to recognize an object in a visual representation are the same or at least directly based on the heuristics that are used to recognize objects in the real world. Although this might not be a surprise, I hold, this shows that the recognition of visual representation is not conventional as Goodman (1976) suggested. It is the result of repeated experiences of physical and semantic regularities that lead to the derivation of heuristics of perception and interpretation.

This conclusion is supported by many studies that assess the comprehensibility of pictograms and other visual representations in HCI. In general, pictograms are faster and more correctly interpreted if they are more concrete. In other words, the more similar they are to the real world the easier they are understood and the more abstract they are the more difficult the interpretation is (Curry et al. 1998, Koutsourelakis and Chorianopoulos 2010, Satcharoen 2018, pp. 109–110, Schröder and Ziefle 2008, p. 90). This effect is independent of the cultural backgrounds of the study participants (Pappachan and Ziefle 2008, p. 336), and it seems independent of their age. Even children react more to more realistic visual representations (Pierroutsakos and DeLoache 2003, p. 147), and adults identify objects more easily, for example, if the objects are represented suggesting three dimensions, rather than two-dimensionality. We can assume, this is the case because well-developed perceptual heuristics are be applied with concrete pictograms—in contrast to more complex and abstract visual representations for which heuristics might not (yet) exist and interpretation requires cognitive work (e.g., in case of "the everchanging conventions of artistic representation" Cavanagh 2005, p. 301). Consequently, if heuristics of visual perception are applied to interpret and comprehend visual representations that are similar to the real world, and we consider the human optical system as much as basic perceptual heuristics to be universal, intuitive, and permanent, then, I suggest, a design system that is grounded in the human optical system and in perceptual heuristics might be universally, intuitively, and permanently comprehensible (see Ware 2013, p. 14, too).

However, although infants are able to distinguish real-world objects from objects in visual representations (cf. Yonas et al. 2005, p. 147), they are not able to understand the concept of visual representation. That is, they are not able to understand the concept of a two-dimensional object representing a three-dimensional scene that itself might refer to an abstract meaning:

> [I]t takes several years for children to sort out the full nature of picture–referent relations. Preschool children sometimes confuse the properties of objects and pictures, indicating, for example, that a photograph of an ice cream cone could be cold to touch and even occasionally lapsing into manual behavior toward pictures. (DeLoache et al. 1998, p. 210)

Children learn progressively what visual representations are and how to interact with them. That is, they need experience with visual representations in order to understand not only the difference between a real-world object and its representation but to learn the meaning and consequences of that difference, too (DeLoache et al. 2003, p. 117, Pierroutsakos and DeLoache 2003, p. 155). I claim that the difference between the representation and the meaning is, in fact, the reference relation, as described in Sect. "Defining Basic Concepts: Representation, Similarity, and Sign Relations". Consequently, while recognition of the content of visual representations might be based on the process of visual perception, that is, perceptual heuristics, humans need to acquire additional understanding through experience or through learning to comprehend visual representations in their entirety. That is, humans require to learn and comprehend the various categories of reference relations that I mentioned above to comprehend visual representations of more complex or abstract meanings (see Avgerinou and Pettersson 2011, 8–9, 12, Ware 2013, pp. 7–9, and Sect. "Conceptualizing the Relations of Design and of Reference").

Along those lines, as much as for visual perception, the perception of visual representations is influenced by experience. Even small children use the experience they have with the real world to interpret a visual representation and the object or scene that the representation refers to (DeLoache et al. 2003, p. 118). Even the most basic processes of perception of visual representations are influenced by experience and knowledge, for example, when a beholder learns to perceive motion in a static representation (again, according to Gibbs 2005, pp. 55–57, this is an embodied cognitive process). Subsequently, the beholder's skill in interpreting cues that signal motion increases. Melcher and Cavanagh (2013, p. 379) gave the following example: Two groups of participants, one naïve and one familiar with art history, were presented with two stimuli. The first stimulus were chronophotographs by Étienne-Jules Marey, the second, artistic experiments by famous artists Marcel Duchamp and Giacomo Balla. While the areas in the brain that process motion were active in both groups when looking at the chronophotographs, only the experts in art history showed active motion-processing when looking at the artistic experiments (Kim and Blake 2007). The study showed that experience with visual representations influences how the representations are processed by our visual perceptual system. However, the study indicated, too, that the most basic heuristics of the perception of visual representations are independent of cultural influences. For that reason, both groups were able to perceive motion in the chronographs, that is, in representations that are similar to real-world objects and events. As Melcher and Cavanagh (2013) pointed out: "[T]he influence of individual experience and culture is greater at the level of complex perceptions, such as the interpretations of particular movements" (p. 383). In contrast, the influence on basic abilities, for example, to perceive contour lines or depth, is marginal because it is based on the earliest experiences in life, shared by most human beings.

Basic Requirements for a Universal, Intuitive, and Permanent Design System

In summary, visual perception is the result of repeated experiences of physical and semantic regularities perceived through the human optical system. These experiences lead to the automatic derivation of perceptual heuristics and the subsequent intuitive application of these heuristics. If a visual representation is similar to the real world, the same (or very similar) heuristics are used to comprehend the representation. However, visual perception and the perception and interpretation of visual representations are influenced by culture, and only basic perceptual heuristics might be universal.

Based on this discussion, I am now able to determine basic requirements for a universal, intuitive, and permanent design system. As described, in human visual perception as much as in the perception and interpretation of visual representations, the optical system, perceptual heuristics, and cultural influences interact. Consequently, all three aspects need to be taken into account when developing such a design system.

First, the visual stimuli that are perceived by the optical system, that is, the patterns of light that are reflected by a visual representation should be designed in a way that they are similar to the visual stimuli reflected by the real-world object that is the content of the representation. As described above, this is in line with current empirical research suggesting that pictogram recognition is faster and more accurate if pictograms are more similar to the real world. In addition, it is in line with the two poles of design relations that I discussed in Sect. "Approaching the design relation".

Second, if a representation is similar to the real world, the human perceptual system will apply the same perceptual heuristics that it applies to the real world (see Sect. "Grounding Visual Design in Visual Perception"). Since these perceptual heuristics are considered intuitive, I propose that further rules and regularities of a design system should be derived from these perceptual heuristics in order to be intuitive (Pappachan and Ziefle 2008, pp. 331–332).

Third, since perceptual heuristics are influenced by culture, it is important to avoid cultural specificity. On the one hand, this needs to be taken into account when deriving design guidelines from perceptual heuristics. To that end, only heuristics may be considered that are universal, that is, heuristics that are based on experiences shared by all human beings (Ware 2013, p. 14). On the other hand, culture-specific regularities and conventions that facilitate complex interpretations must be excluded, for example, language, reading direction, gender stereotypes, and specific skin colors. This might be achieved through deductive reasoning (see Sect. "Guidelines for Universal Visual and Pictogram Design").

In conclusion, I suggest that a universal and intuitive design system should be grounded in the human optical system, it should be derived from perceptual heuristics, and it should avoid culture specificity. If this is achieved, I suggest, the design system might be permanently comprehensible, too, because the physical world and the human body are considered not to change over time. This is in line with other current trends in HCI that I have previously mentioned, such as reality-based interaction (Jacob et al. 2008), image schemata (Hurtienne 2017), and visual thinking (Ware 2013). In the next section, I derive guidelines for the development of the UIPP design system and for the production of the pictogram prototypes, on the basis of these requirements.

Let me add one aspect. I have previously discussed that the UIPP project focuses on cross-cultural design, not inclusive design, although this is a drawback. This holds for my discussion of visual perception and the requirements for a universal, intuitive, and permanent design system, too. In the discussion, I assume that all people share the same optical system and the same perceptual heuristics. Of course, this is not the case, for example, for elderly people or people with disabilities. Since elderly people and people with disabilities are not addressed specifically in the UIPP project, neither the design system nor the resulting pictogram prototypes may be considered completely universal, intuitive, or permanent. However, as described, I had to make the choice to focus on cross-cultural design because of limited resources, and I made the choice with the intention to provide a good basis for subsequent research on individual capabilities (see, e.g., Sect. "Universal, Intuitive, and Permanent Pictogram Project: Two Main Goals").

Guidelines for Designing Universal, Intuitive, and Permanent Pictogram Contents

The previous section has shown that visual perception can tell us a lot about visual representations (Ware 2008, p. x). As a result, I conducted a literature review of research on visual perception, on perceptual heuristics, and on the perception and interpretation of visual representations, in particular of pictograms. In that review, I avoided culture specificity through deductive reasoning. I followed the seven-step model proposed by Cooper (2016). Cooper's model focuses on quantitative meta-analyses and comparisons of quantitative results. Consequently, I used two adaptions: the integrative literature review method (Whittemore and Knafl 2005) and the best-evidence synthesis (BES) method (Slavin 1986, Slavin 1987, Slavin 1995). Both are based on Cooper's model.

The integrative review method introduces two main features. First, it allows for the inclusion of a wide range of research, from experimental data to non-experimental papers. Second, it includes the categorization of research and the drawing of conclusions about research. In other words, it "is a form of research that reviews, critiques, and synthesizes representative literature on a topic in an integrated way such that new frameworks and perspectives on the topic are generated" (Torraco 2005, p. 356). Using the integrative review method seemed appropriate because the review focused on the derivation of practice-oriented guidelines for design from experimental research on visual perception. That is, it involved at least two distinct research disciplines.

BES introduces one main feature. It suggests focusing on the best available evidence regarding the research question. That is, while all available research should be reviewed, only the best evidence should be presented. As Slavin (1995) argued:

> [A]ll other things being equal, far more information is extracted from a large literature by clearly describing the best evidence on a topic (as determined by objective standards) than by using limited journal space to describe statistical analyses of the entire methodologically and substantively diverse literature. (p. 13)

However, what is considered the best evidence depends on the scientific field, the available research, and the research question. For that reason, BES does not provide a formal, rigid model for the review process. Instead, it is based on the reviewer's judgment. In that, it emphasizes that the judgment must be based on the available evidence, and it must be explicit and replicable. In some cases, the reviewer might even "conclude that the evidence currently available does not allow for any conclusions" (Slavin 1995, p. 17). BES seemed appropriate for UIPP because the literature review focused on the derivation of guidelines for content design, not on the presentation of all the available literature. Thus, instead of presenting all the literature, presenting only the best evidence seemed sufficient. Furthermore, the method had already been used successfully by other researchers to review literature on pictogram design (see, e.g., Carney et al. 1998, pp. 8–9).

The UIPP literature review was conducted as an iterative process, including going back and forth between steps. In the following, I describe the seven steps of the process:

1. Formulating the problem
2. Searching the literature
3. Gathering information from studies
4. Evaluating the quality of studies
5. Analyzing and interpreting the outcomes of studies
6. Interpreting the evidence
7. Presenting the results (Cooper 2016, p. 13)

In the first step, the research problem is described and a research question is formulated (see Cooper 2016, Cooper et al. 2019, Templier and Paré 2015, and Whittemore and Knafl 2005, for step descriptions). This is considered the basis for subsequent selection of relevant research. In the previous sections, I have described the research problem in detail. For the review process, I used the following research question: How should pictogram contents be designed to achieve universal, intuitive, and permanent comprehensibility, according to scientific research? Consequently, relevant research should address pictogram design, and it should be empirical and scientific.

In the second review step, procedures for literature search are chosen, sources for relevant research are identified, and literature scoping is performed. I chose to use online databases and subsequent hand searching for literature search. I identified and used the following online databases as sources: ACM Digital Library (Association for Computing Machinery 2020), Google Scholar (Google LLC), ScienceDirect (Elsevier B.V.), and Web of Science (Clarivate Analytics 2020). I assumed, they cover the majority of publications in the relevant scientific fields, that is, cognitive psychology, computer science, design, ergonomics, HCI, and human factors. I searched these databases using various search terms and combinations of terms, for example, cross-cultural, design, graphic, guideline, icon, image, interface, interpretation, intuitive, perception, pictogram, picture, symbol, visual, universal. I did not use a time frame. However, only publications in English were considered. I sorted the results by relevance, using the databases' algorithms, and by number of citations. Since papers are often relevant that are cited frequently, there were many duplicates in the resulting lists. However, publication date is important for relevancy, too. That is, more recent publications are considered more relevant. Following the integrative review method, I scoped for approximately the 100 highest ranked papers, articles, meta-analyses and books that were listed by the databases for each search term. In addition, I hand searched papers and books referenced in the literature that I included in the review after Review Step 4 because they addressed the same keywords.

In Review Step 3, papers listed by the online databases are scanned, and relevant information provided by these papers is identified. In this step, first, I scanned the titles of the papers and books listed by the databases for information on their research questions. Second, I scanned the abstracts of the papers and books that seemed relevant to my research question, based on the criteria described in the next step.

Step 4 consists in the definition of criteria and the subsequent inclusion or exclusion of studies from the review, according to the criteria. One criterion is the quality of a paper. The quality of a paper is assessed by examining internal validity, for example, research design and methods, and by examining external validity, for example, generalizability of the results. As an example, I excluded studies that made universal claims about pictogram interpretation based on culture specific samples. I defined additional criteria specific to my research question. The second criterion included that a study should examine specific properties of the design of visual representations, for example, perspective projection, color, and content sizes. For that reason, studies that evaluated complete sets of pictograms without evaluating specific properties independently were excluded. The third criterion specified that only empirical and scientific studies, meta-analyses, and handbook articles that summarize scientific research should be included. Consequently, guidelines that do not provide scientific reference, as discussed in Sect. "Review of Existing Guidelines for Pictogram Design", were excluded. Fourth and finally, I did not take papers into account that address abstract visualizations (see Sect. "Categories of Visual Representations"), because the pictogram contents that were derived in Study 1 and 2 are real-world objects and actions that require to be represented based on similarity (for research on visualization see, e.g., Hansen and Johnson 2011, Kosslyn 2006, Munzner 2015, Sedig and Parsons 2013, Spence 2014, Tversky 2011, Ware 2013). After this step, references provided by meta-analyses and handbooks included in the review were hand searched, as described in Steps 2 and 3. Then, these references were included or excluded based on the criteria above. Subsequently, I included more than 200 papers and articles in the next review step.

In Review Step 5, methods for synthesizing results should be chosen, and they should be applied in the review process. As described above, I chose BES as the method for literature synthesis. In this step, I examined the main contents of the papers, articles, and so forth, that I had included in the previous step. I created summaries of the findings, and I created groups of findings and coded categories according to the properties of pictograms that the findings addressed. These categories are represented by the sections of guidelines presented below.

In Step 6, the groups of findings are summarized and synthesized, and conclusions are drawn regarding the research question. Following BES and the integrative review method, in this step, I synthesized the grouped and categorized findings, and I included explicit details of primary sources. Finally, I formulated the design guidelines.

In the final, seventh review step, a framework for the presentation of the results is chosen, and the results are presented. Consequently, in the following section, I present the results of the literature review. In the presentation, I follow BES, using the framework by Lidwell et al. (2010). That is, I present the best evidence by synthesizing the central findings of one or multiple studies, I provide the references, and I formulate a design guideline that I derived from the findings (see Sect. "Appendix J" for a table of all the cited literature per guideline). Following my description in the previous section, the guidelines address the human optical system, basic perceptual heuristics, and more complex aspects that can be influenced by culture. According to the categories of groups of findings that I coded during the review process, there are six categories of guidelines: how to project a three-dimensional real-world object onto a two-dimensional surface, how to represent the pictogram content, how to design general aspects of visual representations, how to use color, how to represent motion, and how to choose which exemplar of a pictogram content to represent.

How to Represent Three-Dimensional Objects on a Two-Dimensional Surface (G1–G8)

G1: Use an adapted linear perspective for content projection

Linear perspective reproduces the way in which a pattern of light that is reflected or emitted by an object is received in the eye (Giardino and Greenberg 2015, p. 21). It is a mathematically defined way of projecting a three-dimensional scene onto a two-dimensional surface (Palmer 1999, p. 20). In general, linear perspective is considered the best way of projection. However, in some cases, linear perspective might represent a scene in a way that appears false to a user. Melcher and Cavanagh (2013) described:

> Leonardo da Vinci, for example, distinguished between mathematical perspective and true psychological perspective. One problem noticed by Leonardo was that a picture of a building with frontal columns that was made using linear perspective would result in columns of unequal width. (p. 369)

As a consequence, when designing a pictogram content, linear perspective should be used, however, it might need to be adapted in marginal zones to suit the expectations of a user.

G2: Pictogram contents should not be too realistic, but they should be represented as line drawings of their contours

Line drawings are not conventional. Instead, they represent the contours , that is, the edges of real-world objects. Contours do not exist in the real world, however, they "are important to the brain. The initial stages of visual processing focus on finding discontinuities in brightness, colour, and depth" (Melcher and Cavanagh 2013, p. 362). Neural activity patterns suggest that perceived real-world scenes are processed based on the edges of the included objects. Thus, cognitive processing of line-drawings is similar to the processing of real-world scenes (Sayim and Cavanagh 2011, pp. 1–2). This is supported by evidence that more detailed representations, for example, colored photographs are not faster or more accurately recognized than line drawings. Instead, too realistic representations might be confounded with the objects that they represent and not interpreted as representations that refer to more abstract meanings, for example, through semantic association (Biederman and Ju 1988, p. 63, Liu et al. 2012, p. 146, Medhi et al. 2007, p. 876, Walther et al. 2011, 9661, 9665, Willats 2005, p. 160). However, although contours are fundamental, it is not fully understood how to determine which contours exactly should be represented (Giardino and Greenberg 2015, pp. 18–19). Representing too few of them might impede recognition, just like representing too many contours. At least three mathematically defined approaches exist: first, suggestive contours and highlight lines; second, ridges and valley lines; and, third, apparent ridges (see Fig. 1). Suggestive contours and highlight lines (DeCarlo et al. 2003) can be "understood as those lines which would become occluding contours if the viewpoint is only slightly changed" (Hörr et al. 2010, p. 4). Ridges and valley lines "are formed by local extrema of surface curvature along one of the principal curvature directions (…) and might be considered a generalization

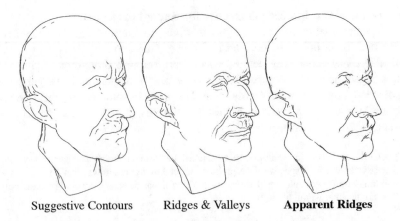

Suggestive Contours   Ridges & Valleys   **Apparent Ridges**

Fig. 1 Judd et al. (2007, p. 5) presented the abovementioned three approaches to line drawings and argued that apparent ridges—their approach—yields the best results. However, other authors find that apparent ridges "exaggerate curvature in some cases and tend to be noisy" (Cole et al. 2008, p. 2)

of sharp creases to smooth surfaces" (Cole et al. 2009, p. 2). Apparent ridges (Judd et al. 2007) "are the set of those points having a maximal view-dependent curvature" (Hörr et al. 2010, p. 4). Among scholars, there is considerable debate about which approach is the most appropriate. In contrast, experienced designers seem to have tacit knowledge of the contours that should be represented (Cole et al. 2008, p. 2, Sayim and Cavanagh 2011, pp. 1–3), and they still achieve results superior to the mathematically defined approaches (Cole et al. 2009, pp. 8–9). Consequently, designers should produce line drawings for pictograms relying on their experience instead of following strict definitions. Walther et al. (2011, pp. 9661–9665) suggested that long contours should be focused in contrast to short contours because the former represent the global structure of a scene.

G3: Only contours of shapes should be represented, not contours of shadows or colors

Contours in real-world scenes can result from color variation or random illumination. If contours of illuminations are represented in line drawings, they can suggest depths or slants that do not exist. "As a result, the whole image is corrupted, deviating from the structure of the original objects" (Sayim and Cavanagh 2011, p. 2). The same applies to colors (Cavanagh 2005, p. 303). Consequently, in pictograms, contours of shadows and colors should be avoided.

G4: Shadows should be omitted, or they should be darker than their surroundings

In general, shadows are not necessary (Melcher and Cavanagh 2013, p. 374). If shadows are represented in pictograms, they must be darker than their immediate surroundings, unlike, for example, in the case of inversion or other abstract designs. Otherwise, there are "few if any other deviations from realism [that] affect the recovery of shape from shadows" (Cavanagh 2005, p. 302).

G5: Lighting and reflection do not need much attention

If lighting and reflections are used, keep in mind that studies suggest "that inconsistent direction of lighting is not readily noticed" (Cavanagh 2005, p. 302). The same applies to reflections as long as the reflection pattern matches "the average properties of natural scenes and curve in concert with the implied curvature of the shiny surface" (Cavanagh 2005, p. 306). However, do not use too many elements to represent lighting and reflection as this will interfere with G3, G15, and G18, among others.

G6: Line junctions should not be in conflict

Junctions , that is, the points where contours touch or intersect, are crucial to representations of real-world objects and scenes as line drawings. There are three types of junctions: "a T-junction is formed when one object interrupts the contours of another object behind it (the contours meet in a junction as in the letter T); a Y-junction is seen at the front corner of a cube" (Sayim and Cavanagh 2011, p. 3). For X-junctions, Cavanagh gave the following example: "When a transparent

Fig. 2 "When a transparent surface covers a contour in the object behind it, the contour of the transparent surface and the underlying contour cross to form an X-junction" (Cavanagh 2005, p. 304). On the right, no X-junction, thus, no transparency is visible. Other aspects of transparency, like refraction, are not important

surface covers a contour in the object behind it, the contour of the transparent surface and the underlying contour cross to form an X-junction" (Cavanagh 2005, p. 304) (see Fig. 2). Junctions provide information that is fundamental to our perceptual system to infer the three-dimensional object that was the basis of the representation. Consequently, in pictograms, it is crucial to not draw conflicting junctions, in particular, when aiming for simplicity, because they might impede content recognition (see Willats 1997, pp. 112–123 for more details on how junctions can be used to represent objects).

G7: Use black lines on a white ground and high contrast
The processing of black line drawings on white ground is similar to real-world visual perception. In contrast, "white lines on black ground are not nearly so effective. White lines on a black ground provide luminance ridges in the optic array" (Willats 2006, p. 10). If it is not possible to use black lines on white ground when designing pictograms, use high contrast between the represented content and its background, for example, by means of colors, in order to achieve faster and more accurate recognition of the content (Huang 2008, p. 241).

G8: Use lines in the direction of the principal curvature
Studies suggest that the directions of drawn lines that represent surfaces influence content recognition. "This is especially the case when other techniques (shading, silhouetting) do not present sufficient shape information. The psychology literature suggests that lines in the principal directions of curvature may communicate surface shape better than lines in other directions" (Girshick et al. 2000, p. 43). See, for example, Fig. 3.

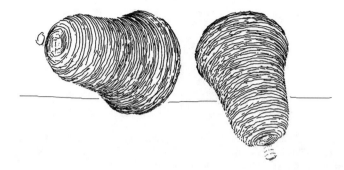

Fig. 3 Girshick et al. (2000, p. 50) gave an example of how principal direction line drawings can lead to easily recognizable pictogram contents. In the example, lines representing the object's curvature from the bottom to the top would create confusion. However, the presented drawing remains ambiguous: It represents pears but could be interpreted as bells, too. This indicates the importance of considering further guidelines in the design process (e.g., G2, G9, and G12)

How to Represent the Pictogram Contents (G9–G12)

G9: Contents should be represented with a focus on a few invariant and distinguishing properties

A visual representation is always partial compared to a real-world object because the real-world object is three-dimensional and can be viewed from different angles. In order to allow for accurate and fast recognition of the content (Gatsou et al. 2012, p. 96, Goonetilleke et al. 2001, pp. 755–756), the content should be represented in a way that its invariant properties are perceptible, that is, properties that are unaffected by variations in viewpoint (Goldstein 2010, p. 820, Willats 2005, p. 160). Other properties should be excluded (Melcher and Cavanagh 2013, 365, 367) as much as characteristics that are created accidentally, for example, by an inappropriate viewpoint. Furthermore, properties that are characteristic of the content should be focused (see G15 and G34). Unnecessary, too many, or too complex content details render recognition slow and inaccurate (Thompson et al. 2011, pp. 588–591) [408]. Willats (2006, pp. 16–19) provides further guidance on designing unambiguous pictograms.

G10: Contents and representations should be designed regularly and symmetrically

Regular and symmetrical shapes are more easily matched, remembered, and described. This is called figural goodness (Palmer 1999, pp. 398–402). In addition, balanced and symmetrically designed representations are preferred by users (Chang and Nesbitt 2006, p. 8). However, the content design should be based on the contours of real-world objects (see G2) that might be irregular and unsymmetrical. Then, an average of the contours should be used (see G34). Figure 4 offers an example of a compromise between regularity and similarity to the real world (a), in contrast to an established, symmetrical pictogram (b).

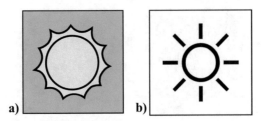

Fig. 4 Pictograms with the content *sun* and the meaning *day*. a) is a prototype designed using the presented guidelines, especially G2, 9–11, 17–19, 22–25. b) is an established pictogram by the manufacturer Bosch (Bosch Thermotechnik GmbH 2018, p. 24)

G11: Represent contents in their canonical sizes

Real-world objects have typical sizes . When we imagine an object, we usually imagine it in that size, and users prefer visual representations that adhere to that size. See Fig. 5 for examples by Konkle and Oliva (2011). They argued that the canonical, that is, typical size of an object can be defined using the ratio between the represented object and the white space that frames the object. These "systematic visual size ratios were observed across different mental processes and across observers (…). For instance, the canonical visual size of a chair is not a specific visual angle but rather is 38% of a surrounding spatial envelope" (Konkle and Oliva 2011, p. 11). Pictogram design should respect these canonical sizes and should not represent contents of different sizes in the same size.

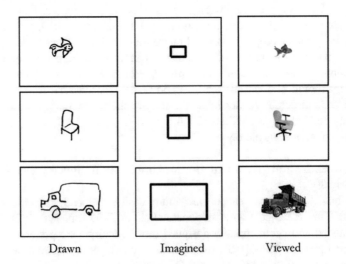

Fig. 5 "Example drawings of a fish, chair, and dump truck for a single observer. The average imagined size and preferred size across observers are shown for these same objects in the adjacent columns" (Konkle and Oliva 2011, p. 12)

G12: Contents should be represented from three-quarters canonical viewpoints

Studies have shown that participants prefer three-quarters viewpoints on objects. Figure 6 is a set that Palmer et al. (1981, p. 139) used to study the phenomenon first, including the preferred viewpoint on the left. These so-called canonical viewpoints allow for most parts of the object to be seen. It is assumed that humans store visual mental representations of objects accordingly. Recognition is faster if an object is represented from these viewpoints, and recognition time increases with increasing deviation (Palmer 1999, pp. 421–424, Thompson et al. 2011, pp. 606–609). Willats (2005) calls these "possible views of objects" (p. 160).

How to Design General Aspects of Visual Representations (G13–G21)

G13: Use similarity and proximity in order to group elements

"Elements will tend to be grouped together if their attributes are perceived as related (…). For example, with [sic] visual displays elements will be grouped together, if the lightness (…), hue, size, orientations or shape are closely related with each other" (Chang and Nesbitt 2006, p. 6). The same holds for proximity (Palmer et al. 2003). If elements of pictograms are represented close to each other, they are interpreted as belonging together (Ware 2013, pp. 182–183).

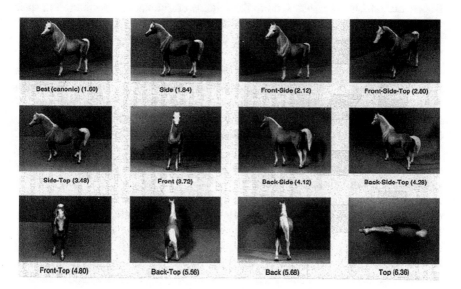

Fig. 6 Examples from a set showing 12 viewpoints by Palmer et al. (1981, p. 139) who studied the phenomenon first. Best viewpoint is left

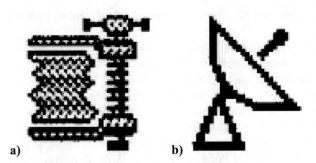

Fig. 7 A complex pictogram (a: file compression) that includes at least 8 distinguishable elements in contrast to a simpler pictogram (b: communications) that includes 3 elements (Curry et al. 1998, p. 1592)

G14: Separate elements of a content should be represented separately

If the content of a representation consists of multiple, separate elements, the content is more easily recognized if these elements are distinguishable and represented separately (Biederman 1987, p. 139, Wogalter et al. 2006, p. 162). For example, elements in pictograms should not overlap.

G15: Pictograms should include the least possible elements and may not exceed 7 ± 2 elements

In general, humans are able to store 7 ± 2 items or chunks of information in their short-term memory. Fewer chunks of information increase the probability that users will need less cognitive effort to comprehend a representation (Yee et al. 2012, p. 837).

See, for example, Fig. 7. Curry et al. (1998) found that a concrete pictogram with fewer elements was more accurately recognized than a concrete pictogram with more elements. Consequently, pictograms should include the least possible and not more than 7 ± 2 distinguishable elements. See also my definition that pictograms consist of only few separate elements in Sect. "Various Terms and Definitions".

G16: Use the regularity of patterns and shapes to indicate the continuation of these patterns and shapes

If similar patterns can be identified in a pictogram, users tend to interpret separate elements with these patterns as belonging together. As a result, users will assume that the patterns continue even when some parts of the patterns are missing. For example, they might interpret two separate patterns as one pattern that is partially occluded. The same applies to shapes. Take Fig. 8 as an example. Users tend to interpret two similar lines as one continuous line that is partially occluded (Chang and Nesbitt 2006, pp. 6–7, 9, Ware 2013, pp. 183–184).

G17: Be aware of attracting attention with irregularities

Elements can attract attention if these elements differ from other elements, for example, because of irregular shapes or colors. If so, they might become focal

Fig. 8 Pictogram with two similar lines that are interpreted as one continuous line

points and, thus,—inadequately or adequately—gain importance in the interpretation of the representation (Chang and Nesbitt 2006, p. 7). Take Fig. 5 in Chap. "Step 2: Understanding Visual Representation(s)" as an example, in comparison to Fig. 7 in Chap. "Step 2: Understanding Visual Representation(s)". The Bliss pictogram might become a focal point because of its irregular shape.

G18: Pay attention to shapes because they may suggest unintended meanings
Shapes influence the interpretation and preference of users, irrespective of the content of the representation. For example, sharp corners can represent danger and may be associated with fear. This is so because sharp real-world objects are potentially dangerous, like knives and fangs (see G22). In Fig. 5, pictogram a) might appear sharper, thus, more dangerous than pictogram b), although both represent the same content (Bar and Neta 2006, pp. 646–647, Lidwell et al. 2010, p. 62, Melcher and Cavanagh 2013).

G19: Use blurry, less detailed representations for faster emotional responses and sharp, more detailed representations for slower conscious recognition
Studies have shown that the center of emotions in the brain is more active when a participant is presented with blurry representations. In contrast, more details trigger cognitive processes of recognition. This is observable, for example, with impressionist and expressionist paintings (Cavanagh 2005, p. 305, Melcher and Cavanagh 2013, pp. 367–368).

G20: Each pictogram should be unique and distinctive
Often, pictograms are used together with other pictograms, for example, as a set for a single GUI, as is the case in UIPP. In order to decrease recognition time, pictograms should be designed in a way that they are distinguishable from other pictograms with which they might be used together (Barker and van Schaik 2000, pp. 162–163, Goonetilleke et al. 2001, pp. 755–756). However,

what is perceived as similar or dissimilar can change markedly from one situation to the next. For example, items that seem quite different (e.g., children and jewelry) can be rated as highly similar when they are placed in a context that highlights possible similarities. (McDougall et al. 2000, p. 292)

See G9 in this context, too.

G21: The size of a pictogram should be about 0.7° of visual angle

Lindberg and Näsänen (2003) showed that the "size of icons (interface elements) should not be less than 0.7° of visual angle, which corresponds to about 0.5 cm at a viewing distance of 40 cm, and about 0.9 cm at a viewing distance of 70 cm" (p. 119). Otherwise, recognition will be slower and less accurate. This is often constrained by the application for which the pictograms are designed.

How to Use Color (G22–G26)

G22: Use colors that are similar to the represented real-world object or scene

Studies show that visual representations of objects are more easily and more accurately recognized if they are colored similarly to the real-world object that they represent (Bramao et al. 2010, 50, 60, 62, Pierroutsakos and DeLoache 2003, p. 147) (see, e.g., Fig. 4).

G23: Be aware of unintended meanings of colors

Colors can stimulate the limbic system, thus evoking preconscious reactions based on sensorimotor experiences. For example,

> red is the colour of blood or raw meat, it is the colour of ripe fruit and dangerous animals. In other words, it makes sense to be aware of the colour red and to associate this colour with the reward system in order to survive. (Melcher and Cavanagh 2013, p. 388)

As a consequence, in visual representations, colors, like red, can suggest unwanted interpretations if the colors are associated preconsciously with other meanings.

G24: If colors are used in a representation, use a blue background

The human fovea only has a limited number of cones that are sensitive to the wavelength of the color blue. As a result, it is difficult for the eye to focus on blue. If the color blue is used as background, cognitive fatigue is reduced because the color does not distract the user (Durrani and Durrani 2009, p. 164, Lidwell et al. 2010, p. 48). See, for example, Fig. 4. Here, the background might have been designed in white or transparent, too.

G25: Avoid the colors red and green together

Users might suffer from color blindness. Consequently, red and green should not be used together (Yee et al. 2012, p. 838).

G26: Use as few colors as possible

Humans can store 7 ± 2 items in their short-term memory (see G15). This applies to colors, too. In order to reduce cognitive load, the number of colors should be limited accordingly (Durrani and Durrani 2009, p. 164). The fewer colors are integrated, the less a user needs cognitive effort to interpret the pictogram.

How to Represent Actions and Movements (G27–G33)

G27: Prefer animated representations over static representations

Studies in cognitive psychology have shown that neurons that are specialized in motor responses are activated when movement is indicated by static images or sculptures. Even muscle tone can increase (Melcher and Cavanagh 2013, p. 381). Consequently, it is possible to perceive movement in representations although real-world movement is not happening. This is the case for many established pictograms. However, studies in HCI have shown that animated visual representations , that is, "rapidly changing static displays, giving the illusion of temporal and spatial movement " (Scaife and Rogers 1996, p. 190) are preferred and faster and more accurately identified than static drawings or static photographs (Jones 1993, pp. 44–45), (Medhi et al. 2007, pp. 876–878). For that reason, in case an action or event is the content of a representation, animated pictograms should be designed instead of static pictograms. See Fig. 9 for an example. Here, animation was used instead of, for example, one of the presented frames as a static pictogram.

G28: Animations should be similar to the represented actions, but segmented

The representation of an action or event should last as long as the real-world action or event. That is, it should not be faster or slower, and it should have the same sequential order. For example, the order should not be inverted. However, "animations should lean toward the schematic and away from the realistic" (Tversky et al. 2002, p. 258) (see Fig. 9, for an example). Recognition and comprehension of events, actions, and movements are better if the latter are segmented and only the relevant segments are represented (Thompson et al. 2011, 670, 674–675) because human beings process perceived real-world actions and movements as sequences of discrete steps. Consequently, a "step-by-step presentation is more congruent to the way the mind understands and represents continuous organized action than continuous presentation" (Tversky 2011, p. 526; furthermore, see Tversky et al. 2006, p. 4), for example, a cinematic representation of 24 frames per second.

Fig. 9 A UIPP prototype with the meaning *[warmth] goes wrong, is wrong*, designed using the described guidelines (see Section *Presentation of the Design System*, p. 255, too). The first frame is presented for 450 ms, the last for 650 ms. All other frames are presented for 350 ms

G29: To represent causation, do not exceed a 0.14 s interval between the involved events

The "[m]aximum interval between events for perception that one event caused another event [is]: 140 ms" (Johnson 2014, p. 201). Thompson et al. (2011, pp. 662–665) mentioned 0.2 s. This period should be respected when designing pictograms that represent events in which one element causes the reaction of another (see G30).

G30: To represent motion, use about 100 ms as the interval between segments

Apparent motion , that is, perceived motion that did not happen physically, is a result of the interval between the perception of two stimuli in different locations (Ramachandran and Anstis 1986). For example, if the interval between the presentation of two lights is about 25 ms, the lights appear to be flickering. If the interval is about 100 ms, one light appears to be moving between the positions of the two lights. At about 500 ms, movement no longer is perceived, and the two lights appear to be turned off and on alternately (Palmer 1999, pp. 471–480). Since animated pictograms do not move in reality, use the aforementioned intervals to design apparent motion of elements in pictograms (see G29).

G31: Elements that change or move similarly are perceived as belonging together

Elements of a pictogram "that change at the same time or move in a similar way will be grouped together (…). For example, animated visual elements that move in the same direction, with the same speed will be seen as related" (Chang and Nesbitt 2006, p. 9) (see G13). Elements that change their state, for example, by blinking, will be grouped together, too (see G30). This should be considered when pictograms are designed that integrate various animated elements.

G32: Do not use reading directions. Instead, use appropriate spatial relations

Reading directions have a high influence on interpretations, especially those related to the concept of time (Tversky 2011, p. 512, Tversky et al. 1991, pp. 545–547). At the same time, reading directions are culture specific. For that reason, they must be avoided (Honeywill 1999, pp. 63–64, Horton 1993, p. 683). This holds for animation as well as for pictograms with multiple parts. Instead, other appropriate spatial relations between elements in pictograms should be used to convey abstract relations because the capability to understand them can be found "in Children as young as 5 in diverse cultures" (Tversky et al. 2002, p. 249).

G33: If animation is not possible, use two-part representations

If animation of pictograms is not possible, for example, because of technical constraints, two-part visual representations, that is, static pictograms that represent two aspects or states of a content at once, should be designed. Two-part pictograms are comprehended better than pictograms that represent only one aspect or state of a content (Adams et al. 2010, Theo Boersema and Adams 2017, p. 310) (see Fig. 9).

How to Choose Which Exemplar of a Pictogram Content to Represent (G34)

The guidelines presented in the previous section indicate in which way the content of a pictogram should be designed. However, one important question remains: Which exemplar of a content should be represented for the pictogram to be universally, intuitively, and permanently comprehensible? Take, for example, the meaning *coldness*. In Step 3, I derived that the content of a pictogram for the meaning *coldness* might be *a snowflake* (see Sect. "Discussion, Limitations, and Future Research"). However, it remains unclear which exemplar of a snowflake should be represented. Virtually, an infinite number of snowflakes exist.

In answering this question, at least three important requirements should be considered. First, the representation of a content may not be too specific. If it is too specific, the representation will be interpreted as referring to an existing real-world object (based on similarity), not to a more abstract meaning (e.g., through semantic association). This is so because specific representation inhibits generalization, according to Tversky (2011, p. 516). If the representation of the snowflake is too specific, the pictogram will be interpreted as representing a specific snowflake, that fell in a specific place on a specific date, not as a representation of the more abstract meaning of *coldness*. Instead, the representation of the snowflake must be comprehensible as representing the general category of snowflakes (Rosch et al. 1976, p. 383). Take the like button in Fig. 4 in Chap. 2 for another example. The pictogram does not represent a specific hand or thumb of a specific human being. Instead, it represents a hand and a thumb in general. Only because of that, the representation might be interpreted as referring to the more abstract meaning of *liking something*.

Second, the representation must be specific enough to be comprehended as a general category, not a broader or narrower category (Ware 2008, p. 121). For example, the content of the pictogram for *coldness* should be recognizable as the category of *snowflake* and not be confused with the broader category of *precipitation* or the narrower category of, for example, *sectored plates snowflakes* (Libbrecht 2006). In the second example of the like button, the content of the pictogram should be recognizable as representing the category *hand* and not be confused with the broader category of *limb* or the narrower category of, for example, *child's hand*.

Third, the representation of the category must be universal. This is in line with the guidelines for avoiding cultural specificity by Horton (1994, pp. 241–268, 1993, pp. 684–689). One important recommendation that Horton made is to generalize visual representations by suppressing details that are not important and by representing generic people and best-known versions of objects (Horton 1994, pp. 252–253). He argued,

> we should pick the version most widely recognized. If one version of an object is more common throughout the world, show that version. (...) If there is no international version, then pick the most common version familiar to the largest number of users. (Horton 1994, p. 256)

Take for example the category *tree*. The best-known version of a tree might be very different, for example, in Scandinavia compared to Africa (Barsalou 1993). Consequently, the represented best-known version of the content *tree* must be general enough to be comprehended as the category *tree* by all humans, from all cultures, of all ages, and with all capabilities.

Considering these requirements, the question arises, how to determine the best-known version, that is, the most representative exemplar, of a category. To answer this, I look again at research in cognitive sciences. For a visual representation to be comprehensible , Tversky et al. (2006, p. 3) suggested that the content of the representation should correspond to the user's mental representation of the represented object or scene. In other words, in order to recognize an object, creature, characteristic, or action, humans require prior knowledge of that object, creature, and so forth, to which the perceived visual pattern can be compared (Ranta 2000, p. 214). If a person has a mental representation of a given content, then she is able to recognize and comprehend the content fast and accurately. In contrast, without prior knowledge, the person will spend much time and effort interpreting the representation without being certain to reach a correct conclusion (Durrani and Durrani 2009, p. 159). It is assumed that humans do not only have mental representations of individual objects, creatures, or scenes, but they have mental representations of typical representatives of categories , too (Ranta 2000, p. 215). These typical representatives, or best-known versions, are also called *prototypes*. However, I do not use the term here because it might be confused with the artifacts that are produced in a design production process. Mental representations of typical representatives of a category are developed based on experiences with multiple members of that category. For example, through experiences of many individual trees, human beings develop a mental representation of a typical representative of the category *tree*. Rosch et al. (1976) argued that these mental representations of typical representatives are developed according to one principle: "[A]n item is judged to be prototypical of a category, the more attributes it has in common with other members of the category and the fewer attributes in common with members of contrasting categories" (p. 433). This applies in particular to attributes like shape and movement (Harnad 1990, p. 342, Palmer 1999, p. 419, Rosch et al. 1976, p. 405). In other words, in order to fulfill the first requirement, the representation of a content must have the most possible of the characteristics that all members of that category share and, at the same time, have the least possible characteristics of other categories. If this is the case, the content might be interpreted as a typical representative of that category, not a specific object.

The second requirement addresses the structure of categories. Cognitive categories of objects, creatures, characteristics, and actions are structured hierarchically. With regard to the category *tree*, for example, *fir* is a subordinate category, and *plant* is a superordinate category. Studies have shown that most people recognize objects first at the intermediate level in this hierarchy (Palmer 1999, pp. 416–418). Rosch et al. (1976) called this the *basic-level category* . They suggested that typical basic-level objects are easier to recognize and that even very young children recognize them (Rosch et al. 1976, p. 429) (see the collected data in Study 1 that consist almost exclusively in basic-level category objects and scenes). Basic-level categories are not universally definable. However, Palmer (1999, p. 419) gave one guideline to identify them. He said, only for basic-level categories will the average shape of all the objects in that category be recognizable. For other categories, that is, superordinate or subordinate categories, this is not the case. Pictogram contents should be designed accordingly. That is, I suggest that the content of pictograms should be designed as typical basic-level category objects by averaging the shapes of all objects in that category.

As mentioned above, humans develop mental representations of typical representatives based on prior experience, for example, in case of the category *tree*. Through repeated experience of many individual trees, a typical representative of the category *tree* is developed. However, humans in one region will have experiences with distinct types of objects and scenes than humans in other regions. For example, humans in Scandinavia have distinct experiences with trees than humans in Africa or in the Amazon. Consequently, their mental representations of a typical representative of the category *tree* will be different (e.g., Kress 2003, p. 29). This holds for all categories and for all typical representatives (Durrani and Durrani 2009, pp. 159–160). For that reason, with regard to requirement three, shapes and characteristics should be represented that are shared by all members of a category worldwide—not only by members present in a specific culture or region. Only then, the represented content might be a typical representative of a universal basic-level category. Of course, in a design project, this might be difficult to achieve, and designers, researchers, and businesses might need (or want) to aim for characteristics that are shared in a specific group of cultures. However, if a typical representative of a universal basic-level category were achieved, I suggest, the content might be universally and intuitively comprehensible. Furthermore, it might be permanently comprehensible, too, because the physical world and its flora and fauna might not change significantly in the next few thousand years. This brings me to the final design guideline for universal, intuitive, and permanent pictogram contents:

G34: Represent typical basic-level contents.

The Pictogram Design Production Process

In Step 3, I have developed an approach to the reference relation, I have presented the UIPP meanings prescribed by the UCUI project, and I have derived and evaluated content candidates for the UIP Pictograms. In Step 4, so far, I have developed an approach to the design relation, and I have presented guidelines for the design of pictogram contents. In the following section, I describe the design production process in which the previous results were applied.

The UIPP Design Production Process as a Research Through Design Project

As described in Sect. "The UIPP Design Process and the Chapters of this Book", UIPP performs a complete human-centered design process for universal, intuitive, and permanent pictograms. Regarding HCD processes, two main problems need close consideration. First, there is still a lack of studies that go "the full cycle of a human-centred design process. In particular, the transition from requirements to design solutions has been identified as a problem for design" (Hurtienne et al. 2015, pp. 239–240). That is, studies on human-centered design do not explain "how a designer transforms the information gathered about users and their work into an effective user interface design" (Wood 1998, p. 10). In other words, they do not close the design gap (see Sect. "Universal, Intuitive, and Permanent Pictogram Project: Two Main Goals"). As a result, it is not clearly understood how designers proceed, and how they achieve their results. Second, since it is not clearly understood how designers proceed, their production process cannot be integrated optimally in the HCD process (e.g., Cash 2018, Zimmerman et al. 2007). For example, it remains unclear how strictly designers should adhere to scientific findings (Hurtienne 2017, pp. 15–16). This is a problem because the work of experienced designers is still superior to, for example, the results of mathematically described approaches (e.g., Cole et al. 2009, pp. 8–9, Sayim and Cavanagh 2011, p. 3), thus, the work of designers cannot be substituted (Hurtienne 2017, p. 15).

UIPP addresses these problems by usinga research through design (RTD) approach to the pictogram design production process. In the following, I describe the approach. Famously, Frayling (1993, p. 5) distinguished between research into art and design, research for art and design, and research through art and design. Almost at the same time, Archer (1995, p. 11) addressed the same categories as research about practice, research for the purposes of practice, and research through practice.[2] Frayling and Archer defined the first category, that is, research into design practice, as the historical, social, economic, material, or perceptual research concerning design and its products. The second category, research for design, is defined as the activity of collecting material "where the end product is an artefact – where the thinking is, so to speak, embodied in the artefact" (Frayling 1993, p. 5). In that category, research is not realized in written or spoken language but as a visual, tangible, or multimodal product. Although the activity of research for design might be scientific, the realization of the product should not be considered research, according to Archer (1995, p. 11). However, today, gathering and interpreting scientific findings and user studies are considered research for design, too

---

[2]Archer has coined the phrase as early as in 1981, according to Findeli et al. (2008, p. 71).

(Stappers and Giaccardi 2017). Third, research through design is a practical process of experimentation. Archer (1995) said that

> [t]here are circumstances where the best or only way to shed light on a proposition, a principle, a material, a process or a function is to attempt to construct something, or to enact something, calculated to explore, embody or test it. (p. 11)

Consequently, research through design is a production process. This process is situation-specific, that is, it "is pursued through action in and on the real world, in all its complexity, its findings only reliably apply to the place, time, persons and circumstances in which that action took place" (Archer 1995, p. 12). The result of that process is an artifact, for example, a metal object or the customization of a given technology. Although the results are generalizable only to a small degree, they "can advance practice and can provide material for the conduct of later, more generalisable, studies" (p. 12). Research through design occurs frequently in disciplines with a strong practical focus, and it is based on the practitioner's tacit knowledge.

Since these early definitions, RTD has developed into an independent research approach and, at the same time, an attempt to integrate design practice into more scientific disciplines, for example, HCI (Zimmerman et al. 2007, p. 493). RTD addresses the abovementioned two problems of HCD processes by reflecting on the designer, the production process, and the best use of the skills of designers. In addition, it generates innovative artifacts that embody theory and technical possibilities allowing for new ways of interaction (Gaver 2012, pp. 941–942, Stappers and Giaccardi 2017, Zimmerman et al. 2007, p. 498).

The UIPP design production process was structured as an RTD project. In that, Findeli's project-grounded model was followed (Findeli 2010). Findeli's approach has already been used successfully in other RTD projects (see., e.g., Hemmert 2014). In contrast to Frayling and Archer, Findeli does not distinguish between research for and research through design. He says that RTD "must be understood as having the virtues of both" (Findeli et al. 2008, p. 71). According to Findeli, "the central distinction that needs to be made is between a research question and a design question" (Findeli 2010, p. 294). Design projects often start with a design question. Then, the initial step is to create a research question from the design question. The second step consists in the creation of a design answer, considering the design project the field of research. Finally, the design answer will contribute to the research answer. Findeli calls his approach project-grounded research and argues that it can contribute to the knowledge of any phenomenon (Findeli 2010, p. 299). In UIPP, the design question was the question, how to design universal, intuitive, and permanent pictograms. Following Findeli's model, the steps in the design production process were considered the research questions. These steps were planned according to ISO 9241:210 (see Sect. "The UIPP Design Process and the Chapters of this Book"). In each step, the research questions were answered through design. Consequently, the produced design prototypes were considered the design answers. Subsequently, the design answers were transformed into research answers by evaluating the interaction of the users with the pictogram prototypes in Step 5 (Findeli 2010, p. 289).

Approaching the Research Questions: The HCD Production Process

The production of design prototypes is Step 4 in a human-centered design process. ISO 9241:210 suggests several intermediate steps for the process. In Table 1, I describe the intermediate steps (iSteps) according to that framework. Furthermore, ISO 9241:210 recommends taking other design methods and principles into account. Consequently, I describe established methods and guidelines that were used in the UIPP process to specify further and give reasons for each step. In addition, I describe the practical approach in the IBIS project (in German: Gestaltung intuitiver Benutzung mit Image Schemata) which I consider a best-practice example of a complete human-centered design process that uses the theory of embodied cognition for the production of intuitive user interface prototypes (Fetzer et al. 2013, Löffler et al. 2013, Löffler et al. 2013).

Table 1 Intermediate steps (iSteps) 1–4 in the design production process according to HCD

Intermediate step number and title	
Source	Content
iStep 1.1: Specification of context of use and user requirements	
ISO 9241:210	ISO 9241:210 defines the context of use as the "users, tasks, equipment (…), and the physical and social environments in which a product is used" (International Organization for Standardization 2010, p. 2). The understanding of the context of use, the users, their requirements, and the user tasks are considered the first intermediate step in the production process. According to ISO 9241:210, the production process relies on them (International Organization for Standardization 2010, p. 15). Furthermore, the understanding achieved in this intermediate step must be transferred to the production process and communicated to the people that are involved in the process.
Hartson and Pyla, Sharp et al., Shneiderman et al.	Shneiderman et al. (2017, 133–134), Hartson and Pyla (2012, pp. 161–180), and Sharp et al. (2019, pp. 41–49) described the process similarly to ISO 9241:210.
iStep 1.2: Planning tasks and interaction between user and system	
ISO 9241:210	The first intermediate step also includes the planning of the design that will be produced in the process. Furthermore, decisions are made, how the design will be approached in order to fulfill the previously described user requirements with regard to the context of use and the tasks that need to be carried out. Individual design tasks are identified. ISO 9241:210 states that "decisions at this point can include issues such as the choice of modality (e.g. auditory, visual and tactile) and the choice of media (e.g. text versus graphics, dialogue boxes versus wizards, mechanical versus electronic controls)" (International Organization for Standardization 2010, p. 15). The order in which the tasks are completed can be changed, according to the design process.

(continued)

Table 1 (continued)

Intermediate step number and title	
Source	Content
Sharp et al.	Sharp et al. (2019, pp. 434–445) called this step conceptual design. They said, it focuses on the development of a conceptual model of the design solution.
IBIS	In IBIS, it was noted that it is important to decide at the beginning of the production process which one of the image schematic metaphors should be produced as a prototype (Löffler et al. 2013, p. 39). IBIS' image schematic approach is similar to UIPP's approach.
iStep 1.3: Reviewing state of the art solutions and guidelines	
ISO 9214:210	ISO 9241:210 states that the team members should look at "the established state of the art in the application domain, design and usability guidelines and standards" (International Organization for Standardization 2010, p. 14) in the beginning of the production process.
iStep 2.1: Production of design solutions	
ISO 9214:210	The second intermediate step is the production of designs, using the specification, reviews, and plans made in Intermediate Step 1. Here, the designs are made "more concrete (for example making use of scenarios, simulations, prototypes or mock-ups)" (International Organization for Standardization 2010, pp. 15–16), thus, allowing explicit interaction with the proposed design products and subsequent discussion. It is advised to produce several designs.
Cooper et al., Macbeth et al., Nielsen, Sharp et al., Shneiderman et al.	Sharp et al. (2019, pp. 445–446) called this step concrete design . Cooper et al. (2014, p. 37) said that it should start with a kickoff meeting in which the product is discussed, and the stakeholders and designers are introduced. There are various methods for the production of designs. Two options are focus groups and production groups. In focus group design, a group of participants generates ideas, and each participant creates a design. Then, the group decides which design solution is the best. In production group design, participants create independently designs. Then, a designer evaluates the designs and creates a final design solution from these designs. Macbeth et al. (2000, p. 329) found that focus groups yield better results. Nielsen (1993, pp. 86–87) recommended parallel design as a design method. In a parallel design process, multiple designers work independently on the same project at the same time in order to produce distinct options that can be compared, discussed, and refined subsequently. Shneiderman et al. (2017, pp. 142–144) described yet another method: ideation and creativity also called convergent thinking. This approach includes the continuous specification of possible designs. Shneiderman et al. (2017) considered it suitable for teams of designers "who each bring their own expertise and visions to the table" (p. 143).

(continued)

Table 1 (continued)

Intermediate step number and title	
Source	Content
IBIS	In IBIS, it was recommended to create a project plan during the kickoff meeting (Löffler, Heß, Maier, & Schmitt, 2013, p. 40). Furthermore, nine roles are described that are involved in the design process with the intention to allow for a quick understanding of the skills that are needed for specific activities. Not all roles are always needed for a design process, and one person can take over multiple roles. Here, I only describe the roles that are involved in the UIPP production process: The requirements engineer gives information on the technical system requirements; the theory expert (IBIS called this role image schema expert) knows the theoretical background and must be able to revise the design solutions with regard to the theory; the designer develops ideas and creates prototypes from these ideas; and the developer implements the prototypes (Löffler et al. 2013, p. 7).
iStep 2.2: Producing prototypes	
ISO 9214:210	ISO 9241:210 recommends creating prototypes in iStep 2. Prototypes are simplified and limited design products that allow exploring "alternative design solutions. While there can be substantial benefit in making the design solutions as realistic as possible, the level of detail and realism should be appropriate to the issues that need to be investigated. Investing too much time or money in producing a detailed working prototype can lead to a reluctance to change the design" (International Organization for Standardization 2010, p. 16).
Hartson and Pyla, Hemmert, MacKenzie, Nielsen	Nielsen (1993, pp. 93–99) recommended prototyping, too, because intermediate evaluation and subsequent refinement are only possible with produced prototypes, not through abstract discussions and guidelines. In addition, it is fast and less costly to work with prototypes. Hemmert (2014, p. 68) considered prototypes the central object in the design process. One suitable form of prototype is the paper mock-up, that is, drawings or printouts of digital, on-screen designs (see Hartson and Pyla 2012, pp. 391–425 and MacKenzie 2013, pp. 128–129, too).
IBIS	In IBIS, sketches were drawn (Löffler et al. 2013, p. 55).
iStep 3: Iteration	
ISO 9241:210	Intermediate Step 3, according to ISO 9241:2010, is the continuous refinement of the designed prototypes. Refinement can be achieved through iterative evaluations. Reiterations are useful because human–computer interactions are complex and can hardly be specified in their entirety at the beginning of a development process. Many requirements will emerge only during the process. In each iteration, the prototype must be evaluated, and feedback must be given which is integrated subsequently through an alteration of the prototype. The alteration should be evaluated, too. Furthermore, "[p]roject plans should allow sufficient time for making the changes as a result of such feedback" (International Organization for Standardization 2010, p. 16).

(continued)

Table 1 (continued)

Intermediate step number and title	
Source	Content
Nielsen	Nielsen (1993, pp. 105–109) recommended iterative design, too, and gave practical examples. He suggested that a detailed evaluation of the solutions might not be feasible in each iteration, but iterations are fruitful even if they are exclusively an occasion for trying out the prototypes in different settings. For each iteration, he recommends making design decisions explicit and documenting the reasons for the decisions.
IBIS	In IBIS, the drawn sketches were continuously developed and refined into production prototypes (Löffler et al. 2013, p. 55). They called one step is in this process "MetaphernCheck" (Löffler et al. 2013, p. 40). This step specifically addressed the evaluation of the suitability of the designed image-schematic content, that is, whether the prototypes convey the intended meanings.
iStep 4: Communicating the design products for implementation	
ISO 9241:210	The final intermediate step in the design production process is the adequate communication of the design products to the team that is responsible for the implementation of the designs. ISO 9241:210 states that the most appropriate means for communicating the results "vary from providing appropriate documentation, to producing revised prototypes, to embedding experts in human-centred design in the design and development team" (International Organization for Standardization 2010, p. 16).

Presentation of the UIPP Design Team

Cooper et al. (2014, pp. 146–147) recommended small expert teams that focus on a specific task for the design production process. Consequently, the UIPP design team consisted of three designers, each holding a university degree in design. Two designers were experts not only in pictogram design but also in interaction design. Both worked for a design agency, one of them coleading the agency. Both designers were remunerated through the UCUI project. The third designer was the author of this book. According to Findeli et al. (2008, pp. 76–80), the design team should be multidisciplinary. ISO 9241:210 adds that the team does "not have to be large, but the team should be sufficiently diverse to collaborate over design and implementation trade-off decisions at appropriate times" (International Organization for Standardization 2010, p. 8). The team should include people with various skills and disciplinary backgrounds, for example, in human–computer interaction, user interface design, user research, technical support, and software engineering. All those skills and backgrounds were found in the UIPP design team. In addition, scholarship in semiotics and the cognitive sciences was brought into the team by the author of this book.

Technical Constraints by UCUI

In addition to the guidelines presented in Sect. "Guidelines for Designing Universal, Intuitive, and Permanent Pictogram Contents", technical constraints for pictogram design were set by the UCUI interface prototype (see Sect. "Universal, Intuitive, and Permanent Pictogram Project: Two Main Goals"). These constraints are not universal, but they were requirements for the UIPP production process, in addition to the requirements derived in the previous steps. For that reason, they are presented in the following (M. Huber, personal communication, August 9 – 10, 2018):

- Pictograms should have 125 × 125 px and 120 dpi.
- Files should have SVG format. However, PNG and GIF are possible.
- Pictograms should be black and white, or they should have more than two colors.
- Several pictograms can be displayed at the same then, however, then, pixels must be reduced accordingly.
- Up to 3 animations are possible at the same time.
- Animation speed can be set from 0.1 s to 25.4 s.

Design Answers: Report of the UIPP Design Production Process

In general, it is agreed that the documentation of an RTD process is central to the RTD approach (e.g., Hemmert 2014, pp. 66–67, Zimmerman et al. 2010, p. 316). The actions and the reasons for the actions, that is, the design rationale, should be documented in order for designers and researchers to be able to reproduce them. This holds although "there is no expectation that others following the same process would produce the same or even a similar final artifact" (Zimmerman and Forlizzi 2014, p. 168). In Table 2a–g, I report the UIPP design production process. I do so by presenting the procedure of the UIPP design team. That is, I describe the designers' meetings, plans, and ways to approach the previously described intermediate steps in the production process in order to produce design answers to the RTD research questions. In addition, for each step, I report the designers' findings and decisions based on their practical experience, tacit knowledge, and skills.

Table 2a   Report of the UIPP design production process

Phase Date iSteps	Content
kickoff meeting January 24, 2018 1 h iStep 2.1	The design production process started with an early kickoff meeting (iStep 2.1). For this meeting, the UIPP design production team came together for the first time. The team members were introduced. Prior to the meeting, the two designers working for the design agency received a paper that explained the UIPP project. During the meeting, the agency's designers asked further questions regarding details and goals of the project. A production process plan was developed which is presented in Fig. 10. The following roles were to be involved in the process, according to the plan: requirements engineer (prior to the production process), theory expert, designer, and developer (after the production process).
Decisions and findings	In the meeting, it was decided that the production process would start after the completion of the derivation of the pictogram contents and of the design guidelines. The kickoff meeting took place during Study 2.

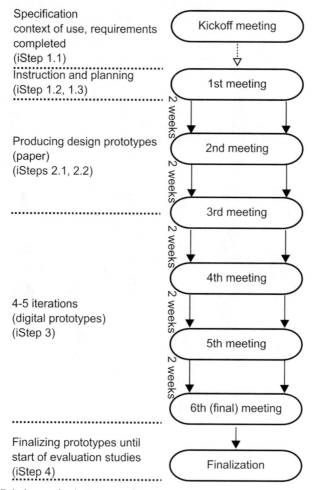

Fig. 10   UIPP design production process plan

Table 2b Report of the UIPP design production process

Phase Date iSteps	Content
1st meeting August 14, 2018 2 h iSteps 1.1, 1.2, 1.3	In UIPP, examining suitable theories, specifying visual representation, and deriving content candidates as much as the guidelines for content design are considered the specification of the context of use and the user requirements (iStep 1.1). These intermediate steps were completed prior to the design production process. Consequently, the design team was briefed about the results in writing prior to the beginning of the production process. Established pictograms were reviewed at the beginning of the first meeting (iStep 1.3). See Fig. 11 for an example of the presentation of established pictograms. The design team discussed approaches to the design of the pictograms (iStep 1.2), and it discussed the further organization of the production process.
Decisions and findings	It was decided that a parallel design method would be used to produce the design prototypes. Furthermore, it was decided that the team would start with a small set of pictograms and not tackle all pictograms at the same time in order to prevent confusion. It was found that the design system could not be developed independently from the pictogram prototypes. Consequently, the design system should be specified as a result of the process. In the discussion, the established pictograms were considered highly abstract and conventional (see Sect. "Conceptualizing the Relations of Design and of Reference"). Following the content taxonomy that was developed in Study 1 (Sect. "Study 1.1: German-speaking Participant Group"), It was decided that two groups of UIPP pictograms were needed. On the one hand, pictograms that represent a content and, on the other hand, pictograms that represent a content through another content. The first group was called simple, the second group was called compound (see Sect. "Presentation of the Design System and of the Pictogram Prototypes").

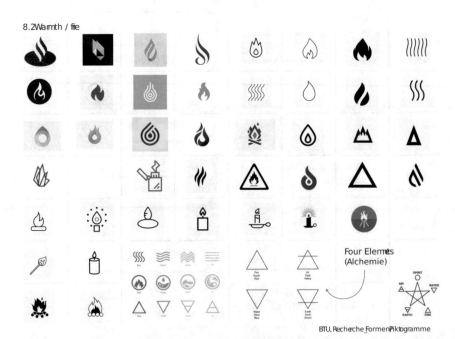

Fig. 11 Presentation of established pictograms for the meaning *warmth*

Table 2c Report of the UIPP design production process

Phase Date iSteps	Content
2nd meeting planned: August 29, 2018 took place: August 22, 2018 2 h iSteps 1.3, 2.1, 2.2	Following the parallel design method, the designers worked independently on their designs between each meeting (iStep 2.1). Furthermore, they chose independently the pictogram contents for their designs (iStep 1.3). Sketches were drawn (see Fig. 12), and the first digital prototypes were designed (iStep 2.2). The designers were motivated by the project goals and worked faster than planned. As a result, they met one week earlier. During the meeting, the designs were presented, discussed, and each designer gave feedback. Furthermore, the chosen pictogram contents were discussed. At this point, the designed prototypes were still rather abstract and similar to established pictograms. It was emphasized that the pictograms should be designed according to the UIPP design guidelines—not imitating established designs. Real-world objects and actions should be represented as pictogram contents, not conventional signs, for example, pictorial runes that can be found in comics (Forceville 2011). At the end of the meeting, the next steps and design options were determined (iStep 2.1).
Decisions and findings	The designers decided independently from each other which of the pictogram contents that were derived and ranked in Studies 1 and 2 they considered most suitable for the prototypes. However, they discussed together whether the contents *a big, muscular man or a male arm with flexing biceps* might be less suitable for the meaning power in the context of use of a heating system user interface than the content lightning bolt. The subject arose because, in Study 1, contents were derived without informing participants about a specific context of use. The designers decided to use the content *a male arm with flexing biceps* in order to aim for universal use of the pictograms. It was considered difficult by the designers to ignore the established pictogram designs because the designers were very familiar with them. As a consequence, they used the familiar designs intuitively instead of adhering to the UIPP guidelines. Several properties of pictogram contents were discussed, for example, whether representing the face of a smiling girl for the meaning *[something] is good, positive* is sexist, despite the fact that the content was derived in Study 1 (see Fig. 12). Furthermore, it was discussed that a fire might not be a suitable pictogram content for the meaning *warmth* because fire might suggest danger. It was determined that a pleasant and harmless fire should be represented, for example, a campfire. The content *piece by piece [something] is taken away* was not considered suitable because it suggested the interpretation of *[something] is disappearing* when represented visually. Finally, it was discussed that compound pictograms such as *[something] begins* or *[something] is everywhere* require to represent their content as being currently in a process in order to be able to convey the intended meaning. Take the example *[warmth] begins*. The content of the pictogram *[something] begins is a baby being born or the rising sun*. It was found that not birth or sun should be represented as the content. Instead, the beginning of warmth must be represented through the representation of *warmth* as being in the process of being born, like a baby, or as being in the process of rising, like a sun. This applies to all pictograms in this group.

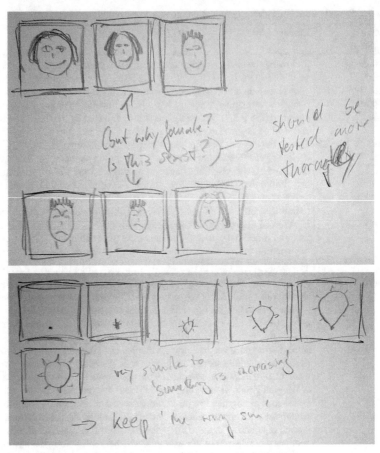

Fig. 12 Examples of sketches drawn for the meanings *[something] is good, positive, [something] is bad, negative, and [something] begins*

Table 2d Report of the UIPP design production process

Phase Date iSteps	Content
3rd meeting planned: August 29, 2018 took place: September 3, 2018 2 h iSteps 2.1, 2.2, 3	This time, the meeting was planned earlier, after one week, but was post-poned because of illness. The meeting was considered the first reiteration meeting (iStep 3). The refinements of the designs that were presented in meeting 2 were discussed, and new designs and content representations were added (iSteps 2.1 and 2.2). Digital prototypes of the pictograms were produced. Other than that, the procedure was the same as in meeting 2. See Fig. 13 for examples of digital prototypes for a pictogram of a pleas-ant fire that radiates warmth and for the pictograms *power, [warmth] is increasing, and [power] is increasing.*

(continued)

Table 2d (continued)

Phase Date iSteps	Content
Decisions and findings	It was decided to use *[something or someone] is approaching very fast* as the representational content for the pictogram *[something] is dangerous*, although it was not ranked low (see Sect. "Discussion, Limitations, and Future Research") because other contents could not be represented visually in suitable ways (see findings of meeting 2). Furthermore, it was emphasized that contours and movements should be curvy and irregular because real-world shapes of objects are curvy and irregular (see Guideline 2). Shapes should not be straight, symmetrical, or angular (cf. Guideline 10) although this is the established way of designing pictograms. Reproducing conventional designs should be avoided in UIPP (see Fig. 14). To achieve this, photographs of real-world objects, creatures, and actions from the microstock website Shutterstock (Shutterstock Inc.) [383] were used as the bases of the content designs. In addition, in line with Guideline 36, multiple photographs were used in order to design averaged shapes for typical basic-level contents and to avoid cultural specificity. Fig. 15 is a screenshot of the prototype refinement process aiming for basic-level designs of contents. Furthermore, it was decided that colors should not be used in UIPP, although this is Guideline 22. The decision was made after a long discussion within the design team. As mentioned above, it was a technical constraint by the UCUI interface prototype that the pictograms should be black and white, or they should have more than two colors. The latter constraint seemed to go against Guideline 11 because including at least three colors even if an object could be represented in one color seemed to include too many unnecessary details, thus, impede fast recognition. Furthermore, it was argued that the use of real-world colors of objects is not new. Real-world colors have been used for decades, and they are still in use today. Take for example the basic pictograms in Windows, MacOS, and Android operating systems and the Minspeak representation system (Baker 1982). In contrast, the most innovative guidelines proposed by UIPP seemed to be the guidelines regarding real-world shapes (Guideline 8) and animation (Guideline 27). Since pictogram characteristics are closely interrelated (McDougall et al. 2009, p. 62), the designers assumed that it would increase the difficulty of evaluating the impact of these innovative guidelines if colors were added (see Fig. 16). This holds, in particular, because the manufacturer pictograms that were reviewed in the first meeting and to which the UIP Pictograms will be subsequently compared (see Section Presentation of the Manufacturer Pictograms, p. 273) are black and white. In other words, the design team was concerned that the impact of adding the common characteristic of real-world colors would render the evaluation of the innovative characteristics of real-world shapes and animation imprecise. Consequently, it was decided that the UIP Pictograms should be black and white, just like the established manufacturer pictograms.

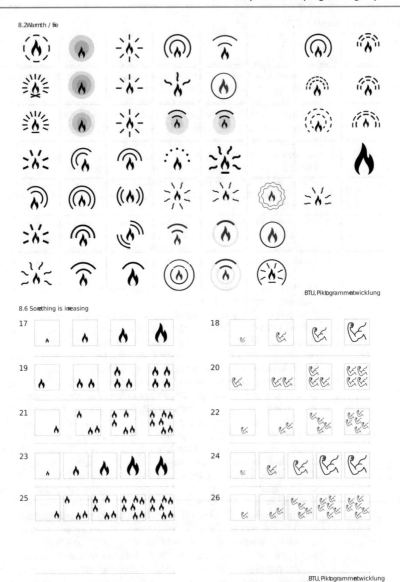

8.2 Warmth / fire

BTU, Piktogrammetwicklung

8.6 Something is increasing

BTU, Piktogrammetwicklung

Fig. 13 Examples of prototypes for the pictogram warmth and the pictograms *[warmth] is increasing* and *[power] is increasing*

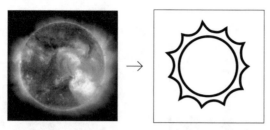

Die Sonne ist mit ihrer fließenden Aurora amorph
und nicht symmetrisch.

Die Flammenstruktur eines Feuers wird optisch
als Fläche klarre

Fig. 14 Internal document by the design team regarding the curvy and irregular design of pictogram contents

Fig. 15 Screenshot during the design of the pictogram *[something] is bad, negative*, using the freeware software Inkscape (The Inkscape Project 2019)

Fig. 16 Examples of colored pictograms that were not further refined in favor of real-world shapes and animated pictograms

Table 2e Report of the UIPP design production process

Phase Date iSteps	Content
4th meeting September 13, 2018 2 h iStep 3	The structure of the fourth meeting was identical to the structure of meeting 3 (iStep 3). More pictograms were added and more design characteristics, for example, the sizes of the contents, were discussed.
Decisions and findings	With regard to Guideline 12, it was decided that pictogram contents that are big in reality, for example, the sun, should be 10% bigger than normal sized contents, for example, a person. Small contents, for example, a snowflake, should be 10% smaller than normal sized contents. Furthermore, with the intention to design basic-level representations of human beings (Guideline 36), it was decided that faces and people should not be distinguishable with regard to their gender although one derived content for the pictogram *[something] is good, positive was the face of a laughing, smiling girl*. However, facial expressions were used because they were assumed to be universal (Plocher et al. 2012, p. 166). Finally, with the intention to prevent confusion due to reading direction, it was decided that animations should avoid specific directions. Succession should be indicated by representing contents one after another where possible.

Table 2f Report of the UIPP design production process

Phase Date iSteps	Content
5th meeting September 25, 2018 2 h iStep 3	The structure of this meeting was identical to the structure of meeting 3 (Step 3). See Fig. 17 for examples of the pictogram prototypes that were refined and discussed further.
Decisions and findings	Decisions were made for individual pictograms, for example, regarding the duration and speed of animations. Furthermore, it was decided that animations should always loop. However, there should be two kinds of loops . First, loops that convey to the user that there are a beginning and an ending, thus, indicating that an animation is repeated. Second, loops that appear to run continuously, that is, with no apparent beginning or ending. The first group should be interpreted as representations of actions, for example, *[something] is increasing*. The second as representations of characteristics, for example, *[something] is good, positive*. For the meaning *[something or someone] is busy*, it was decided that two versions should be designed (see Figs. 32 and 40) in order to determine in Study 3 which version is better suited. Finally, for the pictogram of *[something] goes wrong, is wrong* it was determined that it should break into four pieces instead of three because the three-piece version could not be adapted to the design of all additional contents (see Fig. 18).

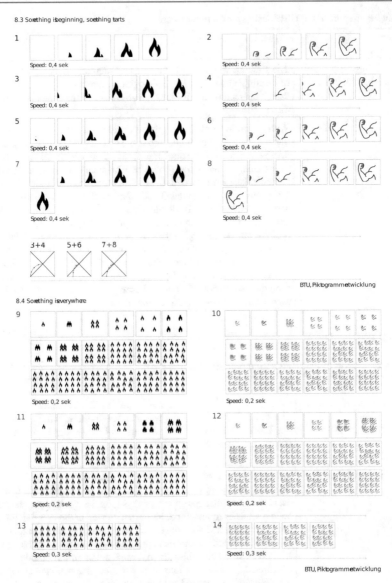

8.3 Something is beginning, something starts

8.4 Something is everywhere

BTU, Piktogrammentwicklung

Fig. 17 Examples of refined and discussed prototypes in an internal document by the design team

Ein weiteres Beispiel für eine natürliche Bewegung ist das Fallen oder Ein stürzen eines Gegenstands gemäß des natürlichen Vorbilds. Stürzt z.B. ein Gebäude in sich zusammen, so fallen die oberen Teile nach innen wodurch die unteren Teile am Boden nach außen gedrückt werden. Daraus lässt sich folgen des Fallschema ableiten, das vier Bereiche der Zeichnungsfläche und deren Fallverhalten definiert.

Abgeleitetes Fallschema

Daraus folgt die konkrete Sequenzierung:

Sequenz: „Something is beginning" mit Piktogramm „Wärme"

Fig. 18 Internal document of the design team that discusses the animation of the compound pictogram *[something] goes wrong, is wrong*

Table 2g Report of the UIPP design production process

Phase Date iSteps	Content
6th, final meeting October 10, 2018 1 h	Prior to the final meeting, new prototypes were sent via e-mail (on October 8, 2018) to be able to discuss them during the meeting. The structure of the meeting was identical to the structure of meeting 3 (Step 3), except, only minor changes were discussed that should be made during the finalization of the pictogram prototypes.
Decisions and findings	The designers discussed the finalization of the pictograms. It was argued that the pictograms should be more similar to each other if they were designed for the market. Only then, they would be recognizable as belonging to a set. Since they were not produced for the market, the idea was not implemented.
Finalization Until the start of the evaluation studies: March 23, 2019 iStep 4	The pictogram prototypes were finalized and prepared for evaluation (iStep 4) by the author of this book. In the finalization process, the freeware software Inkscape (The Inkscape Project 2019) was used for the design, and the freeware software GIMP (The GIMP Team 2018) was used for animation. Freeware software was used with the intention to enable designers, researchers, and businesses with limited resources to follow the process, in contrast to expensive established software. The final contribution by the agency's designers was on October 28, 2018, via e-mail.

Discussion of the Design Production Process

At the end of the design production process, the designers discussed and evaluated the process. It was found that the entire production process was characterized by continuous iteration , that is, back and forth and by leaps between pictogram designs. This is was considered typical for research through design projects (Hemmert 2014, p. 154). Although the designers considered the process productive, in the beginning, they found it challenging to follow the guidelines mainly because of three reasons: the number of guidelines was considered large, the designers were not very familiar with the guidelines, and the guidelines were often in contrast to established ways of designing pictograms. However, in the course of the process, the designers became familiarized with the guidelines by evaluating before, during, and after the design of prototypes whether these prototypes followed the guidelines. If this was not the case, the prototypes were adapted according to the guidelines that were not followed. Since some guidelines might contradict each other with regard to specific design problems, the designers decided which guidelines to follow based on their skills and tacit knowledge. Furthermore, the design system was considered a result of the process and could not be developed independently from the pictogram prototypes. For that reason, the system was specified at the end of the process. In conclusion, the designers considered the design production process fruitful and instructive for future processes.

Presentation of the Design System and of the Pictogram Prototypes

In this section, the developed design system and the finalized pictogram prototypes are presented. The presentation follows IEC 80416-1:2008 (Deutsches Institut für Normung 2009, pp. 10–13). IEC 80,416–1:2008 proposes a basic square pattern of 75 mm length and width for pictogram design. The basic size of the pictogram contents should be 50 mm. However, the contents should be as big a possible but not beyond the borders of the 75 mm square (see Fig. 19). Line thickness should be between 2 and 4 mm.

Since UIPPs were designed for a GUI, instead of millimeters, pixels were used as units of measurement. The UIPP design system obeys the following rules and regularities:

- The basic square pattern of the pictograms is 125×125 px in size.
- The pictogram contents are projected using adapted linear perspective and photographs as their bases.
- The contents are represented as contours, based on photographs. However, the designers choose the contours.
- Multiple photographs are used to design average basic-level objects and creatures.

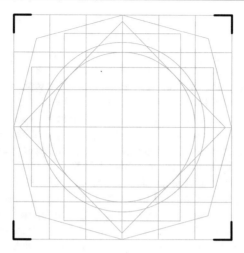

Fig. 19 Basic pattern for pictogram design, according to IEC 80,416–1:2008 (International Organization for Standardization 2007)

- The contents are represented curvy and irregular, as they are in the real world.
- The lines are black, the pictogram background is white.
- The basic thickness of lines is 2 px but can be adapted according to real-world contours.
- The contents are represented from a canonical viewpoint.
- In general, the contents are centered.
- In general, the contents' sizes are 80% of the pictogram (100 px). However, contents that are big in the real world are 10% bigger (i.e., 88% of the pictogram or 110 px), and contents that are smaller in the real world are 10% smaller (i.e., 72% or 90 px).
- Actions and movements, too, are based on real-world actions and movements. However, they are segmented.
- Compound contents do not overlap.
- (In other projects that are not subject to the constraints of the UCUI project: Contents are colored similar to the real-world object or scene that they represent.)

Following the adapted taxonomy from Step 3 (Sect. "Results"), the pictogram prototypes were categorized into two groups. The first group contained pictograms that represent a countable object or creature as their content, for example, the pictogram for *warmth* that represents a flame. I call these pictograms simple pictograms . The second group contained pictograms that represent actions, characteristics, or uncountable objects as their contents because these contents require an additional object or creature that has the characteristic or that performs the action in order to be visually representable. I call these pictograms compound pictograms (cf. Bezuayehu et al. 2014, p. 41). One example is *[something] is increasing.*

The content of the pictogram is *the level of [something] is rising*. In order for the content, that is, the action of *a level that is rising*, to be visually representable, an additional object is required. In the finalized pictogram prototype, *a male arm with a flexing biceps* that refers to the meaning of *power* was used as the additional object. Consequently, the meaning of the finalized pictogram prototype is *[power] is increasing*. The central part of the meaning is *is increasing*, and *power* might be replaced. In the pictogram meanings, the part that can be replaced is indicated with brackets. Since the simplest pictogram meanings consist of only one object, action, or characteristic (as described in Sect. "Deriving UIP Pictogram Meanings"), and compound pictograms consist by definition of multiple, thus, complex meanings, I hypothesize that compound pictograms are more difficult to comprehend (Löffler 2017, p. 191). This was examined in Study 3. In line with my discussion in this step, I contend that the design relation of the UIP Pictograms is based on similarity because they were produced using the developed design system. In the following, the 22 finalized prototypes are presented, including their meaning, the content that was chosen by the designers, and the category on which their reference relation is based (see Sect. "Conceptualizing the Relations of Design and of Reference").

Simple Pictograms

Fig. 20 Pictogram meaning: *coldness*. The represented content is *snowflake*. The reference relation is based on the semantic association type semantic narrowing

Fig. 21 Pictogram meaning: *day*. The represented content is *the shining sun*. The reference relation is based on the semantic association type semantic narrowing

Fig. 22 Pictogram meaning: *power*. The represented content is *a male arm with flexing biceps*. The reference relation is based on the semantic association type semantic narrowing

Fig. 23 Pictogram meaning: *hand*. The represented content is *hand*. The pictogram was not derived in Chap. "Step 3: Grounding, Deriving, and Evaluating Pictogram Contents" However, it was designed as a part of the pictogram for *[something or someone] is busy*. The reference relation is iconic

Fig. 24 Pictogram meaning: *night*. The represented content is *bright moon and stars*. The reference relation is based on the semantic association type semantic narrowing

Fig. 25 Pictogram meaning: *person*. The represented content is *a person standing or sitting alone*. The reference relation is iconic

Fig. 26 Pictogram meaning: *warmth*. The represented content is *fire*. The reference relation is based on the semantic association type semantic narrowing

Compound Pictograms

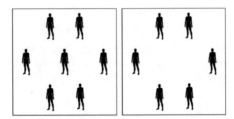

Fig. 27 Pictogram meaning: *[person] is absent, not here*. The represented content is an *empty space in the middle of people*. This is a conflation of the two contents *an empty seat in the middle of people* and *an empty space in the middle*. The reference relation is based on the semantic association type temporal decomposition. The first frame is presented for 1,000 ms, the second for 4,500 ms. The loop appears to be continuous

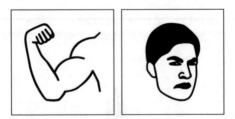

Fig. 28 Pictogram meaning: *[power] is bad, negative*. The represented content is *an angry, frowning face*. The reference relation is based on the semantic association types semantic narrowing and metaphor. The first frame is presented for 1,250 ms, the second for 1,150 ms. The loop appears to be continuous

Fig. 29 Pictogram meaning: *[warmth] begins*. The represented content is the rising sun. The reference relation is based on the semantic association types semantic narrowing, metaphor and temporal decomposition. Each frame is presented for 500 ms, except the last frame which is presented for 1500 ms. The loop is apparently repeated

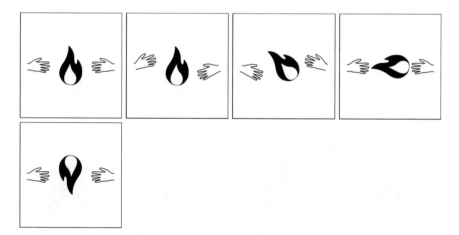

Fig. 30 Pictogram meaning: *[warmth] is busy* (Version A). The represented content is hands performing an action. The reference relation is based on the semantic association type semantic narrowing. Each frame is presented for 150 ms. The loop appears to be continuous

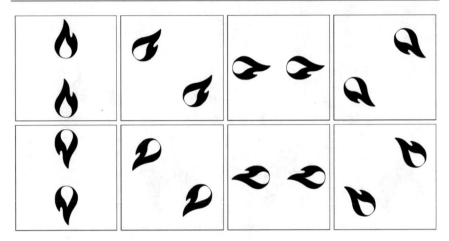

Fig. 31 Pictogram meaning: *[warmth] is busy* (Version B). The represented content is a confla-tion of the contents *[something] is moving around fast and an action is performed over and over again*. The reference relation is based on the semantic association type semantic narrowing. Each frame is presented for 100 ms. The loop appears to be continuous

Fig. 32 Pictogram meaning: *[warmth] is dangerous*. The represented content is *[something] is approaching very fast*. The reference relation is based on the semantic association type semantic narrowing. The first frame's presentation time is 80 ms. Presentation time decreases for each fol-lowing frame by 5 ms. The last frame is presented for 30 ms. The loop is apparently repeated

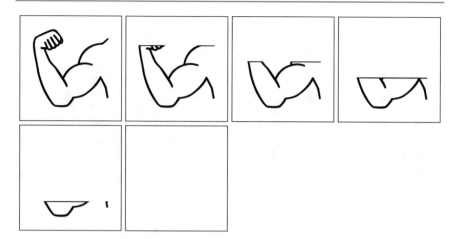

Fig. 33 Pictogram meaning: *[power] is decreasing*. The represented content is *the level of [something] is sinking*. The reference relation is based on the semantic association type semantic narrowing. All frames are presented for 600 ms except for the last frame which is empty. It is presented for 1,200 ms. The loop is apparently repeated

Fig. 34 Pictogram meaning: *[coldness] ends*. The represented content is *[something] becomes darker until it is black*. The reference relation is based on the semantic association types semantic narrowing and temporal decomposition. All frames are presented for 800 ms, except the last which is presented for 1,200 ms. The loop is apparently repeated

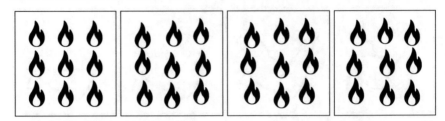

Fig. 35 Pictogram meaning: *[warmth] is everywhere*. The reference relation is based on the semantic association type contiguity. The represented content is *air*. Each frame is presented for 300 ms. The loop appears to be continuous

Fig. 36 Pictogram meaning: *[coldness] is good, positive*. The represented content is *a smiling, laughing face*. The reference relation is based on the semantic association types semantic narrowing and metaphor. The first frame is presented for 1,250 ms, the second for 1,150 ms. The loop appears to be continuous

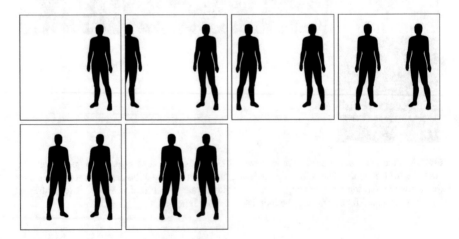

Fig. 37 Pictogram meaning: *[person] is here, on-site*. The represented content is a conflation of the two contents *[someone] is arriving* and *[someone] is standing in front of oneself*. The reference relation is based on the semantic association type temporal decomposition. The first frame is presented for 800 ms, the following for 400 ms, and the last frame for 4,500 ms. The loop is apparently repeated

Fig. 38 Pictogram meaning: *[coldness] is important*. The represented content is *[something] is flashing*. The reference relation is based on the semantic association types contiguity. Each frame is presented for 500 ms. The loop appears to be continuous

Fig. 39 Pictogram meaning: *[warmth] is increasing*. The represented content is *[something] is growing upward*. The reference relation is based on the semantic association type semantic narrowing. All frames are presented for 800 ms, except for the last frame, which is presented for 1,200 ms. The loop is apparently repeated

Fig. 40 Pictogram meaning: several, a group of [people]. The represented content is [some people] standing together in a circle. The reference relation is iconic

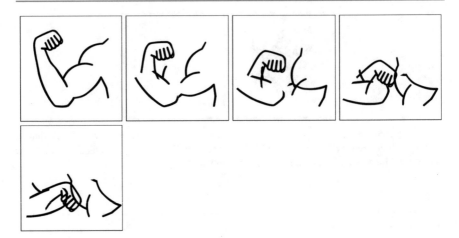

Fig. 41 Pictogram meaning: *[power] goes wrong, is wrong*. The represented content is *[something] collapses*. The reference relation is based on the semantic association type semantic narrowing. The first frame is presented for 450 ms, the last for 650 ms. All other frames are presented for 350 ms. The loop is apparently repeated

Summary and Conclusion of the Chapter

This chapter constitutes the fourth step in the UIPP process, that is, the approach to the design relation. First, I reviewed existing guidelines for visual and pictogram design, and I argued that they are not suitable. Second, I explained the UIPP approach, which is grounded in visual perception. I argued that the process of visual perception is suitable because it is in general assumed to be universal, intuitive, and permanent. Third, I argued that perception, recognition, and interpretation of visual representation is based on visual perception, too. For that reason, a universal, intuitive, and permanent design system should be grounded in the process of visual perception. Fourth, I proposed guidelines for pictogram content design that I derived from research on visual perception. Fifth, I explained and reported the design production process of the UIP Pictogram prototypes, which was conducted as a research through design (RTD) project. Finally, I presented the developed UIPP design system and the produced pictogram prototypes.

One goal of the UIPP project was to develop a process that can be performed and adopted by other designers, researchers, and businesses in their projects. I hold that this is achieved for Step 4. This is so because I have described and explained the derived design guidelines and the production process in detail. In addition, the guideline, the proposed RTD approach, and the design system might be used for any required content and meaning. Consequently, designers, researchers, and businesses should be able to apply Step 4 in their own project—using the contents and meanings that they have previously derived in Step 3. Furthermore, the process might be used for localization and for more specific contexts of use.

However, then, designers, researchers, and businesses might need to review and derive additional guidelines specific to their project. In other words, if the pictograms are intended for a specific user interface system, criteria that influence perception and interpretation of that interface system need to be reviewed, and additional design guidelines must be derived. Then, the design system should be adapted. In addition, market-related requirements might need to be considered. For example, if the pictograms are produced for a specific business, designers might need to consider brand guidelines. Nevertheless, if designers, researchers, and businesses do not have the resources available required for the derivation of additional guidelines, they can adapt the presented design system or the guidelines based on their expert knowledge. Finally, I propose that the process in this step might be adapted to other categories of representations, for example, to contents of auditory representations. However, to that end, a complete review of research on auditory perception would be required, and, subsequently, guidelines for the design of contents of auditory representations must be derived.

The production of design prototypes is the fourth step in a human-centered design process, as described by ISO 9241:210 (International Organization for Standardization 2010). In this step, prototypes are produced by a design team based on previous findings and on existing guidelines (see Sect. "The UIPP Design Process and the Chapters of this Book"). I consider this fourth step completed (see Fig. 42). In the next chapter, I present the evaluation of the produced prototypes. This is Step 5 of the UIPP process.

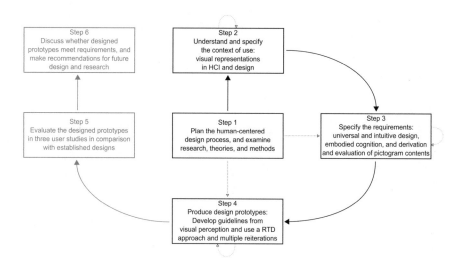

Fig. 42 The UIPP human-centered design process. Step 4 is completed. Dotted arrows indicate iterations

Step 5: Evaluating the UIP Pictograms

Abstract

According to ISO 9241:210, in the fifth HCD step, the designed prototypes are evaluated by users. All previously derived requirements should be fulfilled. While several evaluation studies were conducted during the entire UIPP process, Chapter 5 reports four user studies that evaluated in detail the produced UIP Pictograms by comparing them with established manufacturer pictograms. In these studies, three different approaches were used, consisting of comprehension tests, direct comparisons, and subjective ratings, to determine whether the UIPP prototypes are more suitable than the established pictograms and whether they might be considered universal, intuitive, and permanent. The evaluation studies suggest that the process was successful.

In the previous chapters of this book, I have discussed visual representations, I have argued that two properties, the reference and the design relation, are central to visual representations, and I have presented the UIPP approach to both relations. Finally, 22 pictogram prototypes were designed. In the fifth step of the UIPP process, these prototypes are evaluated. According to ISO 9241:210 (International Organization for Standardization 2010), this is in line with the fifth step of the human-centered design process.

Best-practice methods or procedures for the evaluation of visual representations and GUIs are not established in HCI. In contrast, various methods exist, for example, measuring error rates or completion time, interviews, eye-tracking, and Likert-type evaluation scales (Agrawala et al. 2011, p. 68; Stahl-Timmins 2017). In addition, crowdsourcing offers new possibilities for cross-cultural evaluation that had not been available before (Laursen et al. 2016, p. 2). In UIPP, with the intention to examine the designed pictograms from a broad spectrum

D. Bühler, *Universal, Intuitive, and Permanent Pictograms*,
https://doi.org/10.1007/978-3-658-32310-3_5

187

of viewpoints, three approaches were chosen. These approaches have been used widely in HCI, and they have different empirical foci. The approaches are, first, the ISO 9186:3 standard method for testing symbol referent association which is a comprehension test (International Organization for Standardization 2014); second, an approach used by Jörn Hurtienne and colleagues on various occasions including direct comparison (e.g., Hurtienne 2011, Chapters 5–6); and, third, an approach by McDougall, Isherwood, and colleagues to pictogram characteristics that consists of subjective ratings (e.g., Isherwood et al. 2007, pp. 466–467). In the respective studies, UIPPs were compared with established manufacturer pictograms, and performance data were collected. The latter are research desiderata mentioned by Hurtienne et al. (2015, p. 252). In the studies, only German-speaking participants were recruited. This is a drawback because the UIPP project aimed for cross-cultural design. However, since Study 3 consisted of four separate studies, conducting Study 3 with participants from four continents, as in Study 1 and 2, would have multiplied the required resources, indeed, it would have exceeded them (see Chong 2004, pp. 301–302). Consequently, this was not an option. Nevertheless, I contend that a positive evaluation might suggest universal comprehensibility because the pictograms were not designed specifically for German-speaking participants. Instead, they were derived in studies with participants from four continents. Consequently, if German-speaking participants evaluate the pictograms positively, it seems reasonable to assume that participants from Australia, Canada, South Africa, and the United States might, too. In the following, I first present the manufacturer pictograms. Then, I report the studies, their results, and findings.

Presentation of the Manufacturer Pictograms

To guarantee comparability of UIP Pictograms and established manufacturer pictograms, following Medhi et al. (2007, p. 874), two requirements were met. First, pictograms were chosen from the same context of use to which the UIP Pictograms were to be applied, that is, user interfaces for heating systems (see Sect. "Universal, Intuitive, and Permanent Pictogram Project: Two Main Goals"). Second, the pictograms were normalized, that is, the manufacturer pictograms were scaled to the same size as UIPPs while conserving their original aspect ratio. Furthermore, pictograms were selected that refer to meanings equivalent to UIPP meanings. To that end, a literature review was conducted, and pictograms were extracted from ISO standards, heating system manuals, or design documents by manufacturers. Furthermore, several manufacturers were requested to provide heating interface pictograms. Contacted manufacturers were Bosch, Broetje, Buderus, Remeha, Vaillant, Viessmann, Weishaupt, and Wolf. Finally, Bosch pictograms were chosen because they fulfill all the criteria. Following the example of the UIP Pictograms (see Sect. "Presentation of the Design System and of the Pictogram Prototypes"), the manufacturer pictograms were also separated into two groups: simple and compound pictograms. In the next section, the manufacturer pictograms are presented. For each pictogram, the original meaning (if applicable, with translation), the source, and the equivalent UIPP meaning are stated.

Simple Pictograms

Fig. 1 Pictogram meaning: *cold* (Bosch Thermotechnik GmbH 2018, p. 4). Used as an equivalent to *coldness*

Fig. 2 Pictogram meaning: *day* (Bosch Thermotechnik GmbH 2018, p. 24). Used as an equivalent to *day*

Fig. 3 Pictogram meaning: *energy* (Bosch Thermotechnik GmbH 2017, p. 20). Used as an equivalent to *power*

Fig. 4 Pictogram meaning: *manual operation* (German: Manuelle Bedienung) (Bosch Thermotechnik GmbH 2017, p. 13). Used as an equivalent to *hand*

Fig. 5 Pictogram meaning: *night* (German: *Nacht*) (Bosch Thermotechnik GmbH 2018, p. 24). Used as an equivalent to *night*

Fig. 6 Pictogram meaning: *end user* (German: *Endbenutzer*) (Bosch Thermotechnik GmbH 2018, p. 35). Used as an equivalent to *person*

Fig. 7 Pictogram meaning: *hot* (Bosch Thermotechnik GmbH 2018, p. 4). Used as an equivalent to *warmth*

Compound Pictograms

Fig. 8 Pictogram meaning: *user away* (Bosch Thermotechnik GmbH 2018, p. 25). Used as an equivalent to *[person] is absent, not here*

Fig. 9 Pictogram meaning: *heating on* (Bosch Thermotechnik GmbH 2018, p. 10). Used as an equivalent to *[warmth] begins*

Fig. 10 Pictogram meaning: *heating generator in operation* (German: Wärmeerzeuger in Betrieb) (Bosch Thermotechnik GmbH 2017, p. 7). Used as an equivalent to *[warmth] is busy*

Fig. 11 Pictogram meaning: *danger* (German: *Gefahr*) (Bosch Thermotechnik GmbH 2017, p. 2). Used as an equivalent to *[something] is dangerous*

Fig. 12 Pictogram meaning: *energy consumption* (Bosch Thermotechnik GmbH 2017, p. 38). Used as an equivalent to *[power] is decreasing* (Version A)

Fig. 13 Pictogram meaning: *battery status indicator* (in International Organization for Standardization and International Electrotechnical Commission 2007, p. 25, only a description is provided and not a meaning). Used as an equivalent to *[power] is decreasing* (Version B). The first three frames are presented for 600 ms, the last for 1,200 ms

Fig. 14 Pictogram meaning: *cooling off* (Bosch Thermotechnik GmbH 2018, p. 10). Used as an equivalent to *[coldness] ends*

Fig. 15 Pictogram meaning: *everything okay with your system* (German: Alles okay mit Ihrem System) (Bosch Thermotechnik GmbH 2018, p. 33). Used as an equivalent to *[something] is good, positive*

Fig. 16 Pictogram meaning: *attention* (German: *Vorsicht*) (Bosch Thermotechnik GmbH 2017, p. 2). Used as an equivalent to *[something] is important*

Fig. 17 Pictogram meaning: *temperature up* (Bosch Thermotechnik GmbH 2018, p. 11). Used as an equivalent to *[warmth] is increasing*

Fig. 18 Pictogram meaning: *user at home* (Bosch Thermotechnik GmbH 2018, p. 25). Used as an equivalent to *[person] is here, on-site*

Fig. 19 Pictogram meaning: *multiple users or group* (Bosch Thermotechnik GmbH 2018, p. 35). Used as an equivalent to *several, a group of [people]*

Fig. 20 Pictogram meaning: *error or fault* (Bosch Thermotechnik GmbH 2017, p. 10). Used as an equivalent to *[something] goes wrong, is wrong*

Study 3.1: Comprehension Test

ISO 9186:3 (International Organization for Standardization 2014) describes a method for testing visual representations in HCI. That is, a "procedure for quantifying the degree of understanding of a proposed graphical symbol" (p. 1). While ISO 9186:1 proposes testing pictograms through open-ended questions, and ISO 9186:2 tests for basic identification of represented objects (International Organization for Standardization 2008, 2014), ISO 9186:3 allows to examine whether participants understand correctly to which familiar meaning a given pictogram refers. If a pictogram receives at least 66% correct responses (CRs), it is accepted. If it receives 86% or above correct responses, it is suitable as a safety symbol. This method was developed especially for technical contexts and for the comparison of pictograms (Theo Boersema and Adams 2017, pp. 311–312). Following the example of other studies (e.g., Isaacson et al. 2017), the ISO standard comprehension test was adapted: ISO 9186:3 proposes conducting a familiarity training prior to the test in which participants are familiarized with the pictograms that are tested. In Study 3.1, the training was omitted because UIP Pictograms are intended to be intuitive, that is, comprehensible without familiarization. In addition, response times (RTs) were recorded, and a *none of the above* answer option was deleted from stimuli because participants were not familiar with the pictograms (see Sect. "Stimuli").

Hypotheses

UIP Pictograms were designed using pictogram contents and a design system that were assumed to be as universal, intuitive, and permanent as possible, in contrast to manufacturer pictograms. In addition, it was assumed that simple pictograms are more easily and faster comprehended than compound pictograms because they represent only one countable object or creature (see Sect. "Presentation of the Design System and of the Pictogram Prototypes"). Based on these assumptions, the following hypotheses were made:

H1:   CRs are higher and RTs are shorter with UIP Pictograms than with manufacturer pictograms.
H2:   CRs are higher and RTs are shorter with simple pictograms than with compound pictograms.
H3:   There is no significant interaction between UIPP CRs or UIPP RTs and age, education, pictogram experience, or heating interface experience.

Method

Participants
ISO 9186:3 recommends $n = 25$ or more participants (International Organization for Standardization 2014, p. 3). For this study, sample size was calculated with the effect size calculator G*Power 3.1.9.2 by Faul et al. (2009). One hundred and one participants were included in the study ($n = 101$), ranging in age from 18 to 72 years ($M = 37.20$, $SD = 13.58$). Participants were 49.5% female, 50.5% male, none stated *diverse* as gender. Educational level was high, $Mdn = 3$, $IQR = 1$ (no school leaving certificate $= 0$, primary/national or lower secondary school leaving certificate $= 1$, secondary school leaving certificate $= 2$, high school diploma $= 3$, or university degree $= 4$). Self-reported level of experience with pictograms was high, too, $Mdn = 4$, $IQR = 1$ (use frequency: never $= 1$, rarely $= 2$, occasionally $= 3$, often $= 4$, or always $= 5$). In contrast, the self-reported experience with heating interfaces was low, $Mdn = 1$, $IQR = 2$ (scale identical to pictogram experience). The latter three distributions were highly skewed (see "Appendix K" for bar graphs). Participants were recruited and remunerated through a crowdsourcing process as described in Sect. "Crowdsourcing Cross-Cultural Studies for Universal Associations". In addition, participants were recruited through newsletters addressing German university degree holders. The newsletter recruiting

was used to balance the crowdsourcing participant group which was expected to have a lower educational level (Rau et al. 2011, p. 692). Only participants living in Austria, Germany, or Switzerland and with German as a first language were included. In addition, only participants with normal or corrected-to-normal vision were included. Study 3.1 participants were the same as in Study 3.2.

Materials
All materials were presented in German. In the following, they are translated into English where appropriate.

Stimuli
Stimuli consisted of all pictograms that were introduced in Sects. "Presentation of the Design System and of the Pictogram Prototypes" and "Presentation of the Manufacturer Pictograms", except pictograms with the meanings *hand* and *person* which were parts of compound pictograms. Consequently, 38 pictograms were presented. 20 were UIP Pictograms and 18 were manufacturer pictograms. Of the UIPPs, 5 were simple and 15 were compound. Of the manufacturer pictograms, 5 were simple and 13 were compound (see "Appendix L"). The presentation included four answer options below the pictogram of which one was the intended meaning of the pictogram. Stimuli were presented as follows (Fig. 21).

As described by ISO 9186:3, the answer options were presented below the pictogram (International Organization for Standardization 2014, p. 4). Stimuli were clearly legible and not distorted, this was clarified through pretesting. Presentation of the stimuli was randomized. All stimuli were presented to every participant.

Following the example of other studies (e.g., Isaacson et al. 2017), the standard presentation was adapted. According to ISO 9186:3, stimuli should be presented that do not include the intended meaning of the pictogram in order to examine whether participants were previously correctly familiarized with the items. Consequently, answer options should include a *none of the above* answer. Furthermore, the standard test method includes seven answer options. Since, on the one hand, participants were not familiar with the items and, on the other hand, with the intention to reduce fatigue effects, the *none of the above answer* was omitted and options were reduced to four.

Fig. 21 Study 3.1 presentation of the UIP Pictogram with the meaning *coldness*

In Study 3.1, two versions (A and B) of UIPP *[something or someone] is busy* (see Figs. 30 and 31) were included to determine which version is better suited (see Sect. "Design Answers: Report of the UIPP Design Production Process").

Instructional Page

Participants were not informed about the pictograms beyond their intended context. They were not informed of being presented with two different sets, that is, the UIP Pictograms and the manufacturer pictograms. Participants were presented with the task to choose the best fitting meaning of four and to choose as fast as possible. They were informed that their focus should be on choosing correctly. Participants were told to ignore terms in brackets [ ] of compound pictograms and focus on the part of the meaning that was different in all four answer options. Following ISO 9186:3, participants were asked to not listen to music, watch TV, or do anything that could distract them during the test. Participants were told that their response was not to be judged in any way.

Demographic and Experience Questionnaires

The study included a demographic questionnaire with 5 items and a questionnaire on user experience with pictograms and heating interfaces (2 items). Demographic items were gender (*female*, *male*, or *diverse*), age (continuous variable), education (*no school leaving certificate*, *primary/national or lower secondary school leaving certificate*, *secondary school leaving certificate*, *high school diploma*, or *university degree*), German as a first language (*yes* or *no*), and normal or corrected-to-normal vision (*yes* or *no*). Experience level, that is, familiarity, with pictograms and heating interfaces were ascertained with scales of use frequency (*never*, *rarely*, *occasionally*, *often*, or *always*) (Blackler et al. 2019, p. 69; Hurtienne et al. 2010, p. 479) .

Apparatus

LimeSurvey Version 3.16.1 + 190314 open-source online survey software was used for the creation and design of the study materials (LimeSurvey GmbH 2019).

Since a crowdsourcing process was used in the study, online screen testing was preferred. Previous studies showed that there is no significant difference between paper and screen testing in ISO 9186 tests (Foster et al. 2010, p. 107, pp. 115–116). Because of the online test, participants used their own personal computers in locations of their choice. The survey was designed to support all common computer systems and internet browsers (Andrews et al. 2003, p. 3).

Through a PHP script, participants were rejected if they used a mobile device to access the study. Only use of personal computers was allowed. This was implemented because recent studies suggested that large screens are significantly more efficient than small screens in online questionnaires (Nissen and Janneck 2018), thus, increase reliability of the test.

With the intention to minimize interference by technical setups, participants were asked to close all other browser tabs and all programs running in the background of their computer. For the same reason, latency was measured three times:

when participants were forwarded to the test, in the middle of the test, and at the end of the test. Latency was used afterward for calculating response times.

Pretests

Five consecutive pretests were conducted to optimize the procedure regarding introduction, instructions, stimuli design, and question phrasing. After each test, the participants were interviewed and the material was adapted according to the participant's remarks (Stahl-Timmins 2017, pp. 458–459).

Design

Gender, experience with pictograms, and experience with heating interfaces were considered categorical independent between-subjects variables. Age was raised as an independent continuous control variable. Pictogram set (UIPPs vs. manufacturer pictograms) and meaning complexity (simple vs. compound) were manipulated as independent within-subject variables. Two dependent variables were measured: Correct responses (CR) and response times (RT). Correct responses were measured instead of error rates following ISO 9186:3. Response time was defined as the time interval from the presentation of the pictogram until the participant's click on an answer option. All effects were reported as significant at $p < .05$.

Procedure

First, participants were informed of the study and of the context of use of the pictograms. On the Clickworker website(see Sect. "Crowdsourcing Cross-Cultural Studies for Universal Associations"), participants were presented with an introductory text that included the context for which the pictograms are intended, that is, a heating interface. If the participants chose to participate in the study, they were forwarded to the study website, however, only if they were using a personal computer. Second, on the study website, participants were presented with a demographic questionnaire and a questionnaire on user experience. Third, participants were presented with instructions and, again, with the intended context of the pictogram use. Participants were asked to choose the best fitting answer and to choose as quickly as possible. Fourth, participants were successively presented with the stimuli. The presentation was randomized. Responses were collected and response times were recorded. The test was self-paced. It took about 4 min. Study 3.1 was conducted in the same session as Study 3.2 to minimize testing time for each participant and, again, reduce fatigue effects (MacKenzie 2013, pp. 175–177). After the entire session, participants were presented with a thank-you message and forwarded to the Clickworker website to receive remuneration.

Reliability

A six-week test–retest reliability test was performed with time as the only known source of variance ($n = 12$) (Salkind 2010, pp. 1237–1242). Because of the interval between two tests, it was assumed that participants would not remember the pictogram meanings from the first test. The test had a significant test–retest reliability, Kendall's $\tau = .51$, $p < .001$ (Pearson's $r = .55$, $p < .001$). The reliability is considered *moderate* (Akoglu 2018, p. 92; Dancey and Reidy 2017, pp. 181–189). ISO 9186:3 does not report reliability.

Data Selection, Cleaning, and Reduction

With the intention to minimize interference by the technical setup in the homes of the participants, an aggregated forwarding time was calculated as a mean of the three measured forwarding times of each participant. Then, the aggregated forwarding time was subtracted from the individual aggregated response times of the participants to obtain a cleaned individual aggregated response time (see, e.g., Löffler 2017, p. 200).

There were no missing data because only complete tests were included in the analysis. Consequently, no data were imputed. Participants with total correct responses 2 standard deviations below or above the mean were excluded. Aggregated response times for UIPP and manufacturer pictograms were log-transformed where appropriate, and participants with aggregated response times 2 standard deviations below or above the mean were excluded. Since participants in this study were the same as in Study 3.2, participants with erroneous responses in Study 3.2 were excluded, too. That is, participants who rated all connections identically or who used recognizable rating patterns. In total, 6.48% of participants' responses were excluded.

Results

Data analysis was conducted using JASP Version 0.10.2 (JASP Team 2019) and Microsoft Excel 365 Version 1906 (Microsoft Corporation 2019).

Comparison of UIPP [Something or Someone] is Busy Versions

As described in Section *Design Answers: Report of the UIPP Design Production Process* (p. 243) two versions (A and B) of UIPP *[something or someone] is busy* (see Figs. 30 and 31) were included in Studies 3.1 and 3.2 to determine which version is better suited. In total, Version A received 90.1% correct responses, Version B 96%. Mean aggregated response time for A was 7.7 s ($SD = 4.27$ s), for B 6 s ($SD = 3.34$ s). A McNemar test showed no significant difference in correct responses between the two versions, $\chi^2(1) = 3.00$, $p = .083$. However, a paired samples t-test of the log-transformed response times revealed that response times for B were significantly shorter than for A, $t(100) = 5.80$, p < .001. Consequently, where possible, Version B was used in the analysis.

Correct Response Rates and Response Times

Eighteen UIP Pictograms received correct response rates above 66% of which 13 received CRs above 86%. Consequently, 90% of UIPPs were confirmed of which 72.2% were confirmed as safety symbols, according to ISO 9186:3 (International Organization for Standardization 2014). Only two UIPPs received CRs below 66%. An inspection of these pictograms suggests that answer options were misleading. One answer option for *[something] is important* (CR 53.9%) was *[something] is dangerous*. Since a dangerous creature or situation can be assumed to be important, too, the pictogram might have been confused with a pictogram for the meaning *[something] is dangerous*. Pretests had not revealed this problem. Forty-two point two per cent of the participants chose the answer *[something] is dangerous* instead of *[something is important]*. Both answers together account for 96.1%. This suggests that the pictogram might have been confirmed with more distinct answer options. If the pictogram were included into the group of confirmed pictograms, 95% of UIPPs would have been confirmed of which 73.7% would have been confirmed as safety symbols. If the pictogram is excluded, 94.7% of UIPPs are confirmed, 72.2% as safety symbols. For the pictogram *[something or someone] is absent, not here*, one frequently chosen answer option was *[something or someone] is here*, that is, the opposite meaning. This suggests that the pictogram was ambiguous, thus, not suitably designed. For manufacturer pictograms, 13 received CRs above 66%, seven above 86%, and four below 66%. Thus, 72.2% were confirmed of which 53.8% were confirmed as safety symbols. See Fig. 22 for percentage distributions.

The mean of correct responses per participant in percent for all UIPPs was 87.1 ($SD = 9.3$) and for manufacturer pictograms 78.2 ($SD = 9.2$) (see "Appendix L" for CRs in percent per pictogram). A paired samples t-test showed that CRs for UIPPs were significantly higher than for manufacturer pictograms, $t(100) = 6.51, p < .001$. This suggests a *medium-sized* effect, Cohen's $d = 0.65$ (Cohen 1988).

The mean of aggregated response times per participant for all UIPPs was 7.07 s ($SD = 2.43$ s), for manufacturer pictograms 5.65 s ($SD = 2.13$ s) (see "Appendix M" for RTs per pictogram). A paired samples t-test with log-transformed reactions times showed that RTs for UIPPs were significantly longer than for manufacturer

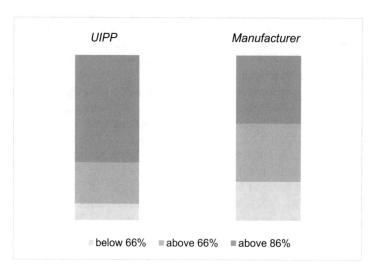

Fig. 22 Percentage distributions of UIPPs and manufacturer pictograms regarding CRs

pictograms, $t(100) = 56.17$, $p < .001$. This is considered a *large* effect, Cohen's $d = 5.59$.

The mean of correct responses per participant in percent for all simple pictograms was 94 ($SD = 5.7$) and for compound pictograms 78.6 ($SD = 8.5$). A paired samples t-test showed that CRs for simple pictograms were significantly higher than for compound pictograms, $t(100) = 14.49$, $p < .001$. This suggests a *large* effect, Cohen's $d = 1.44$. The total mean of aggregated response times per participant for simple pictograms was 4.01 s ($SD = 1.64$ s), for compound pictograms 7.32 s ($SD = 2.50$ s). A paired samples t-test showed that RTs for simple pictograms were significantly shorter than for compound pictograms, $t(100) = -2.93$, $p < .001$. This is considered a *large* effect, Cohen's $d = -2.28$.

The mean of correct responses per participant in percent for simple UIPPs was 97.2 ($SD = 6.9$), for simple manufacturer pictograms 90.7 ($SD = 10.8$), for compound UIPPs 83.5 ($SD = 12.2$), and for compound manufacturer pictograms 72.3 ($SD = 12.6$). Paired samples t-tests showed that CRs for simple and for compound UIPPs were significantly higher than for manufacturer pictograms, $t(100) = 4.63$, $p < .001$ and $t(100) = 5.88$, $p < .001$. This suggests a *close to medium* sized effect for simple pictograms and a *medium* sized effect for compound pictograms, Cohen's $d = 0.46$ and Cohen's $d = 0.59$.

The mean of aggregated response times per participant for simple UIPPs was 4.25 s ($SD = 2.27$ s), for simple manufacturer pictograms 3.78 s ($SD = 1.60$ s), for compound UIPPs 8.08 s ($SD = 2.66$ s), and for compound manufacturer pictograms 6.43 s ($SD = 2.53$ s). Paired samples t-tests showed that log-transformed RTs for simple and for compound UIPPs were significantly higher than for manufacturer pictograms, $t(100) = 20.21$, $p < .001$ and $t(100) = 12.84$, $p < .001$. This suggests for both a *large* effect, Cohen's $d = 2.01$ and Cohen's $d = 1.28$.

Pearson correlational analyses and multiple regression analyses were conducted to analyze interactions between age, pictogram experience, heating interface experience, and simple or compound UIPPs and manufacturer pictograms (CRs and RTs) respectively. A negative correlation was revealed between age and pictogram experience, $r(99) = -.25$, $p = .01$. In addition, pictogram experience was positively correlated with education, $r(99) = .31$, $p = .001$. A positive correlation was revealed between log-transformed age and total aggregated response times (RTs), $r(99) = .44$, $p < .001$. All response times were significantly related to age (see "Appendix N"). Although total correct responses correlated with age, $r(99) = -.3$, $p = .002$, only correlation between age and CRs for UIPPs was significant, $r(99) = -.26$, $p = .01$, in contrast to correlation between age and CRs for manufacturer pictograms, $r(99) = -.14$, $p = .169$.

Linear regression analysis to predict CRs for simple UIPPs showed that only education ($\beta = .21$, $p = .032$) made a significant improvement to the ability of the model, with age not being significant ($\beta = -.19$, $p = .057$). However, both variables accounted only for 8% of the variance within the outcome variable ($R^2 = .084$, $F(2,98) = 4.5$, $p = .014$).

A two-way repeated measures analysis of variance of CRs for pictogram set (UIPP vs. manufacturer) and complexity (simple vs. compound) was conducted with age as a covariate. The ANOVA within subjects effects table showed that there are significant main effects for pictogram set and for complexity both with *medium to large* effects ($F(1,99)=11.71$, $p<.001$, $\eta_p^2=.106$; $F(1,99)=13.86$, $p<.001$, $\eta_p^2=.123$) if adjusted for age. Although there was a statistically significant effect of age ($F(1,99)=10.06$, $p=.002$, $\eta_p^2=.092$), there was no significant interaction between neither pictogram set and age nor complexity and age, $F(1,99)=0.97$, $p=.327$ and $F(1,99)=2.14$, $p=.146$. Main effects were not qualified by an interaction between pictogram set and complexity, $F(1,99)=0.19$, $p=.665$.

A second two-way repeated measures analysis of variance of CRs for pictogram set (UIPP vs. manufacturer) and complexity (simple vs. compound) with age as a covariate and educational level as a between subjects factor revealed that there were significant interactions between complexity and education ($F(3,96)=2.99$, $p=.035$, $\eta_p^2=.085$) and between complexity and age ($F(1,96)=4.38$, $p=.039$, $\eta_p^2=.044$) irrespective of pictogram set. Age ($F(1,96)=15.02$, $p<.001$, $\eta_p^2=.135$) and education ($F(3,96)=4.50$, $p=.005$, $\eta_p^2=.123$) had significant *almost large* effects.

Finally, a two-way repeated measures analysis of variance of log-transformed RTs for pictogram set and complexity was conducted with age as a covariate. The ANOVA within subjects effects table shows that there is no significant main effect for pictogram set if adjusted for age ($F(1,99)=0.32$, $p=.57$) but a significant *medium* sized effect for complexity ($F(1,99)=7.70$, $p=.007$, $\eta_p^2=.072$). Age interacted significantly with pictogram set and with complexity, $F(1,99)=8.87$, $p=.004$, $\eta_p^2=.082$ and $F(1,99)=11.62$, $p<.001$, $\eta_p^2=.105$. Age had a significant effect, $F(1,99)=23.92$, $p<.001$, $\eta_p^2=.195$. Main effects were not qualified by an interaction between pictogram set and complexity, $F(1,99)=1.50$, $p=.224$.

Discussion

Almost all, that is, 90%, of UIP Pictograms were confirmed. Most, that is, 72.2%, had CRs above 86%, thus, are suitable as safety symbols, according to ISO 9186:3 (International Organization for Standardization 2014). In addition, correct response rates for UIPPs were significantly higher than for established manufacturer pictograms with a medium-sized effect. This was the case for simple and for compound UIP Pictograms.

An inspection of an UIP Pictogram with CRs below 66% revealed that answer options were misleading. Forty-two point two per cent of the participants chose an alternate answer that had almost an identical meaning to the correct answer. Both answers together account for 96.1%. This suggests that the pictogram might have been confirmed with more distinct answer options. In that case, 95% of UIPPs would have been confirmed of which 73.7% would have been confirmed as safety symbols. In addition, effect size of difference between correct response rates of UIPPs and manufacturer pictograms would further increase.

Response times are important. They can be an indicator of task difficulty because easy tasks are expected to require fewer mental transformations which result in faster task completion (Tversky et al. 2006, p. 5). However, RTs should be handled with care. It is a noisy variable that needs a large number of trials to gain exact results (Rubinstein 2013, p. 540). Robinson (2007) suggested that this is due to momentary states of the mind. These momentary states are important for response times, but they are unstable. The problem increases because of two reasons. First, the exact setups and circumstances of the experiment in the homes of the participants and the attention given to the test by the participants were not controlled. Consequently, the accuracy of the collected response times cannot be guaranteed although the aggregated forwarding times of each participant's apparatus were subtracted from the individual response times. Second, most UIP Pictograms are animated. For that reason, it must be assumed that the duration of the animations influenced the response times. However, it is not clear how to consider the duration of the animations. Subtracting the duration of the animations from the aggregated response times seemed not an option because it might have distorted the results. For example, some animations of UIPPs are rather long, and participants might have been able to comprehend these pictograms before the end of the animation (e.g., in case of *[warmth] is dangerous*). In contrast, other animations are short loops that appear to run continuously, for example, *[coldness] is good, positive*. In that case, multiple loops might have occurred before participants comprehended the pictogram. In addition, the duration of the animation of some pictograms does not seem to have influenced their RTs, for example, in case of the UIP Pictogram for *[power] is decreasing*. The animation of that pictogram takes 4.8 s. Nevertheless, aggregated response times with the pictogram (6.73 s) were much shorter than for the manufacturer pictogram (8.02 s). Nevertheless, all response times were in the cognitive band, according to Newell (1994, pp. 121–123, 131–139). Although RTs with all UIPPs were longer than with manufacturer pictograms with a large effect, if adjusted for participant's age, no significant effect was revealed. Consequently, H1 was partially confirmed because CRs for UIP Pictograms were higher than for manufacturer pictograms, and there was no significant difference between RTs for UIPPs and for manufacturer pictograms.

H2 was confirmed because CRs for simple pictograms were significantly higher than for compound pictograms in both sets, and RTs were significantly shorter. Age had a significant effect on the difference between RTs for simple and for compound pictogram sets but not on the difference between CRs. This indicates that both are equally comprehended, but compound pictograms take longer to be interpreted with increasing age.

H3 was partially confirmed because UIPP CRs and RTs were not correlated with gender, education, pictogram experience, or heating interface experience but with age. Although age had significant effects on both CRs and RTs, age significantly affected only the differences between RTs for UIPPs and manufacturer pictograms. It did not significantly affect the difference between CRs for UIPPs and manufacturer pictograms. As stated above, this indicates that UIPPs are more successfully comprehended than manufacturer pictograms, independent of age. At the same time, there is no significant difference between RTs if adjusted for age. On the one hand, this is in line with previous studies on intuitive and inclusive design

(Blackler et al. 2012, p. 575). Since physical and cognitive abilities decrease with age (Park and Schwarz 2000), elderly people might have longer response times because they take longer to interpret the pictogram and to click on the correct answer option. On the other hand, various studies suggest that practice or experience, thus, familiarity is a predictor of response times (Robinson 2007, p. 20). Familiarity leads to better cognitive and motor performances (Lee et al. 2014). At the same time, if participants are less confident because of missing practice, they take longer to answer (Lasry et al. 2013, p. 703). Especially abstract and conventional representations benefit from this effect (Goonetilleke et al. 2001, pp. 757–758; Schröder and Ziefle 2008, p. 90). In Study 3, participants were not familiar with UIP Pictograms. Consequently, longer RTs might have been related to a lack of familiarity and missing confidence with UIPPs (in addition to the duration of the animations of the UIP Pictograms, as discussed above). At the same time, it might be assumed that participants were familiar with the established manufacturer pictograms, as indicated by the results of Study 3.3—in contrast to their self-reported low experience with heating interfaces. The self-reported level of experience with pictograms was high. RTs might have been shorter and CRs even higher if participants had a short period of training with UIPPs, and UIPPs would still qualify for intuitive use, as long as the participants are able to interpret the pictograms without direct instruction (see Sect. "Defining intuitive use: prior knowledge and automatic processing"). Studies 3.2 and 3.3 provide further insights into these findings. However, neither age nor experience affected that UIPPs were more successfully comprehended than the established pictograms.

Finally, if adjusted for age, education level affected the difference of CRs between simple and compound pictograms. At the same time, neither pictogram experience, nor age or education interacted with the difference between CRs for UIPPs and for manufacturer pictograms. If we assume that educational levels are related to cognitive abilities and cognitive abilities affect pictogram interpretation (Leontieva et al. 2008), then, this is in line with the discussion above. However, in the study, education and experience levels were not normally distributed.

Study 3.2: Direct Comparison

In Study 3.2, an approach used, for example, by Hurtienne (2011, Chapters 5–6), Löffler (2017, Chapter 5), and Hurtienne et al. (2015) to compare directly image schema instantiations was adapted to compare directly the perceived suitability of UIPPs and manufacturer pictograms.

Hypotheses

The following hypothesis was made:

H1: Suitability ratings are higher than the neutral average in favor of UIP Pictograms.

Method

Participants
Participants were the same as in Study 3.1.

Materials
Apparatus, instructional page, and demographic and experience questionnaires were the same as in Study 3.1, except that participants were asked to rate suitability on a Likert-type scale. Furthermore, the participants could take as long as they wanted. All materials were presented in German. In the following, they are translated into English where appropriate.

Stimuli
Stimuli consisted of 42 pictograms, that is, 21 UIP Pictograms and 21 manufacturer pictograms. Of each set, nine were simple and 12 were compound pictograms. Stimuli included a bipolar 7-point Likert-type scale that ranged from +++ to *** and the pictogram meaning. UIPPs were always left. Higher ratings for UIPP resulted in a higher Likert-type score. Higher ratings for manufacturer pictograms in a lower score. Stimuli were presented as in Fig. 23.

Design
As in Study 3.1, gender, experience with pictograms, and experience with heating interfaces were considered categorial independent between-subjects variables. Age was raised as an independent continuous control variable. Meaning complexity (simple vs. compound) was manipulated as an independent within-subject variable. One dependent variable was collected: Likert-type scale rating with +++=7, ++=6, +=5, 0=4, *=3, **=2, *=1. The rating of 4 indicated a neutral judgment. All effects were reported as significant at $p < .05$. Since the study

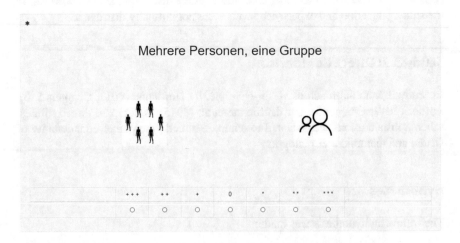

Fig. 23 Study 3.2 presentation of UIPPs and manufacturer pictograms for *several or a group of [people]*

was conducted in the same session as Study 3.1, the results of both studies can be related to each other (MacKenzie 2013, pp. 175–177).

Procedure
Study 3.2 was conducted in the same session as Study 3.1, after Study 3.1. Consequently, it was expected that participants would be more familiar with UIP Pictograms after concluding Study 3.1. Thus, effects of familiarity would be reduced. Participant instruction procedure and demographic questionnaire were the same as in Study 3.1. Participants were asked to rate which of two presented pictograms represented best in their opinion the meaning that was also presented. Participants were successively presented with the pictograms that were introduced in Presentation of the Design System and of the Pictogram Prototypes and Presentation of the Manufacturer Pictograms. The presentation was randomized. Scale ratings were collected. The test took about 3:30 min.

Pretests
Pretests were the same as in Study 3.1.

Reliability
A test–retest reliability test was performed, as described in Study 3.1, with the same participants. The test had a significant test–retest reliability: Kendall's $\tau = .61$, $p < .001$ (Pearson's $r = .73$, p < .001). The reliability is considered *strong* (Akoglu 2018, p. 92; Dancey and Reidy 2017, pp. 181–189).

Data Selection, Cleaning, and Reduction
Data selection, cleaning, and reduction were carried out as described in Study 3.1. The same participants were excluded as in Study 3.1.

Results

Data analysis was conducted using JASP Version 0.10.2 (JASP Team 2019) and Microsoft Excel 365 Version 1906 (Microsoft Corporation 2019).

Comparison of UIPP *[Something or Someone] is Busy* Versions
Again, two versions of UIPP *[something or someone] is busy* (see Figs. 30 and 31) were included to determine which version is better suited. Version A was presented on the left side (see "Appendix O"). Version A was rated lower than Version B, $Mdn = 3$, $IQR = 3$. A one-sample Wilcoxon signed-rank test showed that this was significantly below the neutral average of 4, $p = .004$, *Hodges-Lehmann Estimate* $= -0.50$, *Rank-Biserial Correlation* $= -0.51$. However, a Wilcoxon matched pairs signed-ranks test of both ratings for Version A and B in comparison with manufacturer pictograms did not reveal a significant difference, $p = .252$. Following Study 3.1 where Version B showed shorter RTs, Version B was considered more suitable and used in the analysis where possible.

UIP Pictograms and Manufacturer Pictograms Comparisons

The median of all pictogram comparisons per participant was 3, $IQR = 2$. A one-sample Wilcoxon signed-rank test showed that this was significantly below the neutral average of 4, $p < .001$, *Hodges-Lehmann Estimate* $= -1.50$, *Rank-Biserial Correlation* $= -0.76$. However, a one-sample Wilcoxon signed-rank test of ratings per pictogram was not significant, $p = .368$ (see "Appendix P"). The median of all simple pictogram comparisons was 4, $IQR = 2$. A one-sample Wilcoxon signed-rank test showed that this did not differ significantly from the neutral average of 4, $p = .255$. For compound pictogram comparisons median was 3, $IQR = 2$. This differed significantly from the neutral average, $p < .001$, *Hodges-Lehmann Estimate* $= -1.25$, *Rank-Biserial Correlation* $= -0.65$. See Fig. 24 for a comparison chart of UIPPs and manufacturer pictograms and "Appendix P" for median rank values and *IQRs* per direct pictogram comparison:

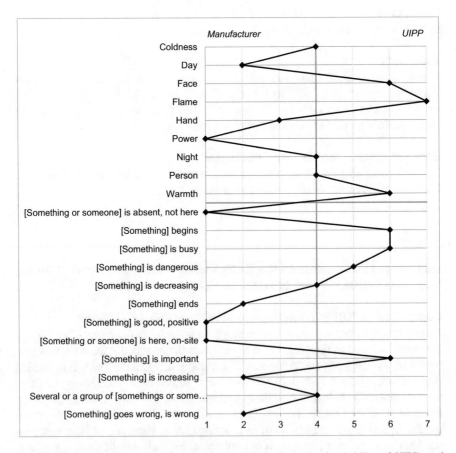

Fig. 24 Chart of median ratings for direct comparison of perceived suitability of UIPPs and manufacturer pictogram

Correlational analyses revealed that ratings of simple pictograms were negatively correlated with pictogram experience, $\kappa(99) = -.19, p = .027$.

Correlational analyses with data from Study 3.1 that was collected in the same session showed that median ratings per participant were negatively correlated with total manufacturer CRs, $\kappa(99) = -.25, p = .002$.

Discussion

Ratings per participant were below the neutral average. Although comparisons per pictogram were not significantly below average, this indicates that UIPPs were perceived as less suitable than the manufacturer set. Consequently, H1 was rejected.

Ratings were negatively correlated with pictogram experience and with manufacturer CRs. This indicates that participants preferred established manufacturer pictograms if they were more experienced, that is, familiar with pictograms. This contrasts with their self-reported level of experience with heating system user interfaces, which was low. I argue, this indicates either that participants did not evaluate correctly their experience with heating system user interfaces, or that the manufacturer pictograms are representative of established pictograms in general. Participants might have not been familiar with manufacturer pictograms because of experience with heating system user interfaces but because of general experience with pictograms. This is in line with Study 3.3 in which participants rated perceived familiarity of manufacturer pictograms high while, at the same time, self-reporting that their level of experience with heating system user interfaces was low. Furthermore, this indicates that participants preferred manufacturer pictograms if participants were more successful in interpreting these pictograms. This is in line with Study 3.1 and with previous research (see, e.g., Raskin 1994, p. 18). In contrast, the ratings did not represent correctly the significantly higher CRs for UIPPs in Study 3.1. I argue, this indicates that participants do not rate correctly the suitability of pictograms if they are asked for their subjective judgment. This is in line with the criticisms that were raised against subjective measures of intuitive use (see Sect. "Subjective Measures of Intuitive Use").

As predicted by the UIPP design team during the design production process (see Sect. "Discussion of the Design Production Process"), ratings of UIP Pictogram *power* were low. During the production process, the design team discussed whether the contents *a big, muscular man* or *a male arm with flexing biceps* might be less suitable for the meaning *power* in the context of use of a heating system user interface than the content *lightning bolt*. In Study 1 and 2, contents were derived and evaluated without informing participants about a specific context of use. However, the designers decided to use the content *a male arm with flexing biceps* in order to aim for universal use of the pictograms. This might have been a disadvantage because in Study 3 participants were informed about the context of use. Consequently, a retest was conducted in Study 3.4.

Study 3.3: Subjective Ratings

In Study 3.3, an approach was used that was developed and applied by McDougall, Isherwood, and colleagues on various occasions (Isherwood 2009; Isherwood et al. 2007; McDougall et al. 2000, 2009). In 2000, they stated that there was a lack of appropriate measures for pictograms, thus, of generalizable results, despite the importance of pictograms in HCI (McDougall et al. 2000, p. 291). Subsequently, they identified and described characteristics that are central to pictogram comprehensibility and usability. While most other studies analyzed one or two characteristics, Isherwood and McDougall examined up to six: concreteness, distinctiveness, visual complexity, familiarity, semantic distance, and appeal. In addition, they did not analyze the effect of each characteristic independently but the interactions between the characteristics. I summarize the characteristics in the following, except appeal, which is not addressed in UIPP.

Concreteness "is the extent to which [the pictogram] depicts real objects, materials, or people" (Isherwood et al. 2007, p. 466). With concrete pictograms, the relation with real-world objects should be evident and an interpreter should be able to apply everyday knowledge. This is in line with my definition of similarity with the real world. As discussed in Sects. "Conceptualizing the Relations of Design and of Reference" and "Basic Requirements for a Universal, Intuitive, and Permanent Design System", similarity with the real world is an important goal of UIPP because more similarity with the real world seems to facilitate more universal, intuitive, and permanent pictograms (Schröder and Ziefle 2008, p. 90).

Distinctiveness, too, was addressed in the design of the UIP Pictograms (see Guidelines 14 and 20 in Sect. "How to Design General Aspects of Visual Representations (G13–G21)"). Distinctiveness addresses how easily pictograms are recognized among others. Distinct pictograms are less easily confused. Distinctiveness is important for users in the selection of the correct pictogram (McDougall et al. 2000, p. 292). In UIPP, besides distinctiveness, un-ambiguity is central because ambiguous pictograms allow more than one interpretation (Gatsou et al. 2012, p. 96).

Visual complexity addresses how many details and forms are present in a pictogram, that is, "the number of lines, letters, and simple shapes an icon contains" (Isherwood et al. 2007, p. 466). Usually, less complex pictograms are easier to identify, and more complex pictograms come with longer response times (Schröder and Ziefle 2008, p. 90). This is in line with Guideline 15 in Sect. "How to Design General Aspects of Visual Representations (G13–G21)", too. According to Curry et al. (1998, pp. 1291–1292), visual complexity is not related to concreteness.

According to Isherwood and McDougall, familiarity addresses, on the one hand, frequency of use of pictograms, that is, experience with a pictogram and, on the other hand, experience with the represented object or meaning. I have discussed familiarity in length in Sect. "Definitions of Intuitiveness in HCI". Familiarity allows for faster access to long-term memory (Ralph et al. 1998), and it improves pictogram recognition. Studies have shown that the positive effect of concreteness and the negative effect of complexity decrease with pictogram familiarity (Forsythe et al. 2008, pp. 116–117, 127; Schröder and Ziefle 2008, p. 90).

Semantic distance is "the closeness of relationship between the icon and the function it represents" (Isherwood et al. 2007, p. 467). McDougall, Isherwood, and colleagues argued that not only pictogram concreteness is crucial for pictogram comprehension but the "conceptual mapping between icon and function" (Isherwood et al. 2007, p. 474). I argue that this is in line with my discussion of the reference relation (see Sect. "Conceptualizing the Relations of Design and of Reference"). However, Isherwood et al. did not specify further what semantic distance is, and they did not distinguish between the relations of reference and of design.

In order to assess UIPPs and manufacturer pictograms, in Study 3.3, the described characteristics were adapted, and two characteristics were added, following Hurtienne et al. (2015, pp. 246–248): intuitiveness and innovativeness. Intuitiveness was operationalized as perceived intuitiveness, based on QUESI (Questionnaire for the subjective consequences of intuitive use), thus, addressing low subjective mental workload, high perceived achievement of goals, low perceived effort of learning, and low perceived error rate (Naumann and Hurtienne 2010, p. 401). Perceived innovativeness was assessed based on the AttrakDiff2 questionnaire (Hassenzahl et al. 2003).

Following McDougall et al. (2000, pp. 296, 305) and Hurtienne et al. (2015, pp. 246–248), subjective ratings by the participants were collected. Six items were developed to evaluate six pictogram characteristics: ambiguity (distinctiveness), complexity, familiarity, suitability (semantic distance), intuitiveness, and innovativeness (see Sect. "Stimuli"). Concreteness was not evaluated because it is the basis of UIPP. Distinctiveness was operationalized with an emphasis on ambiguity. While familiarity was evaluated as described by Isherwood et al. (2007, p. 466), complexity was assessed with an emphasis on the design relation, not on meaning because an emphasis on meanings would address the reference relation. Semantic distance was assessed with an emphasis on a global judgment on suitability (Hurtienne et al. 2015, p. 247). Intuitiveness was assessed using usability magnitude estimation (UME) (McGee 2004). Sauro and Dumas (2009) considered UEM approximately as useful as SMEQ (Subjective Mental Effort Question) or SEA (in German: Skala zur Erfassung von subjektiv erlebter Anstrengung) which were proposed by Hurtienne and Blessing (2007, pp. 6–7) and Wegerich et al. (2012, pp. 9–11). Innovativeness was evaluated by using one item of the AttrakDiff2 questionnaire that refers to said characteristic (Hassenzahl et al. 2003, p. 192).

Hypotheses

Based on previous discussions, reviews, and findings in UIPP, the following hypotheses were made:

H1:   Suitability, intuitiveness, un-ambiguity, un-complexity, and innovativeness rat-
      ings for UIPPs are above the neutral level and familiarity ratings are below.
H2:   Suitability ratings for UIPPs are higher than for manufacturer pictograms, as
      are intuitiveness, un-ambiguity, un-complexity, and innovativeness ratings.
      Familiarity ratings for UIPPs are below familiarity ratings for manufacturer
      pictograms.
H3:   Ratings of suitability are positively correlated with familiarity ratings.
H4:   Simple pictograms are rated higher than compound pictograms with regard
      to intuitiveness, un-ambiguity, and un-complexity.
H5:   There is no significant interaction between age, education, pictogram experi-
      ence, or heating interface experience and ratings.

Method

Participants
Sample size was calculated as described in Study 3.1. Ninety-five participants were included in the study ($n = 95$), ranging in age from 19 to 72 years
($M = 38.01$, $SD = 13.43$). Participants were 51.6% female, 48.4% male, none
stated *diverse* as gender. Educational level was high, $Mdn = 3$, $IQR = 1$.
Experience with pictograms was high, too, $Mdn = 4$, $IQR = 1$. In contrast, experience with heating interfaces was low, $Mdn = 1$, $IQR = 2$. Similar to Studies 3.1 and
3.2, the distributions were skewed and not normally distributed (see "Appendix Q"
for bar graphs). Participants were either registered on the crowdsourcing website
as living in Austria, Germany, or Switzerland or addressed by the newsletter to
German university degree holders. Additional criteria were German as a first language and normal or corrected-to-normal vision. Participants were recruited and
remunerated as described in Study 3.1.

Materials
Apparatus, instructional page, and demographic and experience questionnaires
were the same as in Study 3.1 and 3.2 except that participants were asked to rate
pictograms on Likert-type scales and that the participants could take as long as
they wanted. All materials were presented in German. In the following, they are
translated into English where appropriate.

Stimuli
Stimuli consisted of 37 pictograms, 19 UIP Pictograms and 18 manufacturer
pictograms. Of UIPPs, 5 were simple and 14 were compound. Of manufacturer
pictograms, 5 were simple and 13 were compound. Manufacturer pictograms
were presented with their original meanings (see Sect. "Presentation of the
Manufacturer Pictograms"). Stimuli were presented with six unipolar or bipolar 5-point Likert-type scales below them (see, e.g., Löffler 2017, Chapter 5,
for a similar design). The scale designs were based on the semantic differential technique (SDT), an approach that was developed by Osgood et al. (1957).

SDT strives to ascertain the connotative meaning of objects and concepts (Stoutenborough 2008). Likert-type scales are considered apt means to examine these associations, and they are widely used in HCI (see, e.g., Hurtienne et al. 2015). The literature is inconclusive whether 7-point Likert-type scales should be used over 5-point Likert-type scales. Although 7-point scales allow for more fine-grained divisions, in this study, 5-point scales were used to reduce testing time for each participant, thus, fatigue effects (Joshi et al. 2015, pp. 398–399). Consequently, 3 indicates a neutral judgment.

Suitability was rated on a unipolar scale from *extremely well suited* to *extremely poorly suited*; intuitiveness was rated on a unipolar scale from *very slow and difficult to understand* to *very fast and easy to understand*; ambiguity on a bipolar scale from *completely unambiguous* to *completely ambiguous*; complexity unipolar from *very complex design* to *very simple design*; fifth, innovativeness from *very novel design* to *very conventionally designed*; familiarity was rated on a bipolar scale from *with this meaning already known* to *with this meaning completely unknown* (see Vagias 2006; cf. Isherwood et al. 2007).

The items' response anchors for suitability, ambiguity, and innovativeness were reversed, that is, with the positive characteristic on the left, in order to prevent inattentiveness and fatigue in the participants. Furthermore, reverse coding was applied to simplify the identification of erroneous responses. Stimuli were presented as in Fig. 25.

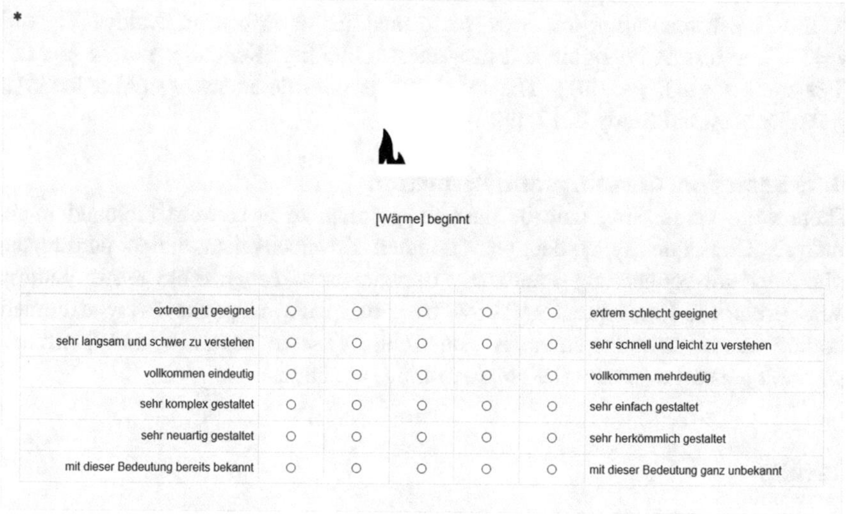

Fig. 25 Study 3.3 presentation of UIPPs and manufacturer pictograms, here, for UIPP *[warmth] begins*

Design

As in Studies 3.1 and 3.2, gender, experience with pictograms, and experience with heating interfaces were considered categorical independent between-subjects variables. Age was raised as an independent continuous control variable. Pictogram set (UIPPs vs. manufacturer pictograms) and meaning complexity (simple vs. compound) were manipulated as independent within-subject variables. Five dependent variables were collected: Likert-type scale ratings for suitability, intuitiveness, un-ambiguity, un-complexity, and familiarity. All effects were reported as significant at $p < .05$.

Procedure

Participant instruction procedure and demographic questionnaire were identical to Studies 3.1 and 3.2. However, in this study, participants were asked to rate pictograms on several scales according to the response anchors. Participants were presented successively with the pictograms that were introduced in Sections *Presentation of the Design System and of the Pictogram* Prototypes and *Presentation of the Manufacturer Pictograms*. The presentation was randomized. Scale ratings were collected. The test took about 13:30 min.

Pretests

Pretests were conducted as described in Study 3.1. Furthermore, Likert-type scale response anchors were tested and optimized through qualitative interviews.

Reliability

A test–retest reliability test was performed as described in Study 3.1 with $n = 12$. The test had a significant test–retest reliability: Kendall's $\tau = .74$, $p < .001$ (Pearson's $r = .83$, p < .001). The reliability is considered *strong* (Akoglu 2018, p. 92; Dancey and Reidy 2017, pp. 181–189).

Data Selection, Cleaning, and Reduction

There were no missing data because only complete tests were included in the analysis. Consequently, no data were imputed. Erroneous data, that is, participants who rated all connections identically or who used recognizable rating patterns were excluded. Consequently, 2.06% of participants' responses were excluded. Coding was reversed for suitability, un-ambiguity, innovativeness, and familiarity to reflect general tendency (i.e., higher ratings are better).

Results

Data analysis was conducted using jamovi Version 1.0.6 (The jamovi project 2019) and Microsoft Excel 365 Version 1906 (Microsoft Corporation 2019).

See Table 1 for median ratings for all, all simple, all compound, complete UIPP set, complete manufacturer set, simple UIPPs, compound UIPPs,

Table 1 Median ratings for suitability (SU), intuitiveness (IU), un-ambiguity (UA), un-complexity (UC), innovativeness (IO), and familiarity (FA) per participant ($n=95$)

Pictograms	SU	IU	UA	UC	IO	FA
All	4	4	4	4	3	3
All simple	5	5	4.5	5	1.5	5
All compound	4	4.5	4	5	2	4
All UIPP	4	3	3	3	4	3
Simple UIPP	4	5	4	4	2	4
Compound UIPP	3	3	3	2	4	2
All manufacturer	5	5	4	5	2	4
Simple manufacturer	5	5	5	5	1	5
Compound manufacturer	4	4	4	4.5	2	4

simple manufacturer, and compound manufacturer pictograms per participant (see "Appendix S" for ratings including *IQR*s).

See "Appendix R" for median ratings per pictogram. UIP Pictogram *power* was rated lowest of simple UIP Pictograms. Furthermore, compound UIP Pictograms that included *power* or *person* were rated lowest of compound UIP Pictograms.

One-sample Wilcoxon signed-ranks tests showed that only median ratings for UIPP un-ambiguity and un-complexity did not differ significantly from a neutral rating (see "Appendix T"). Only ratings for UIPP familiarity and manufacturer pictogram innovativeness were below the neutral rating of 3. All the others were above.

Matched-pairs Wilcoxon signed-ranks tests revealed that all ratings differed significantly between UIPPs and manufacturer pictograms for complete sets, simple, and compound pictograms. While UIPPs were rated lower than manufacturer pictograms for suitability, intuitiveness, un-ambiguity, un-complexity, and familiarity, they were rated higher for innovativeness (see "Appendix U"). Median difference for familiarity was double the median difference for suitability (*Hodges-Lehmann Estimate* $=-2$ and *Hodges-Lehmann Estimate* $=-1$).

In addition, matched-pairs Wilcoxon signed-ranks tests showed that only for un-complexity ratings simple pictograms were not significantly different from compound pictograms. Simple pictograms were rated higher for all characteristics except for familiarity where they were rated lower (see "Appendix V").

Mann-Whitney U test showed that there were significant differences between genders for suitability ratings for all pictograms ($U=1430.00$, $p=.005$, *Rank-Biserial Correlation* $=0.27$) and un-ambiguity ratings for all compound pictograms ($U=1419.50$, $p=.019$, *Rank-Biserial Correlation* $=0.26$), although medians and *IQR*s were identical in both cases: for suitability, $Mdn=4$, $IQR=0$; for un-ambiguity, $Mdn=4$, $IQR=1$.

Correlational analyses were conducted to analyze interactions between age, pictogram experience, heating interface experience, and ratings for suitability, intuitiveness, un-ambiguity, un-complexity, innovativeness, and familiarity (simple and compound UIPPs and manufacturer pictograms). For UIPPs suitability was positively correlated with intuitiveness and un-ambiguity with an *almost strong* effect (see Table 2). Suitability correlated with familiarity with a *weak* effect. Familiarity correlated significantly with all other pictogram characteristics with a *weak* effect. Only for innovativeness, the correlation was negative.

For manufacturer pictograms, all characteristic ratings correlated with each other. The effect between familiarity and suitability is *medium* sized. Familiarity correlated significantly with all other pictogram characteristics with a *medium* effect. Only for innovativeness, the correlation was negative (see Table 3).

Ordinal logistic regression analyses showed that for all simple pictograms there was a 43.3% chance ($b=-.57$, $Z=-2.63$, $p=.008$) that familiarity ratings decrease with increasing pictogram experience. The model was significant, Cox and Snell's $R^2=.010$, Nagelkerke's $R^2=.032$, $\chi^2(1)=6.71$, $p=.01$. However, as for the following models, too, the model accounted only for a low percentage of the variance within the outcome variable.

For suitability ratings for UIPPs, there was a 35% chance ($b=-.43$, $Z=-2.13$, $p=.033$) to decrease with increasing heating interface experience level while having a 65.4% chance ($b=.50$, $Z=2.33$, $p=.02$) to increase with increasing pictogram experience level (Cox and Snell's $R^2=.019$, Nagelkerke's $R^2=.050$, $\chi^2(2)=8.66$, $p=.012$).

Un-complexity ratings for manufacturer pictograms had a 99% chance ($b=.67$, $Z=2.92$, $p=.004$) to increase with pictogram experience (Cox and Snell's $R^2=.03$, Nagelkerke's $R^2=.07$, $\chi^2(1)=8.59$, $p=.003$).

Finally, for innovativeness ratings for manufacturer pictograms, there was a 50.6% chance ($b=.41$, $Z=2.03$, $p=.042$) to increase with heating interface experience while having a 45.6% chance ($b=-.61$, $Z=-2.85$, $p=.004$) to decrease with pictogram experience (Cox and Snell's $R^2=.024$, Nagelkerke's $R^2=.064$, $\chi^2(2)=11.70$, $p=.003$).

Discussion

Low ratings for UIPP compound pictograms including *power* or *person* are further explored in Study 3.4.

Familiarity ratings for manufacturer pictograms were high although self-reported experience with heating system user interfaces was low, in contrast to pictogram experience which was self-reported as high. I argue, this indicates that the established manufacturer pictograms are representative of established pictograms in general, not exclusively of heating system user interface pictograms in particular (see Sect. "Study 3.2: Direct Comparison").

Suitability, intuitiveness, and innovativeness ratings for UIPPs were above the neutral average, familiarity was below. This is in line with H1 and indicates that UIPPs were considered suitable and intuitive by participants, although the pictograms were new, and the participants were not familiar with them. However,

Table 2 Kendall's τ correlations for characteristics ratings for complete UIPP set ($n = 95$)

		Suitability	Intuitiveness	Un-ambiguity	Un-complexity	Innovativeness
Intuitiveness	Kendall's τ	0.64***	—			
	p-value	<.001	—			
Un-ambiguity	Kendall's τ	0.66***	0.60***	—		
	p-value	<.001	<.001	—		
Un-complexity	Kendall's τ	0.10	0.22*	0.11	—	
	p-value	.283	.015	.222	—	
Innovativeness	Kendall's τ	0.09	0.17	0.09	−0.37***	—
	p-value	.345	.059	.331	<.001	—
Familiarity	Kendall's τ	0.28**	0.26**	0.36***	0.29**	−0.19*
	p-value	.002	.003	<.001	.001	.038

Notes: *$p<.05$, **$p<.01$, ***$p<.001$

Table 3 Kendall's τ Correlations for characteristics ratings for complete manufacturer set ($n = 95$)

		Suitability	Intuitiveness	Un-ambiguity	Un-complexity	Innovativeness
Intuitiveness	Kendall's τ	0.74***	—			
	p-value	<.001	—			
Un-ambiguity	Kendall's τ	0.63***	0.68***	—		
	p-value	<.001	<.001	—		
Un-complexity	Kendall's τ	0.49***	0.53***	0.51***	—	
	p-value	<.001	<.001	<.001	—	
Innovativeness	Kendall's τ	−0.30**	−0.41***	−0.34***	−0.62***	—
	p-value	.001	<.001	<.001	<.001	—
Familiarity	Kendall's τ	0.55***	0.60***	0.48***	0.49***	−0.46***
	p-value	<.001	<.001	<.001	<.001	<.001

Notes: *$p<.05$, **$p<.01$, ***$p<.001$

un-ambiguity and un-complexity ratings did not differ significantly from the neutral level. Consequently, H1 is partially rejected.

Suitability, intuitiveness, un-ambiguity, and un-complexity ratings for UIPPs were lower than for manufacturer pictograms. Familiarity ratings were lower, too. Innovativeness ratings were higher. Consequently, H2 is partially rejected. UIPPs were considered more innovative but less suitable than manufacturer pictograms. The literature suggests that this could be related to familiarity with established pictograms, as discussed above. On the one hand, familiarity allows for faster access to memory and improves recognition. On the other hand, positive effects of similarity with the real world, which is the basis of UIPP, decrease with pictogram familiarity (Forsythe et al. 2008, pp. 116–117, 127; Schröder and Ziefle 2008, p. 90). This interpretation is supported by the significant positive correlation of familiarity with all other characteristic ratings, which also confirms H3. In addition, for manufacturer pictograms, correlation effects between familiarity and suitability ratings were much stronger than for UIPPs. Furthermore, the difference between ratings of familiarity for manufacturer pictograms and UIPPs was much larger than the difference between ratings of suitability, Hodges-Lehmann Estimate of median difference for the former characteristic is 2, for the latter 1. This suggests that un-familiarity with UIPPs influenced perceived suitability, but not as strongly as familiarity influenced perceived suitability in manufacturer pictograms. After all, as mentioned above, suitability ratings for UIPPs were above the neutral average.

Simple pictograms were rated higher regarding perceived intuitiveness, un-ambiguity, and un-complexity than compound pictograms, thus, H4 was confirmed.

No interaction between age and pictogram characteristics ratings was revealed. Gender had a significant effect on suitability ratings although medians and *IQR*s were identical for both genders. There was an interaction between ratings and pictogram and heating interface experience. However, the interaction was small. UIPPs were rated less suitable with increasing heating interface experience and more suitable with increasing pictogram experience. The reason could be that users who are familiar with heating interfaces prefer the established pictograms; frequent users of pictograms in general, however, seem more likely to consider UIPPs suitable in comparison to pictograms in general. This interpretation is supported by the high chance of increasing un-complexity ratings for manufacturer pictograms with increasing heating interface experience and the significant chance of decreasing innovativeness ratings for the set with increasing pictogram experience in general. If participants were more familiar with heating interfaces the manufacturer pictograms appeared less complex to them, and if they were frequent users of pictograms, in general, they considered the manufacturer pictograms less innovative. However, it must be considered that distributions of education levels, heating interface experience, and pictogram experience were skewed. Nevertheless, H5 was partially rejected.

Study 3.4: Retest

As described in Sect. "Discussion of the Design Production Process", for UIPP *power* and compound pictograms that include the said pictogram lower ratings were predicted because the content *a male arm with flexing biceps* was expected to be less suitable for the context of use of a heating system user interface than the content *lightning bolt*. Instead, it seemed more suitable for universal use of the pictogram. Since participants were informed about the context of use in Study 3, this might have been a disadvantage. This was partially confirmed in Studies 3.2 and 3.3. Furthermore, the studies revealed that compound pictograms that included *person* (i.e. *[something or someone] is absent, not here* and *[something or someone] is here, on-site*) had lower ratings, too. To determine negative effects on ratings for compound pictograms by less suited exchangeable parts and to evaluate the compound pictograms without these effects, a retest was conducted. In the retest, Studies 3.1 and 3.3 were repeated with a different simple UIP Pictogram—with higher ratings—as the exchangeable part of the mentioned compound UIP Pictograms.

Hypotheses

H1: CRs are higher and RTs are shorter for the pictogram prototypes in this study than they were for the equivalent pictograms in Study 3.1.

H2: Suitability, intuitiveness, un-ambiguity, un-complexity, and innovativeness ratings are higher for the pictogram prototypes in this study than they were for the equivalent pictograms in Study 3.3.

Method

Participants

Twenty-eight participants were included in the study ($n=28$), ranging in age from 25 to 62 years ($M=40.00$, $SD=10.77$). Participants were 46.4% female, 53.6% male, none stated *diverse* as gender. Median of educational level was 3 ($IQR=1$). Median of experience with pictograms was 3 ($IQR=1$), and median of experience with heating interfaces was 1 ($IQR=2$). Demographics were not normally distributed. Only participants who were registered on the crowdsourcing website as living in Austria, Germany, or Switzerland and with German as a first language were included. An additional criterion was normal or corrected-to-normal vision. Participants were recruited and remunerated as described in Study 3.1.

Materials

Materials were as described in Studies 3.1 and 3.3, except that the following pictograms were included with UIPP *warmth* as the exchangeable part of the compound pictogram (Figs. 26, 27, 28, 29 and 30).

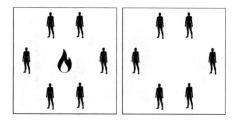

Fig. 26 Pictogram meanings: *[warmth] is absent, not here*. The first frame is presented for 1000 ms, the second for 4500 ms

Fig. 27 Pictogram meanings: *[warmth] is bad or negative*. The first frame is presented for 1250 ms, the second for 1150 ms

Fig. 28 Pictogram meanings: *[warmth] is decreasing*. All frames are presented for 600 ms except the last frame which is empty. It is presented for 1200 ms

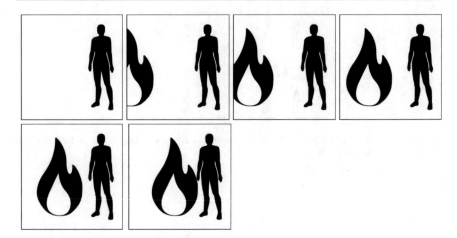

Fig. 29 Pictogram meanings: *[warmth] is here or on-site*. The first frame is presented for 800 ms, the following for 400 ms, and the last frame for 4500 ms

Fig. 30 Pictogram meanings: *[warmth] goes wrong or is wrong*. The first frame is presented for 450 ms, the last for 650 ms. All other frames are presented for 350 ms

Design
Design was as in Studies 3.1 and 3.3.

Procedure
Procedure was as in Studies 3.1 and 3.3. Both tests were conducted in the same session by each participant.

Data selection, cleaning, and reduction
Data selection, cleaning, and reduction were conducted as described in Study 3.1. All participants' responses were included in the analysis.

Table 4 Correct responses (CRs) in percent and response times (RTs) in seconds for UIP Pictograms with *warmth* vs. with *power* or *person*

Correct response rates	Warmth	Power or person
[Something or someone] is absent or not here	35.7	53.9[pe]
[Something] is bad or negative	78.6	67.6[po]
[Something] is decreasing	92.9	86.3[po]
[Something or someone] is here or on-site	78.6	94.1[pe]
[Something] goes wrong or is wrong	89.3	86.3[po]
Response times		
[Something or someone] is absent or not here	10.44	10.52[pe]
[Something] is bad or negative	6.38	10.27[po]
[Something] is decreasing	5.34	6.73[po]
[Something or someone] is here or on-site	9.01	11.46[pe]
[Something] goes wrong or is wrong	7.35	8.87[po]

Notes: [po] = power, [pe] = person

Results

Data analysis was conducted using JASP Version 0.10.2 (JASP Team, 2019) and Microsoft Excel 365 Version 1906 (Microsoft Corporation, 2019).

Table 4 presents CRs and RTs per pictogram. While mean CRs for pictograms with *warmth* were lower than for equivalent pictograms with *person*, mean CRs for pictograms with *warmth* instead of *power* were higher (Fig. 31). Mean RTs in both cases were shorter (Fig. 32).

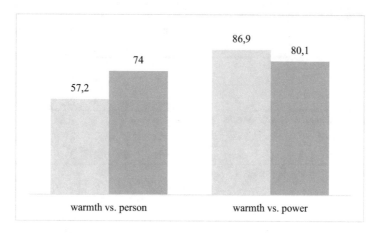

Fig. 31 Mean CRs in percent for pictograms with *warmth* vs. with *power* or *person*

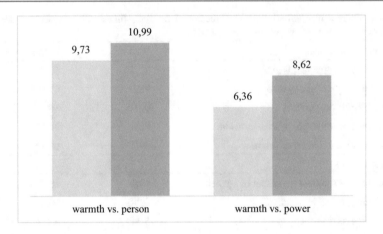

Fig. 32 Mean RTs in seconds for pictograms with *warmth* vs. with *power* or *person*

Table 5 presents characteristic ratings per pictogram.

A matched-pairs Wilcoxon signed-ranks test showed that all characteristic ratings for pictograms with *warmth* were significantly higher than for pictograms with *power* or *person*, $W = 277.00$, $p = .007$, *Hodges-Lehmann Estimate* $= 1$, *Rank-Biserial Correlation* $= 0.58$.

Table 5 Median ratings for pictogram characteristics

Pictogram		SU	IU	UA	UC	IO	FA
[Something or someone] is absent, not here							
	Warmth	3	3	2.5	3	3	1.5
	Person	2	2	2	2	4	2
[Something] is bad, negative							
	Warmth	3	3	3	3	3	2.5
	Power	2	2	2	2	4	1
[Something] is decreasing							
	Warmth	4	4	4	4	3	3
	Power	3	3	3	2	4	2
[Something or someone] is here, on-site							
	Warmth	2	2	2	3	3	2
	Person	2	2	2	2	4	2
[Something] goes wrong, is wrong							
	Warmth	3	3	3	4	3	3
	Power	2	2	2	2	5	1

Notes: SU = suitability, IU = intuitiveness, UA = un-ambiguity, UC = un-complexity, IO = innovativeness, FA = familiarity

Discussion

CRs were higher for compound pictograms with *warmth* instead of *power*, but they were lower with *warmth* instead of *person*. Consequently, H1 was partially rejected. RTs are shorter for all pictograms with *warmth*, thus, H2 was confirmed. H3 was confirmed, too, because all characteristic ratings were higher for compound pictograms with *warmth* instead of *power* or *person*.

The analyses show that compound pictograms with *warmth* as the exchangeable part are better than pictograms with *power* as the exchangeable part. This indicates that UIPP *power* is less suited for the context of use of a heating system user interface, as it was predicted in Sect. "Discussion of the Design Production Process". However, UIPP *power* as a simple pictogram had high CRs and ratings (see Sects. "Results" and "Results"), indicating that it is suitable for universal use.

Since CRs for *[something or someone] is here, on-site* were high in both cases, and CRs could not be improved with *warmth* instead of *person*, I conclude that the UIP Pictogram *[something or someone] is absent, not here* is not suitable and needs improvement. Improved characteristic ratings for both compound pictograms with *warmth* could result from higher ratings for *warmth* compared to *person* (see, e.g., Sect. "Results").

General Discussion and Conclusion

Let me summarize. Up to 95% of UIP Pictograms were confirmed, 73.7% as safety symbols, according to ISO 9186:3 (International Organization for Standardization 2014). UIPPs had significantly higher comprehension rates than the manufacturer pictograms with a medium-sized effect. This was the case for simple and for compound UIP Pictograms. In addition, no significant difference was revealed between response times if adjusted for participant's age. This holds although UIPPs were animated, and although participants were familiar with the established manufacturer pictograms but not with UIPPs. Previous research showed that familiarity has an important influence on success and speed of human–computer interaction in general and of pictogram comprehension in particular (see Sect. "Definitions of Intuitiveness in HCI", Lasry et al. 2013, p. 703; Lee et al. 2014; Miller and Stanney 1997, p. 129; Pappachan and Ziefle 2008, p. 336; Schröder and Ziefle 2008, p. 90, and so forth). With increasing familiarity, correct response rates increase, and response times shorten. On the one hand, this suggests that CRs might further increase and RTs shorten if participants become familiar with UIPPs. On the other hand, UIPPs had already higher CRs than manufacturer pictograms and equally short RTs despite being new and despite being animated. I consider this evidence that UIPPs are more suitable than established manufacturer pictograms.

The reason for this, I argue, is that the UIP Pictograms are grounded in embodied cognition and visual perception. In the UIPP process, pictogram contents were derived from universal sensorimotor experiences with the intention to achieve universal, intuitive, and permanent semantic association (see "Step 3: Grounding, Deriving, and Evaluating Pictogram Contents"). In addition, guidelines for content design were derived from principles of visual perception to develop a universal, intuitive, and permanent design system (Step 4). Since UIPPs were new, study participants could only interpret them based on universal sensorimotor experiences and on the principles of visual perception, not based on prior experience with the pictograms. Although the evaluation studies in this chapter were not conducted cross-culturally, I contend, this suggests that UIPPs might yield similar results in other cultures and on other continents. This is so because the pictograms were not designed for a specific culture. Instead, participants from other cultures might use the same universal experiences and principles that the participants used in Study 3. Consequently, I hold that the UIP Pictograms might be universally comprehensible.

Furthermore, as mentioned above, Study 3.1 showed that UIPPs had higher comprehension rates than the manufacturer pictograms and equally short response times. RTs for both were in the cognitive band (see Sect. "Discussion"). This holds although UIPPs were animated, and participants were not familiar with UIPPs but with manufacturer pictograms. On the one hand, I assume that CRs for UIPPs might further increase and RTs might shorten if participants were familiar with UIPPs. On the other hand, equally long RTs still qualify UIPPs for intuitive use because a short period of training is acceptable as long as the participants are able to interpret the pictograms without direct instruction (Löffler et al. 2013, p. 1). Since participants were able to interpret the UIP Pictograms without instruction, that is, exclusively based on previous sensorimotor experiences and on principles of visual perception, I suggest that UIPPs are intuitively comprehensible (see Sect. "Definitions of Intuitiveness in HCI").

Permanent comprehensibility, of course, was not examined in the studies. However, again, the UIPP contents as much as the design system might be considered permanent because they are based on sensorimotor experiences and on principles of visual perception that are considered permanent. Consequently, I argue that the UIP Pictogram prototypes might be permanently comprehensible, too. In conclusion, I suggest that UIPPs are as universally, intuitively, and permanently comprehensible as possible—considering the context of this project.

In contrast to research on image schemata (cf. Hurtienne 2017, p. 9), in the UIPP project, it was confirmed that age affects the ability to interpret pictograms (Schröder and Ziefle 2008, p. 91). In Study 3.1, regarding UIPPs, with increasing age, CRs decreased and RTs lengthened. Furthermore, there was a significant interaction between age, education, and CRs for complex pictograms. I assume, this is because of lesser cognitive abilities. For elderly people, this is called the *cognitive decline* (Bishop et al. 2010). However, the effect was revealed for both sets, and CRs for UIPPs were still high and RTs were short with elderly people and people with lower educational levels. If we consider the capability to correctly interpret new designs related to cognitive abilities and cognitive abilities related to age (and educational levels), then, I argue, lower CRs and longer RTs cannot be avoided with new pictograms with people with lower cognitive abilities. Even if the new pictograms are universally, intuitively, and permanently comprehensible, they will have lower CRs and longer RTs than with familiar pictograms just because they are new. Consequently, I argue that this does not rule out the inclusiveness of UIPPs because an effect of lower cognitive abilities cannot be avoided, and CRs were still high and RTs were short. However, of course, this needs further investigation.

When directly compared in Study 3.2 and when subjectively rated in Study 3.3, manufacturer pictograms were rated higher than UIPPs by participants. On the one hand, these results might have been affected by low ratings of the pictogram *power*. On the other hand, this contradicts high CRs in Study 3.1. In line with results of previous studies, participants favored pictograms that they were familiar with (Goldstein and Gigerenzer 2002; Jung and Myung 2006, p. 182; Pappachan and Ziefle 2008, p. 336). I suggest, this confirms previous criticism of subjective measures that participants do not judge objectively the suitability of pictograms (Still and Still 2019, pp. 56–58). It does not suggest that manufacturer pictograms are more suitable than UIPPs. In other words, interacting with a system might be intuitive although a user might not be satisfied when interacting with that system, just because the user is not familiar with that system. These results contradict Hurtienne's (2011) definition of intuitive use as "resulting an effective and satisfying interaction using a minimum of cognitive resources" (p. 29) (see Sect. "Definitions of Intuitiveness in HCI"). Instead, the results suggest that the experience of satisfaction when using a system is less closely related to intuitive use than it is related to a user's familiarity with that system.

Finally, previous research suggested that complex meanings, for example, compound qualitative concepts, like *[coldness] is good, positive*, are more difficult to interpret than simple concepts (Löffler 2017, p. 191). This was indicated by the studies in this chapter, too. In all studies, simple pictograms that represent a single countable object or creature as their content, for example, *a snowflake* in the case of the concept *coldness* (see Sect. "Presentation of the Design System and of the Pictogram Prototypes"), were rated higher, received higher CRs, and had shorter RTs than compound pictograms.

Limitations and Future Research

As already discussed, in the studies, only German-speaking participants were recruited. This is an important drawback because the UIPP project aimed for universal, that is, cross-cultural design. Lee et al. (2014) showed that pictograms "can be interpreted very differently in different cultures. Thus, it is necessary to test symbols across countries in their development process" (p. 17). This was beyond the scope of the UIPP project. Since Study 3 consisted of four separate studies, conducting the study with participants from four continents—as in Study 1 and 2—would have exceeded the available resources. Consequently, this was not an option. Instead, the studies focused on one culture—with the intention to provide viable results as a basis for future studies (Chong 2004, pp. 301–302). However, cross-cultural evaluation studies should be conducted in the future to confirm the successful evaluation of UIPPs in multiple cultures and worldwide.

In the studies, familiarity had a strong effect on CRs, RTs, and ratings. I assume that CRs and RTs might improve further, and suitability ratings of UIPP pictograms might surpass the ratings of manufacturer pictograms if participants were equally familiar with both sets. This should be examined in the future, for example, through prior familiarization of participants with UIPPs (see International Organization for Standardization 2010, pp. 18–19, regarding long-term monitoring). In addition, since the results indicate that CRs, RTs, and suitability ratings are closely related to a user's familiarity with a system, future studies should research fast and effective ways of familiarization with HCI systems.

In addition, not all guidelines were followed in the design production process. For example, it was a technical constraint by the UCUI interface prototype that the pictograms should be black and white, or they should have more than two colors. The designers decided that UIPPs should be black and white—although this is against Guideline 22—because always including three colors in a pictogram might be against Guidelines 22 and, at the same time, against Guideline 11. Furthermore, the manufacturer pictograms are black and white, and including too many pictogram characteristics might impede precise evaluation of the characteristics (McDougall et al. 2009, p. 62).

Results indicate that UIPP are evaluated better with more educated and with younger participants, that is, people that are expected to have higher cognitive abilities. However, demographics were skewed. Future studies should assess whether the findings are confirmed if demographics are normally distributed, and they should further examine the relationship between age and comprehension (Lee et al. 2014). In general, UIPPs should be evaluated with elderly people and, in particular, with people with disabilities in order to assess the inclusiveness of the UIPP prototypes.

Studies 3.2 and 3.3 indicated that subjective measure ratings had been affected by familiarity. In line with previous criticism of subjective measures (Still and Still 2019, pp. 56–58), I argue that objective measures, for example, CRs and RTs as in Study 3.1, should be focused in future studies.

Although I argue that the developed design system was confirmed implicitly through high ratings, high CRs, and short RTs for simple pictograms, the UIPP design system should be evaluated separately in future studies. Then, evaluations should be used to reiterate and improve further the design system in additional design production processes.

In addition, comparison of *[something or someone] is busy* Versions A and B showed that designing and testing multiple pictograms with different contents that represent the same meaning would be useful to determine the most suitable pictograms (see, e.g., Cho et al. 2007). In UIPP, only one pictogram content was chosen by the designers and produced in only one version (except *[something or someone] is busy*). In future studies, prototypes should be further improved by including multiple pictogram contents and multiple design versions that are evaluated and improved iteratively.

In UIPP, meanings were taken from the UCUI project. For that reason, UIPP meanings were not identical to manufacturer pictogram meanings—although they were very similar. To guarantee complete identity for subsequent direct comparison, futures research might initiate the complete UIPP design process with meanings that are taken from established manufacturer pictograms.

Finally, although only personal computers were allowed, response times were cleaned, and participants were asked to focus on the studies, the exact setup for participants could not be controlled. A large sample was chosen to reduce noise effects (see Sect. "Data Selection, Cleaning, and Reduction"). However, future studies with more resources should consider conducting evaluation studies on-site in a controlled setting.

Summary and Conclusion of the Chapter

This chapter constitutes the fifth step in the UIPP process. The studies that I reported in this chapter evaluated the UIPP prototypes in comparison to established manufacturer pictograms. The studies were based on three evaluative approaches: comprehension testing (Study 3.1), direct comparison (Study 3.2), and subjective rating (Study 3.3). Study 3.4 was a retest. The goals were to determine whether UIPPs are better suited than manufacturer pictograms and whether UIPPs might be considered universally, intuitively, and permanently comprehensible. I hold that the evaluation was successful.

I suggest that designers, researchers, and businesses perform and adopt the presented evaluation studies in their projects. In that, I propose that they focus on Study 3.1 and, to some extent, on Study 3.3. This is so because users do not judge objectively the suitability of interaction systems. Instead, they prefer systems that they are familiar with. Since the goal of the UIPP project was to develop a process for the design of suitable pictograms, focusing on objective measures (i.e., Study 3.1) seems sufficient. However, of course, user satisfaction in general is important. Consequently, if satisfaction of users is a central goal, I suggest conducting Study 3.3, too. Nevertheless, in order to achieve user satisfaction, I propose focusing on innovative and satisfying ways of familiarization—instead of producing designs that are similar to already established design (see Sect. "Limitations and Future Research"). To produce suitable designs, I recommend using the UIPP process.

At the end of this chapter, I hold that I completed the fifth step in the UIPP human-centered design process, following ISO 9241:210 (International Organization for Standardization 2010), that is, the evaluation of the produced designs (see Fig. 33).

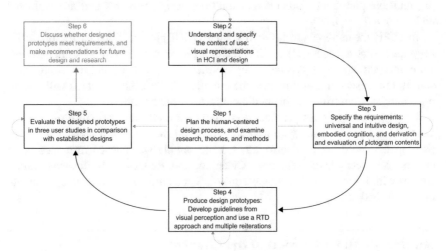

Fig. 33 The UIPP human-centered design process. Step 5 is completed. Dotted arrows indicate iterations

Step 6: Conclusion, Implications, and Future Research

Abstract

Finally, ISO 9241:210 suggests that the conformity of the designed prototypes with the previously derived requirements should be discussed, and recommendations regarding future designs and processes should be made. To that end, this final chapter summarizes the UIPP design process, it discusses drawbacks, and it proposes implications for future designs and studies. In conclusion, the chapter proposes a technical process for the design of suitable pictograms that can be adopted by by other designers, researchers, and businesses.

The UIPP project was structured as a human-centered design process, following the technical standard ISO 9241:210 (International Organization for Standardization 2010). Consequently, in the first step ("Step 1: Introduction, Goals, and Summary of the Process"), the project goals were presented, previous research was reviewed, and the process was planned.

In the second step ("Step 2: Understanding Visual Representation(s)"), the context of use was analyzed. This step usually consists in the close examination of the real situations in which existing products are used by actual users. In UIPP, the context of use was specified by the Universal Cognitive User Interface (UCUI) project as the universal use of pictograms in HCI. Consequently, in Step 2, I discussed universal characteristics of visual representations in HCI, and I described the central properties and relations that are involved in visual representation. I suggested that two relations are central: the reference relation and the design relation. The reference relation is the way in which the content of a representation refers to the intended meaning. The design relation is the way in which the content of a representation is designed. I argued that both the reference and the design relation require to be comprehensible for a visual representation to be comprehensible. Consequently, I suggest that both relations should be universally, intuitively,

D. Bühler, *Universal, Intuitive, and Permanent Pictograms*,
https://doi.org/10.1007/978-3-658-32310-3_6

and permanently comprehensible for a visual representation to be universally, intuitively, and permanently comprehensible. I completed the second step proposing a taxonomy for visual representations based on various categories of the two relations.

The third step ("Step 3: Grounding, Deriving, and Evaluating Pictogram Contents") consisted in the UIPP project's approach to the reference relation. First, I discussed general approaches to universality and intuitiveness in HCI, and I presented approaches that are suitable. These approaches are grounded in the theory of embodied cognition. Second, I presented the theory of embodied cognition, and I developed requirements for universal, intuitive, and permanent pictogram contents relying on the theory. Third, I reported two empirical studies that were conducted to derive and evaluate suitable content candidates for universal, intuitive, and permanent pictograms. In Study 1, 1,015 people in seven countries on four continents participated, and 143,446 words were collected as raw data. I conducted a two-step process to analyze the data and derived 182 content candidates. In Study 2,952 participants from the same population rated these candidates. The high degree of similarity between continents was remarkable. In conclusion, I created a comprehensive ranking of contents for subsequent design.

Step 4 ("Developing a Design System and Producing the UIP Pictograms") consisted in the UIPP approach to the design relation. First, I reviewed existing guidelines for pictogram design, and I argued that they are not appropriate. Second, I discussed the process of visual perception, and I showed that visual representations are perceived and interpreted based on the process of visual perception. Since visual perception is considered to be universal, intuitive, and permanent, I suggest that a design system for pictogram contents should be grounded in visual perception in order to be universal, intuitive, and permanent. Consequently, third, I derived guidelines for the design of pictogram contents from research on visual perception. Fourth, I reported a research through design process in which the UIP Pictogram prototypes were produced, using the guidelines. Finally, I presented the produced design system and the pictogram prototypes.

In the fifth step ("Step 5: Evaluating the UIP Pictograms"), the designed prototypes were evaluated. I conducted four separate studies consisting of comprehension tests, direct comparisons, subjective ratings, and a retest. The goals of these studies were to determine whether the UIP Pictograms are more suitable than established pictograms and whether UIPPs might be considered universal, intuitive, and permanent. The UIPP prototypes were evaluated successfully although, of course, drawbacks exist.

In the remainder of this book, that is, Step 6 ("Conclusion, Implications, and Future Research"), I discuss the drawbacks, the project goals, the implications for design, and directions for future research. In addition, I propose a technical process for the design of suitable pictograms. This is the sixth and final step of a human-centered design process, according to ISO 9241:210 (International Organization for Standardization 2010).

Conclusion and the UIPP Technical Process

In Step 1 (Sect. "Universal, Intuitive, and Permanent Pictogram Project: Two Main Goals"), I described two main goals of the UIPP project. The first goal was to produce pictograms that are as universal, intuitive, and permanent as possible—although I argued that completely universal, intuitive, and permanent comprehension is hardly achievable. The second goal was to develop a technical process for the design of suitable pictograms that might be performed and adopted by other designers, researchers, and businesses. I propose that I have achieved these goals.

First, up to 95% of UIP Pictograms were confirmed of which 73.7% were confirmed as safety symbols. UIPPs had higher comprehension rates than the manufacturer pictograms and equally short response times—despite the fact that UIPPs were animated and participants were familiar with the established manufacturer pictograms but not with UIPPs. In addition, the results suggest that CRs might increase further and RTs shorten if participants become familiar with UIPPs. Consequently, I consider the UIP Pictograms more suitable than the established manufacturer pictograms. Furthermore, since UIPPs were new, people could only interpret them based on sensorimotor experiences and principles of visual perception—not based on prior experience. Since these sensorimotor experiences and principles of visual perception are considered to be universal, I propose that UIPPs might be universal. Since the experiences and principles are applied intuitively—as suggested by RTs and CRs—I suggest that UIPPs might intuitive. Finally, since the sensorimotor experiences and principles of visual perception on which the UIPP contents and their design were based might be permanent, I suggest that the UIPP prototypes might be permanently comprehensible, too. In conclusion, I contend that the produced pictogram prototypes are as universal, intuitive, and permanent as possible—considering the context of this project.

Second, researchers have criticized that studies in HCI do not perform complete design processes and that they only provide few methods and technical processes for design, in particular when relying on embodied cognition. Instead, "there has been more work that deconstructs existing systems than (…) generates guidelines for informing the design of such systems." (Antle et al. 2009, p. 67). The UIPP project addressed these issues by including all steps of a human-centered design process from theoretical underpinnings, to requirements analyses, to the production of design prototypes, and to the subsequent evaluation of these prototypes. In addition, each step was grounded firmly in scientific theory to achieve more technical designs, and empirical data were raised to arrive at data-driven designs. Finally, theories, methods, and procedures were described and explained in detail to enable repeatability (Hemmert 2014, pp. 65–66; cf. ISO/IEC 11581–10:2010, International Organization for Standardization and International Electrotechnical Commission 2010, p. 19), drawbacks were discussed, and suggestions to adapt the process were made in the summaries of the chapters. For example, I argued that the process might be used for any required meaning, it might be used for localization instead of universal design, and it might be adapted to other representations,

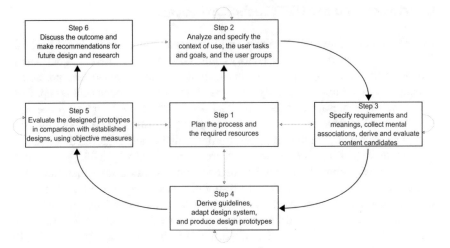

Fig. 1 The UIPP technical design process. Dotted arrows indicate iterations

for example, to auditory representations, too. These characteristics suggest that the UIPP process is viable and that it might be performed and adopted by other designers, researchers, and businesses in their specific projects. I conclude by proposing the following technical process for the design of suitable pictograms in HCI (Fig. 1 and Table 1):

In summary, I conclude that the UIPP project was a success. The UIP Pictograms are as universal, intuitive, and permanent as possible, and the UIPP technical process might be performed by other designers, researchers, and businesses to produce suitable pictograms.

Table 1 UIPP technical process for the design of suitable HCI pictograms

Step	Content	Description
1.1	Plan process	Plan the design process including the steps, studies, and production processes that need to be adapted from UIPP, for example, if specific contexts of use or specific user groups are aimed at.
1.2	Plan required resources	Calculate required time, financing, and personnel for the process. Following UIPP, at least two experimenters and two designers should be involved.
2.1	Analyze context of use, user tasks, and user goals	If the pictograms are not developed for universal use, as in UIPP, identify, describe, and analyze the intended context of use as much as the user goals and tasks. To do so, examine real situations in which existing products are used by actual users, using one of the various existing approaches (e.g., contextual inquiry, creative methods, expert evaluation, focus groups, interviews, observation, questionnaires, or think-aloud protocols).

(continued)

Table 1 (continued)

Step	Content	Description
2.2	Analyze user groups	If the pictograms are not developed for all users, independent of culture, age, and capabilities, identify, describe, and analyze the intended user groups and the specificities of the users in real situations.
3.1	Specify meanings	Specify the required pictogram meanings by deriving them from the intended context of use and from the intended user tasks and goals (Step 2.1).
3.2	Collect universal and intuitive mental associations	Follow UIPP Study 1 by conducting crowdsourced association tests and by recruiting participants in the previously specified user groups. Specify the intended context of use in the studies (Steps 2.1–2.2).
3.3	Derive content candidates	Conduct the UIPP two-step (quantitative and qualitative) analysis: Lemmatize, count, and code data into categories. Derive content candidates by using the six UIPP requirements and the proposed content taxonomy.
3.4	Evaluate content candidates	Evaluate candidates by using crowdsourced perceived suitability ratings, by recruiting participants in previously specified user groups, and by specifying the intended context of use in the evaluation studies. Present all content candidates to all participant groups.
3.5	Create ranking	Create a ranking of the evaluated content candidates, using UIPP ranking rules.
4.1	Derive guidelines	If distinct contexts of use and distinct users are aimed at than in the UIPP project (Steps 2.1–2.2) and distinct meanings were derived (Step 3.1), appropriate guidelines for pictogram content design should be derived from research on perception in that intended context (e.g., if abstract visualizations are required or pictograms are intended for use in a specific system). If resources are not available to derive guidelines, proceed to Step 4.2.
4.2	Adapt design system	If additional guidelines were derived or guidelines were adapted (Step 4.1), use these guidelines to adapt the UIPP design system. If resources to derive guidelines were not available in Step 4.1, adapt the design system based on the expert knowledge of experienced designers.
4.3	Produce design prototypes	Use the (adapted) UIPP design system (Step 4.2) and the ranking of content candidates (Step 3.5) to produce design prototypes in a parallel research through design process.
5	Evaluate prototypes	Evaluate the prototypes (Step 4.3) in comparison with established pictograms, by conducting crowdsourced comprehension tests, following UIPP Study 3.1. Participants should be recruited in the previously specified user groups, that is, the same population as in Studies 1 and 2. The intended context of use should be specified in the evaluation studies (Steps 2.1–2.2).

(continued)

Table 1 (continued)

Step	Content	Description
6.1	Discuss outcome	Discuss conformity of the produced pictograms with the requirements, the intended context of use, and the users.
6.2	Make recommendations	Make recommendations for appropriate use of the pictograms, for possible adaptions, and future improvements of the designs.
#	Refine designs	The process must include many iterations, in each step as much as between steps, to refine continuously the designed prototypes. If the result of any step is not optimal, the process should be resumed at a previous step (Steps 1–5).

Implications for Design

Besides proposing a technical process that can be performed and adopted by other designers, researchers, and businesses, I propose that the findings in UIPP might be relevant for HCI in general and for pictogram design in particular. Today, visual representations are ubiquitous. In fact, they might be the most important mode of communication and interaction, and the number of situations in which we encounter them is still growing. In addition, in the course of recent technological developments, markets have become increasingly connected just as people's lives in general. Consequently, means of interaction are required that allow for interaction between people, independent of their culture, age, and capabilities. However, there is a lack of understanding of visual representations, there is a lack of research on universal and intuitive design, and there is a lack of knowledge about how to apply scientific findings to design. By building on UIPP, I argue, not only users might profit because their interaction might be more successful, and they might be able to interact with people from all over the world. Researchers might profit because the findings of this project will contribute to research on universal and intuitive design. Finally, businesses might profit because they will be able to apply the findings to their production of more innovative and successful designs.

In addition to more specific implications that I have discussed throughout this book, I suggest the following general implications for design, building on UIPP:

1. *Research and design projects that focus on visual representations should always consider both the reference and the design relation.*
   Only if both relations are designed in suitable ways, the representation might be suitable. Consequently, the relations should not be confused, and research and design should always address both relations separately. Then, researchers and designers might be able to understand better the process of visual representation, and they might be able to improve their designs. To that end, I propose, they use my taxonomy of visual representations (Sect. "Categories of

Visual Representations") and my adapted taxonomy of pictogram contents (Sect. "Study 1.1: German-speaking Participant Group").

2. *Familiar designs should not be adhered to only because they are familiar.*
   At first, new designs might appear less suitable because they are less familiar (Raskin 1994, p. 18). However, they might be better suited, as shown in UIPP. Exclusively adhering to established designs because they are familiar might result in designs that are unsuitable to users who are not familiar with the designs. In particular, this is important with people of distinct ages and with people from distinct cultures because they might be familiar with distinct technologies or they might not have certain technologies. Thus, adhering to established designs might exclude them from interaction.

3. *Designs should be grounded in theory and scientific research, in particular in cognitive theories.*
   Humans, their physical and cognitive abilities, and their personal and cultural experiences are far too complex, and technology is developing too fast, for one person or even a group of people to have knowledge and understanding of them all. For that reason, neither design nor research should be based on personal experience or unverified assumptions. Instead, they should be based on theory and scientific research to arrive at more technical designs. In UIPP, this was addressed with regard to visual and pictogram design because guidelines in that field sometimes are vague, without empirical bases, and they might be culture specific. I suggested grounding design in scientific research on cognition, in particular, on embodied cognition, and on research on visual perception because the requirements and guidelines that I derived from scientific research led to prototypes that were evaluated superior to established pictogram designs. I propose that the approach might be fruitful to others, too.

4. *Design processes should be based on empirical data, and they should be evaluated using objective measures.*
   In UIPP, I contend, using empirical data that were collected with hundreds of participants on four different continents was one important prerequisite for the successful evaluation. In addition, in line with previous studies, UIPP has confirmed that subjective evaluations are not reliable (Still and Still 2019, pp. 56–58). Instead, objective measures that are grounded in scientific research yield more reliable results. Consequently, I suggest that design processes should use empirical data as much as objective measures to arrive at more data-driven designs (Costa et al. 2014; Tan et al. 2017).

5. *Design processes should include many iterations, within and between steps, and various prototypes should be designed.*
   Of course, this is a central recommendation of design handbooks, it has been mentioned by ISO 9241:210, and it was part of UIPP, too. However, a discussion of the UIPP project showed that design processes should include many more iterations than performed in UIPP to evaluate and refine the designs continuously. In addition, multiple prototypes and variations should be produced in order to evaluate which prototypes are best suited. Evaluating many prototypes to refine them in multiple iterations considerably improves the results.

6. *The work of experienced designers cannot be substituted.*
Grounding the design process in scientific theories and research as much as using empirical data and objective measures to evaluate the designs seems crucial and might lead to good results. However, the experience and expert knowledge of skilled designers cannot be substituted (see Sect. "Future Research", too). In UIPP, a team of designers conducted a research through design process over several months that was characterized by a continuous back and forth and by leaps. Only because of this process, it was possible to develop a design system and to produce the design prototypes. That is, only thanks to the work of the designers, the UIP Pictogram prototypes exist.

Drawbacks

Inclusive design is central to HCI. At the same time, it is difficult to achieve, and research on inclusive design is missing. It is an important drawback that UIPP does not focus on inclusive design. I have addressed the drawback throughout this book, and I have discussed this project's findings in relation to inclusive design on various occasions. The choice to focus on cross-cultural design had to be made because of limited resources. I made the choice because research on cross-cultural design is scarce, too. In addition, I hoped that the focus on similarities between people might provide a good basis for subsequent research on their individual capabilities, that is, for inclusive design. Future studies, of course, should address directly elderly people and people with disabilities. That is, they should develop methods and procedures to derive, produce, and evaluate pictogram contents, design systems, and prototypes for inclusive design.

With regard to cross-cultural design, it was a drawback to recruit only German-speaking participants in Study 3. This was due to limited resources, too. However, UIPPs were not designed for a specific culture, and, I hold, they might yield similar results in other cultures. Nevertheless, Study 3 should be conducted with participants from the same cultures in which the pictogram contents were derived. Furthermore, I suggest that Studies 1 and 2 should be conducted with participants from additional cultures with additional first languages, in particular, cultures that are even more distinct from western cultures, like the Indian or the Chinese culture. Including these non-western cultures seems crucial to be able to produce completely universal designs. At the same time, recruiting participants from these cultures seems viable because crowdsourcing can be used easily with these cultures, too. However, of course, there are challenges regarding the translation process (see Sect. "Deriving UIP Pictogram Meanings").

In order to avoid challenges in the translation process, future studies should develop empirical approaches to the presentation, collection, analysis, and evaluation of visual material and data. As discussed in Sect. "Experimental Materials and Data: Linguistic, not Visual", presenting linguistic stimuli and collecting linguistic data might have produced a bias in UIPP—although it seemed the best option for the project, and results were validated subsequently. Nevertheless, not being required to switch modes of communication in the studies and being able to address directly visual mental associations might lead to even better results.

In order to further improve the results, I argue that future studies should choose a specific context of use at the beginning of the process and not adjust the context of use in the course of the process. In UIPP, with the intention to derive content candidates for universal use that are, at the same time, suitable for heating system user interfaces, in Study 1 and 2, participants were not informed about the context of use of the heating system. However, in Study 3, informing participants about the context of use was required in order to allow for comparison with established manufacturer pictograms. This was a drawback. Although simple UIP Pictogram *power* had high CRs and high subjective ratings, thus, indicating that it is suitable for universal use, Study 3 showed that it is less suited for a heating system user interface. That is, the pictogram was rated much lower than the equivalent manufacturer pictogram that represented the content *lightning bolt*. In addition, pictograms that included *power* had lower ratings and CRs. These results were predicted by the UIPP designers during the design production process. They assumed that the content *lightning bolt* would be better suited for the context of use of a heating system. Consequently, as proposed in the UIPP technical process (Sect. "Conclusion and the UIPP Technical Process"), in Step 2, a specific context of use should be analyzed as much as the users, their tasks and goals. This specific context of use should be used throughout the process.

It was an important drawback that the design team could not follow all UIPP guidelines in the design production process. As discussed in Sect. "Technical Constraints by UCUI", it was a constraint by the UCUI interface prototype that the pictograms should be black and white, or they should have more than two colors. The designers decided to design the UIPP prototypes in black and white— although this is against Guideline 22—because including constantly three colors in a pictogram might be against Guidelines 22, too, and it might be against Guideline 11. Furthermore, the manufacturer pictograms to which UIPPs were subsequently compared were also black and white, and too many novel pictogram characteristics might impede precise evaluation of the characteristics (McDougall et al. 2009, p. 62). Nevertheless, it seems crucial that future projects follow all the derived guidelines and that they evaluate the designed prototypes accordingly.

Along those lines, it seems important that future studies develop empirical methods and procedures to evaluate distinct pictogram characteristics individually, for example, color, animation, complexity, and so forth. Since pictogram characteristics are closely interrelated, this is a challenging task. Although suggestions were made in UIPP Step 5, methods should be developed, for example, to assess in more detail which pictogram characteristics lead to better results for certain pictogram prototypes than for others. In addition, it should be assessed which characteristics lead to rejections, as in the case of the pictogram *person* (Hurtienne et al. 2009, p. 67).

Following my Implication for Design Number 5, I suggest that future studies should include many more iterations. In addition, they should produce multiple variations of prototypes. Although multiple iterations were done during the

UIPP design production process, only one iteration was done in Step 5: Study 3.4 is a retest with adapted UIP Pictogram prototypes. Future studies should include additional iterations of design production processes after the evaluation studies in Step 5 to refine the prototypes continuously (Hurtienne et al. 2015, p. 252). In addition, during the design production process, designers made decisions based on their tacit knowledge. For example, sometimes, they used content candidates that were ranked lower than other content candidates because the lower-ranked content candidates seemed more suitable for pictogram design. I propose that future studies should produce multiple pictogram prototypes with distinct contents, and they should produce distinct variations of pictogram prototypes with the same content to evaluate subsequently which prototypes are best suited—as it was done with the UIPP versions of *[something or someone] is busy* in Study 3.

Future Research

Finally, I propose two directions for future research. First, in UIPP, simple meanings were derived from use scenarios prescribed by UCUI. In future studies, the scope of represented meanings should be extended. For example, meanings should be used that are more complex and abstract. As Hornecker (2012) noted: "Digital systems are *not* the real world; it is their very strength to offer functionality unavailable in the real world" (p. 178). For that reason, using real-world sensorimotor experience might work only to a certain point. Future research should take meanings as its starting points that do not have an equivalent in the real world. Then, for example, the use of abstract visualizations might be required, that is, design systems that are categorized farther towards the abstract pole of design systems but that are still based on semantic association (see Sect. "Categories of Visual Representations"). In that case, in Step 4, research and theories must be taken into account that have not been addressed in UIPP (e.g., Hansen and Johnson 2011; Kosslyn 2006; Munzner 2015; Sedig and Parsons 2013; Spence 2014; Tversky 2011; Ware 2013). Furthermore, more complex meanings should be used that consist of combinations of other meanings. In other words, future research should examine how pictograms might be combined to refer to complex meanings. This seems important, in particular, for interaction between people because, most of the time, people communicate complex combinations of meanings rather than simple meanings. Take the example of compound meanings like *[warmth] is everywhere* (Fig. 35). In future studies, combinations of more than two meanings should be researched, like the meaning *[warmth] begins everywhere* that consists of a combination of *warmth, [something] is everywhere,* and *[something] begins.* One approach might be to integrate pictograms for all three meanings in a single pictogram. A second approach might be based on modularity, that is, pictograms for *[warmth] begins* and for *[warmth] is everywhere* might be presented one after another in an animation, or they might be presented next to each other. In that case, of course, further design guidelines are required that have not been considered in UIPP, for example, with regard to spacing of pictograms. One example is Lindberg and Näsänen's (2003, pp. 118–119) study in which they showed that participants preferred spacings for visual representations on GUIs in the size of one representation. The second best spacing is half the size of a representation. Of course, this needs further investigation.

Second, I suggest that future research might address the automation of the UIPP process. Automation of design processes has been sparking interest for some decades (Tzonis and White 1994), especially in instructional design (Fernandes 1995). However, in recent years, design automation, in particular of visual and interface design, has become a buzzword because of new possibilities thanks to artificial intelligence and machine learning. In that context, Adobe seems a driving factor (see, e.g., Adobe's Advertising Cloud, Adobe Inc. 2020; O'Donovan et al. 2015). At the beginning of this chapter, I have argued that UIPP describes a viable technical approach to the design of universal, intuitive, and permanent pictograms. The project includes all steps of a human-centered design process, it is firmly grounded in scientific theory and empirical research, and it explains in detail its methods and procedures. While the production process by designers cannot (yet) be substituted by mathematically described approaches—as discussed in Step 1 and Step 4—many parts of the UIPP process might be suitable for automation. For example, in Step 3, participants might be recruited and presented automatically with previously designed materials through the crowdsourcing process. In Study 1, data might be annotated and coded, and categories of content candidates might be derived automatically, either through programming or through machine learning, if suitable rules are defined, based on the previously developed requirements. Automatic annotation and analysis, of course, are important topics in computational and corpus linguistics, and methods and approaches could be derived from these disciplines (Ide and Pustejovsky 2017; Lu 2014; McEnery and Wilson 2001). In addition, crowdsourcing has been used for annotation on many occasions (see Sabou et al. 2014, for an overview). In Study 2, after presenting participants automatically with the stimuli, I suggest that the creation of a comprehensive ranking of the content candidates might be easily mathematically described. However, to that end, all content candidates should be presented to all participant groups, even if they were not derived in that specific group. In Step 4, the work by designers cannot be substituted because it is still superior, for example, to the results of mathematically described approaches (e.g., Cole et al. 2009, pp. 8–9; Sayim and Cavanagh 2011, p. 3). However, mathematically described approaches already yield good results, in particular in the field of non-photorealistic rendering (NPR) (Judd et al. 2007, p. 2). In NPR, line drawings are an important topic (e.g., Cole et al. 2008; DeCarlo et al. 2003; Hörr et al. 2010). These approaches might be used to support the design production process and the designers. For example, they might be used to automate the creation of average shapes of real-world objects and creatures to achieve typical basic-level contents. In the process, they might use microstock photographic footage and the previously defined rules and regularities of the UIPP design system, similar to the approach followed in UIPP. In Step 5, again, the crowdsourcing process might be conducted automatically once an appropriate study design is created for online testing.

At the end of this book, I suggest that I have completed the sixth and final step in a human-centered design process, according to ISO 9241:210 (International Organization for Standardization 2010). The sixth step consists in the discussion of the conformity of the designed prototypes with the developed requirements and in recommendations for future design and research. By completing the sixth, I have completed the UIPP human-centered design process (see, again, Fig. 1).

Appendix A

Table A.1 UCUI scenarios and derived UIPP meanings

Scenarios	Actual state	Target state	Meaning(s)
Default setting: Day	Time of day and desired temperature unknown to the system	Time of day and heating temperatures stored according to user requirements	Day
Basic setting: Lowering	Time and desired temperature unknown to the system	Times and heating temperatures stored according to user requirements	Night
I am cold!	Current room temperature in the entire house is perceived as too low	System informs users about current room temperature	Coldness, everywhere, wrong
I'm hot!	Current room temperature in the entire house is perceived as too high	System informs users about current room temperature	Warmth, everywhere, wrong
I'm cold! Individual	Current room temperature in certain rooms (e.g., bathroom) is perceived as too low	System informs users about the current room temperature in the concerned room	Warmth, here, single, wrong
I'm hot! Individual	Current room temperature in certain rooms (e.g., bedrooms) is perceived as too high	System informs users about the current room temperature in the concerned room	Coldness, here, single, wrong
Increase temperature now	Current room temperature is perceived as too low—in certain rooms or the whole house	System increases temperature according to user requirements—in the room or the whole house	More/increasing, warmth, everywhere, here

(continued)

Table A.1 (continued)

Scenarios	Actual state	Target state	Meaning(s)
Lower temperature now	Current room temperature is perceived as too high—in certain rooms or the whole house	System lowers temperature according to user requirements—in the room or the whole house	Less/decreasing, warmth, everywhere, here
Visitor mode	User expects visitors (with overnight stay), current heating times and temperature not appropriate	System changes heating times and temperatures in the house accordingly	More/increasing, warmth, night, group
Visitor mode II	User expects visitors for a celebration, current heating times and temperature not appropriate	System changes heating times and temperatures in the house accordingly	More/less, warmth, night, group
Individual visitor mode	User expects visitors, current heating times and temperature not appropriate in certain rooms	System changes heating times and temperatures in desired rooms (e.g., guest rooms) accordingly	More, warmth, here, day/night, group
Earlier from work	Stored times of day for day and lower operation not appropriate	System starts up earlier from lowering to daytime operation	More/increasing, warmth, begins
Later from work	Stored times of day for day and lower operation not appropriate	System will shut down later from day mode to lower operation	Less/decreasing, warmth, ends
Absence individual	Certain people (e.g., child) leave the house for several days, current heating times and temperature are not appropriate	System heats certain rooms (e.g., children's rooms) at a lowered temperature during absence	Absent, single
Voice input	System is processing voice input just received	System informs user about current processing—User is waiting	Busy
Input via gestures	System is processing just received input via gestures	System informs user about current processing—User is waiting	Busy
Energy consumption okay	Current energy consumption is efficient	System informs users about current energy consumption	Power, good
Energy consumption too high	Current energy consumption is inefficient	System informs users about current energy consumption	Power, bad, less/decreasing, dangerous, important

Notes: Scenarios were provided by UCUI in German and translated to English where appropriate

Appendix B

Table B.1 English and German UIPP meanings derived from UCUI scenarios

English	German
[Something or someone] is absent, not here	[Etwas oder jemand] is abwesend, nicht hier
[Something] is bad, negative	[Etwas] ist schlecht, negativ
[Something] begins	[Etwas] fängt an
[Something or someone] is busy	[Etwas oder jemand] ist beschäftigt
Coldness	Kühle, Kälte
[Something] is dangerous	[Etwas] ist gefährlich
Day	Tag
[Something] is decreasing	[Etwas] wird weniger
[Something] ends	[Etwas] endet
[Something] is everywhere	[Etwas] ist überall
[Something] is good, positive	[Etwas] ist gut, positiv
[Something or someone] is here, on-site	[Etwas oder jemand] ist hier, vor Ort
[Something] is important	[Etwas] ist wichtig
[Something] is increasing	[Etwas] wird mehr
Night	Nacht
Power	Leistung, Stärke
Several, a group of [some things or some people]	Mehrere, eine Gruppe von [Dingen oder Menschen]
[Something or someone] is single, solitary	[Etwas oder jemand] ist einzeln
Warmth	Wärme
[Something] goes wrong, is wrong	[Etwas] geht schief, stimmt nicht

Notes: Meanings are in alphabetical order of first major words in English. Brackets indicate that the meaning requires specification

Appendix C

Dear participant,

below, we will present you with a variety of different terms and situations.
Please, **close your eyes immediately after reading** each word or description.

Please do not listen to music, watch TV or anything similar - that would considerably distort the results.

Your task will be to **describe the images** that **spontaneously** come to your mind,
i.e. that appear **before 'your inner eye' within the first 15 seconds** after reading each term or situation.
We recommend to start your answer with: "I see..."

It is necessary that you describe the pictures accurately and **very extensively**.
For example, colors, forms, places, persons, objects, etc.
Describe all the images that come to your mind without evaluating them or checking them for potential criticism. Neither
will we judge your responses.

It is necessary that you do not name abstract concepts (such as emotions) but describe visual images -
that is, things you can see or touch.
Do not name couple terms, analogies, opposites, or the like - otherwise the payment cannot be credited to you.
Please note: Only serious and careful answers can be remunerated.

If after a short period of time (about 15 seconds) you cannot think of anything more,
please proceed to the next term or scenario.

Thank you very much for your participation!

Fig. C.1 Instructional page for Study 1.2. In Study 1.1 an identical German translation was presented

Appendix D

Table D.1 Open-ended response data for the meaning *[something] is important* from German-speaking participant group

#	Response
1	Zwei Hände die sich fest halten
2	Geld
3	Ein Dokument liegt auf einem Schreibtisch. Daneben befindet sich ein schwarzer Stift.
4	Ich hatte meinen Terminplan vor Augen, bei dem ein Termin rot markiert war
5	Eine To-Do-Liste. Es ist rot markiert und steht ganz oben. Die restlichen Punkte sind schon durchgestrichen
6	Gespräch mit Chef—Lohnerhöhung, Auto muss repariert werden
7	Einen digitaler wecker, die schrift grün leuchten
8	Hinweis zum Geburtstag meiner besten Freundin groß & bunt im Tischkalender notiert und umrahmt
9	Rufzeichen, Post it, Großbuchstaben, Straßenschild
10	Bildung ist wichtig
11	Ein Uhr an der Wand… danach ein Mensch der auf die Armbanduhr schaut
12	Mir fallen meine Freunde und Familie ein
13	Mein Engel, Schwitzt gestresst und ist krank
14	Ich sehe meine Frau, wie sie sich freut mich zu sehen
15	Ein kleiner gelber Zettel, der mitten auf dem Schreibtisch platziert wurde
16	Das Wort Achtung in roter Schrift auf einem Schild
17	Da sehe ich vor meinem inneren Auge ein Ausrufezeichen, schwarz und dick gezeichnet

(continued)

D. Bühler, *Universal, Intuitive, and Permanent Pictograms,* https://doi.org/10.1007/978-3-658-32310-3

Table D.1 (continued)

#	Response
18	Ich sehe einen grauen Kieselstein mit unebener Oberfläche auf einem Blatt Papier. Das Papier liegt an den Enden auf zwei Ziegelsteinen und wird vom Gewicht des auf ihm liegenden Steines durchgedrückt, aber nicht bis auf den Boden.
19	Kein konkretes Bild, sorry…
20	Ein rot blinkendes Licht am Festnetztelefon zeigt an, dass jemand angerufen hat.
21	Nicht vergessen
22	Familie, Arbeit, Geld, Gesundheit
23	Meine Frau, meine Religion
24	Leben
25	Das Guthaben auf meinem Konto
26	Ich sehe eine Hand an der der Zeigefinger ausgestreckt ist. Die Hand zeigt gerade nach oben.
27	Dreieckiges Warnschild gelb mit schwarzem rand und schwarzer aufschrift, nicht erkennbar
28	Bedeutsam
29	Arbeit, karriere, wichtige personen
30	Rot, ausrufezeichen
31	Das Büro einer Firma. Es kommt zu einem Vorstellungsgespräch. Ein sehr wichtiger Termin für jemanden, der die Stelle unbedingt haben möchte.
32	Nicht vergessen
33	Notizzettel am Kühlschrank
34	Geld
35	Ich sitze vor dem Computer, ich schreibe einen Text, ich sehe mein Handy, einen Laserdrucker, weißes Papier, Kugelschreiber und einen braunen Schreibtisch
36	Ich sehe meine Familie
37	Die erwartung von akzeptanz zu nicht neher erklärten schverhalten verbunden mit der erwartung von bevorzugter behandlung.
38	Ein dunkles Ausrufezeichen auf hellem Grund
39	Ich sehe meine Freundin, meine Familie.
40	Natur
41	Die Beziehung zu den Eltern
42	Ein Polizist übergibt einen Brief und salutiert dabei
43	Hausaufgaben, Noten
44	Ein Lehrer vor der Klasse mit roter Kreide in der Hand.
45	Eine Prüfung, welche für das weitere Berufsleben, studiumfortschritt von Bedeutung ist

(continued)

Table D.1 (continued)

#	Response
46	Ein rot hervorgehobener Kreis bewegt sich vor meinen Augen hoch und runter
47	Das mädel was ich liebe und freunde
48	Was
49	Lottoschein, Auto, Familie
50	Familie
51	Muss am Treffen um 6 Uhr teilnehmen
52	Ein adressierter Brief mit einem Klarsicht-Adressfeld
53	Eine Straße, ein Geschäft, ein Ereignis … es ist noch etwas einzukaufen … Gäste sind am Abend zu Besuch. Ist alles vorbereitet? Werden die Gäste zufrieden sein? Ich gehe in den Laden … was habe ich vergessen.
54	Freunde
55	Terminplaner
56	Ich überreiche meinem Chef einen Stapel Unterlagen,rote Blätter
57	Eine wichtige unterhaltung zwischen zwei personen.
58	Eine unbezahlte Rechnung auf meinem Schreibtisch
59	Ein Bote bringt einen Brief, der Umschlag ist mit einer schön geschwungenen Schrift beschriftet.
60	Auf dem silbernen Kühlschrank klebt ein gelber Post-it-Zettel, auf dem mit schwarzem Filzstift das Wort "Kaffee kaufen" mitsamt drei Ausrufungszeichen geschrieben ist.
61	Diese Sache ist äußerst dringend.
62	Eine Mutter die ihrem Sohn erklärt wie wichtig es ist, dass er seine Hausaufgaben gewissenhaft macht.
63	Meine Kinder sind das wichtigste
64	Arbeit, Gesundheit
65	Priorität
66	Beziehung zu Freunden und Familie, Arbeiten/Geld verdienen, eine Wohnung haben
67	Sich täglich für seine Umwelt zu interessieren, Zeitung und andere seriöse Nachrichtenquellen benutzen sowie seine Meinung zu vertreten, ist enorm wichtig.
68	Mein Chef weist auf die Wichtigkeit einer Kundenanfrage mehrmals hin.
69	Jemand sitzt im Parlament als Politiker
70	Gespanntes und aufmerksames Gesicht
71	Ein Meeting, eine Abgabefrist für einen Kunden etc.…
72	Der mit Nachdruck drängende Chef
73	Familie
74	Abiturklausur

(continued)

Table D.1 (continued)

#	Response
75	Steht auf den Erinnerungszetteln ganz oben, steht auf der ersten Seite der Zeitung, kommt gleich in den Nachrichten.
76	Ich muss heute noch Tabletten gegen Heuschnupfen nehmen.
77	Ein rotes Ausrufezeichen
78	Koffer mit Geld
79	Freude am leben
80	Ein gelbes Dreieck, Spitze oben mit schwarzem Ausrufezeichen und schwarzen Rand
81	Todo-Liste
82	Achtung
83	Ein Blatt Papier wird in eine Plastikhülle gesteckt und in eine Pappmappe gelegt.
84	Es ist wichtig, dass wir für unseren Garten in unserer Abwesenheit jemanden haben, der uns die Blumen/Pflanzen gießt.
85	Ein Post it welches an einem Bildschrim klebt. Es ist rot. Darauf eine Notiz die Unterstrichen ist. Sie endet mit Ausrufezeichen
86	Aufgeschlagener Kalender, Hand hält einen Stift und fängt gerade an zu schreiben.
87	Leben, freunde, besitz
88	Toll
89	Ich sehe meine Familie und meine Freunde. Alle haben Essen. Jeder lacht.
90	Freunde behalten, kämpfen, nicht aufgeben
91	Geld von meinem Konto überweisen
92	Gesundheit
93	Ein Objekt blinkt in einem regelmäßigem Takt in einer hellen, edelen Farbe (Gold oder Weiß)
94	Langweilig
95	Die Seite eines Notizkalenders, in dem sämtlicher Freiraum durch Schrift, teils blau, teils schwarz, auch mit Markierungen, überfüllt ist.
96	Ein Ofen in dem gerade ein Schweinsbraten liegt, daneben meine Lernunterlagen
97	Der Termineintrag ist mit roter Farbe markiert.
98	Rechnungen für Telefon, Versicherung jeden Monat rechtzeitig zu zahlen
99	Eintreffende E-Mail mit hoher Wichtigkeit
100	Familie, Geburtstag.
101	Bedeutungsvoll, Aufmerksamkeit, Dringlichkeit
102	Etwas von Bedeutung
103	Eine Sonne
104	Ich sehe einen Rettungswagen auf der Autobahn. Der Wagen fährt mit Blaulicht und es wird eine Rettungsgasse gebildet.

(continued)

Table D.1 (continued)

#	Response
105	Ein dreieckiges Warnschild (weißer Grund, roter Rand) mit einem Ausrufungszeichen in der Mitte
106	Eine Person in einem Anzug steht vor einer verschlossenen Tür und hält einige Zettel in der Hand und schaut auf seine Armbanduhr.
107	Ich sehe meine Mutter lächelnd vor mir. Ich nehme sie in den Arm
108	Nihilismus
109	Gezeichnete Ausrufe zeichen
110	Hohe aufmerksamkeit
111	Eine Statue schaut auf einen Platz hinab. Ein Platz wie er in der Mitte einer Hauptstadt steht die früher einmal internationale Grösse hatte.
112	Das Sparschwein für den Führerschein
113	Eigenes Zuhause
114	Eine Mathematik klausur mit einer schlechten Note.
115	Meine Mutter während sie lächelt
116	Anmerkung in Großbuchstaben und roter Schrift
117	Ein Mann im roten Hemd mit einem Klemmbrett in der einen Hand telefoniert mit seinem Handy in der andern Hand.
118	Ich sehe einen Terminkalender, an einzelnen Tagen sind mit Kugelschreiber Zeit und Ablauf festgehalten.
119	Ein rotes Ausrufezeichen. Es sieht aus wie ein Schild und schwebt in einem ansonsten leeren Raum. Es pulsiert, wird laufend größer und kleiner.
120	Ich sehe viele Goldbarren in einem Banktresor liegen
121	Ich habe das unbestimmte Gefühl, dass irgendeine wichtige Aufgabe ansteht. Ich erinnere mich ungenau, dass bis zu einem bestimmen Zeitpunkt etwas erledigt werden muss. Da mir nicht einfällt, was genau ich zu tun habe, durchsuche ich meine Unterlagen und meine Notizen, aber ich finde nicht, wonach ich suche. Ich frage meine Kollegen in den anderen Büros. Keiner kann mir jedoch sagen, welchen Abgabetermin ich vermutlich soeben verpasse.
122	Höchste Priorität, Arbeit, Leben, Liebe
123	Genau
124	Geburtstag
125	Ausrufezeichen
126	Jemand schreibt etwas auf seine Hand. Er möchte es nicht vergessen. Auf der Hand trägt er es immer bei sich und kann jederzeit nachlesen an was er denken muss
127	Familienbild
128	Familie, Freunde, Verlobte, Ehe-mann/-frau
129	Ich sehe ein Zettelchen und das der Termin darauf vergessen wurde das passt mir selten

(continued)

Table D.1 (continued)

#	Response
130	Ein Termin muss eingehalten werden Terminkalender liegt vor mir Zu sehen ist der Termin der eingetragen wurde
131	Ein Raum, ich zusammen mit einer Person, Arm und Arm, ruhig, entspannt, sicher
132	Mein leben
133	Lernen, Gesundheit, Basenreiche Ernährung, Ehrlichkeit, Zahnpflege,
134	Ich sehe eine Studentin vor mir, die daran denkt, dass sie bald eine wichtige Abgabefrist einhalten muss.
135	Ein Notizzettel, der an meinem Bildschirm klebt. Der Text darauf hat mehrere Ausrufezeichen
136	Meine Familie, die gesund und glücklich an einem Tisch sitzt
137	Den richtigen weg zu finden
138	Notiz mit Ausrufezeichen, rote Markierung
139	Unruhe, Zeit, Druck, notwendigkeit, Sorge, Angst
140	Geld, 50 € Scheine
141	Wartezimmer, Termin beim Arzt nicht vergessen, Impfung ist wichtig vor der Reise
142	Mein Leben, meine Familie und Freunde, dass sie alle gesund und glücklich bleiben
143	Familie, Menschen reden miteinander
144	Die Familie ist wichtig. Die gibt Halt und Freude
145	Ich sehe meinen Freund und meinen Hund. Ich sehe das Gesicht meines Freundes und das glänzende braune Fell meines Hundes.
146	Hart arbeiten um Geld zu verdienen
147	Dazu fällt mir zuallererst meine Tochter ein
148	Ein großes rotes Ausrufezeichen steht neben einem Termin im Kalender.
149	Brief
150	Ich sehe meinen Partner vor mir, er ist das Wichtigste für mich. Er lächelt und ich bin froh, dass er da ist
151	Meine Kinder, viel Zeit mit meinen Kindern zu verbringen
152	ToDo Liste
153	Keine Idee
154	Es isst wichtig einen klaren Tagesablauf zu haben und Ordnung zu halten.
155	Familie
156	Notizzettel. Der Text darauf ist rot angestrichen und enthält mehrere Ausrufezeichen.
157	Mein leben, mein partner
158	Wichtig ist mir, Zeit für mich zu haben. Ich sitze auf dem Balkon und lese
159	Der Postbote bringt ein Einschreiben

(continued)

Table D.1 (continued)

#	Response
160	Rote Farbe; wie ein Schild mit Text und Ausrufezeichen
161	Ich sehe einen grauen Notizblock mit einem schwarzen Ausrufezeichen, jemand hat dieses darauf notiert. Er liegt auf einem Tisch, weiter ist nichts darauf zu sehen.
162	Eheurkunde, Geburtsurkunde
163	Ich renne über die Straße und versuche noch rechtzeitig die Post zu erreichen um einen wichtigen Brief wegzubringen. Die Autos bremsen und die Menschn schauen mir hinterher. Meine Haare werden ganz zerzaust, aber ich renne weiter.
164	Meine Familie ist mir wichtig.
165	Meine Kinder
166	Ein Schüler bekommt ein Heft zurück und springt freudig in die Luft. Die anderen Schüler applaudieren. Auf der ersten Seite steht eine 1, darunter ein paar Formeln. Er steckt das Heft in seinen schwarzen Rucksack mit einem Totenkopfanhänger. An der Tafel steht neben der 1 nur ein Strich.
167	Beruflicher Termin, ich darf nicht zu spät kommen
168	Das weiße Kaninchen starrt gehetzt auf seine Uhr
169	Ich sehe meine Familie
170	Liebe, Familie, Gesundheit
171	jemand hastet mit einem Zettel in der Hand einen Flur entlang, ist außer Atem, viele Bürotüren, Fensterfront
172	Klausur
173	Ich setze mich dafür ein, ich arbeite an der Situation
174	Eine wichtige Postsendung vom Amt
175	Ein wichtiger Termin, den man nicht verschieben kann.
176	Meine Freunde sind mir wichtig; die Traditionen zu Weihnachten wie ich si evon früher her kenne; mein Garten ist wichtig, in dem ich mich erholen kann und viel eRosen einen betörenden Duft verströmen
177	Gesundheit ist wichtig, wich ich nach dem Tod einer Angehörigen durch krebs weiß, ohne Gesundheit kann man alles ander enicht genießen
178	Prioritäten zu setzen ist verhältnissmässig schwer denn alles ist wichtig;wir werden mit Wissen übeladen denn eigentlich so etwas wie das Genug an Wissen ist nicht existent aber der Prozess der Filtrierung der Infos ist aufwändig und zeitraubend
179	Ich sehe einen Bildschirm mit Emaileingang und eine Email mit einem roten Ausrufezeichen
180	Die Arbeit
181	Familie ist wichtig
182	Auf Urlaub zu sein
183	Eine Frau, die an ihrem Schreibtisch sitzt und sehr konzentriert ein Schriftstück durchliest, dabei wenn nötig unbekannte Begriffe im Internet sucht, um ganz sicher zu sein, auch alles richtig verstanden zu haben, bevor sie eine Entscheidung trifft.

(continued)

Table D.1 (continued)

#	Response
184	Treffen der G20 Regierungschefs, alle schütteln sich fürs Foto die Hände
185	Podest mit einer leuchtenden Kugel oben
186	Schule
187	Familie
188	Das wichtigste für uns ist, dass wir gesund bleiben und das mein Ehemann nicht seine Arbeit verliert, wichtig für uns, ist dass wir genug Geld haben um unser Haus abzuzahlen
189	Ich sehe das Angabenblatt einer Seminararbeit, die ich noch nicht geschrieben habe, vor mir liegen.
190	Kein Bild
191	In einem großen Konferenzraum ist das komplette Führungsteam versammelt. Sie sitzen an einem langem Tisch, schwarz glänzend der Tisch - fünf Meter lang. Einige Flaschen und Gläser stehen pro Meter auf dem Tisch. Die Männer und Frauen haben auf den grauen Stühlen Platz genommen. Jeder hat ein Namensschild vor sich auf dem Tisch. Sie wirken angespannt. Alle sind im Businessoutfit erschienen. Männer in grauen Anzügen, die Frauen in grauen Kostümen. Niemand greift zu den Getränken. Die Smartphone liegen auf der Tischplatte. Die Tür am entgegengesetzten Eingang geht auf.
192	Im Kalender kontrollieren, ob alle Termine eingetragen sind.
193	etwas hat eine besondere Bedeutung
194	Familie
195	Ich sehe meine Partnerin, die mir sehr wichtig ist. Sie steht vor mir und sieht mich lächelnd an.
196	Ein gelblicher Notiezblock mit unleserlicher schrift darauf, daginter hat jemand ein rotes Ausrufezeicgen gemalt
197	Eine Akte auf dem Schreibtisch
198	Ein Mund mit pink farbenen Lippen der einen Kussmund darstellt auf weißem Hintergrund
199	Menschen sind das Wichtigste auf der Welt. Man sollte nicht zu viel Zeit mit Nebensächlichkeiten verbringen. Beispielsweise kann man abend statt Fernsehen einen lieben Menschen besuchen, der sonst ganz allein wäre.
200	Ich sehe Ausrufezeichen und ein blinkendes Alarmsignal. Außerdem habe ich meinem Handy-Terminkalender und meinen physischen Terminkalender (Buch) vor Augen, in dem ich mir einen Termin einspeichere bzw. eintrage. "Das darfst du nicht vergessen" geht mir durch den Kopf.
201	Ich darf meinen Termin nicht vergessen.
202	Sehe angespannte Gesichter und mahnende Blicke; fühle mich aufgefordert auf einen bestimmten Punkt zu schauen
203	Wichtig ist,dass ich gesund bleibe und für meine Tiere sorgen kann
204	"Man denkt, ohne etwas geht es nicht weiter…
205	Ein schwarzes Telefon. Daneben liegt ein Block und ein schwarzer Stift

(continued)

Table D.1 (continued)

#	Response
206	Ein Termin ist sehr wichtig.
207	Ich suche meinen Terminkalender. Dort habe ich notiert, wann ich zum Routine-Check beim Hausarzt muss.
208	Ein Wahrndreieck mit einem großen Ausrufezeichen
209	Ein Schloss (zum Verschließen), ein Schlüssel, etwas wird bewacht, beschützt.
210	Terminkalender mit vielen eingetragenen Terminen
211	Eine Frau schaut sich ununterbrochen den Ring an ihrer Hand an, der golden ist und einen kleinen weißen Stein in der Mitte hat. Sie lächelt über den Ring und berührt ihn immer wieder gedankenverloren. Ein Mann hält ein Baby in den armen und wiegt es leicht hin und her. Es schaut sich das Kind immer wieder an und küsst es sanft auf die Stirn.
212	Eine Angestellte im Büro trägt einen Termin in ihren Kalender ein. Im Kalender steht: "Besprechung mit dem Chef". Diesen Satz unterstreicht sie dreimal und macht mit einem Rotstift drei Ausrufezeichen dahinter.
213	Meine Familie, mein Freund und meine Freunde sind das wichtigste für mich
214	Merken, darf nicht vergessen werden, stress, muss klug wirken, Warnsignal
215	Ein rotes Ausrufezeichen
216	Meinen ehering nicht zu verlieren
217	Roter Alarmknopf
218	Ausrufezeichen, Chef
219	Der Flug muss rechtzeitig bekommen werden
220	Ich sehe eine Medaille vor mir. Sie ist aus Gold und glänzt unheimlich schön. Sie ist sehr schwer und fühlt sich dadurch auch sehr wertvoll an. Außerdem sehe ich eine Urkunde, sie ist aus sehr festem Papier und gerollt.
221	Familie, Kinder, Freunde
222	Ich sehe eine schwarze Aktentasche mit goldenen Schnallen auf einem Schreibtisch, daneben ein Stapel Papiere, auf denen ein Füller liegt.
223	Ich sehe einen Möbelwagen und Männer, die Umzugskisten tragen.
224	Es ist wichtig für mich und meine Familie zu sorgen und mir selbst treu zu bleiben
225	Arbeit, Termin einhalten, Familie, oberste Priorität
226	Keine Gedanken
227	Helle Farben, viel rot/orange
228	Ich denke daran, wie wichtig es ist, später noch Zivilrecht für die bevorstehende Klausur zu lernen, und wie wichtig mir mein Studium ist. Es ist wichtig, von Anfang an mitzulernen, um das Examen bestehen zu können.
229	Kalender, Aufgabenliste, Briefkuvert, Amt,
230	Dazu fällt mir leider nichts ein.

(continued)

Table D.1 (continued)

#	Response
231	liste, nach prioritäten geordnet, ausrufezeichen, unterstrichen, rot markiert, schwarze schrift, eingekreist, anmerkungen, groß geschrieben
232	Liebe zwischen zwei Menschen ist sehr wichtig und bildet die Basis einer Beziehung.
233	Meine Familie ist mir wichtig
234	Hoffnung und Glaube an eine bessere Welt
235	Ein großes Ausrufezeichen in Farbe rot
236	Treffen
237	Wenn etwas hohe Priorität hat und bevorzugt behandelt wird. Es muss schnell erledigt werden und die Konsequenzen sind bedeutend.
238	Dreieckiges weißes Symbol, in dessen Mitte ein rotes Ausrufezeichen ist
239	Eine Mutter, die ihr Kind an der Hand hält an einem Sommertag in der Stadt
240	Termine einzuhalten ist wichtig oder wenn etwas dazwischen kommt rechtzeitig um eine Verlegung des Termins bitten.
241	Morgen habe ich einen Termin beim Zahnarzt. Der ist sehr wichtig, weil dann die Fäden gezogen werden.
242	Die Organisation der freuberuflichen Selbständigung für einen gesunden Start ins Berufsleben, um die geplanten Kinder versorgen zu können.
243	Vieles ist wichtig, aber etwas ganz besonders das hier und jetzt mit meinen Kindern die ich sehe wenn ich die Augen schließe.
244	Terminplaner an der Wand, termin mit roten Ausrufezeichen markiert
245	Ein Kalerderblatt, das Datum ist nicht zu erkennen. Das Papier ist weiß und hat blaue Linien. Über das ganze Blatt ist ein Ausrufezeichen in schwarz gemalt.
246	Ich sehe meine familie, wir verbringen zeit und lachen
247	Lesezeichen und Unterstreichungen in Büchern
248	Die Bewerbung ist wichtig für mich und ich brauche dringend mehr Geld. Das Geld reicht mir nicht. Daher wäre der Job wichtig.
249	Gott und die Familie
250	Höchste Priorität
251	Ich schreibe mir auf einen Post it eine Notiz und hefte sie an meinen Arbeitslaptop gut sichtbar in die Mitte.
252	Geld abheben
253	Gott steht an erster Stelle, danach kommt die Familie
254	Ein gedruckter Text mit Paragraphen-Zeichen
255	Die Eltern stehen hinter ihren Kindern und sind Sportlich-Schick gekleidet. Die Kinder sind zwischen 5 und 15 Jahren alt und alle Blond, Hellblond das Mädchen und Dunkelblond- braun die Jungs "
256	Ein E-Mailpostfach: viele E-Mails haben darin das rote Ausrufungszeichen

(continued)

Table D.1 (continued)

#	Response
257	Staffelei mit weißem Papier in einem Gebäude, Altbau. Es ist ein rundes Zimmer, mit weißen Fenstern und goldenen Fenstergriffen. Auf dem weißen Papier ist mit bunten Farben gemalt. Mit großem, flachen Pinsel breite bunte Streifen gemalt. Längsstreifen.
258	Ich sehe einen Text, in dem eine einzelne Zeile gelb markiert ist.
259	Essen Trinken
260	Angespannte Gesichtszüge
261	Ein kleiner, offener Terminkalender mit weißen Seiten und dunkelgrauer Schrift auf einem Holztisch. Ein Datum ist eingekreist.
262	Eltern mit einem Kind auf dem Arm
263	Gesundheit
264	Ich erkenne einen gelben zettel, der an einem Kühlschrank hängt. Darauf ist ein rotes Ausrufezeichen.
265	Eine Notiz die an der Pinnwand hängt
266	Ein mann mit hellblauem hemd und schwarzer stoffhose eilt mit einem brief in der hand zu einem gelben briefkasten
267	Ein Kalender, der an der Wand hängt und das aktuelle Monat zeigt. Ein Datum ist mit rotem Filzstift umkreist und mehrere Ausrufezeichen sind in den Kreis gemalt. Ein Foto von zwei kleinen Kätzchen ist am Kalender abgebildet und außer der roten Markierung gibt es keine weiteren Einträge.
268	Am Notizbrett klemmt eine wichtige Notiz, in leuchtenden Farben, so dass sie nicht vergessen werden kann
269	Früh aufstehen, Kaffee trinken, klare Gedanken haben
270	Im Kalender ist das heutige Datum mit einem roten Kreis markiert.
271	Liebe, auskommen, gesundheit
272	Dringend
273	Meinen Mann, mein Kind und Hund;)
274	Wichtige Unterlagen (z. B. Bewerbungsunterlagen, Pass, Ausweis)
275	Arbeitsmaterialien—Materialien auf ein Meeting vorbereiten
276	Gesundheit, Ehrlichkeit, Pünktlichkeit, Bescheindenheit
277	Ausrufezeichen, dringlich, volle Aufmerksamkeit
278	Ausrufezeichen
279	Freunde, Familie, Katze, Arbeit, Geld, Wohnung
280	Das rote Ausrufezeichen bei Outlook, mit dem eine Email als wichtig markiert ist..
281	Ich sehe das Arztrezept, dass ich heute vergessen habe mitzunehmen und das hinter mir liegt. Es liegt auf dem kleinen Sofatisch und ich muss es morgen mit in die Stadt nehmen.
282	Ein rotes Ausrufezeichen neben einer eMail.
283	Etwas steht ganz oben auf der Liste. Etwas hat höchste Priorität.

(continued)

Table D.1 (continued)

#	Response
284	Ein Notizzettel klebt an der Küchentür, damit es nicht bergessen wird.
285	Eine Geldbörse liegt allein auf einem Tisch.
286	In einem Terminkalender ist ein Eintrag dick rot unterstrichen und mit Ausrufezeichen versehen.

Notes: Participants with erroneous response and participants without response were deleted

Appendix E

Dear participant,

below, we will present you with a variety of different terms and situations.

Please, **picture those terms and situations before 'your inner eye'.**

Your task will be to **rate the connection between the terms and situtations on a scale.**

Your responses will not be judged.

Please do not listen to music, watch TV, or anything similar––that would considerably distort the results.

Please note: Only serious and careful answers can be remunerated.

Thank you very much for your participation!

Fig. E.1 Instructional page for Study 2.2 to 2.4. In Study 2.1, an identical German translation was presented

Appendix F

Table F.1 Median ratings per content candidate in Austrian, German, and Swiss participant group

Meaning (Group)	
Contents	Rating
[Something or someone] is absent, not here (E.4)	
An empty seat	6 (IQR = 2)
A person is standing alone and far away	5 (IQR = 3)
[Something] is bad, negative (E.4)	
An angry face	6 (IQR = 2)
[Something] is dark, black	4 (IQR = 2)
An overcast, rainy sky	4 (IQR = 2)
A sad face	6 (IQR = 2)
Spoiled food	6 (IQR = 2)
[Something] begins (E.1)	
A baby being born	7 (IQR = 1)
[Something] becomes bright, brighter	4 (IQR = 2)
The rising sun	6 (IQR = 1)
[Something or someone] is busy (E.3)	
An action is repeated over and over again	5 (IQR = 3)
Hands performing an action	6 (IQR = 2)
Many [people or things] perform many actions, all at the same time	5 (IQR = 3)
Coldness (E.3)	
Blue background	3.5 (IQR = 3)
Snow, ice	7 (IQR = 1)
Snowflake	6 (IQR = 1)

(continued)

D. Bühler, *Universal, Intuitive, and Permanent Pictograms,*
https://doi.org/10.1007/978-3-658-32310-3

Table F.1 (continued)

Meaning (Group)	
Contents	Rating
A snowy landscape with mountains	7 (IQR = 1)
White, blue	4 (IQR = 3)
[Something] is dangerous (E.2)	
[Something] is big	3 (IQR = 2)
An animal that could kill a human being	6 (IQR = 2)
[Something] is dark, black	3 (IQR = 3)
Fire	6 (IQR = 1)
Doing something by night	3 (IQR = 2)
A deep abyss	6 (IQR = 2)
[Something] is red	4 (IQR = 4)
[Something or someone] is running fast and approaching	4 (IQR = 2)
Teeth and jaws	5 (IQR = 3)
Day (E.3)	
The blue sky	6 (IQR = 1.25)
Brightness and light	6 (IQR = 2)
A meadow with flowers	4 (IQR = 3)
The shining sun	7 (IQR = 1)
[Something] is decreasing (E.4)	
Something big is getting smaller and smaller	6 (IQR = 2)
Bit by bit [something] is taken away	7 (IQR = 1)
A full container is emptied continuously	7 (IQR = 1)
[Something] ends (E.4)	
[Something] gets slowly darker until it turns black	5 (IQR = 3)
The last of a row or a set	6 (IQR = 2)
A path or a road ends	6 (IQR = 1)
People leave a place	5 (IQR = 2)
Tears	4 (IQR = 2)
[Something] is everywhere (E.1)	
Air	6 (IQR = 2)
Particles suspended in the air	5 (IQR = 2)
The blue sky	4 (IQR = 3)
[Something] is good, positive (E.4)	
The face of a laughing, smiling girl	6 (IQR = 2)
A green meadow	5 (IQR = 2)

(continued)

Table F.1 (continued)

Meaning (Group)	
Contents	Rating
Light and bright colors	5 (IQR = 2)
The shining sun	6 (IQR = 1)
A smiling face	6 (IQR = 1)
[Something or someone] is here, on-site (E.3)	
[Someone or something] is arriving, entering	5 (IQR = 3)
[Someone] is sitting someplace	4 (IQR = 3)
[Someone or something] is standing in front or next to oneself	7 (IQR = 1)
[Something or someone] is standing someplace	3.5 (IQR = 3)
[Something] is important (E.2)	
[Something] is big	4 (IQR = 3)
[Something] is bright, shining	4 (IQR = 3)
[Something] is flashing, blinks	5 (IQR = 2)
[Something] is in the middle	3 (IQR = 2)
[Something] is on top	4 (IQR = 3)
[Something] is red	4 (IQR = 3)
[Something] is increasing (E.1)	
[Something] is getting denser	5 (IQR = 3)
[Something] is growing upwards	5 (IQR = 2)
Pregnancy, birth	5 (IQR = 3)
Night (E.3)	
Dark, black, blue	6 (IQR = 2)
Many stars shining bright	7 (IQR = 1)
The moon shining bright	7 (IQR = 1)
Power (E.1)	
A dark tree	3 (IQR = 2)
A male arm with tensed biceps muscle	6 (IQR = 1)
A tree	4 (IQR = 2)
Several, a group of [some things or some people] (E.2)	
[Some people or some things] standing together, all doing the same thing	6 (IQR = 2.5)
[Some people or some things] standing together, all looking the same	6 (IQR = 3)

(continued)

Table F.1 (continued)

Meaning (Group)	
Contents	Rating
[Some people or some things] standing together in a circle	6 (IQR = 2)
[Some people or some things] standing together, each in a different color	5 (IQR = 2)
[Some people or some things] standing together randomly in a square	4 (IQR = 2)
[Something or someone] is single, solitary	
A person standing alone	n.t
Warmth (E.1)	
Fire	7 (IQR = 1)
A red fire	6 (IQR = 1)
Sun	7 (IQR = 1)
A sweating person	6 (IQR = 2)
[Something] goes wrong, is wrong (E.3)	
[Something] collapses	5 (IQR = 2)
[Something] falls and breaks, shatters	6 (IQR = 2)
Hands dropping [something] that breaks, shatters	6 (IQR = 2)
[Something] is red	2 (IQR = 3)

Notes: n.t. = not tested. Meanings and contents are in alphabetical order of major words

Appendix G

Table G.1 Median ratings per content candidate in U.S. and Canadian participant group

Meaning (Group)	
Contents	Rating
[Something or someone] is absent, not here (NA.4)	
[Something] is black	2 (IQR=4)
A hole in the middle	5 (IQR=4)
An empty seat in an empty room	6 (IQR=3)
An empty seat in the middle of sitting people	6 (IQR=3)
An empty space in the middle	5 (IQR=3)
[Something] is white	2 (IQR=3)
[Something] is bad, negative (NA.4)	
An angry, frowning face	6 (IQR=2)
[Something] is black	4 (IQR=3)
Dark clouds	5 (IQR=2)
People fighting and yelling at each other	7 (IQR=1)
[Something] is red	4 (IQR=4)
A sad, crying face	6 (IQR=2)
Spoiled food	6 (IQR=2)
[Something] begins (NA.2)	
A baby being born	7 (IQR=1)
A hatching egg	6 (IQR=2)
The rising sun	6 (IQR=2)
A sprouting plant	6 (IQR=2)
[Something or someone] is busy (NA.3)	
Bees are flying around	5 (IQR=4.25)
[Someone or something] is doing the same over and over again	5 (IQR=3.25)

(continued)

Table G.1 (continued)

Meaning (Group)	
Contents	Rating
Hands performing an action	5 (IQR = 3)
[Someone or something] is moving around fast	6 (IQR = 2.25)
[Someone or something] is moving back and forth	4 (IQR = 4)
[Some people or some things] perform actions all at the same time	5 (IQR = 4)
[Some people or some things] are standing in a queue	3 (IQR = 3.5)
Coldness (NA.2)	
Breath freezing	7 (IQR = 1.5)
[Something] is dark, black	3 (IQR = 4)
Ice and snow	7 (IQR = 0.5)
Icicle	7 (IQR = 1)
Glacier	7 (IQR = 1)
A snow-covered mountain	6 (IQR = 2)
Snowflake	7 (IQR = 1)
[Something] is white, blue	4 (IQR = 4)
[Something] is dangerous (NA.2)	
An animal that could kill a human being	7 (IQR = 1)
[Someone or something] is approaching very fast	4 (IQR = 2.5)
[Something] is black	2 (IQR = 3)
A cliff	6 (IQR = 2)
Fire	6 (IQR = 2.5)
Knife	5 (IQR = 3)
[Something] is red	3 (IQR = 3.5)
Sharp teeth and jaws	6 (IQR = 2)
Day (NA.2)	
The blue sky	6 (IQR = 1)
Light shining bright through an opening in the wall	6 (IQR = 2.5)
A meadow with flowers and trees	4 (IQR = 3.5)
The shining sun	7 (IQR = 0)
[Something] is decreasing (NA.3)	
[Something or someone] is going farther away	4 (IQR = 4)
The level of [something] is sinking	6 (IQR = 2)
Piece by piece [something] is taken away	6 (IQR = 2)
The size of [something] is shrinking	7 (IQR = 1)
A vessel is emptying	6 (IQR = 3)
[Something] ends (NA.4)	
[Something] becomes continuously darker until it is black	4 (IQR = 4)

(continued)

Table G.1 (continued)

Meaning (Group)

Contents	Rating
The end of a rope or string	6 (IQR = 3)
The last of a row or a quantity	5 (IQR = 2)
The linear movement of [someone or something] comes to a stop	5 (IQR = 3)
A road ends	7 (IQR = 2)
[Someone] walks away	5 (IQR = 3)
[Something] is everywhere (NA.1)	
Air	7 (IQR = 2)
Ants	3 (IQR = 3)
The blue sky	4 (IQR = 4)
Light shining bright	4 (IQR = 4)
Ocean	5 (IQR = 4)
Particles in the air or light	5 (IQR = 3)
[Something] is spread all over a surface	6 (IQR = 2.5)
[Something] is good, positive (NA.4)	
A flower	5 (IQR = 2)
Tasty food	6 (IQR = 2)
[Something] is green	4 (IQR = 3)
People sitting together eating	5 (IQR = 3)
A smiling, laughing face	7 (IQR = 1)
The shining sun	5 (IQR = 3)
[Something] is white	4 (IQR = 3)
[Something or someone] is here, on-site (NA.3)	
[Someone or something is arriving	6 (IQR = 3)
[Someone or something] is standing behind someone or something else	4.5 (IQR = 3.25)
[Someone or something] is standing in front of oneself	5 (IQR = 4)
[Something] is important (NA.1)	
[Something] is big	5 (IQR = 3.5)
[Something] is black	2 (IQR = 3)
[Something] is bright	4 (IQR = 3)
[Something] is flashing	5 (IQR = 2)
[Something] is red	4 (IQR = 3)
[Something] is increasing (NA.2)	
[Something] is falling onto a pile while the pile is getting bigger	6 (IQR = 2)
[Something] is growing upward	6 (IQR = 2)
The level of [something] is rising	7 (IQR = 1)

(continued)

Table G.1 (continued)

Meaning (Group)	
Contents	Rating
Night (NA.1)	
Bright moon and stars	7 (IQR = 1)
Clouds in the dark sky	5 (IQR = 3)
[Something] is dark, black, blue	5 (IQR = 3)
An owl	6 (IQR = 2)
Power (NA.2)	
A big, muscular man	7 (IQR = 1)
A fist	6 (IQR = 2)
A male arm flexing biceps	6 (IQR = 2)
Lightning bolt	6 (IQR = 2)
Several, a group of [some things or some people] (NA.3)	
[Some people or some things] jointly moving around	6 (IQR = 3)
[Some people or some things] standing together in a circle	7 (IQR = 1)
[Some people or some things] standing together jointly doing the same	7 (IQR = 2)
[Some people or some things] standing together looking the same	6 (IQR = 2)
[Something or someone] is single, solitary	
A person standing or sitting alone	n.t
Warmth (NA.1)	
Fire	7 (IQR = 1)
Beach	6 (IQR = 2)
Blanket	7 (IQR = 1)
A drinking vessel with a hot drink	6 (IQR = 1)
[Something] is red	4 (IQR = 4)
The shining sun	7 (IQR = 1)
[Something] is yellow	5 (IQR = 2)
[Something] goes wrong, is wrong (NA.1)	
[Something] collapses	6 (IQR = 1)
[Something] falls and breaks	6 (IQR = 2)
Fire	4 (IQR = 3)
[Something] is flashing brightly	4 (IQR = 3.5)
[Something] is red	2 (IQR = 2)
[Something] spills over onto the ground	5 (IQR = 3)
A sad, crying face	6 (IQR = 2.5)

Notes: n.t. = not tested. Meanings and contents are in alphabetical order of major words

Appendix H

Table H.1 Median ratings per content candidate in South African participant group

Meaning (Group)	
Contents	Rating
[Something or someone] is absent, not here (SA.4)	
[Something] is black	3 (IQR=3)
A hole in the middle	5 (IQR=2.25)
An empty seat in an empty room	6 (IQR=2.25)
An empty seat in the middle of sitting people	7 (IQR=1.25)
An empty space in the middle	5.5 (IQR=3)
[Something] is white	1 (IQR=2.25)
[Something] is bad, negative (SA.4)	
An angry, frowning face	6 (IQR=1)
[Something] is black	4 (IQR=3.25)
Dark clouds	5 (IQR=3)
People fighting and yelling at each other	7 (IQR=1)
[Something] is red	4 (IQR=3.25)
A sad, crying face	6.5 (IQR=1)
Spoiled food	6 (IQR=2)
[Something] begins (SA.2)	
A baby being born	7 (IQR=1)
A hatching egg	7 (IQR=1)
The rising sun	7 (IQR=2)
A sprouting plant	7 (IQR=1)
[Something or someone] is busy (SA.3)	
Bees are flying around	5 (IQR=4)
[Someone or something] is doing the same over and over again	5 (IQR=2)

(continued)

Table H.1 (continued)

Meaning (Group)	
Contents	Rating
Hands performing an action	6 (IQR = 2)
[Someone or something] is moving around fast	6 (IQR = 3)
[Someone or something] is moving back and forth	5 (IQR = 2)
[Some people or some things] perform actions all at the same time	6 (IQR = 3)
[Some people or some things] are standing in a queue	4 (IQR = 4)
Coldness (SA.2)	
Breath freezing	7 (IQR = 1)
[Something] is dark, black	3 (IQR = 4)
Ice and snow	7 (IQR = 0)
Icicle	7 (IQR = 1)
Glacier	7 (IQR = 1.5)
A snow-covered mountain	7 (IQR = 1)
Snowflake	7 (IQR = 1)
[Something] is white, blue	4 (IQR = 2)
[Something] is dangerous (SA.2)	
An animal that could kill a human being	7 (IQR = 1)
[Someone or something] is approaching very fast	5 (IQR = 3)
[Something] is black	2 (IQR = 3)
A cliff	6 (IQR = 3)
Fire	6 (IQR = 2)
Knife	6 (IQR = 2)
[Something] is red	5 (IQR = 3)
Sharp teeth and jaws	7 (IQR = 1)
Day (SA.2)	
The blue sky	7 (IQR = 1)
Light shining bright through an opening in the wall	6 (IQR = 2)
A meadow with flowers and trees	4 (IQR = 3)
The shining sun	7 (IQR = 0)
[Something] is decreasing (SA.3)	
[Something or someone] is going farther away	4 (IQR = 3)
The level of [something] is sinking	6 (IQR = 1.75)
Piece by piece [something] is taken away	7 (IQR = 1)
The size of [something] is shrinking	7 (IQR = 1)
A vessel is emptying	6.5 (IQR = 2)

(continued)

Table H.1 (continued)

Meaning (Group)	
Contents	Rating
[Something] ends (SA.4)	
[Something] becomes continuously darker until it is black	6 (IQR = 2.25)
The end of a rope or string	7 (IQR = 3)
The last of a row or a quantity	6 (IQR = 2)
The linear movement of [someone or something] comes to a stop	6 (IQR = 2.25)
A road ends	7 (IQR = 1)
[Someone] walks away	5 (IQR = 3)
[Something] is everywhere (SA.1)	
Air	7 (IQR = 2.75)
Ants	3 (IQR = 4)
The blue sky	4 (IQR = 4.75)
Light shining bright	3 (IQR = 3)
Ocean	5 (IQR = 3)
Particles in the air or light	5 (IQR = 4)
[Something] is spread all over a surface	6 (IQR = 2)
[Something] is good, positive (SA.4)	
A flower	5 (IQR = 2)
Tasty food	6 (IQR = 2.25)
[Something] is green	5.5 (IQR = 2)
People sitting together eating	5 (IQR = 2)
A smiling, laughing face	7 (IQR = 1)
The shining sun	6 (IQR = 3)
[Something] is white	4 (IQR = 3)
[Something or someone] is here, on-site (SA.3)	
[Someone or something is arriving	6 (IQR = 2.75)
[Someone or something] is standing behind someone or something else	4 (IQR = 3)
[Someone or something] is standing in front of oneself	6 (IQR = 3)
[Something] is important (SA.1)	
[Something] is big	4 (IQR = 2)
[Something] is black	1 (IQR = 2)
[Something] is bright	4 (IQR = 2.75)
[Something] is flashing	6 (IQR = 3)
[Something] is red	5 (IQR = 2)
[Something] is increasing (SA.2)	
[Something] is falling onto a pile while the pile is getting bigger	7 (IQR = 1)

(continued)

Table H.1 (continued)

Meaning (Group)	
Contents	Rating
[Something] is growing upward	7 (IQR=2)
The level of [something] is rising	7 (IQR=1)
Night (SA.1)	
Bright moon and stars	7 (IQR=0)
Clouds in the dark sky	6 (IQR=3)
[Something] is dark, black, blue	6 (IQR=2)
An owl	6 (IQR=2)
Power (SA.2)	
A big, muscular man	7 (IQR=1)
A fist	6 (IQR=2)
A male arm flexing biceps	6 (IQR=1.5)
Lightning bolt	5 (IQR=2.5)
Several, a group of [some things or some people] (SA.3)	
[Some people or some things] jointly moving around	6 (IQR=2.75)
[Some people or some things] standing together in a circle	7 (IQR=1)
[Some people or some things] standing together jointly doing the same	6 (IQR=2)
[Some people or some things] standing together looking the same	6 (IQR=1)
[Something or someone] is single, solitary	
A person standing or sitting alone	n.t
Warmth (SA.1)	
Fire	7 (IQR=1)
Beach	5 (IQR=2)
Blanket	7 (IQR=0.75)
A drinking vessel with a hot drink	6 (IQR=1.75)
[Something] is red	4 (IQR=2)
The shining sun	7 (IQR=1)
[Something] is yellow	4 (IQR=2)
[Something] goes wrong, is wrong (SA.1)	
[Something] collapses	7 (IQR=1.75)
[Something] falls and breaks	6 (IQR=2.75)
Fire	4 (IQR=3.75)
[Something] is flashing brightly	4.5 (IQR=3.75)
[Something] is red	4 (IQR=3)
[Something] spills over onto the ground	5 (IQR=2.75)
A sad, crying face	7 (IQR=1)

Notes: n.t.=not tested. Meanings and contents are in alphabetical order of major words

Appendix I

Table I.1 Median ratings per content candidate in Australian participant group

Meaning (Group)	
Contents	Rating
[Something or someone] is absent, not here (A.4)	
[Something] is black	3 (IQR = 4)
A hole in the middle	5 (IQR = 3)
An empty seat in an empty room	5.5 (IQR = 2)
An empty seat in the middle of sitting people	6 (IQR = 2)
An empty space in the middle	5 (IQR = 2)
[Something] is white	2 (IQR = 2)
[Something] is bad, negative (A.4)	
An angry, frowning face	6 (IQR = 1)
[Something] is black	4 (IQR = 4)
Dark clouds	5 (IQR = 2)
People fighting and yelling at each other	7 (IQR = 1)
[Something] is red	4 (IQR = 3)
A sad, crying face	6 (IQR = 1.25)
Spoiled food	6 (IQR = 1)
[Something] begins (A.2)	
A baby being born	7 (IQR = 2)
A hatching egg	6.5 (IQR = 1)
The rising sun	6 (IQR = 2)
A sprouting plant	6 (IQR = 1)
[Something or someone] is busy (A.3)	
Bees are flying around	5 (IQR = 3)
[Someone or something] is doing the same over and over again	5 (IQR = 3)

(continued)

Table I.1 (continued)

Meaning (Group)	
Contents	Rating
Hands performing an action	5 (IQR = 3)
[Someone or something] is moving around fast	6 (IQR = 1)
[Some people or some things] perform actions all at the same time	5 (IQR = 3)
[Some people or some things] are standing in a queue	4 (IQR = 3)
Coldness (A.2)	
Breath freezing	7 (IQR = 1)
[Something] is dark, black	3 (IQR = 3)
Ice and snow	7 (IQR = 0.25)
Icicle	7 (IQR = 1)
Glacier	7 (IQR = 1)
A snow-covered mountain	7 (IQR = 1)
Snowflake	6.5 (IQR = 1)
[Something] is white, blue	5 (IQR = 2)
[Something] is dangerous (A.2)	
An animal that could kill a human being	6 (IQR = 1)
[Someone or something] is approaching very fast	5 (IQR = 3)
[Something] is black	2 (IQR = 2)
A cliff	5 (IQR = 2)
Fire	5 (IQR = 2)
Knife	5 (IQR = 3)
[Something] is red	5 (IQR = 3.25)
Sharp teeth and jaws	6 (IQR = 2)
Day (A.2)	
The blue sky	7 (IQR = 1)
Light shining bright through an opening in the wall	5 (IQR = 1)
A meadow with flowers and trees	5 (IQR = 3)
The shining sun	7 (IQR = 0)
[Something] is decreasing (A.3)	
[Something or someone] is going farther away	4 (IQR = 2)
The level of [something] is sinking	6 (IQR = 2)
Piece by piece [something] is taken away	6 (IQR = 1)
The size of [something] is shrinking	6 (IQR = 1)
A vessel is emptying	6 (IQR = 2)
[Something] ends (A.4)	
[Something] becomes continuously darker until it is black	6 (IQR = 2.25)

(continued)

Table I.1 (continued)

Meaning (Group)	
Contents	Rating
The end of a rope or string	6 (IQR = 2.25)
The last of a row or a quantity	5 (IQR = 1)
The linear movement of [someone or something] comes to a stop	6 (IQR = 2)
A road ends	6 (IQR = 2)
[Someone] walks away	5 (IQR = 2.25)
[Something] is everywhere (A.1)	
Air	6 (IQR = 2)
Ants	4 (IQR = 3)
The blue sky	4 (IQR = 4)
Light shining bright	4 (IQR = 3)
Ocean	5 (IQR = 3)
Particles in the air or light	5 (IQR = 2)
[Something] is spread all over a surface	5 (IQR = 1)
[Something] is good, positive (A.4)	
A flower	5 (IQR = 2)
Tasty food	6 (IQR = 1)
[Something] is green	5 (IQR = 2)
People sitting together eating	5 (IQR = 3)
A smiling, laughing face	7 (IQR = 1)
The shining sun	6 (IQR = 2)
[Something] is white	4 (IQR = 2)
[Something or someone] is here, on-site (A.3)	
[Someone or something] is arriving	5 (IQR = 2)
[Someone or something] is standing behind someone or something else	4 (IQR = 4)
[Someone or something] is standing in front of oneself	4 (IQR = 2)
[Something] is important (A.1)	
[Something] is big	4 (IQR = 2.5)
[Something] is black	2 (IQR = 2)
[Something] is bright	4 (IQR = 3)
[Something] is flashing	6 (IQR = 1)
[Something] is red	4 (IQR = 4)
[Something] is increasing (A.2)	
[Something] is falling onto a pile while the pile is getting bigger	6 (IQR = 2)
[Something] is growing upward	6 (IQR = 2)
The level of [something] is rising	6 (IQR = 1)

(continued)

Table I.1 (continued)

Meaning (Group)	
Contents	Rating
Night (A.1)	
Bright moon and stars	7 (IQR = 0)
Clouds in the dark sky	5 (IQR = 3)
[Something] is dark, black, blue	5 (IQR = 2)
An owl	6 (IQR = 0)
Power (A.2)	
A big, muscular man	6 (IQR = 1)
A fist	5 (IQR = 2)
A male arm flexing biceps	6 (IQR = 2)
Lightning bolt	5 (IQR = 1.5)
Several, a group of [some things or some people] (A.3)	
[Some people or some things] jointly moving around	6 (IQR = 1)
[Some people or some things] standing together in a circle	6 (IQR = 1)
[Some people or some things] standing together jointly doing the same	6 (IQR = 2)
[Some people or some things] standing together looking the same	6 (IQR = 2)
[Something or someone] is single, solitary	
A person standing or sitting alone	n.t
Warmth (A.1)	
Fire	7 (IQR = 1)
Beach	5 (IQR = 2)
Blanket	7 (IQR = 1)
A drinking vessel with a hot drink	6 (IQR = 2)
[Something] is red	5 (IQR = 3)
The shining sun	7 (IQR = 1)
[Something] is yellow	4 (IQR = 2)
[Something] goes wrong, is wrong (A.1)	
[Something] collapses	6 (IQR = 2)
[Something] falls and breaks	6 (IQR = 1.5)
Fire	4 (IQR = 3)
[Something] is flashing brightly	4 (IQR = 4)
[Something] is red	4 (IQR = 3)
[Something] spills over onto the ground	5 (IQR = 2)
A sad, crying face	6 (IQR = 2)

Notes: n.t. = not tested. Meanings and contents are in alphabetical order of major words

Appendix J

Table J.1 Guidelines and cited references, following best-evidence synthesis method

Guideline section	
Guideline	Cited literature
How to Represent Three-Dimensional Objects on a Two-Dimensional Surface (G1–G8)	
G1 G2 G3 G4 G5 G6 G7 G8	Giardino and Greenberg (2015, p. 21), Melcher and Cavanagh (2013, p. 369), Palmer (1999, p. 20) Biederman and Ju (1988, p. 63), Cole et al. (2009, pp. 8–9), Cole et al. (2008, p. 2) DeCarlo et al. (2003), Giardino and Greenberg (2015, pp. 18–19), Hörr et al. (2010, p. 4), Judd et al. (2007, p. 5), Liu et al. (2012, p. 146), Medhi et al. (2007, p. 876), Melcher and Cavanagh (2013, p. 362), Sayim and Cavanagh (2011, pp. 1–3), Walther et al. (2011, pp. 9661–9665), Willats (2005, p. 160) Cavanagh (2005, p. 303), Sayim and Cavanagh (2011, p. 2) Cavanagh (2005, p. 302), Melcher and Cavanagh (2013, p. 374) Cavanagh (2005, pp. 302, 306) Cavanagh (2005, p. 304), Sayim and Cavanagh (2011, p. 3), Willats (1997, pp. 112–123) Huang (2008, p. 241), Willats (2006, p. 10) Girshick et al. (2000, p. 4)
How to Represent the Pictogram Contents (G9–G12)	
G9 G10 G11 G12	Gatsou et al. (2012, p. 96), Goldstein (2010, p. 820), Goonetilleke et al. (2001, pp. 755–75), Melcher and Cavanagh (2013, pp. 365, 367), Thompson et al. (2011, pp. 588–591), Willats (2006, pp. 16–19), Willats (2005, p. 160) Chang and Nesbitt (2006, p. 8), Palmer (1999, pp. 398–402) Konkle and Oliva (2011, pp. 11–12) Palmer (1999, pp. 421–424), Palmer et al. (1981, p. 139), Thompson et al. (2011, pp. 606–609), Willats (2005)

(continued)

Table J.1 (continued)

Guideline section

Guideline	Cited literature
How to Design Representations in General (G13–G21)	
G13	Chang and Nesbitt (2006, p. 6), Palmer et al. (2003), Ware (2013, pp. 182–183)
G14	Biederman (1987, p. 139), Wogalter et al. (2006, p. 162)
G15	Curry et al. (1998), Yee et al. (2012, p. 837)
G16	Chang and Nesbitt (2006, pp. 6–7, 9), Ware (2013, pp. 183–184)
G17	Chang and Nesbitt (2006, p. 7)
G18	Bar and Neta (2006, pp. 646–647), Lidwell et al. (2010, p. 62), Melcher and
G19	Cavanagh (2013)
G20	Cavanagh (2005, p. 305), Melcher and Cavanagh (2013, pp. 367–368)
G21	Barker and van Schaik (2000, pp. 162–163), Goonetilleke et al. (2001, pp. 755–756), McDougall et al. (2000, p. 292)
	Lindberg and Näsänen (2003, p. 119)
How to Use Color (G22–G26)	
G22	Bramao et al. (2010, pp. 50, 60, 62), Pierroutsakos and DeLoache (2003, p. 147)
G23	Melcher and Cavanagh (2013, p. 388)
G24	Durrani and Durrani (2009, p. 164), Lidwell et al. (2010, p. 48)
G25	Yee et al. (2012, p. 838)
G26	Durrani and Durrani (2009, p. 164)
How to Represent Actions and Movements (G27–G33)	
G27	Jones (1993, pp. 44–45), Medhi et al. (2007, pp. 876–878), Melcher and
G28	Cavanagh 2013, p. 381), Scaife and Rogers (1996, p. 190)
G29	Thompson et al. (2011, pp. 670, 674–675), Tversky (2011, p. 526), Tversky et al.
G30	(2006, p. 4), Tversky et al. (2002, p. 258)
G31	Johnson (2014, p. 201), Thompson et al. (2011, pp. 662–665)
G32	Palmer (1999, pp. 471–480), Ramachandran and Anstis (1986)
G33	Chang and Nesbitt (2006, p. 9)
	Honeywill (1999, pp. 63–64), Horton (1993, p. 683), Tversky (2011, p. 512), Tversky et al. (2002, p. 249), Tversky et al. (1991, pp. 545–547)
	Adams et al. (2010), Theo Boersema and Adams (2017, p. 310)
How to Choose Which Exemplar of a Pictogram Content to Represent (G34)	
G34	Barsalou 1993, Durrani and Durrani (2009, pp. 159–160), Harnad (1990, p. 342), Horton (1994, pp. 241–268, 1993, pp. 684–689), Kress (2003, p. 29), Palmer (1999, pp. 416–419), Ranta (2000, pp. 214–215), Rosch et al. (1976, pp. 383, 405), Tversky (2011, p. 516), Tversky et al. (2006, p. 3), Ware (2008, p. 121)

Notes: Cited references are in alphabetical order

Appendix K

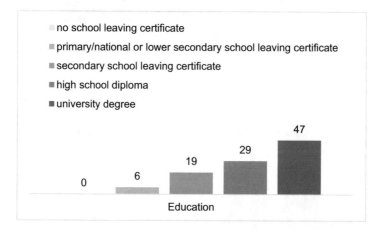

Fig. K.1 Distribution of educational levels of participants ($n = 101$). None mentioned *no school leaving certificate*

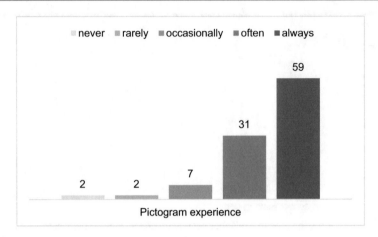

Fig. K.2 Distribution of use frequency of pictograms by participants ($n = 101$)

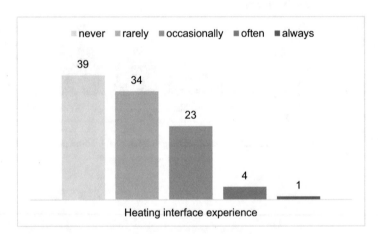

Fig. K.3 Distribution of use frequency of heating interfaces by participants ($n = 101$) for pictograms

Appendix L

Table L.1 Correct responses (CRs) in percent for UIPPs and manufacturer pictograms ($n = 101$)

Simple Pictograms	UIPP	Manufacturer
Coldness	100	100
Day	92.2	94.1
Night	95.1	99.0
Power	99.0	99.0
Warmth	100	61.8
Total	97.3 ($SD = 3.1$)	90.8 ($SD = 14.6$)
Compound Pictograms	UIPP	Manufacturer
[Something or someone] is absent or not here	53.9	76.6
[Something] is bad or negative	67.6	–
[Something] begins	96.1	43.1
[Something or someone] is busy	96.1	78.4
[Something] is dangerous	82.4	21.6
[Something] is decreasing	86.3	59.8
[Something] ends	74.5	86.3
[Something] is everywhere	90.2	–
[Something] is good or positive	85.3	91.2

(continued)

D. Bühler, *Universal, Intuitive, and Permanent Pictograms,*
https://doi.org/10.1007/978-3-658-32310-3

Table L.1 (continued)

[Something or someone] is here or on-site	94.1	99.0
[Something] is important	53.9	84.3
[Something] is increasing	96.1	85.3
Several or a group of [some things or some people]	97.1	77.5
[Something] goes wrong or is wrong	86.3	80.4
Total	82.9 ($SD = 14.4$)	73.6 ($SD = 21.0$)
Grand Total	86.7 ($SD = 13.8$)	78.9 ($SD = 20.7$)

Notes: The pictogram *[something] is decreasing*, taken from International Organization for Standardization and International Electrotechnical Commission (2007, p. 25) [216], was excluded because a pictogram from a manufacturer with the same meaning was included. The ISO 24,755:2007 pictogram's meaning was correctly chosen by 92.2% of the participants

Appendix M

Table M.1 Aggregated and cleaned response times (RTs) in seconds for UIPPs and manufacturer pictograms (n = 101)

Simple Pictograms	UIPP	Manufacturer
Coldness	3.12 (SD = 0.19)	3.25 (SD = 1.62)
Day	5.88 (SD = 6.27)	3.93 (SD = 0.74)
Night	3.47 (SD = 0.82)	3.09 (SD = 1.21)
Power	4.75 (SD = 2.28)	3.71 (SD = 0.78)
Warmth	3.79 (SD = 1.19)	4.67 (SD = 2.45)
Total	4.20 (SD = 1.00)	3.73 (SD = 0.56)
Compound Pictograms	UIPP	Manufacturer
[Something or someone] is absent, not here	10.52 (SD = 3.92)	6.47 (SD = 2.85)
[Something] is bad, negative	10.27 (SD = 4.97)	–
[Something] begins	7.72 (SD = 2.33)	7.51 (SD = 4.23)
[something or someone] is busy	5.94 (SD = 2.13)	6.05 (SD = 2.59)
[Something] is dangerous	6.97 (SD = 2.36)	4.57 (SD = 1.68)
[Something] is decreasing	6.73 (SD = 1.92)	8.02 (SD = 4.30)
[Something] ends	8.91 (SD = 2.79)	6.54 (SD = 3.45)
[Something] is everywhere	6.20 (SD = 2.42)	–
[Something] is good, positive	6.87 (SD = 1.82)	6.53 (SD = 2.03)
[Something or someone] is here, on-site	11.46 (SD = 4.60)	4.94 (SD = 0.98)

(continued)

D. Bühler, *Universal, Intuitive, and Permanent Pictograms*, https://doi.org/10.1007/978-3-658-32310-3

Table M.1   (continued)

[Something] is important	8.78 (SD = 2.85)	5.36 (SD = 1.66)
[Something] is increasing	6.47 (SD = 2.01)	5.98 (SD = 2.98)
Several or a group of [some things or some people]	6.51 (SD = 2.01)	8.58 (SD = 3.54)
[Something] goes wrong, is wrong	8.87 (SD = 3.05)	5.97 (SD = 2.79)
Total	8.02 (SD = 1.73)	6.38 (SD = 1.14)
Grand Total	7.01 (SD = 7.22)	5.60 (SD = 5.74)

Notes: RTs and SDs were subtracted by the mean of the aggregated forwarding times for all participants. The pictogram *[something] is decreasing*, taken from International Organization for Standardization and International Electrotechnical Commission (2007, p. 25) [216], was excluded because a pictogram from a manufacturer with the same meaning was included. RT for ISO 24,755:2007 pictogram was 5.8 s (*SD* = 2.89 s)

Appendix N

Table N.1 Pearson's Product Moment Correlations for Age with CRs and RTs

Correct Responses		Age
Total		−.30**
UIPP		
	Total	−.26**
	Simple	−.20*
	Compound	−.22*
Manufacturer		
	Total	−.14
	Simple	−.00
	Compound	−.14
Response Times[a]		Age[a]
Total		.44***
UIPP		
	Total	.44***
	Simple	.39***
	Compound	.44***
Manufacturer		
	Total	.42***
	Simple	.41***
	Compound	.40***

Notes: $*p < .05$, $**p < .01$, $***p < .001$. [a]Data was log-transformed

Appendix O

Fig. O.1 Presentation of Version A and B of UIPP *[warmth] is busy*

Appendix P

Table P.1 Median ranks and IQRs of comparisons between UIPPs and manufacturer pictograms ($n = 101$)

Simple Pictograms	Rank
Coldness	4 (*IQR*=2)
Day	2 (*IQR*=2)
Face	6 (*IQR*=3)
Flame	7 (*IQR*=1)
Hand	3 (*IQR*=2)
Night	4 (*IQR*=3)
Person	4 (*IQR*=4)
Power	1 (*IQR*=1)
Warmth	6 (*IQR*=3)
Total	4 (*IQR*=3.5)
Compound Pictograms	**Rank**
[Something or someone] is absent, not here	1 (*IQR*=1)
[Something] begins	6 (*IQR*=2)
[Something or someone] is busy	6 (*IQR*=2)
[Something] is dangerous	5 (*IQR*=4)
[Something] is decreasing	4 (*IQR*=4)
[Something] ends	2 (*IQR*=4)

(continued)

Table P.1 (continued)

[Something] is good, positive	1 (*IQR* = 1)
[Something or someone] is here, on-site	1 (*IQR* = 1)
[Something] is important	6 (*IQR* = 1)
[Something] is increasing	2 (*IQR* = 4)
Several or a group of [some things or some people]	4 (*IQR* = 4)
[Something] goes wrong, is wrong	2 (*IQR* = 1)
Total	2 (*IQR* = 4.5)
Grand Total	4 (*IQR* = 4)

Notes: The UIPP comparison with the pictogram *[something] is decreasing*, taken from International Organization for Standardization and International Electrotechnical Commission (2007, p. 25) [216], was excluded because a manufacturer pictogram with the same meaning was included. The median for ratings of the UIP Pictogram compared with the ISO 24,755:2007 pictogram was 1 (*IQR* = 1)

Appendix Q

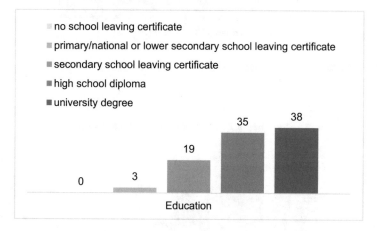

Fig. Q.1 Distribution of educational levels of participants ($n=95$). None mentioned *no school leaving certificate*

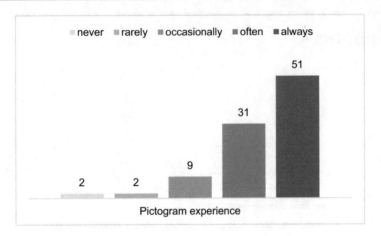

Fig. Q.2 Distribution of use frequency of pictograms by participants ($n = 95$)

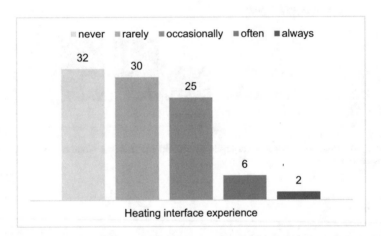

Fig. Q.3 Distribution of use frequency of heating interfaces by participants ($n = 95$) for pictograms

Appendix R

Table R.1 Median ranks for suitability (SU), intuitiveness (IU), un-ambiguity (UA), un-complexity (UC), innovativeness (IO), and familiarity (FA) per UIPP and manufacturer pictogram ($n = 95$)

Simple Pictograms	SU	IU	UA	UC	IO	FA
Coldness						
UIPP	5	5	5	4	2	5
Manufacturer	5	5	5	5	1	5
Day						
UIPP	4	4	4	4	3	4
Manufacturer	5	5	5	5	1	5
Night						
UIPP	5	5	5	4	2	5
Manufacturer	5	5	5	5	1	5
Power						
UIPP	3	3	3	3	4	2
Manufacturer	5	5	5	5	1	5
Warmth						
UIPP	5	5	4	5	2	5
Manufacturer	4	4	4	5	2	4
Total	5 ($IQR = 0.75$)	5 ($IQR = 0.75$)	5 ($IQR = 1$)	5 ($IQR = 1$)	2 ($IQR = 1$)	5 ($IQR = 0.75$)

(continued)

© The Editor(s) (if applicable) and The Author(s), under exclusive license to
Springer Fachmedien Wiesbaden GmbH, part of Springer Nature 2021
D. Bühler, *Universal, Intuitive, and Permanent Pictograms*,
https://doi.org/10.1007/978-3-658-32310-3

Table R.1 (continued)

Compound Pictograms	SU	IU	UA	UC	IO	FA
[Something or someone] is absent, not here						
UIPP	2	2	2	2	4	2
Manufacturer	4	4	3	4	2	3
[Something] is bad, negative						
UIPP	2	2	2	2	4	1
[Something] begins						
UIPP	4	4	3	3	4	2
Manufacturer	3	3	2	5	2	3
[Something or someone] is busy						
UIPP	3	3	3	2	4	2
Manufacturer	4	4	4	4	2	3
[Something] is dangerous						
UIPP	4	4	3	3	3	3
Manufacturer	5	5	5	5	1	5
[Something] is decreasing						
UIPP	3	3	3	2	4	2
Manufacturer	3	2	2	4	3	2
[Something] ends						
UIPP	3	3	3	2	4	2
Manufacturer	4	4	4	4	2	4
[Something] is everywhere						
UIPP	4	4	3	3	4	2
[Something] is good, positive						
UIPP	4	3	3	2	4	2
Manufacturer	5	5	5	5	1	5
[Something or someone] is here, on-site						
UIPP	2	2	2	2	4	2
Manufacturer	5	5	4	5	2	4
[Something] is important						
UIPP	3	3	3	3	3	3
Manufacturer	4	4	4	5	2	4
[Something] is increasing						
UIPP	4	4	4	4	3	3
Manufacturer	5	5	4	5	2	4
Several or a group of [some things or some people]						
UIPP	4	4	4	3	3	3
Manufacturer	4	4	4	4	2	4

(continued)

Table R.1 (continued)

[Something] goes wrong, is wrong						
UIPP	2	2	2	2	5	1
Manufacturer	5	5	4	5	1	5
Total	4 (IQR = 1)	4 (IQR = 1)	3 (IQR = 1)	3.5 (IQR = 2.75)	3 (IQR = 2)	3 (IQR = 2)
Grand Total	4 (IQR = 2)	4 (IQR = 2)	4 (IQR = 1)	4 (IQR = 2)	2 (IQR = 2)	3 (IQR = 3)

Notes: The pictogram *[something] is decreasing*, taken from International Organization for Standardization and International Electrotechnical Commission (2007, p. 25) [216], was excluded because a pictogram from a manufacturer with the same meaning was included. The ISO 24,755:2007 pictogram's medians were: SU = 5, IU = 5, UA = 5, UC = 5, IO = 2, FA = 5

Appendix S

Table S.1 Median ranks for suitability (SU), intuitiveness (IU), un-ambiguity (UA), un-complexity (UC), innovativeness (IO), and familiarity (FA) per participants ($n = 95$)

Pictograms	SU	IU	UA	UC	IO	FA
All	4	4	4	4	3	3
	($IQR = 0$)	($IQR = 0$)	($IQR = 1$)	($IQR = 1.5$)	($IQR = 1$)	($IQR = 1$)
All simple	5	5	4.5	5	1.5	1
	($IQR = 1$)	($IQR = 1$)	($IQR = 1$)	($IQR = 1$)	($IQR = 1$)	($IQR = 1$)
All compound	4	4.5	4	5	2	2
	($IQR = 1$)	($IQR = 1$)	($IQR = 1$)	($IQR = 1$)	($IQR = 1$)	($IQR = 1$)
All UIPP	4	3	3	3	4	2
	($IQR = 1$)	($IQR = 1$)	($IQR = 1.5$)	($IQR = 1.5$)	($IQR = 1$)	($IQR = 1$)
Simple UIPP	4	5	4	4	2	4
	($IQR = 1$)	($IQR = 1$)	($IQR = 1$)	($IQR = 2$)	($IQR = 1$)	($IQR = 2$)
Compound UIPP	3	3	3	2	4	2
	($IQR = 1.5$)	($IQR = 2$)	($IQR = 1.5$)	($IQR = 1$)	($IQR = 0.5$)	($IQR = 1.5$)
All manufacturer	5	5	4	5	2	4
	($IQR = 1$)	($IQR = 1$)	($IQR = 1$)	($IQR = 1$)	($IQR = 1$)	($IQR = 1$)
Simple manufacturer	5	5	5	5	1	5
	($IQR = 1$)	($IQR = 1$)	($IQR = 1$)	($IQR = 0$)	($IQR = 1$)	($IQR = 0$)
Compound manufacturer	4	4	4	4.5	2	4
	($IQR = 0.75$)	($IQR = 1$)	($IQR = 0.75$)	($IQR = 1$)	($IQR = 1.5$)	($IQR = 1$)

Appendix T

Table T.1 One-sample Wilcoxon signed-rank tests for UIPP and manufacturer ratings (test value $= 3$)

	V	p	Hodges-Lehmann Estimate	Rank-Biserial Correlation
UIPP				
Suitability	1775.00	< .001	1.00	−0.22
Intuitiveness	1382.00	< .001	1.00	−0.39
Un-ambiguity	870.00	.230	2.064e-5	−0.62
Un-complexity	753.00	.088	−4.375e-5	−0.67
Innovativeness	2412.5	< .001	1.00	0.06
Familiarity	248.50	< .001	−1.00	−0.89
Manufacturer				
Suitability	3984.50	< .001	1.50	0.75
Intuitiveness	3470.50	< .001	1.50	0.52
Un-ambiguity	3169.50	< .001	1.50	0.39
Un-complexity	4005.00	< .001	1.50	0.76
Innovativeness	115.50	< .001	−1.50	−0.95
Familiarity	3418.50	<.001	1.50	0.50

Appendix U

Table U.1 Matched-pairs Wilcoxon signed-ranks test for UIPP and manufacturer ratings

UIPP vs. Manufacturer set		*W*	*p*	*Hodges-Lehmann Estimate*	*Rank-Biserial Correlation*
Complete					
	Suitability	104.00	<.001	−1.00	−0.92
	Intuitiveness	64.50	<.001	−1.50	−0.95
	Un-ambiguity	211.00	<.001	−1.50	−0.84
	Un-complexity	16.50	<.001	−2.00	−0.99
	Innovativeness	3368.50	<.001	2.00	0.98
	Familiarity	28.00	<.001	−2.00	−0.98
Simple					
	Suitability	30.00	<.001	−1.00	−0.89
	Intuitiveness	159.00	.006	−1.00	−0.50
	Un-ambiguity	275.00	<.001	−1.00	−0.53
	Un-complexity	57.00	<.001	−1.50	−0.91
	Innovativeness	1732.50	<.001	1.50	0.89
	Familiarity	149.50	<.001	−1.00	−0.71
Compound					
	Suitability	106.50	<.001	−1.25	−0.93
	Intuitiveness	97.00	<.001	−1.50	−0.94
	Un-ambiguity	264.50	<.001	−1.50	−0.83
	Un-complexity	23.50	<.001	−2.00	−0.99
	Innovativeness	3604.00	<.001	2.00	0.97
	Familiarity	39.50	<.001	−2.00	−0.98

Appendix V

Table V.1 Matched-pairs Wilcoxon signed-ranks test for UIPP and manufacturer ratings

Simple vs. compound	W	p	Hodges-Lehmann Estimate	Rank-Biserial Correlation
Suitability	980.00	< .001	0.75	0.74
Intuitiveness	806.00	< .001	0.75	0.70
Un-ambiguity	1076.50	< .001	0.75	0.91
Un-complexity	248.00	0.14	0.25	0.31
Innovativeness	280.00	0.03	−0.50	−0.38
Familiarity	1210.50	< .001	0.75	0.83

References

Abdullah R, Hübner R 2006 Pictograms, icons & signs: A guide to information graphics. Thames & Hudson, London

Adams A, Boersema T, Mijksenaar M 2010 Warning symbology: Difficult concepts may be successfully depicted with two-part signs. Information Design Journal 18:94–106. https://doi.org/10.1075/idj.18.2.01ada

Adobe Inc. 2020 Adobe Advertising Cloud. https://www.adobe.com/advertising/adobe-advertising-cloud.html

Agrawala M, Li W, Berthouzoz F 2011 Design principles for visual communication. Commun. ACM 54:60. https://doi.org/10.1145/1924421.1924439

Akoglu H 2018 User's guide to correlation coefficients. Turk J Emerg Med 18:91–93. https://doi.org/10.1016/j.tjem.2018.08.001

Alty JL, Knott RP, Anderson B, Smyth M 2000 A framework for engineering metaphor at the user interface. Interacting with Computers 13:301–322. https://doi.org/10.1016/S0953-5438(00)00047-3

Amazon 2018 Mechanical Turk. https://www.mturk.com/. Accessed 26 February 2020

American Psychological Association 2013 Publication manual of the American Psychological Association, 6th edn. American Psychological Association, Washington, DC

Anderson JR 2014 Cognitive Psychology and Its Implications, 8th edn. W.H. Freeman & Co Ltd, New York

Andrews D, Nonnecke B, Preece J 2003 Conducting Research on the Internet: Online Survey Design, Development and Implementation Guidelines. International Journal of Human-Computer Interaction 16:1–31

Anthony L 2019 AntConc. Waseda University, Tokyo, Japan. https://www.laurenceanthony.net/software/antconc/

Antle AN, Corness G, Droumeva M 2009 What the body knows: Exploring the benefits of embodied metaphors in hybrid physical digital environments. Interacting with Computers 21:66–75. https://doi.org/10.1016/j.intcom.2008.10.005

Apple Inc. 2019 Custom Icons: MacOS. https://developer.apple.com/design/human-interface-guidelines/macos/icons-and-images/custom-icons/. Accessed 22 April 2019

Apple Inc. 2019 System Icons: iOS. https://developer.apple.com/design/human-interface-guidelines/ios/icons-and-images/system-icons/. Accessed 24 April 2019

Apple Inc. 2020 Apple Events. https://www.apple.com/de/apple-events/. Accessed 22 April 2020

Archer B 1995 The Nature of Research. Codesign 2:6–13

Arnheim R 1974 Art and visual perception: A psychology of the creative eye ; the new version, 2nd edn. University of California Press, Berkeley, Calif.

Arterberry ME 2008 Infants' Sensitivity to the Depth Cue of Height-in-the-Picture-Plane. Infancy 13:544–555. https://doi.org/10.1080/15250000802329545

Association for Computing Machinery 2020 ACM Digital Library. https://scholar.google.com/

Averbukh VL 2001 Visualization Metaphors. Programming and Computer Software 27:227–237. https://doi.org/10.1023/A:1012333025189

Averbukh VL, Bakhterev M, Baydalin A, Ismagilov D, Trushenkova P 2007 Interface and Visualization Metaphors. In: Jacko JA (ed) Human-Computer Interaction. Interaction Platforms and Techniques, vol 4551. Springer Berlin Heidelberg, Berlin, Heidelberg, pp 13–22

Avgerinou MD, Pettersson R 2011 Toward a Cohesive Theory of Visual Literacy. Journal of Visual Literacy 30:1–19. https://doi.org/10.1080/23796529.2011.11674687

Baatard G 2012 A Technical Guide to Effective and Accessible Web Surveys. The Electronic Journal of Business Research Methods 10:101–109

Baker B 1982 Minspeak: A semantic compaction system that makes self-expression easier for communicatively disabled individuals. Byte 7:186–202

Bar M, Neta M 2006 Humans prefer curved visual objects. Psychol Sci 17:645–648. https://doi.org/10.1111/j.1467-9280.2006.01759.x

Barker PG, van Schaik P 2000 Designing and Evaluating Icons. In: Yazdani M, Barker PG (eds) Iconic communication. Intellect, Bristol, UK, Portland, OR, USA, pp 161–177

Barr P, Biddle R, Noble J 2002 A taxonomy of user-interface metaphors. In: Jones M, Jones S, Masoodian M (eds) Proceedings of the SIGCHI-NZ Symposium on Computer-Human Interaction - CHINZ '02. ACM Press, New York, New York, USA, pp 25–30

Barr P, Noble J, Biddle R 2003 Icons R Icons. In: Robert Biddle, Bruce H. Thomas (eds) User Interfaces 2003: Fourth Australasian User Interface Conference (AUIC2003). Australian Computer Society, pp 25–32

Barr P, Biddle R, Noble J 2004 A Semiotic Model of User-Interface Metaphor. In: Liu K (ed) Virtual, Distributed and Flexible Organisations, vol 12. Kluwer Academic Publishers, Dordrecht, pp 189–215

Barsalou LW 1993 Flexibility, structure, and linguistic vagary in concepts: Manifestations of a compositional system of perceptual symbols. In: Collins AF, Gathercole SE, Conway MA, Morris PE (eds) Theories of memory. Lawrence Erlbaum Associates, Inc, Hillsdale, NJ, US, pp 29–101

Barsalou LW 1999 Perceptual symbol systems. Behav Brain Sci 22:577-609; discussion 610-60. https://doi.org/10.1017/s0140525x99002149

Barsalou LW 2003 Situated simulation in the human conceptual system. Language and Cognitive Processes 18:513–562. https://doi.org/10.1080/01690960344000026

Barsalou LW 2008 Grounded cognition. Annu Rev Psychol 59:617–645. https://doi.org/10.1146/annurev.psych.59.103006.093639

Beardon C 1995 Discourse structures in iconic communication. Artif Intell Rev 9:189–203. https://doi.org/10.1007/BF00849179

Behrend TS, Sharek DJ, Meade AW, Wiebe EN 2011 The viability of crowdsourcing for survey research. Behav Res Methods 43:800–813. https://doi.org/10.3758/s13428-011-0081-0

Bezemer J, Kress GR 2016 Multimodality, Learning and Communication: A social semiotic frame. Routledge, Milton Park, etc, New York. etc

Bezuayehu L, Stilan E, Peesapati ST 2014 Icon Metaphors for Global Cultures. In: Dwivedi A, Blashki K, Isaias P (eds) Emerging Research and Trends in Interactivity and the Human-Computer Interface, vol 16. IGI Global, pp 34–53

Biederman I 1987 Recognition-by-components: A theory of human image understanding. Psychological Review 94:115–147. https://doi.org/10.1037/0033-295X.94.2.115

Biederman I, Ju G 1988 Surface versus edge-based determinants of visual recognition. Cogn Psychol 20:38–64

Bishop NA, Lu T, Yankner BA 2010 Neural mechanisms of ageing and cognitive decline. Nature 464:529–535. https://doi.org/10.1038/nature08983

Blackler AL 2008 Intuitive Interaction with Complex Artefacts: Empirically-Based Research. VDM Verl. Dr. Müller, Saarbrücken

Blackler AL 2019 Intuitive Interaction: An Overview. In: Blackler AL (ed) Intuitive Interaction: Research and Application. CRC Press (Taylor and Francis), Boca Raton (FL), pp 3–17

Blackler AL, Hurtienne J 2007 Towards a unified view of intuitive interaction: Definitions, models and tools across the world. MMI-Interaktiv 13:36–54

Blackler AL, Popovic V 2015 Towards Intuitive Interaction Theory. Interacting with Computers 27:203–209. https://doi.org/10.1093/iwc/iwv011

Blackler AL, Popovic V, Mahar DP 2010 Investigating users' intuitive interaction with complex artefacts. Appl Ergon 41:72–92. https://doi.org/10.1016/j.apergo.2009.04.010

Blackler AL, Popovic V, Mahar DP, Reddy R, Lawry S 2012 Intuitive interaction and older people. In: Israsena P, Tangsantikul J, Durling D (eds) Research : Uncertainty, Contradiction and Value. Proceedings Design Research Society (DRS) 2012. Department of Industrial Design, Faculty of Architecture, Chulalongkorn University, Chulalongkorn University, Bangkok, pp 560–578

Blackler AL, Popovic V, Mahar DP 2014 Applying and testing design for intuitive interaction. International Journal of Design Sciences and Technology 20:7–26

Blackler AL, Vesna Popovic, Shital Desai 2019 Research Methods for Intuitive Interaction. In: Blackler AL (ed) Intuitive Interaction: Research and Application. CRC Press (Taylor and Francis), Boca Raton (FL), pp 65–88

Blackwell AF 2006 The reification of metaphor as a design tool. ACM Trans. Comput.-Hum. Interact. 13:490–530. https://doi.org/10.1145/1188816.1188820

Bliss CK 1978 Semantography (Blissymbolics): A simple system of 100 logical pictorial symbols, which can be operated and read like 1+2=3 in all languages, 3rd enl. ed. Semantography (Blissymbolics) Publications, Sydney

Blissymbolics Communication International 2019 Full symbol sets in various formats. www.blissymbolics.org/index.php/resources. Accessed 21 December 2019

Böhm V, Wolff C 2013 Usability Engineering-Methoden im interkulturellen Kontext. In: Susanne Boll, Susanne Maaß, Rainer Malaka (eds) Mensch & Computer 2013: Interaktive Vielfalt, Interdisziplinäre Fachtagung, 8.-11. September 2013, Bremen, Germany - Workshopband. Oldenbourg Verlag, pp 457–462

Borghi AM, Caruana F 2015 Embodiment Theory. In: Wright JD (ed) International Encyclopedia of the Social & Behavioral Sciences. Elsevier, pp 420–426

Bosch Thermotechnik GmbH 2017 Bosch Thermotechnology: Icon for Products and Product related User Interfaces:1–39

Bosch Thermotechnik GmbH 2017 Installations- und Bedienungsanleitung: Fernbedienbarer Regler EasyControl CT 200:1–12

Bosch Thermotechnik GmbH 2018 Bosch Thermotechnology: Relevant Bosch Icons:1–47

Bourges-Waldegg P, Scrivener SA 1998 Meaning, the central issue in cross-cultural HCI design. Interacting with Computers 9:287–309. https://doi.org/10.1016/S0953-5438(97)00032-5

Bovet D, Vauclair J 2000 Picture recognition in animals and humans. Behavioural brain research 109:143–165

Brabham DC 2013 Crowdsourcing. The MIT Press essential knowledge series. The MIT Press, Cambridge, Massachusetts, London, England

Bramao I, Inacio F, Faisca L, Reis A, Petersson KM 2010 The Influence of Color Information on the Recognition of Color Diagnostic and Noncolor Diagnostic Objects. The J. of General Psych. 138:49–65. https://doi.org/10.1080/00221309.2010.533718

Brugger C 1990 Advances in the international standardisation of public information symbols. Information Design Journal 6:79–88. https://doi.org/10.1075/idj.6.1.05bru

Bühler D, Hemmert F, Hurtienne J 2020 Universal and intuitive? Scientific guidelines for icon design. In: Preim B, Nürnberger A, Hansen C (eds) Proceedings of Mensch und Computer 2020 - MuC'20. ACM Press, New York, New York, USA, pp 91–103

Bundesministerium für Bildung und Forschung UCUI: Entwicklung eines universellen Hardware-Moduls für eine intuitive Interaktion mit beliebigen Geräten. http://www.technik-zum-menschen-bringen.de/projekte/ucui. Accessed 26 February 2020

Bußmann H, Trauth G 1996 Routledge dictionary of language and linguistics, [Online-ausg.]. Routledge reference. Routledge, London

Callahan E 2005 Interface design and culture. Ann. Rev. Info. Sci. Tech. 39:255–310. https://doi.org/10.1002/aris.1440390114

Caplin S, Alastair C 2001 Icon design. Stiebner, München

Carney C, Campbell JL, Mitchell EA 1998 In-Vehicle Display Icons and Other Information Elements: Literature Review

Carroll JM, Mack RL, Kellogg WA 1988 Interface Metaphors and User Interface Design. In: Helander M (ed) Handbook of Human-Computer Interaction. Elsevier, pp 67–85

Casasanto D 2009 When is a linguistic metaphor conceptual metaphor? In: Evans V, Pourcel S (eds) New Directions in Cognitive Linguistics, vol 24. John Benjamins Publishing Company, Amsterdam, pp 127–145

Casasanto D 2011 Different Bodies, Different Minds. Curr Dir Psychol Sci 20:378–383. https://doi.org/10.1177/0963721411422058

Casasanto D 2013 Development of Metaphorical Thinking: The Role of Language. In: Dancygier B, Borkent M, Hinnell J (eds) Language and the creative mind. Center for the Study of Language and Information, Stanford, pp 3–18

Casasanto D 2014 Experiential origins of mental metaphors: Language, culture, and the body. In: Landau M, Robinson MD, Meier BP (eds) The power of metaphor: Examining its influence on social life. American Psychological Association, Washington, pp 249–268

Casasanto D 2017 The Hierarchical Structure of Mental Metaphors. In: Hampe B (ed) Metaphor: Embodied Cognition and Discourse. Cambridge University Press, Cambridge, pp 46–61

Casasanto D, Chrysikou EG 2011 When left is "right". Motor fluency shapes abstract concepts. Psychol Sci 22:419–422. https://doi.org/10.1177/0956797611401755

Cash PJ 2018 Developing theory-driven design research. Design Studies 56:84–119. https://doi.org/10.1016/j.destud.2018.03.002

Cavanagh P 2005 The artist as neuroscientist. Nature 434:301–307. https://doi.org/10.1038/434301a

Cavanagh P 2011 Visual cognition. Vision Res 51:1538–1551. https://doi.org/10.1016/j.visres.2011.01.015

Chandler J, Mueller P, Paolacci G 2014 Nonnaïveté among Amazon Mechanical Turk workers: consequences and solutions for behavioral researchers. Behav Res Methods 46:112–130. https://doi.org/10.3758/s13428-013-0365-7

Chandler D 2018 Semiotics: The basics, 3rd. The basics. Routledge, New York, NY

Chang D, Nesbitt KV 2006 Developing Gestalt-based design guidelines for multi-sensory displays. In: Proceedings of the 2005 NICTA-HCSNet Multimodal User Interaction Workshop-Volume 57, pp 9–16

Cho H, Ishida T 2011 Exploring Cultural Differences in Pictogram Interpretations. In: Ishida T (ed) The Language Grid, vol 7. Springer Berlin Heidelberg, Berlin, Heidelberg, pp 133–148

Cho H, Ishida T, Yamashita N, Inaba R, Mori Y, Koda T 2007 Culturally-Situated Pictogram Retrieval. In: Ishida T, Fussell SR, Vossen PTJM (eds) Intercultural Collaboration, vol 4568. Springer Berlin Heidelberg, Berlin, Heidelberg, pp 221–235

Chong M 2004 Designing the user experience for international web users. In: Kaplan M (ed) Cultural Ergonomics, 1st edn., vol 4. Elsevier JAI, Amsterdam, Boston, pp 281–316

Choong Y-Y, Salvendy G 1998 Design of icons for use by Chinese in mainland China. Interacting with Computers 9:417–430. https://doi.org/10.1016/S0953-5438%2897%2900026-X

Christian A 2017 Piktogramme: Tendenzen in der Gestaltung und im Einsatz grafischer Symbole. Kommunikationswissenschaft. Herbert von Halem Verlag, Köln

Cienki A 1998 STRAIGHT: An image schema and its metaphorical extensions. Cognitive Linguistics 9:107–150. https://doi.org/10.1515/cogl.1998.9.2.107

Clarivate Analytics 2020 Web of Science. https://apps.webofknowledge.com/. Accessed 26 February 2020

Clemmensen T, Shi Q, Kumar J, Li H, Sun X, Yammiyavar P 2007 Cultural Usability Tests – How Usability Tests Are Not the Same All over the World. In: Hutchison D, Kanade T, Kittler J, Kleinberg JM, Mattern F, Mitchell JC, Naor M, Nierstrasz O, Pandu Rangan C, Steffen B, Sudan M, Terzopoulos D, Tygar D, Vardi MY, Weikum G, Aykin N (eds) Usability and Internationalization. HCI and Culture, vol 4559. Springer Berlin Heidelberg, Berlin, Heidelberg, pp 281–290

Clemmensen T, Hertzum M, Hornbæk K, Shi Q, Yammiyavar P 2009 Cultural cognition in usability evaluation. Interacting with Computers 21:212–220. https://doi.org/10.1016/j.intcom.2009.05.003

clickworker GmbH clickworker. https://www.clickworker.de/. Accessed 21.12.19

Cohen J 1988 Statistical Power Analysis for the Behavioral Sciences, 2nd. Taylor and Francis, Hoboken

Cole F, Golovinskiy A, Limpaecher A, Barros HS, Finkelstein A, Funkhouser T, Rusinkiewicz S 2008 Where Do People Draw Lines? ACM Trans. Graph. 27:1-11. https://doi.org/10.1145/1360612.1360687

Cole F, Sanik K, DeCarlo D, Finkelstein A, Funkhouser T, Rusinkiewicz S, Singh M 2009 How well do line drawings depict shape? ACM Trans. Graph. 28:1–9. https://doi.org/10.1145/1531326.1531334

Cooper A, Reimann R, Cronin D, Noessel C 2014 About face: The essentials of interaction design, Fourth edition. John Wiley & Sons, Hoboken

Cooper HM 2016 Research synthesis and meta-analysis: A step-by-step approach, 5th edn. Applied social research methods series, vol 2. Sage, Los Angeles, London, New Delhi, Singapore, Washington DC

Cooper HM, Hedges LV, Valentine JC (eds) 2019 Handbook of research synthesis and meta-analysis, 3rd edition. Russell Sage Foundation, New York

Coppock A 2018 Generalizing from Survey Experiments Conducted on Mechanical Turk: A Replication Approach. PSRM 349:1–16. https://doi.org/10.1017/psrm.2018.10

Costa T, Dalton J, Burnette A, Stearns C 2014 The Data-Driven Design Revolution. https://www.forrester.com/report/The+DataDriven+Design+Revolution/-/E-RES115903

Cresnar G Multimedia Collection Icon Pack: Icons made by Grewgor Cresnar from www.flaticon.com. https://www.flaticon.com/authors/gregor-cresnar

Crystal D 2011 A dictionary of linguistics and phonetics, 6. ed., [repr.]. The language library. Blackwell, Malden, Mass.

Curry MB, McDougall SJ, Bruijn O de 1998 The Effects of the Visual Metaphor in Determining Icon Efficacy. Proceedings of the Human Factors and Ergonomics Society Annual Meeting 42:1590–1594. https://doi.org/10.1177/154193129804202212

Czaja SJ, Boot WR, Charness N, Rogers WA 2019 Designing for older adults: Principles and creative human factors approaches, Third edition. Human factors & aging series. CRC Press, Boca Raton, FL

Dancey CP, Reidy J 2017 Statistics without maths for psychology. Pearson, New York

de Castro Salgado, Luciana Cardoso, Leitão CF, de Souza CS 2013 A Journey Through Cultures. Human–Computer Interaction Series. Springer London, London

de Souza CS 1993 The semiotic engineering of user interface languages. International Journal of Man-Machine Studies 39:753–773. https://doi.org/10.1006/imms.1993.1082

de Souza CS 2005 Semiotic Engineering of Human-computer Interaction (Acting with technology). MIT Press

de Souza CS, Barbosa SDJ, Prates RO 2001 A semiotic engineering approach to HCI. In: Tremaine M (ed) CHI '01 - Human Factors in Computing Systems. Extended Abstracts. ACM Press, New York, New York, USA, pp 55–56

DeCarlo D, Finkelstein A, Rusinkiewicz S, Santella A 2003 Suggestive contours for conveying shape. ACM Trans. Graph. 22:848. https://doi.org/10.1145/882262.882354

DeepL GmbH DeepL. https://www.deepl.com/. Accessed 26 February 2020

Del Galdo EM, Nielsen J (eds) 1996 International user interfaces. John Wiley & Sons, New York

DeLoache JS, Pierroutsakos SL, Uttal DH, Rosengren KS, Gottlieb A 1998 Grasping the Nature of Pictures. Psychol Sci 9:205–210. https://doi.org/10.1111/1467-9280.00039

DeLoache JS, Pierroutsakos SL, Uttal DH 2003 The Origins of Pictorial Competence. Curr Dir Psychol Sci 12:114–118. https://doi.org/10.1111/1467-8721.01244

Deutsches Institut für Normung 2009 Allgemeine Grundlagen für graphische Symbole auf Geräten und Einrichtungen –: Teil 1: Gestaltung graphischer Symbole für die Registrierung 01.080.20(80416-1:2009)

Deutsches Institut für Normung, International Organization for Standardization 2008 Graphische Symbole auf Einrichtungen: Index und Übersicht 01.080.20(7000:2008-12)

Diefenbach S, Ullrich D 2015 An Experience Perspective on Intuitive Interaction: Central Components and the Special Effect of Domain Transfer Distance. Behaviour & Information Technology 27:210–234. https://doi.org/10.1093/iwc/iwv001

Difallah D, Filatova E, Ipeirotis P 2018 Demographics and Dynamics of Mechanical Turk Workers. In: Chang Y, Zhai C, Liu Y, Maarek Y (eds) Proceedings of the Eleventh ACM International Conference on Web Search and Data Mining - WSDM '18. ACM Press, New York, New York, USA, pp 135–143

Docampo Rama M 2001 Technology generations handling complex user interfaces, Department of Industrial Engineering & Innovation Sciences

Dourish P 2001 Where the action is: The foundations of embodied interaction. Bradford Book. MIT Press, Cambridge, London

Drucker J 2014 Graphesis: Visual forms of knowledge production. Harvard University Press, Cambridge, Massachusetts

Duncker E, Theng YL, Mohd-Nasir N 2000 Cultural Usability in Digital Libraries. Bul. Am. Soc. Info. Sci. Tech. 26:21–22. https://doi.org/10.1002/bult.162

Durrani S, Durrani QS 2009 Applying Cognitive Psychology to User Interfaces. In: Tiwary US, Siddiqui TJ, Radhakrishna M, Tiwari MD (eds) Proceedings of the First International Conference on Intelligent Human Computer Interaction. Springer India, New Delhi, pp 156–168

Elkins J 2001 The domain of images. Cornell Paperbacks. Cornell Univ. Press, Ithaca, NY

Elsevier B.V. ScienceDirect. https://www.sciencedirect.com/. Accessed 26 February 2020

Evers V 1998 Cross-cultural understanding of metaphors in interface design. In: Ess C, Sudweeks F (eds) Proceedings CATAC'98: Cultural Attitudes towards Technology and Communication, pp 1–11

Evers V 2002 Cross-cultural applicability of user evaluation methods. In: Terveen L, Wixon D (eds) CHI '02 Human factors in computing systems. ACM Press, New York, New York, USA, p 740

Evers V, Kukulska-Hulme A, Jones AC 1999 Cross-Cultural Understanding of Interface Design: A Cross-Cultural Analysis of Icon Recognition. In: Prabhu GV, del Galdo E (eds) Proceedings of the International Workshop on Internationalization of Products and Systems

Fahlenbrach K 2016 Embodied metaphors in film, television, and video games: Cognitive approaches, Paperback edition. Routledge research in cultural and media studies, vol 76. Routledge, Taylor & Francis Group, New York, London

Faul F, Erdfelder E, Buchner A, Lang A-G 2009 Statistical power analyses using G*Power 3.1: tests for correlation and regression analyses. Behav Res Methods 41:1149–1160. https://doi.org/10.3758/BRM.41.4.1149

Fazio RH, Williams CJ, Powell MC 2000 Measuring Associative Strength: Category-Item Associations and Their Activation from Memory. Political Psychology 21:7–25. https://doi.org/10.1111/0162-895X.00175

Fernandes M 1995 Using Digital Technologies to Automate Instructional Design. Educational Media International 32:230–236. https://doi.org/10.1080/0952398950320410

Fetzer K, Heß A, Lange K, Löffler D, Maier A, Schmitt H, Weber S 2013 Gestaltung intuitiver Benutzung mit Image Schemata: IBIS

Findeli A 2010 Searching for Design Research Questions: Some Conceptual Clarifications. In: Chow RWY, Jonas W, Joost G (eds) Questions, hypotheses & conjectures: Discussions on projects by early stage and senior design researches. iUniverse Inc, New York, pp 278–293

Findeli A, Brouillet D, Martin S, Moineau C, Tarrago R 2008 Research Through Design and Transdisciplinarity: A Tentative Contribution to the Methodology of Design Research. In: Aebersold R, Minder B, Scheuermann A (eds) Focused - current design research projects and methods: Swiss Design Network Symposium 2008, 30 - 31 May 2008, Mount Gurten, Berne, pp 67–91

Forceville C 2011 Pictorial runes in Tintin and the Picaros. Journal of Pragmatics 43:875–890. https://doi.org/10.1016/j.pragma.2010.07.014

Forceville CJ 2008 Metaphor in pictures and multimodal representations. In: Gibbs RW (ed) The Cambridge handbook of metaphor and thought. Cambridge University Press, New York, pp 462–482

Forceville CJ 2009 Non-verbal and multimodal metaphor in a cognitivist framework: Agendas for research. In: Forceville CJ, Urios-Aparisi E (eds) Multimodal metaphor. M. de Gruyter, Berlin, New York, pp 19–44

Forceville CJ, Urios-Aparisi E (eds) 2009 Multimodal metaphor. Applications of cognitive linguistics, vol 11. M. de Gruyter, Berlin, New York

Forsythe A, Mulhern G, Sawey M 2008 Confounds in pictorial sets: the role of complexity and familiarity in basic-level picture processing. Behav Res Methods 40:116–129

Foster J, Koyama K, Adams A 2010 Paper and on-line testing of graphical access symbols in three countries using the ISO 9186 comprehension test. Information Design Journal 18:107–117. https://doi.org/10.1075/idj.18.2.02fos

Frayling C 1993 Research in Art and Design. Royal College of Art research papers, vol. 1, no. 1. Royal College of Art, London

Frege G, Textor M (eds) 2007 Funktion - Begriff - Bedeutung, 2nd edn. Sammlung Philosophie, vol 4. Vandenhoeck & Ruprecht, Göttingen

Gatsou C, Politis A, Zevgolis D 2011 Text vs Visual Metaphor in Mobile Interfaces for Novice User Interaction. Inf. Serv. Use 31:271–279

Gatsou C, Politis A, Dimitrios Z 2012 The importance of mobile interface icons on user interaction. International Journal of Computer Science and Applications 9:92–107

Gaver W 2012 What should we expect from research through design? In: Konstan JA, Chi EH, Höök K (eds) Proceedings of the 2012 ACM annual conference on Human Factors in Computing Systems - CHI '12. ACM Press, New York, New York, USA, pp 937–946

Giardino V, Greenberg G 2015 Introduction: Varieties of Iconicity. Rev.Phil.Psych. 6:1–25. https://doi.org/10.1007/s13164-014-0210-7

Gibbs RW 2005 Embodiment and cognitive science. Cambridge Univ. Press, Cambridge

Gibbs RW 2005 Embodiment in Metaphorical Imagination. In: Pecher D, Zwaan RA (eds) Grounding Cognition. Cambridge University Press, pp 65–92

Gibbs RW 2011 Evaluating Conceptual Metaphor Theory. Discourse Processes 48:529–562. https://doi.org/10.1080/0163853X.2011.606103

Gibson JJ 1978 The Ecological Approach to the Visual Perception of Pictures. Leonardo 11:227. https://doi.org/10.2307/1574154

Giessner SR, Schubert TW 2007 High in the hierarchy: How vertical location and judgments of leaders' power are interrelated. Organizational Behavior and Human Decision Processes 104:30–44. https://doi.org/10.1016/j.obhdp.2006.10.001

Girshick A, Interrante V, Haker S, Lemoine T 2000 Line direction matters: An Argument For The Use Of Principal Directions In 3D Line Drawings. In: Fekete J-D, Salesin D (eds) Proceedings of the first international symposium on Non-photorealistic animation and rendering - NPAR '00. ACM Press, New York, New York, USA, pp 43–52

Gittins D 1986 Icon-based human-computer interaction. International Journal of Man-Machine Studies 24:519–543. https://doi.org/10.1016/S0020-7373(86)80007-4

Glenberg AM, Schroeder JL, Robertson DA 1998 Averting the gaze disengages the environment and facilitates remembering. Mem Cognit 26:651–658. https://doi.org/10.3758/BF03211385

Goldstein EB 2010 Pictorial Depiction and Perception. In: Goldstein EB (ed) Encyclopedia of perception. SAGE Publications, Thousand Oaks, Calif, pp 819–824

Goldstein EB 2010 Sensation and perception, 8th edn. Wadsworth Cengage Learning, Belmont, Calif.

Goldstein DG, Gigerenzer G 2002 Models of ecological rationality: The recognition heuristic. Psychological Review 109:75–90. https://doi.org/10.1037//0033-295X.109.1.75

Gómez Reynoso J, Olfman L 2012 The impact of combining Gestalt theories with interface design guidelines in designing user interfaces. AMCIS 2012 Proceedings

Goodman N 1976 Languages of art: An approach to a theory of symbols, 2nd edn. Hackett, Indianapolis, Ind.

Google LLC Google Scholar. https://scholar.google.com/. Accessed 26 February 2020

Goonetilleke RS, Shih HM, Kai On H, Fritsch J 2001 Effects of training and representational characteristics in icon design. International Journal of Human-Computer Studies 55:741–760. https://doi.org/10.1006/ijhc.2001.0501

Göritz AS 2014 Determinants of the starting rate and the completion rate in online panel studies 1. In: Callegaro M, Baker R, Bethlehem J, Göritz AS, Krosnick JA, Lavrakas PJ (eds) Online Panel Research. John Wiley & Sons, Ltd, Chichester, UK, pp 154–170

Grady JE 1997 Foundations of Meaning: Primary Metaphors and Primary Scenes. Dissertation, University of California at Berkeley

Grady JE 1999 A typology of motivation for conceptual metaphor: correlation vs. resemblance. In: Gibbs RW, Steen GJ (eds) Metaphor in Cognitive Linguistics, vol 175. John Benjamins Publishing Company, Amsterdam, 79-

Graham L 2008 Gestalt theory in interactive media design. Journal of Humanities and Social Sciences 2:1–12

Green SB, Salkind NJ 2014 Using SPSS for Windows and Macintosh: Analyzing and understanding data, 7. ed. Pearson, Boston

Greenberg G 2011 The semiotic spectrum. Dissertation, Rutgers, The State University of New Jersey

Greenberg G 2013 Beyond Resemblance. Philosophical Review 122:215–287. https://doi.org/10.1215/00318108-1963716

Greifenstein S, Horst D, Scherer T, Schmitt C, Kappelhoff H, Müller C (eds) 2018 Cinematic Metaphor in Perspective: Reflections on a Transdisciplinary Framework. Cinepoetics - English Edition Ser, v. 5. De Gruyter, Inc, Berlin/Boston

Gunstone RF 1980 Word association and the description of cognitive structure. Research in Science Education 10:45–53. https://doi.org/10.1007/BF02356308

Hansen CD, Johnson CR (eds) 2011 Visualization Handbook. Elsevier Science, San Diego

Harnad S 1990 The symbol grounding problem. Physica D: Nonlinear Phenomena 42:335–346. https://doi.org/10.1016/0167-2789(90)90087-6

Hartson R, Pyla PS 2012 The UX book: Process and guidelines for ensuring a quality user experience. Morgan Kaufmann, Amsterdam

Hassenzahl M, Burmester M, Koller F 2003 AttrakDiff: Ein Fragebogen zur Messung wahrgenommener hedonischer und pragmatischer Qualität. In: Szwillus G, Ziegler J (eds) Mensch & Computer 2003, vol 57. Vieweg+Teubner Verlag, Wiesbaden, pp 187–196

Heer J, Bostock M 2010 Crowdsourcing graphical perception. In: Mynatt E, Schoner D, Fitzpatrick G, Hudson S, Edwards K, Rodden T (eds) Proceedings of the 28th international conference on Human factors in computing systems - CHI '10. ACM Press, New York, New York, USA, pp 203–212

Heimgärtner R 2013 Intercultural User Interface Design – Culture-Centered HCI Design – Cross-Cultural User Interface Design: Different Terminology or Different Approaches? In: Hutchison D, Kanade T, Kittler J, Kleinberg JM, Mattern F, Mitchell JC, Naor M, Nierstrasz O, Pandu Rangan C, Steffen B, Sudan M, Terzopoulos D, Tygar D, Vardi MY, Weikum

G, Marcus A (eds) Design, User Experience, and Usability. Health, Learning, Playing, Cultural, and Cross-Cultural User Experience, vol 8013. Springer Berlin Heidelberg, Berlin, Heidelberg, pp 62–71

Heimgärtner R 2014 Intercultural User Interface Design. In: Dwivedi A, Blashki K, Isaias P (eds) Emerging Research and Trends in Interactivity and the Human-Computer Interface, Vol. 6769. IGI Global, pp 1–33

Heimgärtner R 2017 Interkulturelles User Interface Design: Von der Idee bis zum erfolgreichen Produkt. Springer Vieweg, Berlin, [Heidelberg]

Hemmert F 2014 Encountering the Digital: Representational and Experiential Embodiment in Tangible User Interfaces. Dissertation, Universität der Künste Berlin

Heß A, Maier A, Löffler D 2013 Die IBIS- Methode. Softwaretechnik-Trends 33:17–18. https://doi.org/10.1007/BF03323538

Hiniker A, Hong SR, Kim Y-S, Chen N-C, West JD, Aragon C 2017 Toward the operationalization of visual metaphor. Journal of the Association for Information Science and Technology 68:2338–2349. https://doi.org/10.1002/asi.23857

Hirth M, Hoßfeld T, Tran-Gia P 2011 Anatomy of a Crowdsourcing Platform - Using the Example of Microworkers.com. In: 2011 Fifth International Conference on Innovative Mobile and Internet Services in Ubiquitous Computing. IEEE, pp 322–329

Hofstede G 1997 Cultures and organizations: Software of the mind - intercultural cooperation and its importance for survival, 1st edn. McGraw-Hill, New York

Hofstede G 2001 Culture's consequences: Comparing values, behaviors, institutions, and organizations across nations, 2nd edn. Sage, Thousand Oaks, Calif.

Hofstede G 2011 Dimensionalizing Cultures: The Hofstede Model in Context. Online Readings in Psychology and Culture 2. https://doi.org/10.9707/2307-0919.1014

Hofstede G, Hofstede GJ, Minkov M 2010 Cultures and organizations: Software of the mind - intercultural cooperation and its importance for survival, 3rd edn. McGraw-Hill, New York

Hollingworth A 2005 Memory for object position in natural scenes. Visual Cognition 12:1003–1016. https://doi.org/10.1080/13506280444000625

Holtzblatt K, Beyer H 2015 Contextual design: Evolved. Synthesis lectures on human-centered informatics, #24. Morgan & Claypool, San Rafael

Honeywill P 1999 Visual language for the World Wide Web. Intellect, Exeter

Hornecker E 2012 Beyond affordance: Tangibles' Hybrid Nature. In: Vertegaal R, Fernaeus Y, Girouard A, Jordà S, Spencer SN (eds) Proceedings of the Sixth International Conference on Tangible, Embedded and Embodied Interaction - TEI '12. ACM Press, New York, New York, USA, pp 175–182

Hörr C, Brunnett G, Vix C 2010 Line Drawings vs. Curvature Shading:Scientific Illustration of Range Scanned Artefacts. In: Jepp P, Deussen O (eds) Computational Aesthetics in Graphics, Visualization, and Imaging. The Eurographics Association

Horton WK 1993 The Almost Universal Language: Graphics for International Documents. Technical Communication 40:682–693

Horton WK 1994 The icon book: Visual symbols for computer systems and documentation. Wiley, New York, Chichester

Hsieh HC, Holland R, Young M 2009 A Theoretical Model for Cross-Cultural Web Design. In: Kurosu M (ed) Human Centered Design, vol 5619. Springer Berlin Heidelberg, Berlin, Heidelberg, pp 712–721

Huang K-C 2008 Effects of computer icons and figure/background area ratios and color combinations on visual search performance on an LCD monitor. Displays 29:237–242. https://doi.org/10.1016/j.displa.2007.08.005

Hurtienne J 2011 Image Schemas and Design for Intuitive Use, Technische Universität Berlin

Hurtienne J 2017 How Cognitive Linguistics Inspires HCI: Image Schemas and Image-Schematic Metaphors. International Journal of Human–Computer Interaction 33:1–20. https://doi.org/10.1080/10447318.2016.1232227

Hurtienne J 2017 ISCAT - Image Schema Database. http://zope.psyergo.uni-wuerzburg.de/iscat. Accessed 26.02.20

Hurtienne J, Blessing L 2007 Design for Intuitive Use: Testing image schema theory for user interface design. In: Bocquet J-C (ed) Proceedings of the 16th International Conference on Engineering Design, pp 1–12

Hurtienne J, Israel JH 2007 Image schemas and their metaphorical extensions. In: Ullmer B, Schmidt A (eds) Proceedings of the 1st international conference on Tangible and embedded interaction - TEI '07. ACM Press, New York, New York, USA, p 127

Hurtienne J, Meschke O 2016 Soft Pillows and the Near and Dear. In: Bakker S, Hummels C, Ullmer B, Geurts L, Hengeveld B, Saakes D, Broekhuijsen M (eds) Proceedings of the TEI '16: Tenth International Conference on Tangible, Embedded, and Embodied Interaction - TEI '16. ACM Press, New York, New York, USA, pp 324–331

Hurtienne J, Israel JH, Weber K 2008 Cooking up real world business applications combining physicality, digitality, and image schemas. In: Schmidt A, Gellersen H, van den Hoven E, Mazalek A, Holleis P, Villar N (eds) Proceedings of the 2nd international conference on Tangible and embedded interaction - TEI '08. ACM Press, New York, New York, USA, p 239

Hurtienne J, Stößel C, Weber K 2009 Sad is heavy and happy is light. In: Villar N, Izadi S, Fraser M, Benford S (eds) Proceedings of the 3rd International Conference on Tangible and Embedded Interaction - TEI '09. ACM Press, New York, New York, USA, p 61

Hurtienne J, Stößel C, Sturm C, Maus A, Rötting M, Langdon P, Clarkson J 2010 Physical gestures for abstract concepts: Inclusive design with primary metaphors. Interacting with Computers 22:475–484. https://doi.org/10.1016/j.intcom.2010.08.009

Hurtienne J, Klockner K, Diefenbach S, Nass C, Maier A 2015 Designing with Image Schemas: Resolving the Tension Between Innovation, Inclusion and Intuitive Use. Interacting with Computers 27:235–255. https://doi.org/10.1093/iwc/iwu049

IBM Icon Library. https://www.ibm.com/design/v1/language/resources/icon-library/. Accessed 22 April 2019

IBM 2019 Pictograms. https://www.ibm.com/design/language/elements/pictograms/contribute/#producing-an-pictogram. Accessed 22 April 2019

Ide N, Pustejovsky J (eds) 2017 Handbook of Linguistic Annotation. Springer Netherlands, Dordrecht, s.l.

International Organization for Standardization 2002 Ergonomics of human-system interaction: Usability methods supporting human-centred design 13.180(16982:2002)

International Organization for Standardization 2007 Graphical symbols for use on equipment: Symbol Registration Instructions and Form. https://isotc.iso.org/livelink/livelink?func=ll&ob jId=2166869&objAction=browse&viewType=1. Accessed 22 March 2020

International Organization for Standardization 2008 Graphical symbols - Test methods: Part 2: Method for testing perceptual quality 01.080.10(9186-2:2008)

International Organization for Standardization 2010 Ergonomics of human-system interaction: Human-centred design for interactive systems 18.180(9241-210:2010)

International Organization for Standardization 2011 Graphical symbols -- Safety colours and safety signs: Part 1: Design principles for safety signs and safety markings 01.080.10(3864-1:2011)

International Organization for Standardization 2014 Graphical symbols - Test methods: Part 3: Method for testing symbol referent association 01.080.10(9186-3:2014)

International Organization for Standardization 2014 Graphical symbols - Test methods: Part 1: Method for testing comprehensibility 01.080.10(9186-1:2014)

International Organization for Standardization 2014 Graphical symbols for use on equipment: Registered symbols 01.080.20(7000:2014)

International Organization for Standardization, International Electrotechnical Commission 2007 Information technology: Screen icons and symbols for personal mobile communication devices 35.240.20(24755:2007)

International Organization for Standardization, International Electrotechnical Commission 2010 Information technology — User interface icons —: Part 10: Framework and general guidance 35.240.20(11581-10:2010)

International Organization for Standardization, International Electrotechnical Commission 2011 Information technology -- User interface icons: Part 1: Introduction to and overview of icon standards 35.240.20(11561-1:2011)

International Organization for Standardization, International Electrotechnical Commission 2017 Information technology: Universal Coded Character Set (UCS) 35.040.10(10646:2017)

Isaacson JJ, Frantz J, Hall SM, Burhans CG 2017 Tools for Symbol Development – Safety Symbol Response Taxonomy and Graphic Compatibility Verification. Proceedings of the Human Factors and Ergonomics Society Annual Meeting 61:489–493. https://doi.org/10.1177/1541931213601605

Isherwood S 2009 Graphics and Semantics: The Relationship between What Is Seen and What Is Meant in Icon Design. In: Harris D (ed) Engineering Psychology and Cognitive Ergonomics, vol 5639. Springer Berlin Heidelberg, Berlin, Heidelberg, pp 197–205

Isherwood SJ, McDougall SJP, Curry MB 2007 Icon identification in context: the changing role of icon characteristics with user experience. Hum Factors 49:465–476. https://doi.org/10.1518/001872007X200102

Ishii H, Ullmer B 1997 Tangible bits: Towards Seamless Interfaces between People, Bits and Atoms. In: Pemberton S (ed) Proceedings of the SIGCHI conference on Human factors in computing systems - CHI '97. ACM Press, New York, New York, USA, pp 234–241

Ittelson WH 1996 Visual perception of markings. Psychon Bull Rev 3:171–187. https://doi.org/10.3758/BF03212416

Jacob RJK, Girouard A, Hirshfield LM, Horn MS, Shaer O, Solovey ET, Zigelbaum J 2007 Reality-based interaction: Unifying the New Generation of Interaction Styles. In: Rosson MB, Gilmore D (eds) CHI '07 Extended Abstracts on Human Factors in Computing Systems. ACM, New York, NY, p 2465

Jacob RJK, Girouard A, Hirshfield LM, Horn MS, Shaer O, Solovey ET, Zigelbaum J 2008 Reality-based interaction: A Framework for Post-WIMP Interfaces. In: Czerwinski M, Lund A, Tan D (eds) Proceeding of the twenty-sixth annual CHI conference on Human factors in computing systems - CHI '08. ACM Press, New York, New York, USA

Jagne J, Smith SG, Duncker E, Curzon P 2006 Cross-cultural interface design strategy. Univ Access Inf Soc 5:299–305. https://doi.org/10.1007/s10209-006-0048-6

JASP Team 2019 JASP (Version 0.10.2), Amsterdam. https://jasp-stats.org/

Johnson M 1987 The body in the mind: The bodily basis of meaning, imagination, and reason. University of Chicago Press, Chicago

Johnson J 2014 Designing with the mind in mind simple: Simple guide to understanding user interface design guidelines, Second edition. Elsevier, Morgan Kaufmann is an imprint of Elsevier, Amsterdam, Boston

Jokisch O, Huber M 2018 Advances in the development of a cognitive user interface. MATEC Web Conf. 161:1003. https://doi.org/10.1051/matecconf/201816101003

Jones T 1993 Recognition of animated icons by elementary-aged children. ALT-J 1:40–46. https://doi.org/10.1080/0968776930010105

Joshi A, Kale S, Chandel S, Pal D 2015 Likert Scale: Explored and Explained. BJAST 7:396–403. https://doi.org/10.9734/BJAST/2015/14975

Judd T, Durand F, Adelson E 2007 Apparent ridges for line drawing. ACM Trans. Graph. 26:1–7. https://doi.org/10.1145/1276377.1276401

Jung D, Myung R 2006 Icon design for Korean mental models. In: World Scientific and Engineering Academy and Society (ed) Proceedings of the 6th WSEAS International Conference on Applied Computer Science, Tenerife, Canary Islands, Spain, December 16-18, 2006, pp 177–182

Kan IP, Barsalou LW, Solomon KO, Minor JK, Thompson-Schill SL 2003 Role of mental imagery in a property verification task: FMRI evidence for perceptual representations of conceptual knowledge. Cogn Neuropsychol 20:525–540. https://doi.org/10.1080/02643290244000257

Kaushik M, Jain R 2014 Natural User Interfaces: Trend in Virtual Interaction. International Journal of Latest Technology in Engineering 4:141–143

Kennedy JM 1982 Metaphor in pictures. Perception 11:589–605. https://doi.org/10.1068/p110589

Kim C-Y, Blake R 2007 Brain activity accompanying perception of implied motion in abstract paintings. Spat Vis 20:545–560

Kittur A, Chi EH, Suh B 2008 Crowdsourcing user studies with Mechanical Turk. In: Czerwinski M, Lund A, Tan D (eds) Proceeding of the twenty-sixth annual CHI conference on Human factors in computing systems - CHI '08. ACM Press, New York, New York, USA, pp 453–456

Knight E, Gunawardena CN, Aydin CH 2009 Cultural interpretations of the visual meaning of icons and images used in North American web design. Educational Media International 46:17–35. https://doi.org/10.1080/09523980902781279

Kompetenzzentrum Usability Mittelstand 2019 Methodenhandbuch Nutzerzentrierte Entwicklung: Methoden zur nutzerzentrierten Entwicklung betrieblicher Anwendungssoftware in kleinen und mittleren Unterhemen. https://www.usabilityzentrum.de/dokumente/Methodenhandbuch.pdf

Konkle T, Oliva A 2011 Canonical visual size for real-world objects. J Exp Psychol Hum Percept Perform 37:23–37. https://doi.org/10.1037/a0020413

Kosslyn SM 2006 Graph design for the eye and mind. Oxford University Press, New York

Kourtzi Z, DiCarlo JJ 2006 Learning and neural plasticity in visual object recognition. Curr Opin Neurobiol 16:152–158. https://doi.org/10.1016/j.conb.2006.03.012

Koutsourelakis C, Chorianopoulos K 2010 Unaided Icon Recognition in Mobile Phones: A Comparative Study with Young Users. The Design Journal 13:313–328. https://doi.org/10.2752/146069210X12766130824939

Kövecses Z 2005 Metaphor in culture: Universality and variation. Cambridge University Press, Cambridge, UK, New York

Kress GR 2003 Literacy in the New Media Age. Literacies. Routledge, London

Kress GR 2010 Multimodality: A social semiotic approach to contemporary communication. 978-0-415-32061-0--978-0-415-32061-0, 978-, 1st edn. Routledge, London

Lachner F, Nguyen M-A, Butz A 2018 Culturally sensitive user interface design. In: Winschiers-Theophilus H, van Zyl I (eds) Proceedings of the Second African Conference for Human Computer Interaction on Thriving Communities - AfriCHI '18. ACM Press, New York, New York, USA, pp 1–12

Lakoff G 2009 The Neural Theory of Metaphor. Report: January, 2009. An earlier version appeared in: R. Gibbs. 2008 The Metaphor Handbook, Cambridge University Press. http://ssrn.com/abstract=1437794. Accessed 10 July 2016

Lakoff G 2012 Explaining embodied cognition results. Top Cogn Sci 4:773–785. https://doi.org/10.1111/j.1756-8765.2012.01222.x

Lakoff G, Johnson M 1999 Philosophy in the flesh: The embodied mind and its challenge to Western thought. Basic Books, New York, NY

Lakoff G, Johnson M 2003 Metaphors we live by. University of Chicago Press, Chicago, Ill.

Lalanne C, Lorenceau J 2004 Crossmodal integration for perception and action. J Physiol Paris 98:265–279. https://doi.org/10.1016/j.jphysparis.2004.06.001

Landau MJ, Meier BP, Keefer LA 2010 A metaphor-enriched social cognition. Psychol Bull 136:1045–1067. https://doi.org/10.1037/a0020970

Lasry N, Watkins J, Mazur E, Ibrahim A 2013 Response times to conceptual questions. American Journal of Physics 81:703–706. https://doi.org/10.1119/1.4812583

Laursen LF, Koyama Y, Chen H-T, Garces E, Gutierrez D, Harper R, Igarashi T 2016 Icon Set Selection via Human Computation. In: Bajaj C, Thomas Ertl, Tomoyuki Nishita (eds) Proceedings of the 24th Pacific Conference on Computer Graphics and Applications: Short Papers. Eurographics Association, Goslar Germany, Germany, pp 1–6

Lee S, Dazkir SS, Paik HS, Coskun A 2014 Comprehensibility of universal healthcare symbols for wayfinding in healthcare facilities. Appl Ergon 45:878–885. https://doi.org/10.1016/j.apergo.2013.11.003

Leontieva L, Rostova J, Tunick R, Golovko S, Harkulich J, Ploutz-Snyder R 2008 Cross-cultural diagnostic applicability of the Pictogram Test. J Pers Assess 90:165–174. https://doi.org/10.1080/00223890701845286

Levay KE, Freese J, Druckman JN 2016 The Demographic and Political Composition of Mechanical Turk Samples. SAGE Open 6:215824401663643. https://doi.org/10.1177/2158244016636433

Libbrecht KG 2006 Ken Libbrecht's field guide to snowflakes. Voyageur Press, Minneapolis

Lidwell W, Butler J, Holden K, Elam K 2010 Universal principles of design: 125 ways to enhance usability, influence perception, increase appeal, make better design decisions, and teach through design, 2nd edn. Rockport Publishers, Beverly, Mass

Lima PLC 2006 About primary metaphors. DELTA 22:109–122. https://doi.org/10.1590/S0102-44502006000300009

LimeSurvey GmbH 2017 LimeSurvey: An Open Source survey tool: Version 2.72.4+171110. LimeSurvey Project, Hamburg, Germany. http://www.limesurvey.org

LimeSurvey GmbH 2019 LimeSurvey: An Open Source survey tool: Version 3.16.1+190314. LimeSurvey Project, Hamburg, Germany. http://www.limesurvey.org

Lindberg T, Näsänen R 2003 The effect of icon spacing and size on the speed of icon processing in the human visual system. Displays 24:111–120. https://doi.org/10.1016/S0141-9382(03)00035-0

Liu Y-J, Fu Q-F, Liu Y, Fu X-L 2012 2D-Line-Drawing-Based 3D Object Recognition. In: Hutchison D, Kanade T, Kittler J, Kleinberg JM, Mattern F, Mitchell JC, Naor M, Nierstrasz O, Pandu Rangan C, Steffen B, Sudan M, Terzopoulos D, Tygar D, Vardi MY, Weikum G, Hu S-M, Martin RR (eds) Computational Visual Media, vol 7633. Springer Berlin Heidelberg, Berlin, Heidelberg, pp 146–153

Lodding KN 1983 Iconic Interfacing. IEEE Comput. Grap. Appl. 3:11–20. https://doi.org/10.1109/mcg.1983.262982

Löffler D 2017 Color, Metaphor and Culture - Empirical Foundations for User Interface Design: Farbe, Metapher und Kultur - Empirische Grundlagen für die Gestaltung von Benutzeroberflächen, Universität Würzburg

Löffler D, Heß A, Maier A, Hurtienne J, Schmitt H 2013 Developing Intuitive User Interfaces by Integrating Users' Mental Models into Requirements Engineering. In: British Informatics Society Ltd. (ed) Proceedings of the 27th International BCS Human Computer Interaction Conference. British Computer Society, Swinton, UK, UK, 1–10

Löffler D, Heß A, Maier A, Schmitt H 2013 Die IBIS-Methode: Handbuch zur Anwendung von Image Schemas und Metaphern im Designprozess(4.4). http://www.ibis-projekt.de/

Löffler D, Lindner K, Hurtienne J 2014 Mixing languages'. In: Jones M, Palanque P, Schmidt A, Grossman T (eds) Proceedings of the extended abstracts of the 32nd annual ACM conference on Human factors in computing systems - CHI EA '14. ACM Press, New York, New York, USA, pp 1999–2004

Lopes D 1996 Understanding pictures. Oxford philosophical monographs. Clarendon Press; Oxford University Press, Oxford, New York

Lu X 2014 Computational methods for corpus annotation and analysis. Springer, New York

Lyre H 2013 Verkörperlichung und situative Einbettung (embodied/embedded cognition). In: Stephan A, Walter S (eds) Handbuch Kognitionswissenschaft. Verlag J.B. Metzler, Stuttgart, Weimar, pp 186–192

Maassen H 2015 Four Simple Rules for Better Icon Design. https://experience.sap.com/basics/four-simple-rules-for-better-icon-design/. Accessed 22 April 2019

Macbeth SA, Moroney WF, Biers DW 2000 Development and Evaluation of Symbols and Icons: A Comparison of the Production and Focus Group Methods. Proceedings of the Human Factors and Ergonomics Society Annual Meeting 44:327–329. https://doi.org/10.1177/154193120004400209

MacKenzie IS 2013 Human-Computer Interaction: An Empirical Research Perspective. Elsevier, Morgan Kaufmann, Amsterdam, Heidelberg

Madsen KH 1994 A guide to metaphorical design. Commun. ACM 37:57–62. https://doi.org/10.1145/198366.198381

Maglio PP, Matlock T 1999 The Conceptual Structure of Information Space. In: Diaper D, Sanger C, Munro AJ, Höök K, Benyon D (eds) Social Navigation of Information Space. Springer London, London, pp 155–173

Mansoor LE, Dowse R 2004 Design and evaluation of a new pharmaceutical pictogram sequence to convey medicine usage. Ergonmics SA 16:29–41

Marcus A 1995 Principles of Effective Visual Communication for Graphical User Interface Design. In: Baecker R (ed) Readings in Human–Computer Interaction. Elsevier, pp 425–441

Marcus A 1998 Metaphor design for user interfaces. In: Karat C-M, Lund A (eds) CHI 98 conference summary on Human factors in computing systems – CHI '98. ACM Press, New York, New York, USA, pp 129–130

Marcus A 2003 Icons, Symbols, and Signs: Visible Languages to Facilitate Communication. interactions 10:37-43. https://doi.org/10.1145/769759.769774

Marcus A 2007 Global/Intercultural User Interface Design. In: Sears A, Jacko J (eds) The Human-Computer Interaction Handbook. CRC Press, pp 355–380

Marcus A 2015 Icons/Symbols and More: Visible Languages to Facilitate Communication. In: Marcus A (ed) HCI and User-Experience Design. Springer London, London, pp 53–61

Marcus A 2015 Metaphors and User Interfaces in the Twenty-First Century. In: Marcus A (ed) HCI and User-Experience Design. Springer London, London, pp 1–5

Marcus A 2015 Universal, Ubiquitous, User-Interface Design for the Disabled and Elderly. In: Marcus A (ed) HCI and User-Experience Design. Springer London, London, pp 47–52

Marcus A 2015 User-Interface Design and China: A Great Leap Forward. In: Marcus A (ed) HCI and User-Experience Design. Springer London, London, pp 39–45

Marcus A, Gould EW 2000 Crosscurrents: cultural dimensions and global Web user-interface design. interactions 7:32–46. https://doi.org/10.1145/345190.345238

Marshall P, Hornecker E 2013 Theories of Embodiment in HCI. In: Price S, Jewitt C, Brown B (eds) The SAGE Handbook of Digital Technology Research. SAGE Publications Ltd, 1 Oliver's Yard, 55 City Road, London EC1Y 1SP United Kingdom, pp 144–158

Massironi M 2009 The psychology of graphic images: Seeing, drawing, communicating. Psychology Press, New York, London

Masuda T 2010 Cultural Effects on Visual Perception. In: Goldstein EB (ed) Encyclopedia of perception. SAGE Publications, Thousand Oaks, Calif, pp 339–343

McDougall S, Bruijn O de, Curry MB 2000 Exploring the effects of icon characteristics on user performance: The role of icon concreteness, complexity, and distinctiveness. Journal of Experimental Psychology: Applied 6:291–306. https://doi.org/10.1037//1076-898X.6.4.291

McDougall S, Forsythe A, Isherwood S, Petocz A, Reppa I, Stevens C 2009 The Use of Multimodal Representation in Icon Interpretation. In: Harris D (ed) Engineering Psychology and Cognitive Ergonomics, vol 5639. Springer Berlin Heidelberg, Berlin, Heidelberg, pp 62–70

McEnery T, Wilson A 2001 Corpus linguistics: An introduction, 2nd edn. Edinburgh textbooks in empirical linguistics. Edinburgh Univ. Press, Edinburgh

McGee M 2004 Master usability scaling. In: Dykstra-Erickson E, Tscheligi M (eds) Proceedings of the 2004 conference on Human factors in computing systems - CHI '04. ACM Press, New York, New York, USA, pp 335–342

McKay EN 2013 UI is Communication. Elsevier Science

Meade AW, Craig SB 2012 Identifying careless responses in survey data. Psychol Methods 17:437–455. https://doi.org/10.1037/a0028085

Medhi I, Prasad A, Toyama K 2007 Optimal audio-visual representations for illiterate users of computers. In: Williamson C, Zurko ME, Patel-Schneider P, Shenoy P (eds) Proceedings of the 16th international conference on World Wide Web - WWW '07. ACM Press, New York, New York, USA, p 873

Melcher D, Cavanagh P 2013 Pictorial cues in art and in visual perception. In: Bacci F, Melcher D (eds) Art and the senses, 1. publ. in paperback. Oxford Univ. Press, Oxford [u.a.]

Mertens A, Koch-Körfges D, Schlick CM 2011 Designing a User Study to Evaluate the Feasibility of Icons for the Elderly. In: Eibl M (ed) Mensch & Computer 2011, vol 4. Oldenbourg Wissenschaftsverlag GmbH, München, pp 79–90

Messinger H, Fellermayer M (eds) 2007 Langenscheidt Handwörterbuch Englisch: Englisch-Deutsch, 2nd edn. Langenscheidt Handwörterbücher. Langenscheidt, Berlin

Meyer W, Nowack K, Wolff M 2019 Universal Cognitive User Interface (UCUI): Endbericht, Cottbus

Microsoft Corporation 2019 Excel 365: Version 1906, Redmond, U.S.

Miller LA, Stanney KM 1997 The Effect of Pictogram-Based Interface Design on Human-Computer Performance. International Journal of Human–Computer Interaction 9:119–131. https://doi.org/10.1207/s15327590ijhc0902_2

Miyamoto Y, Nisbett RE, Masuda T 2006 Culture and the physical environment. Holistic versus analytic perceptual affordances. Psychol Sci 17:113–119. https://doi.org/10.1111/j.1467-9280.2006.01673.x

Mohs C, Hurtienne J, Israel JH, Naumann AB, Kindsmüller MC, Meyer HA, Pohlmeyer A 2006 IUUI – Intuitive Use of User Interfaces. In: Bosenick T, Hassenzahl M, Peissner M, Müller-Prove M (eds) Tagungsband UP06. Fraunhofer Verlag, Stuttgart, pp 130–133

Moore P, Fitz C 1993 Gestalt Theory and Instructional Design. Journal of Technical Writing and Communication 23:137–157. https://doi.org/10.2190/G748-BY68-L83T-X02J

Mullet K, Sano D 1995 Designing visual interfaces: Communication oriented techniques. Prentice-Hall, Englewood Cliffs, NJ

Munzner T 2015 Visualization Analysis and Design, 1st edition. A K Peters/CRC Press

Nakamura C, Zeng-Treitler Q 2012 A Taxonomy of Representation Strategies in Iconic Communication. International Journal of Human-Computer Studies 70:535–551. https://doi.org/10.1016/j.ijhcs.2012.02.009

Naumann A, Hurtienne J 2010 Benchmarks for intuitive interaction with mobile devices. In: Sá M de, Carriço L, Correia N (eds) Proceedings of the 12th international conference on Human computer interaction with mobile devices and services – MobileHCI '10. ACM Press, New York, New York, USA, pp 401–402

Neale DC, Carroll JM 1997 The Role of Metaphors in User Interface Design. In: Helander MG, Landauer K, Prabhu V (eds) Handbook of Human-Computer Interaction. Elsevier, pp 441–462

Neumann C 2001 Is Metaphor Universal? Cross-Language Evidence From German and Japanese. Metaphor and Symbol 16:123–142. https://doi.org/10.1080/10926488.2001.9678890

Neurath O, Neurath M 1980 International picture language: A facsimile reprint of the (1936) English edition. Department of Typography & Graphic Communication, University of Reading, Reading

Newell A 1994 Unified theories of cognition, [Repr.]. The William James lectures. Harvard Univ. Press, Cambridge, Mass

Niedenthal PM, Barsalou LW, Winkielman P, Krauth-Gruber S, Ric F 2005 Embodiment in attitudes, social perception, and emotion. Pers Soc Psychol Rev 9:184–211. https://doi.org/10.1207/s15327957pspr0903_1

Nielsen J 1993 Usability engineering. Kaufmann, Amsterdam

Nisbett RE, Peng K, Choi I, Norenzayan A 2001 Culture and systems of thought: Holistic versus analytic cognition. Psychological Review 108:291–310. https://doi.org/10.1037//0033-295X.108.2.291

Nissen H, Janneck M 2018 Einfluss des verwendeten Endgeräts auf das Nutzungsverhalten in Online-Befragungen. In: Dachselt R, Weber G (eds) Mensch und Computer 2018, pp 205–214

Norman J 1988 Chinese, 17th print. Cambridge Language Surveys. Cambridge University Press, Cambridge

Norman DA 2008 Signifiers, not affordances. interactions 15:18–19. https://doi.org/10.1145/1409040.1409044

Nöth W 1995 Handbook of Semiotics. Advances in Semiotics. Indiana University Press, Bloomington

Nowack K 2018 More is up – important is central: Impact of developmental origin of image schemas on touch and gesture interaction with computers. International Journal of Human-Computer Studies 120:94–106. https://doi.org/10.1016/j.ijhcs.2018.08.001

O'Brien MA, Rogers WA, Fisk AD 2012 Understanding age and technology experience differences in use of prior knowledge for everyday technology interactions. ACM Trans. Access. Comput. 4:1–27. https://doi.org/10.1145/2141943.2141947

O'Donovan P, Agarwala A, Hertzmann A 2015 DesignScape. In: Begole B, Kim J, Inkpen K, Woo W (eds) Proceedings of the 33rd Annual ACM Conference on Human Factors in Computing Systems - CHI '15. ACM Press, New York, New York, USA, pp 1221–1224

Oppenheimer DM, Meyvis T, Davidenko N 2009 Instructional manipulation checks: Detecting satisficing to increase statistical power. Journal of Experimental Social Psychology 45:867–872. https://doi.org/10.1016/j.jesp.2009.03.009

Ortiz MJ 2011 Primary metaphors and monomodal visual metaphors. Journal of Pragmatics 43:1568–1580. https://doi.org/10.1016/j.pragma.2010.12.003

Osgood CE, Suci GJ, Tannenbaum PH 1957 The measurement of meaning. University of Illinois Press, Urbana-Champaign

Ostroff E 2011 Universal Design: An evolving paradigm. In: Preiser WFE, Smith KH (eds) Universal design handbook, 2nd ed. McGraw-Hill, Maidenhead, pp 34–42

Ota Y 1973 LoCoS: Lovers communications system. Pictorial Institute, Tokyo

Ota Y 2011 The Societal Role and Design of Pictograms as "Kansei Language" (Perceptual Language). In: 2011 International Conference on Biometrics and Kansei Engineering. IEEE, pp 1–13

Palmer SE 1999 Vision science: Photons to phenomenology. MIT Press, Cambridge, Mass.

Palmer SE, Rosch E, Chase P 1981 Canonical perspective and the perception of objects. Attention and performance:135–151

Palmer SE, Brooks JL, Nelson R 2003 When does grouping happen? Acta Psychol (Amst) 114:311–330. https://doi.org/10.1016/j.actpsy.2003.06.003

Pappachan P, Ziefle M 2008 Cultural influences on the comprehensibility of icons in mobile–computer interaction. Behaviour & Information Technology 27:331–337. https://doi.org/10.1080/01449290802228399

Park DC, Schwarz N 2000 Cognitive aging: A primer. Psychology Press, Philadelphia, PA

Persson H, Åhman H, Yngling AA, Gulliksen J 2015 Universal design, inclusive design, accessible design, design for all: different concepts—one goal? On the concept of accessibility—historical, methodological and philosophical aspects. Univ Access Inf Soc 14:505–526. https://doi.org/10.1007/s10209-014-0358-z

Pierroutsakos SL, DeLoache JS 2003 Infants' Manual Exploration of Pictorial Objects Varying in Realism. Infancy 4:141–156. https://doi.org/10.1207/S15327078IN0401_7

Plocher T, Rau P-LP, Choong Y-Y 2012 Cross-Cultural Design. In: Salvendy G (ed) Handbook of Human Factors and Ergonomics. John Wiley & Sons, Inc, Hoboken, NJ, USA, pp 162–191

PONS GmbH PONS. https://de.pons.com/. Accessed 26 February 2020

Popping R 2015 Analyzing Open-ended Questions by Means of Text Analysis Procedures. Bulletin of Sociological Methodology/Bulletin de Méthodologie Sociologique 128:23–39. https://doi.org/10.1177/0759106315597389

Ralph MA, Graham KS, Ellis AW, Hodges JR 1998 Naming in semantic dementia—what matters? Neuropsychologia 36:775–784. https://doi.org/10.1016/S0028-3932(97)00169-3

Ramachandran VS, Anstis SM 1986 The perception of apparent motion. Sci Am 254:102–109. https://doi.org/10.1038/scientificamerican0686-102

Ranta M 2000 Mimesis as the representation of types: The historical and psychological basis of an aesthetic idea. Stockholms universitet, Stockholm

Raskin J 1994 Viewpoint: Intuitive equals familiar. Commun. ACM 37:17–18. https://doi.org/10.1145/182987.584629

Rau P-LP (ed) 2013 Cross-Cultural Design. Cultural Differences in Everyday Life: 5th International Conference, CCD 2013, Held as Part of HCI International 2013, Las Vegas, NV, USA, July 21–26, 2013, Proceedings, Part II. Springer Berlin Heidelberg, Berlin/Heidelberg

Rau P-LP (ed) 2018 Cross-Cultural Design. Methods, Tools, and Users: 10th International Conference, CCD 2018, Held as Part of HCI International 2018, Las Vegas, NV, USA, July 15–20, 2018, Proceedings, Part I. Lecture Notes in Computer Science, vol 10911. Springer International Publishing, Cham

Rau P-LP, Plocher T, Choong Y-Y 2011 Cross-Cultural Web Design. In: Vu K-PL, Proctor RW (eds) Handbook of Human Factors in Web Design, 2nd ed. CRC Press, Hoboken, 677–698

Rau P-LP, Plocher TA, Choong Y-Y 2013 Cross-cultural design for IT products and services. Human factors and ergonomics. CRC Press, Boca Raton, Fla.

Reips U-D 2000 The Web Experiment Method. In: Birnbaum MH (ed) Psychological Experiments on the Internet. Elsevier, pp 89–117

Robbins SS, Stylianou AC 2002 A Study of Cultural Differences in Global Corporate Web Sites. Journal of Computer Information Systems 42:3–9. https://doi.org/10.1080/08874417.2002.11647480

Robinson MD 2007 Lives lived in milliseconds: Using cognitive methods in personality research. In: Robins RW, Fraley RC, Krueger RF (eds) Handbook of research methods in personality psychology. Guilford Press, New York, pp 345–359

Rogers Y 1989 Icons at the interface: their usefulness. Interacting with Computers 1:105–117. https://doi.org/10.1016/0953-5438(89)90010-6

Rogers Y 2012 HCI theory: Classical, modern, and contemporary. Synthesis lectures on human-centered informatics, #14. Morgan & Claypool Publishers, San Rafael

Rogers Y, Oborne DJ 1987 Pictorial communication of abstract verbs in relation to human-computer interaction. British Journal of Psychology 78:99–112. https://doi.org/10.1111/j.2044-8295.1987.tb02229.x

Rosch E, Mervis CB, Gray WD, Johnson DM, Boyes-Braem P 1976 Basic objects in natural categories. Cogn Psychol 8:382–439. https://doi.org/10.1016/0010-0285(76)90013-X

Röse K 2006 Globalization, Culture, and Usability. In: Ghaoui C (ed) Encyclopedia of human computer interaction. IGI Global (701 E. Chocolate Avenue Hershey Pennsylvania 17033 USA), Hershey, Pa, pp 253–256

Ross BH, Perkins SJ, Tenpenny PL 1990 Reminding-based category learning. Cogn Psychol 22:460–492. https://doi.org/10.1016/0010-0285(90)90010-2

Rubinstein A 2013 Response time and decision making: An experimental study. Judgment and Decision Making 8:540–551

Ryan RM 1982 Control and information in the intrapersonal sphere: An extension of cognitive evaluation theory. J Pers Soc Psychol 43:450–461. https://doi.org/10.1037//0022-3514.43.3.450

Sabou M, Bontcheva K, Derczynski L, Scharl A 2014 Corpus Annotation through Crowdsourcing: Towards Best Practice Guidelines. In: European Language Resources Association (ed) Proceedings of the Ninth International Conference on Language Resources and Evaluation (LREC'14). European Language Resources Association (ELRA), Reykjavik, Iceland, pp 859–866

Salkind NJ 2010 Encyclopedia of research design. SAGE reference, Los Angeles [etc.]

Salman YB, Cheng H-I, Patterson PE 2012 Icon and user interface design for emergency medical information systems: a case study. Int J Med Inform 81:29–35. https://doi.org/10.1016/j.ijmedinf.2011.08.005

SAP SE Group. https://sapui5.hana.ondemand.com/sdk/test-resources/sap/m/demokit/iconExplorer/webapp/index.html#/overview/SAP-icons/?tab=grid&icon=group&search=group. Accessed 21.12.19

Satcharoen K 2018 Icon Concreteness Effect on Selection Speed and Accuracy. In: Kavakli-Thorne M (ed) Proceedings of the 2018 10th International Conference on Computer and Automation Engineering - ICCAE 2018. ACM Press, New York, New York, USA, pp 107–110

Sauro J, Dumas JS 2009 Comparison of three one-question, post-task usability questionnaires. In: Olsen DR, Arthur RB, Hinckley K, Morris MR, Hudson S, Greenberg S (eds) Proceedings of the 27th international conference on Human factors in computing systems – CHI 09. ACM Press, New York, New York, USA, pp 1599–1609

Savidis A, Stephanidis C 2004 Unified user interface design: designing universally accessible interactions. Interacting with Computers 16:243–270. https://doi.org/10.1016/j.intcom.2003.12.003

Sayim B, Cavanagh P 2011 What line drawings reveal about the visual brain. Front Hum Neurosci 5:1–4. https://doi.org/10.3389/fnhum.2011.00118

Scaife M, Rogers Y 1996 External cognition: how do graphical representations work? International Journal of Human-Computer Studies 45:185–213. https://doi.org/10.1006/ijhc.1996.0048

Schmid H 1995 Improvements In Part-of-Speech Tagging With an Application To German. In: Elworthy D (ed) In Proceedings of the ACL SIGDAT-Workshop, pp 47–50

Schmid H 2017 TreeTagger: Windows Interface by Ciarán Ó Duibhín. University of Stuttgart. https://www.cis.uni-muenchen.de/~schmid/tools/TreeTagger

Schmid-Isler S 2000 The language of digital genres-a semiotic investigation of style and iconology on the World Wide Web. In: Sprague RH (ed) Proceedings of the 33rd Annual Hawaii International Conference on System Sciences. IEEE Comput. Soc, pp 1–9

Schröder S, Ziefle M 2008 Effects of Icon Concreteness and Complexity on Semantic Transparency: Younger vs. Older Users. In: Miesenberger K, Klaus J, Zagler W, Karshmer A (eds) Computers Helping People with Special Needs, vol 5105. Springer Berlin Heidelberg, Berlin, Heidelberg, pp 90–97

Schröder S, Ziefle M 2008 Making a completely icon-based menu in mobile devices to become true. In: ter Hofte H, Mulder I (eds) Proceedings of the 10th international conference on Human computer interaction with mobile devices and services – MobileHCI '08. ACM Press, New York, New York, USA, pp 137–146

Sedig K, Parsons P 2013 Interaction Design for Complex Cognitive Activities with Visual Representations: A Pattern-Based Approach. THCI 5:84–133. https://doi.org/10.17705/1thci.00055

Shapiro LA 2019 Embodied cognition, Second edition. Routledge, Taylor et Francis group, London, New York

Sharp H, Rogers Y, Preece J 2019 Interaction design: Beyond human-computer interaction, 5th edn. Wiley, Hoboken, N.J.

Shneiderman B 2002 Promoting universal usability with multi-layer interface design. SIGCAPH Comput. Phys. Handicap.:1–8. https://doi.org/10.1145/960201.957206

Shneiderman B, Plaisant C, Cohen M, Jacobs S, Elmqvist N, Author 2017 Designing the User Interface, 6th ed. Pearson Education Limited, Harlow, United Kingdom

Shutterstock Inc. Shutterstock. https://www.shutterstock.com. Accessed 26 February 2020

Slavin RE 1986 Best-Evidence Synthesis: An Alternative to Meta-Analytic and Traditional Reviews. Educational Researcher 15:5–11. https://doi.org/10.3102/0013189X015009005

Slavin RE 1987 Best-Evidence Synthesis: Why Less Is More. Educational Researcher 16:15–16. https://doi.org/10.3102/0013189X016004015

Slavin RE 1995 Best evidence synthesis: An intelligent alternative to meta-analysis. Journal of Clinical Epidemiology 48:9–18. https://doi.org/10.1016/0895-4356(94)00097-a

Solomon KO, Barsalou LW 2001 Representing properties locally. Cogn Psychol 43:129–169. https://doi.org/10.1006/cogp.2001.0754

Spence R 2014 Information visualization: An introduction, Third edition. Springer, Cham, Heidelberg, New York, Dordrecht, London

Stahl-Timmins W 2017 Methods for evaluating information design. In: Black A, Luna P, Lund O, Walker S (eds) Information design: Research and practice. Routledge – Taylor & Francis Group, United States, pp 451–462

Stappers P, Giaccardi E 2017 Research through Design. 43. In: Lowgren J, Carroll JM, Hassenzahl M, Erickson T (eds) The Encyclopedia of Human-Computer Interaction, 2nd edn., https://www.interaction-design.org/literature/book/the-encyclopedia-of-human-computer-interaction-2nd-ed/research-through-design

Stevens CJ, Brennan D, Petocz A, Howell C 2009 Designing informative warning signals: Effects of indicator type, modality, and task demand on recognition speed and accuracy. Adv Cogn Psychol 5:84–90. https://doi.org/10.2478/v10053-008-0064-6

Stewart N, Chandler J, Paolacci G 2017 Crowdsourcing Samples in Cognitive Science. Trends Cogn Sci (Regul Ed) 21:736–748. https://doi.org/10.1016/j.tics.2017.06.007

Still ML, Still JD 2019 Cognitively Describing Intuitive Interactions. In: Blackler AL (ed) Intuitive Interaction: Research and Application. CRC Press (Taylor and Francis), Boca Raton (FL), pp 41–61

Stöppel D 2014 Visuelle Zeichensysteme der Avantgarden 1910 bis 1950: Verkehrszeichen, Farbleitsysteme, Piktogramme. Verlag Silke Schreiber, München

Stoutenborough JW 2008 Semantic Differential Technique. In: Lavrakas PJ (ed) Encyclopedia of survey research methods. SAGE Publications, Thousand Oaks, Calif, pp 810–811

Sukaviriya P, Moran L 1990 User Interfaces for Asia. In: Nielsen J (ed) Designing user interfaces for international use. Elsevier, Amsterdam, pp 189–218

Takasaki T, Mori Y 2007 Design and Development of a Pictogram Communication System for Children Around the World. In: Ishida T, Fussell SR, Vossen PTJM (eds) Intercultural Collaboration, vol 4568. Springer Berlin Heidelberg, Berlin, Heidelberg, pp 193–206

Tan R, King E, Churchill F. Caitlin 2017 Designing with Data. O'Reilly Media, Inc, Sebastopol, United States

Templier M, Paré G 2015 A Framework for Guiding and Evaluating Literature Reviews. CAIS 37. https://doi.org/10.17705/1CAIS.03706

The GIMP Team 2018 GIMP. https://www.gimp.org/

The Inkscape Project 2019 Inkscape. https://inkscape.org/

The jamovi project 2019 jamovi (Version 1.0.6). https://www.jamovi.org

The Merriam-Webster.com Dictionary The Merriam-Webster.com Dictionary. https://www.merriam-webster.com. Accessed 3 December 2019

The Merriam-Webster.com Dictionary 2019 Intuitive. https://www.merriam-webster.com/dictionary/intuitive. Accessed 3 December 2019

The Merriam-Webster.com Dictionary 2019 Meaning. https://www.merriam-webster.com/dictionary/meaning. Accessed 3 December 2019

The Merriam-Webster.com Dictionary 2019 Universal. https://www.merriam-webster.com/dictionary/universal. Accessed 3 December 2019

Theo Boersema, Adams AS 2017 Does my symbol sign work?: International standards for designing and testing graphical symbols. In: Black A, Luna P, Lund O, Walker S (eds) Information design: Research and practice. Routledge - Taylor & Francis Group, United States, pp 303–314

Thompson W, Fleming R, Creem-Regehr S, Stefanucci JK 2011 Visual Perception from a Computer Graphics Perspective. CRC Press, Hoboken

Torraco RJ 2005 Writing Integrative Literature Reviews: Guidelines and Examples. Human Resource Development Review 4:356–367. https://doi.org/10.1177/1534484305278283

Tversky B 2011 Visualizing thought. Top Cogn Sci 3:499–535. https://doi.org/10.1111/j.1756-8765.2010.01113.x

Tversky B, Kugelmass S, Winter A 1991 Cross-cultural and developmental trends in graphic productions. Cogn Psychol 23:515–557. https://doi.org/10.1016/0010-0285(91)90005-9

Tversky B, Bauer Morrison J, Betrancourt M 2002 Animation: Can it facilitate? International Journal of Human-Computer Studies 57:247–262. https://doi.org/10.1006/ijhc.2002.1017

Tversky B, Agrawala M, Heiser J, Lee PU, Hanrahan P, Phan D, Stolte C, Daniele MP 2006 Cognitive design principles: From cognitive models to computer models. Model-based reasoning in science and engineering 2

Tzonis A, White I 1994 Automation based creative design: Research and perspectives. Elsevier Science B.V, Amsterdam, New York

Ullrich D, Diefenbach S 2010 INTUI. Exploring the Facets of Intuitive Interaction. In: Ziegler J, Schmidt A (eds) Mensch & Computer 2010: Interaktive Kulturen. Oldenbourg Verlag, München, pp 251–260

Unicode Consortium 2019 Thumbs up. https://unicode.org/emoji/charts-12.0/full-emoji-list.html#1f44d

Unicode Consortium 2019 Unicode – Basic Info: FAQ. https://home.unicode.org/basic-info/faq/

Vagias WM 2006 Likert-type scale response anchors. http://media.clemson.edu/cbshs/prtm/research/resources-for-research-page-2/Vagias-Likert-Type-Scale-Response-Anchors.pdf

Vallée-Tourangeau F, Anthony SH, Austin NG 1998 Strategies for generating multiple instances of common and ad hoc categories. Memory 6:555–592. https://doi.org/10.1080/741943085

Walther DB, Chai B, Caddigan E, Beck DM, Fei-Fei L 2011 Simple line drawings suffice for functional MRI decoding of natural scene categories. Proc Natl Acad Sci U S A 108:9661–9666. https://doi.org/10.1073/pnas.1015666108

Walton M, Vukovic' V, Marsden G 2002 'Visual literacy' as challenge to the internationalisation of interfaces: A study of South African student web users. In: Terveen L, Wixon D (eds) CHI '02 Human factors in computing systems. ACM Press, New York, New York, USA, pp 530–531

Wang HF, Hung SH, Liao CC 2007 A survey of icon taxonomy used in the interface design. In: Brinkman WP, Ham DH, Wong BLW (eds) Proceedings of the 14th European conference on Cognitive ergonomics invent! explore! – ECCE '07. ACM Press, New York, New York, USA, pp 203–206

Wang EM, Huang AY 2000 A Study on Basic Metaphors in Human-Computer Interaction. Proceedings of the Human Factors and Ergonomics Society Annual Meeting 44:140–143. https://doi.org/10.1177/154193120004400137

Ware C 2008 Visual Thinking for Design, Digital print. The Morgan Kaufmann series in interactive technologies. Elsevier Morgan Kaufmann Publishers, Amsterdam

Ware C 2013 Information Visualization: Perception for Design, 3rd ed. Elsevier; M. Kaufman, Amsterdam [etc.]

Watzman S 2003 Visual Design Principles for Usable Interfaces: The Human-computer Interaction Handbook. In: Jacko JA, Sears A (eds) The Human-Computer Interaction Handbook: Fundamentals, Evolving Technologies and Emerging Applications, Second Edition, 2nd edn. L. Erlbaum Associates Inc, Hillsdale, NJ, USA, pp 263–285

Weblabcenter, Inc. 2020 microWorkers. https://www.microworkers.com/. Accessed 26 February 2020

Wegerich A, Löffler D, Maier A 2012 Handbuch zur IBIS Toolbox: Evaluation Intuitiver Benutzbarkeit. http://www.ibis-projekt.de/icc/assisto/med/9fd/9fd391b9-6dde-541e-43e0-f3206350fd4c,11111111-1111-1111-1111-111111111111.pdf

Whittemore R, Knafl K 2005 The integrative review: updated methodology. J Adv Nurs 52:546–553. https://doi.org/10.1111/j.1365-2648.2005.03621.x

Willats J 1997 Art and representation: New principles in the analysis of pictures. Princeton University Press, Princeton (N.J.)

Willats J 2005 Making sense of children's drawings. Lawrence Erlbaum, Mahwah, N.J.

Willats J 2006 Ambiguity in Drawing. Tracey:1–21

Wilson M 2002 Six views of embodied cognition. Psychon Bull Rev 9:625–636. https://doi.org/10.3758/BF03196322

Wilson RA, Foglia L 2017 Embodied Cognition. In: Edward N. Zalta (ed) The Stanford Encyclopedia of Philosophy, Spring 2017. Metaphysics Research Lab, Stanford University

Wilson AD, Golonka S 2013 Embodied Cognition is Not What you Think it is. Front Psychol 4:1–13. https://doi.org/10.3389/fpsyg.2013.00058

Wogalter MS, Silver NC, Leonard SD, Zaikina H 2006 Warning symbols. In: Wogalter MS (ed) Handbook of Warnings. Lawrence Erlbaum Associates, Mahwah, N.J., pp 159–176

Woike BA 2010 Content Coding of Open-Ended Responses. In: Robins RW, Fraley RC, Krueger RF (eds) Handbook of research methods in personality psychology. Guilford, New York, London, pp 292–307

Wood LE 1998 Introduction: Bridging the Design Gap. In: Wood LE (ed) User Interface Design: Bridging the Gap from User Requirements to Design. Chapman and Hall/CRC, Boca Raton, pp 8–23

Wood JN, Grafman J 2003 Human prefrontal cortex: processing and representational perspectives. Nat Rev Neurosci 4:139–147. https://doi.org/10.1038/nrn1033

Yamazaki AK, Taki H 2010 A comprehensibility study of pictogram elements for manufacturing steps. IJKESDP 2:70. https://doi.org/10.1504/IJKESDP.2010.030467

Yee CK, Ling CS, Yee WS, Zainon WMNW 2012 GUI design based on cognitive psychology: Theoretical, empirical and practical approaches. In: Kwack KD, Ko F, Shin J (eds) 2012 8th International Conference on Computing Technology and Information Management (NCM and ICNIT), vol 2, pp 836–841

Yonas A, Cleaves W, Pettersen L 1978 Development of sensitivity to pictorial depth. Science 200:77–79. https://doi.org/10.1126/science.635576

Yonas A, Granrud CE, Arterberry ME, Hanson BL 1986 Infants' distance perception from linear perspective and texture gradients. Infant Behavior and Development 9:247–256. https://doi.org/10.1016/0163-6383(86)90001-9

Yonas A, Granrud CE, Chov MH, Alexander AJ 2005 Picture Perception in Infants: Do 9-Month-Olds Attempt to Grasp Objects Depicted in Photographs? Infancy 8:147–166. https://doi.org/10.1207/s15327078in0802_3

Zhou H, Fishbach A 2016 The pitfall of experimenting on the web: How unattended selective attrition leads to surprising (yet false) research conclusions. J Pers Soc Psychol 111:493–504. https://doi.org/10.1037/pspa0000056

Zimmerman J, Forlizzi J 2014 Research Through Design in HCI. In: Olson JS, Kellogg WA (eds) Ways of Knowing in HCI, vol 17. Springer New York, New York, NY, pp 167–189

Zimmerman J, Forlizzi J, Evenson S 2007 Research through design as a method for interaction design research in HCI. In: Rosson MB, Gilmore D (eds) Proceedings of the SIGCHI Conference on Human Factors in Computing Systems - CHI '07. ACM Press, New York, New York, USA, pp 493–502

Zimmerman J, Stolterman E, Forlizzi J 2010 An analysis and critique of Research through Design. In: Bertelsen OW, Krogh P (eds) Proceedings of the 8th ACM Conference on Designing Interactive Systems - DIS '10. ACM Press, New York, New York, USA, p 310

Zwaan RA, Madden CJ 2005 Embodied Sentence Comprehension. In: Pecher D, Zwaan RA (eds) Grounding Cognition. Cambridge University Press, pp 224–245

Index

Ihr kostenloses eBook

Vielen Dank für den Kauf dieses Buches. Sie haben die Möglichkeit, das eBook zu diesem Titel kostenlos zu nutzen. Das eBook können Sie dauerhaft in Ihrem persönlichen, digitalen Bücherregal auf **springer.com** speichern, oder es auf Ihren PC/Tablet/eReader herunterladen.

1. Gehen Sie auf **www.springer.com** und loggen Sie sich ein. Falls Sie noch kein Kundenkonto haben, registrieren Sie sich bitte auf der Webseite.
2. Geben Sie die eISBN (siehe unten) in das Suchfeld ein und klicken Sie auf den angezeigten Titel. Legen Sie im nächsten Schritt das eBook über **eBook kaufen** in Ihren Warenkorb. Klicken Sie auf **Warenkorb und zur Kasse gehen**.
3. Geben Sie in das Feld **Coupon/Token** Ihren persönlichen Coupon ein, den Sie unten auf dieser Seite finden. Der Coupon wird vom System erkannt und der Preis auf 0,00 Euro reduziert.
4. Klicken Sie auf **Weiter zur Anmeldung**. Geben Sie Ihre Adressdaten ein und klicken Sie auf **Details speichern und fortfahren**.
5. Klicken Sie nun auf **kostenfrei bestellen**.
6. Sie können das eBook nun auf der Bestätigungsseite herunterladen und auf einem Gerät Ihrer Wahl lesen. Das eBook bleibt dauerhaft in Ihrem digitalen Bücherregal gespeichert. Zudem können Sie das eBook zu jedem späteren Zeitpunkt über Ihr Bücherregal herunterladen. Das Bücherregal erreichen Sie, wenn Sie im oberen Teil der Webseite auf Ihren Namen klicken und dort **Mein Bücherregal** auswählen.

EBOOK INSIDE

eISBN
Ihr persönlicher Coupon

Sollte der Coupon fehlen oder nicht funktionieren, senden Sie uns bitte eine E-Mail mit dem Betreff: **eBook inside** an **customerservice@springer.com**.

Printed in the United States
by Baker & Taylor Publisher Services